Penguin Education

European Integration

Edited by Michael Hodges

Penguin Interdisciplinary Readings

General Editor

Maurice Vile

Advisory Board

Michael Argyle
Ernest Gellner
K. W. Wedderburn
Alan H. Williams

European Integration

Selected Readings

Edited by Michael Hodges

Penguin Books

Penguin Books Ltd, Harmondsworth,
Middlesex, England
Penguin Books Inc, 7110 Ambassador Road,
Baltimore, Md 21207, USA
Penguin Books Australia Ltd,
Ringwood, Victoria, Australia

First published 1972
This selection copyright © Michael Hodges, 1972
Introduction and notes copyright © Michael Hodges, 1972

Copyright acknowledgement for items in this volume
will be found on page 463

Made and printed in Great Britain by
Richard Clay (The Chaucer Press) Ltd, Bungay, Suffolk
Set in Monotype New Times Roman

Series Foreword

The Penguin Interdisciplinary Readings represent an attempt to come to grips with one of the most important areas of study in the Social Sciences today. Although each of the disciplines in the social sciences has made great advances during the past twenty years, there is a danger that they will simply continue to pursue, in greater and greater detail the specialized methods which each of them has evolved. Although this kind of specialized work is necessary, and indeed highly desirable, students of society have become more and more aware of its inherent limitations. The reality of any social situation is that a number of events take place, each of which may have economic, political, sociological and other dimensions; each situation has its historical setting and its own psychological components. Individual disciplines abstract from these events, selecting the data which seem relevant to their own assumptions, and elaborating explanations within their own theoretical framework. However if it is argued that only a partial understanding of the nature of social reality can emerge from such specialized approaches, what are the alternatives?

In the present state of development of the social sciences, there is certainly no integrating theory which can neatly fit together all the pieces to provide a 'complete' picture, if indeed such a complete picture is theoretically possible. Advocates of a holistic social science who reject the fragmented approach of individual disciplines and wish to replace them with a 'global' study of society in all its aspects, simply finish up with a randomly chosen collection of facts. The other alternative is to acknowledge that the study of society must begin by applying the varied techniques of the individual disciplines to 'specific problems' existing in the real world. Such 'problems' may be narrowly conceived or they may be extremely broad in scope. Nevertheless, the existence of a problem to be studied provides the focus for the bringing together of the methods and data of the various disciplines, even if the immediate result is merely to demonstrate how those methods and conclusions conflict, and how each of the disciplines, in pursuing its own particular academic aims, may fail to illuminate the central core of the problem. It is only through such a problem-oriented approach that the beginnings of an integrated social science might emerge.

The books of Readings grew out of the development at the University of Kent of a number of interdisciplinary courses based upon this view of the present state of the social sciences. Each course will attempt to take a particular area or problem in the social sciences and bring to bear upon it the work which has been done in a number of different disciplines. The first volumes in this series are therefore edited by members of the Faculty of Social Sciences at the University of Kent, based upon the courses which they are preparing, but future volumes in the series will be prepared by a wide range of authors, and it is also intended to produce a series of original texts dealing with specific problems in an interdisciplinary way.

Each volume of Readings, therefore, is an attempt by an individual to take a particular problem and to draw from the literature of the subjects concerned those contributions which would seem most likely to illuminate the present state of knowledge in the social sciences relating to that problem, and also to provide the basis for a more integrated understanding of this particular piece of social reality. For each of the editors the selection of the readings must be in one sense a very personal selection, based upon his conception of the nature of the problem, of what is important to the understanding of that problem, and of how the various elements of the different disciplines might eventually be combined to provide such an understanding. Each editor has produced a fairly lengthy introduction which attempts to set his particular choice of materials within the context of the current state of the debate in the disciplines concerned.

If our view of the best way to make progress in the study of the social sciences is correct, this series might provoke the kind of interdisciplinary research, both by groups and by individuals, which may help to make our understanding of the nature of society both more satisfying academically, and more fruitful as a basis for future policy.

M. J. C. Vile

Contents

Part Three
The Dynamics of European Decision-Making 201

Part Four
Sources of Support for European Integration 323

Introduction

For over a quarter of a century there has been no war in Europe; like the nocturnal silence of the dog in the Sherlock Holmes story, this is a curious incident worthy of our attention. Unfortunately, like most non-events, it is very difficult to explain satisfactorily, which is why historians nearly always sanctify as 'Turning Points' things which did happen rather than things which did not. Similarly, European integration is a non-event, inextricably linked with the long period of peace and prosperity which West Europe has enjoyed. It is a non-event in the sense that the growth of a single community in West Europe as a result of collaboration between hitherto autonomous states is a complex, diffuse and unfinished process, almost impossible to pin down.

The greatest achievement of European regional organizations has been to establish patterns of peaceful cooperation in various fields, as preliminary steps to build a community at the international level by negotiation rather than coercion. These experiments in European integration have attracted the interest of social scientists, because they offer an ideal opportunity to test theories of peaceful community-building, but they have thus far failed to capture the imagination of the man on the Strasbourg autobus.

The absence of popular involvement in European integration may partly be explained by the lack of drama in most attempts at international collaboration. Only a few isolated episodes remain in the collective memory – students demolishing the Franco-German frontier barriers when the European Coal and Steel Community was formed in 1952, for example – and the popular image of European integration is probably linked to scenes of headphoned Eurocrats engaged in marathon negotiations over the production of sugar-beet. To the generation born after 1945, 'Europe' is frequently irrelevant or the symbol of a capitalist conspiracy, while to their elders it is often a mere geographical expression or a panacea of dubious validity. The Frenchman who drives a German car assembled by Italian workers is likely to consider the European Community as a remote bureaucratic apparatus, and looks to Paris rather than Brussels to protect his interests and satisfy his demands. The Frenchman is not to be blamed for his lack of supranational loyalty; many Bretons have a similar absence of enthusiasm for the French state, which has been in existence considerably longer than the European Communities.

European integration is in a very early stage of development, and it is impossible to predict what the result of the process will be. As with any contemporary phenomenon, it is difficult to select the most significant aspects and explain how they relate to each other. Richard Mayne, who took an active part in the launching of the European Communities, has remarked that a future historian of European integration is likely to suffer from a surplus of documentation and a shortage of facts:

At once glutted and starved, the historian can only sketchily reconstruct what actually happened; and his account will often seem far too remote, well-ordered and reflectively analytical to those who took part in the muddle and drama of events (Mayne, 1967, p. 350).

A fortiori this applies to analysts of European integration who write in the midst of those events, and possibly explains why most of these analyses have been produced from a single-discipline viewpoint. Such divisions of academic labour are accepted as a necessary expedient in the face of an overwhelming volume of material coming under the rubric of 'European integration', but it is often argued that distinctions between economic, social and political integration are superficial, and that they are interlinked in a complex manner (Streeten, 1964, p. 11).

This volume of readings concentrates on the process of political integration – the formation of a new political system out of several hitherto separate political systems – and the way in which changes in economic and social relationships influence the shift of loyalty and decision-making power from the national to the supranational level. The readings themselves have been chosen because they illustrate the linkages between the political, social and economic aspects of integration, rather than because they provide a comprehensive description of the institutions and policies of the European Community. The principal objective of the readings is to provide sufficient analytical tools for the reader to keep abreast of developments in the European Community and to assess the progress which has been made towards European integration. In this way it may be possible to capitalize on our lack of hindsight: 'When great revolutions are successful their causes cease to exist, and the very fact of their success makes them incomprehensible' (de Tocqueville, 1856, Pt I, ch. 1).

Towards a theory of integration

Regional integration is a comparatively new field of inquiry for social scientists. Consequently a coherent and well-defined body of theory dealing with this phenomenon has yet to emerge. The various political initiatives to integrate West Europe which were made after the Second World War attracted the attention of political scientists and economists because they represented a radical departure from the traditional pattern of relations between nation-states in Europe, which was more notable for conflict than cooperation. The study of regional integration aims, in the words of one of its leading analysts 'to explain the tendency toward the voluntary creation of larger political units, each of which self-consciously eschews the use of force in the relations between the participating units and groups' (Haas, 1970, p. 608). In this emphasis on the process of peaceful, non-coercive, community building at the international level, integration theory has a strong normative element – it is concerned with the creation of new types of political, social and economic communities by methods which are quite different from the coercive efforts which have usually characterized nation and empire building processes in the past.

This normative element, an assumption that the traditional unit of human activity, the nation state, is no longer the most desirable one, has not frequently been made explicit in theories of regional integration. It should, however, be borne in mind when studying such theories, since one of the major difficulties in using the term 'integration' is that it embodies certain values which (like 'democracy') few would care to reject in public. 'Disintegration' has seldom been advocated by anybody, and politicians tend to use words like 'integration', 'cooperation' and 'progress' interchangeably without specifying exactly what they mean. When Churchill, in his famous speech at the University of Zurich in September 1946, called for 'a kind of United States of Europe', it was not immediately obvious that he did not include

Great Britain in such a proposal. If politicians have failed to define what they mean by 'integration', then it must also be said that political scientists have not yet reached a consensus either. Some regard it as the *process* whereby states voluntarily give up certain sovereign powers and evolve new techniques for resolving conflict between themselves, while others consider that integration is the terminal *condition* in such a process, where a new unit is created which subsumes several previously independent units.

This disagreement on the definition of integration has led to different approaches to the study of regional integration, with varying emphasis on the role of institutions, elite and popular attitudes, and social communications in the creation of communities at the international level. Three main approaches may be distinguished: the federalist approach, which emphasizes the role of institutions; the transactionalist approach, which focuses on transactions between people as an indication of their attitudes towards each other; and the neofunctionalist approach, which stresses the ways in which supranational institutions emerge from a convergence of the interests of various significant groups in society.

In assessing the significance of each of these approaches, it is necessary to remember that the function of any theory is to *describe* the process which it covers, identifying the various stages which occur in it, to *explain* why these happen, and to *predict* what will happen under which conditions. As will be seen, none of the three main theoretical approaches to the study of European integration satisfies these criteria, but this is perhaps too much to hope for in what is as yet a youthful branch of the social sciences.

The federalist approach

Federalism, the method of government which divides political power between central and local institutions, each acting autonomously within its own sphere, has been seen as both the ultimate objective of European integration and as a strategy for achieving it (Hay, 1966). Its proponents consider that it provides an institutional arrangement which satisfies the twin criteria of efficiency, by creating central bodies for some functions, and democracy, by decentralizing other activities to ensure greater local control and autonomy. The central assumption of the federalist approach is the primacy of politics – that stable political institutions for a regional federation can be created by an act of political will, and that this political consensus does not depend for its success on the prior resolution of social and economic differences. It is therefore seen as a political solution to the problems posed by the undeniable diversity of interests which exist in a region such as West Europe (de Rougemont, 1965).

The federalist approach is more a strategy for fulfilling a common purpose and common needs than a theory explaining how these integrative forces arise. It assumes that a federal structure can fulfil such common objectives at whatever level it operates, and that institutions which have been effective at the nation-state level in such countries as the USA, West Germany and Switzerland (Muret, 1966) will also be appropriate for supranational groupings. In the context of West Europe, the federalist approach has been seen as a rapid method of achieving integration and contains a strong normative component. Some European federalists saw it as a step toward democratizing society and eventually attaining global integration, while others wished to create a 'United States of Europe' which would stabilize the international system by balancing the existing superpowers of the USA and USSR (Forsyth, 1967). The main requirement for the success of the federalist strategy was a decisive act of collective political will by the governing elites of the various West European states, whereby a federal system would be created. Such a system, it was thought, could withstand or even harmonize regional differences in a way which was impossible for a unitary state, all of whose functions were centralized.

Three events in 1952 formed what has been called West Europe's 'federalist phase' (Spinelli, 1966, p. 19), when it seemed that federalism might be brought about by a piecemeal strategy. The establishment of the European Coal and Steel Community was followed by the signing of the European Defence Community treaty and proposals for a European Political Community. The rejection of the EDC proposals by the French Assembly in 1954, and the consequent abandonment of the EPC, indicated that if there was a common political will, it was to maintain the existing framework of national governments rather than to create supranational institutions (Lerner and Aron, 1957). In Reading 2, Spinelli points out that the political elites in West Europe were not accustomed to thinking of solving European problems on federalist lines, since their only experience of supranationalism had been in the technical, non-political, coordination of armed forces and production of war material during both world wars. The lack of enthusiasm for giving up national sovereignty was intensified by the economic recovery of the West European states and the diminishing likelihood of Soviet expansion in Europe after the Berlin blockade ended in 1949.

After the collapse of EDC the federalist approach in its pure institutional form received less attention. Committed federalists, such as Jean Monnet, Walter Hallstein and Altiero Spinelli remained convinced that a united Europe would necessarily have federal institutions, but that constitutional arrangements for distributing and delimiting political power were only practicable once sufficient consensus had been attained on procedural and substantive issues. Although there is still an active European Federalist Movement, whose 1964 Charter calls for a European Federation as a stage on the way toward federalism, there is no longer much support among the political elites for such a solution. Paul-Henri Spaak, the former Prime Minister of Belgium and one of the moving forces behind the EPC proposals, expressed his disillusionment in an article he wrote in 1967:

The Europe that we wanted, the Europe whose position in the world we intended to restore, the Europe that we hoped to make the equals of the United States and of the Soviet Union, is no longer realizable. . . . My earlier enthusiasms, I can now appreciate, were illusions. We have not known how to halt that decline which has been Western Europe's penalty for the follies of two world wars which originated among us. Today we are paying the price of our errors and of our faults (quoted in Moncrieff, 1967, p. 16).

Nevertheless, the federalist approach still retains some value for students of regional integration, since it posits a system of government which can be used as an ideal type against which to measure progress in political integration. Integration theorists such as Lindberg and Scheingold (1970) stress that one of the most important indicators of political integration is the level at which decision-making takes place, and the range of subjects covered. This emphasis on a division of decision-making power between central and local institutions and the balance between them is inherent in federalism. Federal theorists have responded to criticism of their legalism by affirming that the functions performed by a federal system of government, and the evolution of the interests which determine those functions, are more significant than a legally defined institutional structure (Friedrich, 1968, p. 173). It may be that the federalist approach would also provide a suitable strategy for the final stage of the integration process, 'where the political will exists at the centre and where an alignment of interests has occurred' (Taylor, 1971, p. 15).

The transactionalist approach

In contrast to federalism the transactionalist approach does not concern itself with any specific type of legal and institutional framework, but rather with the conditions necessary to promote and maintain a sense of community among the population of a given region. Its basic premise is that communication is the sole means of achieving the mutual relevance and responsiveness which distinguish organized social groups from random aggregations of individuals. Consequently it looks at West Europe as a whole, in order to assess the degree to which transactions between hitherto separate political entities or nation states indicate a growth in interdependence and therefore in mutual relevance. The more one nation state interacts with another, the more relevant they are to each other; such mutual relevance, however, may not lead to integration unless there is also mutual responsiveness, which may be defined as the ability to respond satisfactorily to the demands expressed in transactions between the nation states.

The foremost exponent of this approach is Karl Deutsch (Deutsch *et al.*, 1957) who has applied the concepts of cybernetics and general systems theory to the study of regional integration. He considers that integration is a condition in which the population of a given region have attained a sense of community, namely an agreement that common problems should be solved without resort to physical coercion. Further, the members of such a community have at their disposal institutions and procedures which are capable of ensuring peaceful change. In Reading 6, Deutsch distinguishes between two types of such a 'security community': firstly, the amalgamated security community, formed by a merger of two or more previously independent units into a single larger unit, with some form of common government; and secondly, the pluralistic security community, where the separate governments retain their legal independence but institutionalize some forms of cooperation.

The crucial factor is not the legal and institutional framework of such communities, but the existence of a sense of community, and in the 1957 study Deutsch and his associates set out to discover the conditions necessary to promote and maintain such a social consensus. They examined ten cases of integration in the

North Atlantic area, ranging from the successful integration of England in medieval times to the disintegration of the Austro–Hungarian empire in the twentieth century. The results of this study are summarized in Reading 6, but it is important to note here that all the cases studied concerned community building at the national level. There is an implicit assumption in Deutsch's work that generalizations derived from this national level are relevant to an understanding of integration at the international level (Pfaltzgraff and Dougherty, 1971).

An examination of the conditions which Deutsch found were necessary to establish and maintain pluralistic and amalgamated security communities (more stringent for the latter) clearly demonstrates the importance of communications in his approach. A community cannot exist unless its members are to some degree interdependent, and interdependence can only be established by a network of mutual transactions. Such transactions are, therefore, a prerequisite for a community, but they are not in themselves sufficient; communications can exacerbate relations as well as improve them, and may well emphasize divergent values and expectations rather than promote common ones.

In addition to the mutual relevance established by a certain level of transactions between units in the region, therefore, the communications system must also promote mutual responsiveness, which may be defined as the probability of getting an adequate response to a communicated demand within an acceptable period of time. This responsiveness depends upon the capability of the actors who control the system and the level of demands made upon them; it is the function of these actors to process these demands by selecting the most relevant information from them, combining this with stored information, and producing responses which will promote the cohesion of the system by satisfying as many demands as possible. Since the needs of the system increase as a result of social, economic and technological change, successful integration can only be ensured if the ability of the system to respond to demands remains equal or superior to the level of those demands, and it possesses the competence to make decisions on them (Deutsch, 1964).

The development of a sense of community at the international level, according to the transactionalist approach, depends upon an effective and significant pattern of communications between national units. As the intensity of communications increases, so will the sense of community, provided demand loads and system capabilities remain in balance. The transactionalist approach therefore aims to measure the level of transactions between units in order to determine the degree of interdependence prevailing within a region. It also aims to measure changes in transaction flows in order to indicate the extent to which mutual responsiveness exists. Thus if an individual enters into a transaction with another and finds the outcome satisfactory, he is more likely to repeat the process than if he were confronted by an unfavourable response; he has, in a sense, learned from his initial experience. Increases in mutual transactions may be seen as the result of a learning process, which through conditioning facilitates the mutual recognition and transfer of stimuli and symbols within a region, and consequently the emergence of common values. In this way the conditioning process implied in a network of communications may increase the cohesion of a region (Teune, 1964).

Transaction analyses of regional integration consequently look for two main patterns of communication which are most characteristic of communities at the international level. Firstly, a high volume of international transactions within the region over a wide range of economic, political, social and cultural activities; thus an increasing volume of such transactions between a group of countries would indicate that the region was a potential international community. Secondly, for a community to emerge, there must be a higher degree of mutual relevance among potential members than between them and non-member countries; therefore the formation of a community is characterized by an increasing divergence between the volume and range of transactions within the prospective community and transactions by the community with the outside world.

The difficulty with such analyses of transaction flows lies in determining which transactions are most significant in developing mutual relevance and potential cohesion within a region. A study of Anglo–American relations during the period 1890–1954 showed that the relative weight of economic transactions steadily diminished, while there was a modest increase in political and military consultations (Russett, 1963, p. 202). Such divergences in transaction flows may be useful in highlighting potential weaknesses in cohesion, by indicating cross-pressures between one type of transaction and another, but until the relative importance of various types of transaction can be defined, comparisons are difficult to make. In a recent study of the prospects for European integration, Deutsch and his associates correlated transaction flows across national boundaries (such as trade, communication by mail and telephone, and tourist movements) with mass and elite attitudes surveyed through interviews, opinion polls and content analysis of editorials in elite newspapers. Deutsch concluded that European integration had slowed since the mid-1950s and has stopped or reached a plateau since 1958, with the increase in mutual transactions being no greater than would be expected from random probability and the increase in prosperity in the countries concerned:

The spectacular development of formal European treaties and institutions since the mid-1950s has not been matched by any corresponding deeper integration of mutual behaviour. . . . The expectable pattern for the next ten years, as suggested by a study of the trends in European transactions between 1928 and 1963, is toward a Europe of national states (Deutsch *et al.*, 1967, p. 17).

This verdict has been questioned by several other analysts, notably Ronald Inglehart (1967) and Donald Puchala (1970). Inglehart takes Deutsch to task for emphasizing the importance of structural integration, such as increases in trade, travel, mail and student exchanges, rather than the degree to which these transaction flows reshape the political aspirations of the major groups in society. He contends that there may be a threshold of structural integration which is high enough for political integration to take place, even if increases in mutual transactions begin to level off as they reach saturation point, as in the case of tourism. Inglehart's own research led him to the conclusion that a limited amount of attitudinal reorientation in favour of 'Europe' has taken place since 1958, and that the most important change is the outlook of the post-1945 generation, who will form the majority of the voting population by the end of the 1970s, and whose pro-European attitudes seem to be more stable and enduring than those of earlier generations. In Reading 16, Inglehart suggests that such public preferences in favour of European integration are likely to constitute an important long-term influence on political decision-makers, and that far from European integration stagnating from 1958 (as Deutsch contends), it may only have moved into full gear since that time. Deutsch himself produced some evidence to support Inglehart's generational theory of attitudes toward integration when he found that junior members of French and German administrative elites tend to be more Europe-oriented than their older superiors (Deutsch *et al.*, 1967).

Puchala (1970) makes the important observation that transaction flow indices are limited to available quantitative data, and that therefore they exclude many transactions which are not readily quantified. Furthermore, while these indices may describe various dimensions of the regional integration process, and thus enable the analyst to monitor the progress of integration in various fields, transaction flows do not cause integration, but are rather a reflection of it. There is, therefore, some risk in predicting the course of integration on the basis of trends in transactions; such predictive exercises assume that transactions are a measure of the perceptions and attitudes underlying human behaviour, and that aggregate transaction flows reflect system-wide behavioural traits. While admitting these limitations, Puchala finds that convergences of attitudes and a modest rise in transactions have continued since 1958, and that Deutsch's pessimism is therefore unjustified.

Even if transaction flow indices do provide some guide to the emergence of what Taylor (Reading 10) calls 'socio-psychological community', it must be remembered that this is only one aspect of the regional integration process. The other component is that of institutional integration, defined as the emergence of new supranational decision-making bodies whose decisions cover a wide range of activities and are regarded as legitimate and authoritative by the merging units. Transaction flows which are useful for monitoring socio-psychological community formation (mass and elite attitudes, trade, mail, tourism, etc.) are not suitable for measuring the growth of institutional channels for international political transactions, and the degree to which such channels are successful in resolving conflicts. Since most of this type of transaction is never made public, there are formidable difficulties in devising appropriate indicators. Even where adequate information exists – for example, joint membership in regional organizations as an indicator of the growth in the capacity of supranational institutions – it is difficult to weigh individual transactions in order to indicate their relative significance. Can one consider membership of the European Launcher Development Organization (ELDO) of equal importance as membership of the EEC?

It is clear that the transactionalist approach has much to offer the student of regional integration, but that it does not yet satisfy the three main criteria for a satisfactory theory of integration. A more refined and comprehensive form of transaction flow analysis may be able to provide an accurate description of the various dimensions of regional integration. The criterion of explanation may be fulfilled if the transactionalist approach can indicate correlations between changes in various types of transaction flow, such as an increase in community formation preceding an increase in institutionalization. Such correlations may reveal patterns of priority in the integration process, but it is doubtful whether causal relationships can be demonstrated by the transactionalist approach. Transaction analysis tends to bypass questions of actor perceptions of present and future benefits, assuming instead that these will be reflected by trends in the transactions themselves. The predictive capability of the transactionalist approach appears to be very limited; Deutsch sees regional integration not as an organic growth process, with a fixed sequence of stages, but rather as an assembly-line process, in which it does not matter in what order the necessary elements are incorporated, so long as they are all included.

The neofunctionalist approach

Whereas the transactionalists are concerned with the development of a sense of community, with an underlying homogeneity of values, the neofunctionalists emphasize the pluralist nature of modern society, composed of competing elites and interest groups. Ernst Haas (Reading 5), the most prominent of the neofunctionalists, has defined integration as:

the process whereby political actors in several distinct national settings are persuaded to shift their loyalties, expectations and political activities towards a new and larger centre, whose institutions possess or demand jurisdiction over the pre-existing national states.

This definition of integration as a process was intended to avoid the difficulties inherent in the transactionalist approach, which treats integration as a condition in which a consensus has already developed, and which therefore cannot make clear distinctions between the situation prior to integration and the situation when the integration process has commenced. The neofunctionalist conception of integration as a process is intended to monitor the changes in values held by politically significant elites (both governmental and non-governmental), as they redefine their interests in terms of a regional rather than a purely national orientation.

The neofunctionalists do not assume that such value-changes are inspired by altruistic motives on the part of such elites, but rather that these elites will see a supranational institution as a means of satisfying their pragmatic interests, and will combine across national frontiers with elites whose interests are similar:

Rather than relying on a scheme of integration which posits 'altruistic' or 'idealistic' motives as the conditioners of conduct, it seems more reasonable – assuming the pluralist basis of politics here used – to focus on interests and values defended by the major groups in the process, experience showing that these are far too complex to be described in such simple terms as 'the desire for Franco-German peace', or the 'will to a United Europe' (Haas, 1958, p. 13).

The neofunctionalist approach concentrates on the development of processes of collective decision-making, and the way in which governmental and non-governmental elites change their tactics and organization as the locus of decision-making shifts from the national to the supranational level.

As the description 'neofunctionalist' implies, theorists of regional integration such as Haas have been influenced by the ideas of the functionalists, a group of political theorists who were active in the period between the two world wars. These functionalist writers, of whom David Mitrany (1943) is probably the most influential, regarded nationalism as the major threat to world peace, and saw the development of international organizations performing human welfare tasks as a means of eroding popular support for nation states and thus diminishing the risk of war. They perceived that in modern political systems there was a growing range of technical, politically neutral, functions which governments had to perform. Many of these tasks, such as control of air transport, or prevention of disease, could not be carried out effectively at the national level, and required international collaboration if they were to be performed successfully.

The functionalist strategy was therefore to encourage governments to entrust the performance of these tasks to non-political technical experts within the framework of an international organization. If the tasks were carried out successfully, then the governments concerned might be encouraged to permit similar collaborative attempts in other fields. In addition, general public support for such international collaboration would be increased if it was seen that such functional international organizations satisfied the common human interest in increased welfare. Thus men would learn from their social environment that international cooperation could satisfy needs which the traditional rivalry of nation states could not fulfil, and the focus of human activity would be shifted away from the political issues which divide states to the technical problems which all states have in common. In this way a transnational web of international welfare organizations would gradually be created, and nationalism would be replaced by allegiance to the world community – a process which Mitrany called 'federalism by instalments'.

The neofunctionalists have found the functionalist concept of incremental decision-making, whereby participants in international organizations 'learn' from success in one field to apply the same techniques in another, an attractive one. They have, however, criticized the functionalist strategy as too ambitious and lacking in clarity. Haas (1964) has questioned the functionalist assumption that there is a fundamental similarity of values in society which produces a universal perception of welfare needs; he contends that perceptions of welfare are shaped by cultural values, with the result that a universal view of welfare is unlikely to emerge from a culturally diverse international organization. Even in strictly technical matters, the views of non-political experts are shaped by the interests and political environment of the nation state which they represent. When discussions on technical standards for colour television took place prior to the introduction of colour transmissions in Europe in 1967, the technical experts had to choose between the West German PAL system and the French SECAM system. The German system was chosen by all the West European countries with the exception of France, despite the fact that the SECAM system was technically inferior and that incompatibility of the two systems would prevent exchange of programmes between France and the other countries of West Europe. The reason for the French decision was that the USSR was unwilling to adopt the West German system, and the French government at that time was anxious to improve its relations with the Soviet bloc (Layton, 1969, p. 72).

The main neofunctionalist criticism of functionalism is that welfare tasks involve the allocation of scarce resources between competing demands, and that this process is a political one, involving the exercise of power. Power, therefore, is inseparable from welfare. Nevertheless, according to Haas, programmes of international collaboration may maximize both welfare and integration, if they are functionally specific (that is, their tasks are economically significant to the member-states) and the national representatives carry some weight in their national decision-making processes. In addition, the countries or groups represented in such organizations should be culturally homogeneous, in order to ensure that a consensus on goals and procedures will emerge. This usually means that regional organizations are more likely to fulfil such conditions than global ones, as Haas found in his study of the International Labour Organization (Haas, 1964, pp. 47–9).

Haas conceives of the integration process as involving 'the gradual politicization of the actors' purposes which were initially considered "technical" or "noncontroversial"' (Haas and Schmitter 1966, p. 262). By this he means that a group of national actors, having decided to collaborate at the international level to further their individual and collective interest in the performance of some technical function, discover that the fulfillment of their original purpose depends upon a widening of the range of means available to them. An agreement among them to broaden the spectrum of means increases the 'controversial component' – namely, the fields of action which require political choices to be made about the amount of national autonomy to be delegated to the international organization. If such politicization is successful, and the national actors perceive that their interests are best served by delegation of national decision-making powers to the new supranational body in one field, it is likely that they will apply the lesson to integrative attempts in other fields.

This is the concept of 'spill-over', which is a central part of the neofunctionalist approach. In his study of economic and political elite activity in the ECSC, from the Schuman Plan of 1950 which proposed the establishment of a coal and steel community, to the signing of the EEC and Euratom Treaties in 1957, Haas (1958) found evidence of spill-over resulting from the interplay of competing interests. While there was no consensus among the elites in the six member countries of the ECSC when it was established, in that there was no widespread ideological commitment to supranationalism, there was a convergence of individual short-term interests which permitted the Schuman Plan to be implemented. Thus for some political parties in France the ECSC represented an opportunity to control German heavy industry, while for the German Christian Democrats it represented a method of removing allied controls over the Ruhr industrial area; for low-cost and efficient producers of coal and steel in all the member countries the ECSC was welcomed as a means of enlarging their markets, while most of the trade unions favoured the ECSC since collaboration at the supranational level improved their bargaining strength in national negotiations.

This fragmentation of opinion, coupled with the absence of divisive political issues, encouraged national elites to seek out like-minded groups elsewhere in the Community. German trade-union leaders, both Socialist and Christian, began lobbying jointly with their counterparts from other member countries, because they perceived their individual interests as being served by establishing through supranational organizations a regulated industrial economy in which labour interests had a permanent and significant influence. Elites in each member state found that economic integration through supranational institutions served their individual interests, and these converging practical goals provided the impetus for extending integration to sectors other than coal and steel. At the same time, the perceptions of governmental elites were being changed, not only because interest-group activity was increasing at the supranational level, but also because the problems which grew out of the initial agreement to set up the ECSC required continuous and ever more extensive contact and consultation between the governmental elites. In these processes of negotiation, the High Authority of the ECSC acted as a supranational honest broker, upgrading common interests by producing package solutions which combined the maximum of short-term satisfaction of interests with the minimum of long-term sacrifice. In performing such a service, the High Authority gained in stature and significance, since it was at the very centre of the bargaining process, and in some cases even encouraged situations in which solutions were only possible through further increases in its competence and the creation of new central policies.

Although the establishment of the EEC and Euratom seemed to confirm the neofunctionalist spill-over hypothesis, the development of the European Communities since 1958 has called many of the assumptions of neofunctionalism into question. Although one study of the governmental and non-governmental elite activities in the EEC found a similar reorientation taking place, it concluded that the bulk of interest-group activity remained oriented towards national goals (Lindberg, 1963, p. 287). Sidjanski (Reading 18) points out that the marginal role of interest groups in supporting integration may be due to the difficulty of achieving a transnational consensus on general policy issues, as distinct from a consensus on purely technical matters such as standards of food purity. Where general policy issues are at stake, interest groups have found it more effective to operate at the national level by putting pressure on their respective governments. Part of the explanation for this seems to be that the member states of the EEC endeavour to come to the negotiating table in Brussels with a coordinated and coherent negotiating position which has been formulated at the national level and is thereafter relatively impervious to pressure by interest groups operating at the supranational level. In addition, European issues have generally been treated as an adjunct of foreign policy, with the foreign affairs ministries assuming prime responsibility for handling them, rather than as a new dimension of activity for the various functional government departments. This has tended to insulate European issues from the normal domestic political processes in which national interest groups are accustomed to participate (see Wallace, Reading 14).

Although such criticisms of neofunctionalism are valid, in that they question the inevitability of political integration arising from gradual economic integration, there are more serious objections to the neofunctionalist approach. Stanley Hoffmann (1966) has argued that the stagnation of European integration in the 1960s is due to the distinction between 'low' politics – involving calculable and relatively insignificant welfare issues – and 'high' politics, involving major foreign policy and defence issues which no government is willing to entrust to an untried supranational institution. The failure of the Six to achieve integration in high politics by means of spillover from economic integration is the result of the diversity of their aims and domestic conditions, and the global character of the international system, in which there are few 'European' issues (as distinct from local or global ones). As Hansen (Reading 9) points out, the very effectiveness of economic integration in stimulating economic growth in the member states of the EEC has strengthened the capacity of those states to undertake independent action in other areas of policy.

Haas has himself recognized that 'pragmatic interest politics concerned with economic welfare has its own built-in limits' (Haas, 1967, p. 327), since such pragmatic interests are based on expectations of economic gain and may be satisfied by relatively limited measures of integration. Without a deep ideological or philosophical commitment to reinforce these material expectations, there is no inherent pressure for further integrative attempts. If integration is to advance, a share political commitment between statesmen and major non-governmental elites is necessary, and this was lacking in Europe; de Gaulle emerged as the opponent of supranationalism because it would undermine national autonomy in important policy areas. Since there was no common political commitment to dramatic advances in integration among the other statesmen of Europe, and the major elites in France and the other member states perceived their interests as being satisfied by gradual economic integration alone, de Gaulle was able to pursue his policy of a 'Europe des patries' without serious opposition. The result of the EEC's constitutional crisis of 1965–6 was an implicit agreement that integration in any given field would not be attempted if a member state considered that this contravened its vital interests – a confirmation of the veto power of member states (Lambert, 1966).

This discontinuity between economic and political integration has led Joseph Nye (1968b) to suggest that the concept of integration should be broken down into economic, political and social components, without making prejudgements as to the links between integration in one field and integration in another. Each component of integration could then be monitored by using measurements most appropriate to it, such as trade and mail flows as indicators of social integration, and it would be possible to distinguish situations in which integration and disintegration were occurring at the same time. Such an approach is useful as a means of describing the integration process, but without hypotheses linking changes in the various components of integration it cannot explain why a certain combination of conditions produces a given result. Lindberg and Scheingold (1970) have offered an alternative approach, in which the key to political integration lies in the extent to which the authority to make decisions is transferred from the national level to the supranational level in various policy areas. They suggest that processes of collective or supranational decision-making may have three possible outcomes: firstly, fulfillment of the original purpose agreed upon by the member states, such as the establishment of the common agricultural policy in the EEC; secondly, retraction from the original purpose because acceptable common rules and policies fail to be produced, as in the case of the abortive EEC transport policy; and thirdly, extension of obligations beyond those originally envisaged, as happened when the Community expanded from a coverage of coal and steel in the ECSC to the general economy in the EEC and Euratom (see Lindberg and Scheingold, Reading 13).

This approach emphasizes the transfer of authority and

legitimacy from member states to Community institutions and procedures, and enables a composite picture to be built up of fulfillment, retraction and expansion in the various issue-areas where integrative attempts have been made. It places much less stress on the shift of elite loyalty to a new centre, which hitherto has been an important part of the neofunctionalist conception of integration, and concentrates on the way in which hitherto independent nation states give up some of the attributes of their sovereignty. Haas himself has come to the conclusion that this process of 'authority-legitimacy transfer' is the master concept under which the various functional issues and tasks of integration can be grouped and evaluated (Haas, 1970, p. 633).

The other major criticism of the neofunctionalist approach is that in concentrating on the activities and aspirations of elites within a region such as West Europe, it neglects the influence of the international environment on those elites. Hoffmann (1966, p. 865) observed that 'the domestic politics are dominated not so much by the region's problems as by purely local and purely global ones, which conspire to divert the region's members from the internal affairs of their own area, and indeed would make an isolated treatment of those affairs impossible'. Kaiser (1968) has pointed out that the European Communities owe a great deal to American encouragement and assistance during the period of their inception, and that the declining possibility of a Soviet threat to their existence had profound effects on the evolution of the EEC and the crises under de Gaulle. There is also some evidence that regional groupings stimulate retaliatory or emulative regional groupings elsewhere, such as the formation of EFTA as a response to the creation of the EEC. Etzioni (1965) has stressed the importance of external elites in the process of political unification, in that they increased the likelihood of unification if their objectives coincided with those of the elites within the region. In the case of the EEC, Etzioni found that the United States used diplomatic, economic and military pressures to encourage unification, but that such pressures proved counter-productive when the United States supported British entry into the EEC in 1962, against the objections of France. The incompatibility of American and French policy objectives thus put a considerable strain on the communities, and had a de-unifying effect.

Although Haas has conceded that 'relations between the regional system . . . and the external world . . . can be of immense importance in explaining integration' (Haas, 1970, p. 620), the neofunctionalist emphasis on the activities and aspirations of regional elites rather than the influence of international environment remains one of the major deficiencies in the approach. This deficiency, however, is one which can be remedied by the inclusion of elite perceptions of extra-regional pressures and environmental factors, and the way in which these influence bargaining styles and strategies in the integration process. With such an enlarged framework of the influences upon elite perceptions, and a reduced emphasis on the possibility of economic, spilling over into political, integration, neofunctionalism provides a valuable approach to the study of regional integration. Its major strength is that it does not assume a conscious desire on the part of elites to undertake a grand design for integration, but rather that most political actors make decisions on the basis of short-term interests without foreseeing the long-term implications of those decisions. These long-term implications may result in further integration; for example, the EEC agreement in 1972 to narrow the exchange rate margins between their own currencies removes a major tool of national economic management, and increases the necessity for supranational economic planning if such a monetary union is to be preserved. There is no guarantee, however, that the political actors will accept such implications, and the advantage of the neofunctionalist approach is that it avoids normative assertions and concentrates on actual actor perception and behaviour in an attempt to discover recurrent patterns of decision-making which result in further integration. Like the other approaches to the study of regional integration, the predictive power of neofunctionalist theory is limited, but this may be strengthened as it is applied to a greater range of decision-making situations.

The study of European integration

This survey makes it clear that none of the major theoretical approaches to European integration is entirely satisfactory, and that a theory of integration is necessary if we are to address ourselves to the most important aspects of the process. At present there are too many competing analytical frameworks and too few directly comparable empirical studies of European integration; the subject is so vast that some methodological synthesis is imperative if duplication of effort is to be avoided. Some progress has been made in this direction (Cobb and Elder, 1970; Alker, 1970), but much more needs to be done before systematic comparisons of integration attempts in various regions are possible. The empirical research which has been accomplished thus far has indicated some of the most significant factors in the integration process, but as yet there is no coherent framework which reveals the relationships between these factors.

As far as West Europe is concerned, we are relatively fortunate that a large number of research projects on integration in the region have been completed or are in progress. Other regions are not being studied so intensively; very little work has been done on Central America and even less on East Africa, for example Nye (1968a). This inhibits further testing of some of the propositions derived from the West European experience, and is therefore an obstacle to the development of a general theory of regional integration.

Even the development of the European Community remains incompletely researched, with most empirical studies concentrated upon the institutional development of the Community rather than the general economic and social consequences of integration. There is a great need for more research on the social effects of labour mobility, for example (Böhning, 1972), and the conflict between the findings of Inglehart's youth survey and Deutsch and his associates' French and German elite interviews indicate that the relationship between integration and attitude formation is not at all clear. An inventory of such gaps in research would be tedious, but the point must be made that we have surprisingly little hard information on the European integration process, and that the search for it will not be fully effective until integration theory has been refined sufficiently to indicate exactly what we must look for.

The growth of the European Community has been and will probably remain a slow, diffuse and extremely complex process. It is important that social scientists come to grips with its development, because it is clear that the European integration movement will have a profound influence upon the conduct of international relations in the future. If a cohesive, centrally-controlled West European political entity develops, analogous to a nation state, this might encourage the emergence of similar regional groupings elsewhere – with unpredictable effects on global security. If West Europe develops a new type of political system, perhaps an extension of the federal type with a high degree of autonomy for local regions, this too may well have a lasting effect upon the political development of other areas. If integration in Europe fails, the prospects for integration else-where are gloomy; European political integration, therefore, is important, not only for the future of West Europe, but also for the future of society in general. It is a truism that man's ability to generate technology outstrips his ability to devise social organ-izations to control it, and the recent experience of the United States suggests that the federal system of government is showing signs of obsolescence. Just as the United States two centuries ago developed a new form of political organization, so West Europe today may have a similar opportunity. We may yet see the old world called into existence to redress the balance of the new.

References

ALKER, H. R. (1970), 'Integration logics: a review, extension and critique', *International Organization*, vol. 24, pp. 869–916.

BÖHNING, W. R. (1972), *The United Kingdom, the European Community and the Migration of Workers*, Oxford University Press.

COBB, R. W., and ELDER, C. (1970), *International Community: a regional and global study*, Holt, Rinehart & Winston.

DEUTSCH, K. W. (1964), 'Communication theory and political integration', in P. E. Jacob and J. V. Toscano (eds.), *The Integration of Political Communities*, Lippincott.

DEUTSCH, K. W. (1967), *Arms Control and Atlantic Unity*, Wiley.

DEUTSCH, K. W. *et al.* (1957), *Political Community and the North Atlantic Area*, Princeton University Press.

DEUTSCH, K. W. *et al.* (1967), *France, Germany and the Western Alliance*, Scribners.

ETZIONI, A. (1965), *Political Unification*, Holt, Rinehart & Winston.

FORSYTH, M. (1967), 'The political objectives of European integration', *International Affairs*, vol. 43, pp. 483–97.

FRIEDRICH, C. J. (1968), *Trends of Federalism in Theory and Practice*, Praeger.

HAAS, E. B. (1958), *The Uniting of Europe*, Stanford University Press.

HAAS, E. B. (1964), *Beyond the Nation State*, Stanford University Press.

HAAS, E. B. (1967), ' "The Uniting of Europe" and the Uniting of Latin America', *J. Common Market Stud.*, vol. 5, pp. 315–43.

HAAS, E. B. (1970), 'The study of regional integration: reflections on the joy and anguish of pretheorizing', *International Organization*, vol. 24, pp. 607–46.

HAAS, E. B., and SCHMITTER, P. C. (1966), 'Economics and differential patterns of political integration', *International Political Communities*, Anchor Books, pp. 259–300.

HAY, P. (1966), *Federalism and Supranational Organizations*, University of Illinois Press.

HOFFMANN, S. (1966), 'Obstinate or obsolete? The fate of the nation state and the case of Western Europe', *Daedalus*, no. 95, pp. 862–915.

INGLEHART, R. (1967), 'An end to European integration?', *Am. Pol. Sci. Rev.*, vol. 61, pp. 91–105.

KAISER, K. (1968), 'The interaction of regional subsystems', *World Politics*, vol. 21, pp. 84–107.

LAMBERT, J. (1966), 'Constitutional crisis 1965–1966', *J. Common Market Stud.*, vol. 4, pp. 195–228.

LAYTON, C. (1969), *European Advanced Technology*, PEP/Allen & Unwin.

LERNER, D., and ARON, R. (1957), *France Defeats EDC*, Praeger.

LINDBERG, L. N. (1963), *The Political Dynamics of European Economic Integration*, Stanford University Press.

LINDBERG, L. N., and SCHEINGOLD, S. A. (1970), *Europe's Would-be Polity*, Prentice-Hall.

MAYNE, R. (1967), 'The role of Jean Monnet', *Government and Opposition*, vol. 2, pp. 329–49.

MITRANY, D. (1943), *A Working Peace System*, Royal Institute of International Affairs.

MONCRIEFF, A. (1967), *Britain and the Common Market 1967*, BBC Publications.

MURET, C. (1966), 'The Swiss pattern for a federated Europe', *International Political Communities*, Anchor Books, pp. 149–74.

NYE, J. S. (1968a), *International Regionalism*, Little, Brown.

NYE, J. S. (1968b), 'Comparative regional integration: concept and measurement', *International Organization*, vol. 22, pp. 855–80.

PFALTZGRAFF, R. L., and DOUGHERTY, J. E. (1971), *Contending Theories of International Relations*, Lippincott.

PUCHALA, D. J. (1970), 'International transactions and regional integration', *International Organization*, vol. 24, pp. 732–63.

DE ROUGEMONT, D. (1965), *The Meaning of Europe*, Sidgwick & Jackson.

RUSSETT, B. M. (1963), *Community and Contention: Britain and America in the Twentieth Century*, MIT Press.

SPINELLI, A. (1966), *The Eurocrats: Conflict and Crisis in the European Community*, Johns Hopkins Press.

STREETEN, P. (1964), *Economic Integration*, Sythoff.

TAYLOR, P. (1971), *International Co-operation Today*, Elek Books.

TEUNE, H. (1964), 'The learning of integrative habits', in P. E. Jacob and J. V. Toscano (eds.), *The Integration of Political Communities*, Lippincott.

DE TOCQUEVILLE, A. (1856), *L'Ancien régime et la révolution.*

Part One
Why Europe? The Origins and Achievements of European Integration

Although the enlargement of the European Community's membership in 1973 marks an important phase in its development, it is clear that the original momentum for greater West European unity has disappeared. Miriam Camps attributes this loss of momentum to the failure of the 'Europeans' to come to terms with changes in the international and domestic environments of the West European countries, which have rendered the original goals of the European experiment either irrelevant or impracticable. She argues that unless new international and domestic priorities can be articulated involving an important and constructive role for the European Community, enthusiasm for European integration will continue to decline.

The absence of a firm political commitment for integration on the part of the West European governments is seen by Altiero Spinelli as the major cause of the failure of European integration to progress beyond limited functional fields. Although this article was written before the formation of the EEC, his prediction that the easing of cold-war tensions and the continuing recovery of West European national economies would erode support for further integration has proved to be accurate.

One of the problems of the European Commission is that it can only play a constructive role in areas which have previously been agreed upon by member governments as appropriate for integration. Despite the Commission's plea for progress beyond the initial objectives laid down in the Rome Treaties, the national governments have firmly retained their powers of initiative. Ralf Dahrendorf aroused some controversy when he suggested that this was desirable, in that national governments are concerned with reaching voluntary agreements on important issues rather than mandatory solutions of relatively insignificant technical matters.

1 Miriam Camps

European Unification in the 1970s

Excerpt from M. Camps, 'European unification in the seventies'
International Affairs (London), vol. 47, 1971, pp. 671–8.

In thinking about the future of the European Community today –
whether one is thinking about institutional reform, the extent of
the integration to be sought among the members of the Community, or the relationship of the Community with the rest of the
world – there is an obvious danger that problems will be looked
at in the context of the late 1950s and early 1960s rather than in
the context of the 1970s. The 'great' debate on joining the Common Market that is taking place in Britain is, for the most part, a
tired replay of that in 1961–3; and the hubbub in Community
circles aroused by the 'Wieland Europa' articles in *Die Zeit*
(9 July, 16 July 1971) did much to confirm the criticisms of the
author who was, it may safely be assumed, trying to rejuvenate,
not to inter, the European construction.

One of the unfortunate, if understandable, by-products of the
long struggle between General de Gaulle and the 'Europeans' of
the Monnet and Hallstein persuasions (which were, of course, not
quite the same) has been the tendency of the 'Europeans' to become conservative and overly doctrinaire. At a time when they
were trying above all to save and protect what they had built, it
was natural enough to resist change and experimentation for
fear that any tampering with their construction would open the
path to its complete destruction. But defensiveness breeds timidity
and leads to sterility of thought. Similarly in the United Kingdom
one effect of having been stalemated for almost a decade has been
to inhibit new thinking. There is a tendency to feel that now, at
last, the old files can be opened, the dust blown off, and the unfinished business put in hand. The temptation to rely on past
thinking is also apparent across the Atlantic: George Ball's recent
article in *The Times* (23 July 1971), giving an American view of
Britain's 'agony' over its decision about joining the European
Community, sounded curiously dated – a charge that can seldom
be made of that articulate advocate.

The European experiment, when it began in 1950 with the announcement of the Schuman Plan, was bold, daring and innovative. It was a brilliant response to the needs of the times: it brought the French and the Germans together in a new creative relationship and it caught the imagination of a battered continent in need of new goals. A 'European Community' could be a catalyst for needed change in the 1970s, but if it is to play that role there must be as much willingness to think new thoughts, experiment with new forms and focus on forging new relationships as there was in the earlier, golden, period of the European movement.

At the risk of reciting the obvious, it is perhaps worth noting some of the things that have changed since the drive for European unity lost its momentum about a decade ago, some of the new factors to which any European Community will have to be responsive if it is again to be both relevant to the problems of the period and a pioneer in the long process of building a more rational global society. Although the dividing lines are inevitably somewhat arbitrary, it is perhaps useful to group these changes under three broad headings: first, changes in the character of the political–security setting; second, changes in the nature of relationships among states and in attitudes within states; and third, changes in the nature of the agenda confronting the enlarged Community.

Perhaps the four outstanding changes in the political–security setting – if one compares the situation today with that of the late 1950s or early 1960s – are:

The recognition of, and acceptance of, strategic parity between the United States and the Soviet Union, and, related to that change, the opening and continuation of the talks between the two powers on the limitation of strategic arms (SALT).

The new triangular relationship between the United States, the Soviet Union and the People's Republic of China.

The *de facto* acceptance of the *status quo* in Central Europe as evidenced, for example, by the Western reaction to the Soviet invasion of Czechoslovakia in 1968, by the German pursuit of *Ostpolitik*, and by the character of the arrangements for Berlin which have recently been negotiated by the four responsible powers.

The emergence of Japan as the third (or fourth, if the European Community is counted as one rather than six) industrial power which some futurologists predict will overtake the Soviet Union by the end of the decade.

Thus, as compared with the picture a decade ago, the situation today is one of greater fluidity, of five main powers – the United States, the Soviet Union, China, Japan and, potentially, Western Europe – with rather greater freedom of movement for each of the five; it is no longer the essentially bipolar world that characterized the 1950s and still dominated thought in the early 1960s.

Turning, next, to the changes in the nature of the relationships among states, I suppose the outstanding change is the rate at which the time and space dimensions of the world are shrinking as a result of scientific and technological progress, a change that was most dramatically demonstrated, not only by the fact of the landing on the moon in the summer of 1969, but also by the fact that this extraordinary event was watched and listened to by millions of people everywhere. Connected with the rate at which modern communications are making the world one, but also an important development in its own right, is the growth in the economic interdependence of countries, especially among the highly developed countries with market economies. This trend was, of course, visible a decade ago, but it is so much more marked today that it is worth emphasizing. Another development – and one which is closely related to the first two and again not totally new but more pronounced and more obvious today than it was a decade ago – is the blurring of the line between internal and external problems, between matters traditionally thought to be of purely domestic concern and those considered to be of foreign or international concern. Again, this is particularly apparent in the relationships among the developed countries; such things as interest rates come immediately to mind. The emergence of new problems – pollution and other aspects of environmental deterioration today, perhaps weather control and genetic manipulation tomorrow – seem bound to accentuate these three trends, thereby shrinking further the time–space dimensions of the globe, intensifying the interactions between countries and smudging further the traditional lines between domestic and foreign concerns.

Then, there is the change within societies, again particularly in the societies of the developed countries: the disenchantment of youth with affluence, its distrust of all forms of organization and its faith in a kind of humanistic anarchism. And related to this, but less identified with youth and most noticeable in the United States, there is a shift in priorities: a growing concern with the quality of domestic life and a growing resistance to overseas involvements.

Finally, when one looks at the internal problems that the enlarged Community will need to tackle in the years ahead – the agenda for the 1970s – one is struck by two things: first, that the decisions that will soon have to be taken about the tasks needing to be done will confront the member countries with large new choices: there is very little hard guidance in the existing agreements. The injunctions in the Treaties of Rome and Paris have either been largely carried out, as is the case with the formation of the customs union; or they have been outlived, as is the case with some of the provisions of the coal and steel treaty; or the attempts to implement them have so clearly run into the sand that they can probably be given new life only by basic new decisions, as is the case with some of the provisions of the Euratom treaty; or they are so general in character that the decisions yet to be taken on how these precepts are to be implemented will constitute the key decisions, as is the case with monetary union and the other statements of intent in the Hague Communiqué of December 1969. Thus there is, inescapably, a critical period of large and very basic decision-making ahead if the Community is not simply to remain on its present plateau.

The second thing that strikes one is that there is very little clear guidance in what might be called the imperatives of the European situation. Today Western Europe is prosperous beyond its wildest post-war dreams; relationships among the Western European countries are sometimes strained, but there is no longer any serious prospect of armed conflict between the ancient rival great powers; and there is little fear of military attack from the East. Even the consequences of the steps towards union already taken, the spill-over effect that for a time seemed likely to give a continuing momentum to the process of integration, although still a factor, is a much less irresistible force than it seemed to be at one time. It is easy enough to enumerate tasks that an enlarged Community *might* now undertake; but it is difficult to list many that either the objective facts of the European situation, or the results of past actions, or the obligations of commitments already entered into *require* it to undertake. British membership is in a very real sense unfinished business. But once that has been achieved, the slate is remarkably clean. This is very different from the situation in the 1950s, or even that of a decade ago when the Community had the timetable laid down in the Treaty of Rome for the transitional period as a clear guide to action. Some convinced 'Europeans' will doubtless rejoin that there are all the imperatives one could wish for in the frequently declared objective of 'uniting Europe'. But this would only be true if the governments concerned had, in effect, bound themselves to a precise form of union which, of course, none of them has done. The rhetoric of European unity is, today, no guide to specific action.

However, if as suggested above, changes in the third category permit an extraordinary amount of freedom for thinking about the future tasks of the Community, the changes that have taken place in the other two categories – in the political–security setting and in the general character of relationships among states and within societies – do suggest certain guidelines for the new thinking that is now called for. Thus the changes noted in the first category suggest that Western Europe has a substantial role to play as a power in the fluid international system that seems in prospect, if it can organize itself to speak collectively. One can go even further. In a curious way, in the realm of geo-political discourse, Western Europe – not France, Germany or the United Kingdom – is already the 'actor'; the question is not whether there is a fifth great power, or more accurately power-grouping, but whether it will organize itself to be an effective 'actor'.[1]

The second group of changes suggests a somewhat different concept of, and role for, a 'uniting Europe'. These changes tend to set, I think, clear limits to the usefulness of thinking about 'Europe' simply as the fifth great power and point to the need to think of 'Europe' as a level between that of the European nation-state on the one hand and more inclusive groupings of states on the other. In other words, certain functions should now be performed at the 'European' level rather than the national level because that is the level that corresponds to the dimension of the problem and not because of some compulsion to push to the European level anything and everything that the concept of 'Europe as a power' might seem to imply. This point is worth some elaboration; for what I am here suggesting is that there will

1. See, for example, the frequent use of the expression 'Western Europe' in President Nixon's second report to the Congress on US Foreign Policy (*US Foreign Policy for the 1970s*, 25 February 1971) and the paucity of references in this document to the individual countries of Western Europe.

be constraints – both from above and from below – on the kind of functions or tasks that are appropriate for handling at the 'European' level.

The growing interdependence, or interrelatedness, of the advanced industrialized countries and the growth of transnational phenomena, like the multinational corporation, that escape national control and treat the world as an incipient single economy, are posing problems with which existing global international institutions built, essentially, on the concept of the autonomy of individual nation-states cannot cope. Increasingly, many problems will either have to be looked at by the advanced industrialized countries, at least, as common problems requiring common action, or the network of economic relationships will deliberately have to be loosened.[2] The recent American action imposing unilaterally and with no prior consultation a 10 per cent surcharge on imports and renouncing its obligation to sell gold (thus, in effect, floating the dollar contrary to the Articles of Agreement of the IMF) was, of course, a move to loosen international economic linkages; it was a big step towards a more national, less international, management of the network of economic relationships in which all the advanced countries are today enmeshed. This was only the first move, however, in what promises to be a long process of modifying the existing rules. As this is being written, the eventual reshaping of the international rules could still be towards closer coordination of policies and more common action among the advanced industrialized countries or towards a deliberate loosening of linkages with more scope for national management and for national protective action. But, whichever way the argument goes in this round, it is difficult to believe that, in the long term, the kind of intimate consultation that has developed in the Group of Ten[3] and Working Party Three of the OECD will not be continued and intensified. If this is so, greater cooperation among the West European countries extending, perhaps, to the point of a monetary union would seem to have

2. Richard Cooper has written extensively on this theme. William Diebold has rightly pointed out that the phenomenon Cooper is discussing is usually not strictly one of interdependence but, rather, of interaction.

3. The Group of Ten is an informal gathering, under the general aegis of the IMF, of Ministers of Finance and Central Bank Governors (or, more usually, their deputies) from the following countries: Belgium, Canada, France, Germany, Italy, Japan, the Netherlands, Sweden, the United Kingdom and the United States (Switzerland, although not originally a member, now normally meets with the Group).

advantages for its members, principally perhaps because it would increase the West European voice in the management of the international system as a whole. But in the long term, European action could not be a substitute for a wider system or for closer coordination of policies among the key members of that wider system.

The general point being made here is this. If one looks ahead, many of the things which today it makes sense for the European countries to treat as common problems and to act on collectively can no longer be handled effectively even by large units like the United States or Western Europe acting alone. Thus although a 'European' approach will frequently be more in accord with the dimensions of today's problems than a purely national approach, there will increasingly be need for cooperation that extends well beyond the European complex and for cooperation that is so close, so continuous and so intimate that it will erode some of the functions of 'Europe as a power' even as it will erode some of the functions of the 'United States as a power'. A forward-looking European Community should, therefore, shun the temptation to clothe itself with those attributes of sovereignty that reason suggests are already threadbare and should soon be cast off.

There are also constraints of a different order on the transfer of functions to the 'European level' – what I have called constraints from below – which also suggest that it would be out of tune with the times simply to take some federal system such as that of the United States as a model and to act by analogy in considering what should be done by 'Europe'. Today, at all levels of society, a pervasive organizational problem is how to combine efficiency with an adequate sense of participation. Alienation and anomy are today particularly marked in the United States, although they are apparent in most highly developed societies. As power has shifted to the federal government and as the government has become larger and more remote and less personal (and with the advent of the computer less personal in a new sense) any effective participation by the individual has become, in fact, extremely difficult. And the situation tends to feed on itself: as the individual loses the feeling that he can affect what happens he loses his sense of responsibility, or opts out, and a bad situation is made worse. Regardless of one's views of the details of the plan, President Nixon's recent proposals for pushing various powers back down to the state and local level is a welcome recognition of the need to re-engage the individual in the process of government through a deliberate decentralization of power and decision-making. There will be a similar need in Europe. And, as functions that can now be handled more appropriately at the European, rather than national, level are transferred upwards, there should be a deliberate process of decentralization and a strengthening of local regional governments within the Community.[4]

Can these two roles be combined? Can 'Europe' be both a world power and a 'layer' or a 'level' in the continuum of organized society? I see no reason why it cannot. And to think about it in these terms, in this dual perspective, seems to me to be in accord with the real needs of the times. But it is a lot harder to break new ground than it is to reproduce known patterns. Moreover, to think adequately about the functions that a European Community will have to perform if it is to play these two quite different roles requires both a conception of the kind of international order one wants to move towards and some minimum level of consensus about the values in domestic society one wants to preserve and to strengthen. These are large issues and not the kind of question that make an instant appeal to pragmatic politicians. But I think it unlikely that the 'Europe of the 1970s' will generate the kind of enthusiasm that was evoked by the 'Europe of the 1950s' unless today's 'Europe of the 1960s' can break out of the uneasy compromise between the 'Europe of Monnet' and the 'Europe of de Gaulle' with which it has been condemned to live, can forget the quarrels of the past and can become again a living experiment in creating new relationships among states and between peoples.

4. If this were done it might well contribute to the easing of various regional ethnic problems that now bedevil some of the individual member states, e.g. Bretons, Welsh, Flemings.

2 Altiero Spinelli

The Growth of the European Movement since the
Second World War

A. Spinelli, 'The growth of the European movement since World War
II', in C. Grove Haines (ed.), *European Integration*, Johns Hopkins
Press, 1957, pp. 37–63.

The forerunners

The question of European unity has been recurring for a number
of centuries in the political literature of the Continent. It was not
until the nineteenth century, however, in the midst of the struggle
for the creation of national democratic states, that this idea of
unity was made more precise and, utilizing the American experience, there was talk of a European federation or, better yet, of a
United States of Europe. But even then men like Mazzini,
Cattaneo, Proudhon, Victor Hugo, and others who advocated
European union were regarded as prophetical or visionary. They
did not think in terms of practical realizations of political action
or understand that problems might be solved by pooling the
respective forces of the various nation-states.

In a certain sense, one may include among the forerunners of
this movement Luigi Einaudi, who between the end of 1918 and
the beginning of 1919 wrote articles arguing against the erroneous
concept of the League of Nations and advocating a federalistic
solution for the European situation. Because of the clarity with
which Einaudi defined the problem, these pages represent federalist thinking of the highest caliber. Unfortunately, these views
were published as personal opinion, and no political movement
developed from them.

The first attempts

Pan-Europe. The first of these proposals for the unification of
Europe was that of Count Coudenhove-Kalergi, which had the
advantage of arousing some unrest in public opinion. Coming
from the Austrian aristocracy, and thus used to the plurinational
idea, Coudenhove-Kalergi became, after the end of the First
World War, the self-appointed paladin of a federated Europe. A
movement called Pan-Europe came into being, but it lacked mass
following and appealed mostly to diplomats and intellectuals of

old Europe, most of whom have since disappeared from the political scene. Its greatest hour came when Briand and Stresemann tried to reconcile the profound differences between their two countries. Coudenhove-Kalergi, backed by his followers, many of whom were men of authority, suggested to Briand that he propose a European federation. Actually Coudenhove-Kalergi himself did not have a very clear idea of what a European federation should mean, since he did not think it at all objectionable to include in such a democratic federation even Fascist Italy, where there was no elected parliament and no political freedom. To add confusion to this already fuzzy program, Briand suggested a project for a European constitution which would set up a little league of nations for Europe. This league provided just as palliative a solution as the big League, since here again member states retained all their sovereign powers.

The Briand project died stillborn, mainly because of British and Italian opposition. With the failure of Franco-German rapprochement and of the Briand-Stresemann policies with it, and with the triumph of national socialism in Germany a few years later, the Pan-Europe movement withered away. Coudenhove-Kalergi is still active today, and still considers himself the leader of Pan-Europe, but his project is no more than a name without any content. Respected as a pioneer of the Pan-Europe movement after the Second World War, he nevertheless has failed to establish an effective collaboration with the present-day federalist movement.

A second and more coherent surge of federalist thinking and activities is represented by the Federal Union movement, which came into being in Great Britain during the years immediately preceding the Second World War. We are used to thinking of the British as completely averse to any idea of federation, and they, themselves, seem to strengthen this impression by often repeating that this is a strictly Latin or a Cartesian idea, very foreign to their method of thinking. The Latin people are supposed to think always in terms of well spelled-out, written constitutions, while the British, whose political system is based on an unwritten constitution, are supposed to apply the empirical approach also in the field of international cooperation. This is not actually so, however. The Latin supranational idea is not an idea of federation, but of empire, of the violent conquest of as many people as possible, bringing them under the law of the strongest. The idea that it is possible to bring about a supranational government by means other than conquest, i.e. through free consent of states, and that it is possible to divide sovereignty, assigning portions of it to different organs of the government, is a typically Anglo-Saxon conception.

The first example of two states uniting by a free decision and without war was the union between England and Scotland, which took place at the beginning of the eighteenth century, and it may be considered as an incipient step to federation. The first real federal constitution was that of the United States, which was written by Englishmen, rebels to their king, of course, but men who had benefited from a British political education. It was this group of people who invented the new constitutional formula, on the basis of which the states keep part of their sovereignty while transferring another part to a higher authority. The British Parliament is, moreover, the only parliament in the world which has created a priori federal constitutions for both Canada and Australia, constitutions which have worked very well. It also took the first steps toward a study from which the federal constitution of India emerged later. The only real example of federation outside the Anglo-Saxon countries is Switzerland. But it is also known that the Swiss, passing in 1847 from the confederate to the federal structure, based their action a great deal upon the experience of the United States Constitution. From this brief résumé, we must conclude that the federal experience is very close to the British political spirit, and also that the British can easily understand the federal concept and its logical political and economic implications. Another proof of this understanding is seen in the federalist literature of the Federal Union, which is of first quality and even today superior to the average Continental literature on the subject, because of the coherence with which problems are presented, obstacles examined, and solutions proposed. It is interesting to note here that the most coherent federalist movement today is the Italian, which has absorbed a great deal from the study of this English federalist literature.

The flowering of the English federalist movement during the 1930s and the sudden abandonment of federalist activities during the following decade must be studied a little more carefully. Many English people at that time had realized that the era in which Great Britain was the political and economic center of the world had definitely come to an end. Following the great economic crisis of 1929, the British Empire had ceased to be the great free market, open to everyone, and it also came to close itself behind protective barriers and preferential tariffs. The economic unity of the world was thus definitely brought to an end. At the same time, the revival of German nationalism showed that England was no longer capable of being, in Europe itself, the decisive element of political equilibrium. It appeared that the First World War and the British victory had been in vain. In Europe there were now two powerful states, too powerful to be either controlled or guided by Great Britain. Country after country set up totalitarian regimes and prepared for war. England, still following its traditional policy, risked being eliminated as a factor in European politics.

Many Britishers, therefore, came to the conclusion that England, in order to put a stop to the economic and political decomposition of the free world, should change its political course and promote a European federal union. This European federation would have created an area of peace and equilibrium around England. Initially, the federation was to be formed by Great Britain, the Low Countries, Belgium, France and the Scandinavian countries, but eventually it was hoped that the Fascist countries might be absorbed after the overthrow of the dictatorships.

Side by side with these proposers of a European federation there were, although less influential, those who favored an Atlantic federation, which looked toward union with the United States, and even those who favored transforming the Commonwealth into a federation. The high mark of British federalism was reached when Churchill proposed to France, crumbling under the onslaught of German military might, a union between the two countries with one parliament and a common citizenship. Churchill's proposal, of course, was dictated by the urgent needs of the situation, which meant that the British government was trying to find a formula which would permit France to continue the war. But it is important to note that if this proposal was a federal proposal, it was due to a great extent to the action and the influence of the Federal Union, which counted among its backers eminent political and cultural personalities, as well as the man in the street. The idea of federation was, so to speak, in the air, and Churchill only had to reach for it.

Among the men who at the time were close to Churchill and who contributed to the inspiration of this proposal, there was a Frenchman whom we shall see later among the fighters for European unity. He was Jean Monnet, who since then has become convinced of the necessity for abandoning the system of national states in favor of a higher, supranational organization. Churchill's proposal, however, caught the French completely unprepared, and, because of its novelty, they considered it absurd. It was also very difficult for the French political mind to admit that there could be a power stronger than France. For this reason, the British proposal for a federal union was unsuccessful, and France accepted capitulation as a vassal state of Germany.

With this French refusal, it can be said that the active cycle of the British federal movement came to an end, although the Federal Union, as a small and insignificant movement, is still in existence. After the fall of France, England found herself alone, facing a Europe conquered by Hitler, in the gravest moment of her national history. In this period we note the consolidation in the British public conscience of two attitudes destined to weigh heavily in the following years. First, there was reappraisal of the value of the British nation as able to hold fast in the moment of greatest danger and to organize the life of the whole nation, counting on the full loyalty of all citizens, thus becoming the absolute center and surest bulwark for the safety of the whole British people. Second, there was a complete loss of faith in Europe, and the old sentiment for unification with Europe was replaced by the firm conviction that no confidence could be placed in the European states.

The entire course of the war strengthened the British in these attitudes. And in order to understand properly the meaning of the Labour party's postwar experience, we must look at it as the result of the rallying of the British nation during the war. The same state which had been capable of mobilizing and organizing all the energies of the country to lead it to victory could also be mobilized to attain higher levels of social justice.

All this meant, too, a strengthening of nationalism – British nationalism to be sure, better-mannered than that of other countries, alien to exaggeration, but nationalism none the less, strengthening the persuasion that outside of national unity there is nothing that has the right to interfere with it. It is clear why, in a situation like this, British federalism has withered away, no longer finding political forces to support it.

The situation following the Second World War

The problem of European unity became acute and pressing following the Second World War, which created an entirely new situation in Europe. To understand the meaning of the movement for European unification and the forces which moved toward this unification, its achievements, its failures and its present prospects, it is advisable to stop for a minute and analyse the situation from which it emerged.

The downfall of the idol of the sovereign national state

A generation ago, during the war of 1914, the Continental European nations went through an experience analogous to that of the British during the Second World War. Some states won and others lost the war, but all, with the exception of the Hapsburg Empire, which had collapsed, managed to maintain their positions as sovereign communities, demonstrating the capacity to survive, to face a perilous political situation, and to organize national life and guide it with a firm hand. The citizens of the various countries were convinced of the value and worth of the national state as the best expression of political life. Even Russia, where the archaic political and economic order had collapsed as a result of the war, succeeded, through a terrible revolution, in emerging as a more dynamic and cohesive political entity, capable of asserting her national unity and defending her independence.

A consequence of these experiences was the rapid spreading of ideals which tended to emphasize and strengthen the power of the state, and to restore to it, even in time of peace, that ascendancy over the population which it had had during the war, and to render it even more detached from the community of nations. Loud voices calling for the continuation and the enhancement of the power of the state were those of Rathenau, Lenin, Mussolini and Hitler, and crowds came to listen. The war had given birth to two new powerful ideologies which glorified the state, communism and fascism.

The experience of the Second World War has had the opposite effect for Continental Europe. With the advance of Germany, all other states involved in the war, whether opponents or allies of Hitler, collapsed and showed they could no longer guarantee a minimum of security and independence to their people; they were turned, voluntarily or reluctantly, into dependencies of the Nazi Empire. Then the German state, which had absorbed the others, was crushed violently, her military power annihilated and her political organization destroyed. Germany became a territory swamped by the victors, and when a few years later the victors attempted to give back to the people some form of political organization, it was discovered that they were not able to re-construct one state, but had to create two.

All European people had experienced military defeat, but this time there were different results; the idol of the national state, which had been respected up to then, aroused disgust and fell to pieces. Hundreds of thousands of Europeans had ignored national loyalties, often fighting against their own countrymen side by side with those who were officially enemies of their country.

After the war, the European states regained formal sovereignty at some point, but the national institutions were unstable, lacked force, and were not capable of facing the problems of reconstruc-ting a normal national life without the protection and pressure of the great victor powers. That the national state was an idol which did not merit that absolute respect which the pressure of political propaganda had enforced had already been pointed out by non-conformist thinkers. To this now had to be added the obvious and irrefutable evidence of the facts.

This elementary experience penetrated the minds of all, even though not all were fully conscious of it, and it brought about a situation which has made possible the spreading of the movement for European unity, that is, the attainment of order which could replace the discredited and obsolete formula of national states.[1]

The leading role of Catholic political parties
After the war there was a tendency for political parties inspired by the Catholic religion to become predominant in all countries of Western Europe. This is not the place to examine the reasons for this predominance, which was further evidence of the declining power of the state and of the increased prestige of its secular antagonist, the Catholic church. What matters here is to note that of all the democratic forces which appeared during the immediate postwar period, the Catholics were the least imbued with a nationalistic point of view.

The forces of nationalism had been swept away by the catas-trophe, and the democratic currents which prevailed were in-

1. From this basic experience one must exclude Great Britain, for reasons which we have seen already, and the neutral countries such as Switzerland and Sweden. English and Swedish influence has also contributed to keeping Denmark and Norway outside the European movement. Spain and Portugal have stayed outside the movement because of their Fascist type of dictator-ships, as have countries of eastern Europe which, transformed into satellites of the USSR, cannot hope to follow roads other than those prescribed by the Kremlin.

spired more or less consistently by liberalism, socialism and the idea of Christian democracy. Men sympathetic to the problem of European unity were to be found in all three, but their respective influence within each of these groups varied because of their differing political traditions, although all three were built on antinationalistic and universalistic ideological foundations.

The liberals who had been the builders of, or at least the inspiration for, the modern European states tended to believe, quite naturally, in the conservation of these states as creatures they loved dearly.

The Socialists had been from the outset strongly antinationalistic, even if only sentimentally so. Their manifesto had stated clearly that 'the proletarians have no fatherland'. But the manifesto had also stated a clear indication of how the Socialist program could evolve: 'In so far as the proletariat of every country ought, above all, to gather all the political power to itself, to raise itself to a national class and to constitute itself as a nation, so it still is and remains national.' The Socialists had, in fact, exerted their political action by inserting the working classes into the national picture. Their political aims increasingly took the form of an ever-growing and consistent program of national planning. A shrewd Socialist like Ignazio Silone said that of all the nationalizations advanced by socialism, the one which has succeeded best has been the nationalization of socialism itself. When, after the Second World War, the democratic states were restored, the Socialists consistently advocated that these states follow a national, socialistic policy, aware perhaps of the fact that abandonment of national sovereignty would weaken their position. The experience of the English Labourites, which seemed to be the great model, made the Socialists deaf to the problem created by the crises of national states.

The hands of the Catholic parties were not quite so tied with respect to their universalistic doctrine, although the church had intrigued to some extent with Fascist regimes. Catholic political forces had kept aloof for a long time from politics in the three most important states of Western Continental Europe. The Third French Republic had been a secular state; the German Reich was Protestant at its beginning and pagan by the end; the kingdom of Italy had a struggle with the Vatican. The Catholics, indeed, had not remained immune from the spread of nationalism, but still remained outside its influence, and it cannot be said that they had much sympathy for the European national states. This explains why, following the war, when the Catholic parties assumed control of various European countries, they did not prove themselves to be jealous custodians of national sovereignties, but were open-minded enough to admit the possibility of unification at the supranational level, even though they had no clear ideas how this should be brought about. It is worth while to note that among the least European-minded Catholics have been the Belgian Social Democrats, and this because, unlike their French, German and Italian counterparts, they had identified themselves for several generations with the forces of their national state.

To this general predispostion to a European union on the part of the Catholic parties must be added another factor which, although accidental, is not without significance. The three men destined to direct French, German and Italian foreign policy after the war, Schuman, Adenauer and De Gasperi, came from borderlands. Two of them in their time had belonged to two different states; the third, Adenauer, had been involved in the separatist movement in the Rhineland after the First World War. All three were fundamentally conservative, but national sovereignty was not one of the values that they were anxious to protect.

Decline of the traditional forces of nationalism

If the respect of the public and of rulers for national sovereignty has fallen, this is also true for administrative, social and economic bodies. Such bodies, which are normally profoundly interested in the maintenance of sovereignty and to whom the system of national states usually gives a strong voice in the conduct of the political life of the state, found themselves in full decline at the end of the war.

The bureaucracies which had represented the backbone of the states and had become to a great extent the organizers of national life were in a position at the end of the war in which they were not even able to satisfy the most elementary needs of the state. The general staffs had either been dissolved or, if still existing, were left without troops to command and certainly were not in a position to claim to be the tutors of national security. The great coalitions of sectional interests, whether representing capitalists or labor, that had obtained from the state a monopoly or had been given a free hand to exploit the national market, were no longer in a position to assure even a reduced movement of the most needed consumer goods and, of course, could not still expect the state to guarantee them the privileged position formerly enjoyed.

In Continental Europe at this time public administration bodies, armed forces and the economic system existed, as it were, disemboweled and incapable of action. That unnoticed force which is continuously generated by the administrative bodies of the national state, and which more often than ideologies and the will of politicians determines the development of national life, had suddenly been found missing. Not until the old mold had been recast could these forces effectively impede the various political tendencies moving toward a reconstruction of Europe along supranational lines.

The great force of Soviet imperialism

After the Second World War Europe had ceased to be the center of world politics and had been replaced by the USSR and the United States as the leaders in world affairs, with England, still important, definitely confined to play a secondary role. An inescapable result of this shift in the power system has been the large influence that the policies of the United States and the USSR have had on European politics.

The USSR through its policy of expansion has contributed indirectly, but none the less effectively, to the development of the ideas of European unity. All of Eastern Europe has fallen under its domination, and progressively, but inevitably, the earlier democratic experiments have suffocated wherever Communist governments, satellites of the Soviet Union, were formed. The Soviet Union never actually concealed the intention of reaching beyond the Trieste-Stettin line. The developments of this policy have been varied, and are known too well to need further discussion here. The power differentials between the European democratic states and the Soviet Union were extremely great, and the fear of affecting the fate of the Russian and Eastern European people was felt very deeply by the majority of Western Europeans. The fear factor, always present in political situations, played a very important role in the development of the European idea after the Second World War. Men and political forces who might have been hostile or indifferent to the idea of European unity understood clearly that this was the only way of giving Europe the necessary strength to preserve its independence. The traditional rivalries among European states, and especially between France and Germany, seemed now anachronistic. The idea of European unity had come up as a means to prevent wars among the people of Europe, but such wars were now pointless, and the real problem was the threatening march of Soviet imperialism. In a certain sense the influence of this great fear on the development of a united European action has been excessive, and we shall see that, after Stalin's death and the subsiding of war jitters, it has had adverse consequences on the European movement.

The American influence

The countries of Western Europe found themselves, thanks to the decisions reached at Yalta, in the zone of Anglo-American influence or, to be more realistic, in the American sphere of influence. Had the United States chosen to follow an imperialistic policy, like the USSR, there would have been no serious resistance to it in Western Europe. Moreover, the Americans disposed of the military power necessary to command obedience and the economic power with which to aid and to corrupt the European populations.

This did not take place, nor indeed was the United States equipped to carry out a policy of imperial conquest, for the American mind, like the Russian, is basically Jacobin, irrespectful of the past, and convinced that the political organization in its own country should serve as a model for the rest of the world. Fortunately, the Americans were enemies of dictatorship under any guise, and the ideas which they brought along were those of federal democracy. They wanted to see Europe forget all its petty nationalism and unite itself in liberty as the American states had done.

American influence has been applied continually and with increasing momentum in favor of a unification of Europe. This was made possible by the great prestige of the United States, which had given ample evidence of its military strength and so much economic aid – so much more than could ever have been expected – to European populations reduced almost to desperation. In fact, it may be said that the American attitude toward the unification of Europe has been a decisive factor in whatever initiatives have been taken by European statesmen in this direction. Indeed, it should be remembered that initiatives of this type were taken by these statesmen not so much in a spirit of loyal dedication to European unity, as through a desire to please the Americans. This duplicity on the part of the European ruling class is another example of the moral degeneration of Europe, and it also explains the many shortcomings of their efforts in bringing about unification. Unfortunately for Europe, the Americans very often have been deceived by the promises and words of European statesmen, trusting that the words were followed by deeds, which in many instances was not the case.

The German problem

The solution of the German problem immediately after the end of the war was a military one and obviously could not last long. A people of seventy million, intelligent and highly developed economically, occupying the heart of Europe, and with such a strong national tradition as to constitute a threat to all Europeans, could not be permanently subjugated. But, on the other hand, it was not advisable to give back to them full sovereignty, as had been done light-heartedly after the First World War. Soviet expansion, moreover, had swallowed part of Germany, while the problem of coexistence had not come any closer to being resolved. The only solution which appeared possible to the average individual called for a restoration of governmental functions to West Germany, minus some of the sovereign attributes, especially those pertaining to the conduct of foreign policy, military matters and economic life in general. But it was to be expected that if these attributes remained in the hands of the visitors for a while, eventually they would of necessity fall back into German hands. For some time German officials and the public in general have been so sincerely disgusted with their past political experience that it would seem they would never again desire to be the possessors of the fatal sovereign power. The idea of European unity, therefore, has been more and more put forth as a solution to the question of what to do with Germany, of how to establish a coexistence with her, recognizing her right to be free while still denying her full sovereignty.

The new force-idea

All the data that we have so far examined constituted at the end of the war the sum of the circumstances which made the problem of European unity so urgent and actual without, however, providing a solution. The solution might, of course, take the form of integration with either the Soviet Union or the United States, or of a restoration of the old national state system, or of a free union of existing European states under a new supranational body superior to that of the national states.

This last possibility has been taken up and has manifested itself in two currents of European political thought, both of which today are striving to gain the support of all who are interested in European unity – federalism and functionalism.

Both of these currents had formulated their programs before the end of the war, when any action was still in the realm of possibility. In the very heart of anti-Fascist conspiracy, during the Resistance, in the prisons, concentration camps and in underground groups, some individuals had come to the conclusion that a pure and simple restoration of sovereign national states would be an absurdity. The two world wars had been the direct consequence of a Europe divided into national states. To restore these states even with a democratic form of government, and leave them in possession of sovereign prerogatives, would mean an inevitable rebirth of political and economic nationalism, thus perpetuating the cause of international conflicts.

The political originality of these first thinkers did not lie in their method for realizing a European federation, for they reverted to the already existing models in the American and Swiss experiences. Their originality was in the proposals to promote a political action which, by demonstrating the impotence of the national sovereign states and the critical conditions in which European states would find themselves after the war, would pave the road for a movement which would create European federal institutions.

When the first such groups began to gather and to elaborate their ideas in illegal underground meetings, no one knew whether in other European countries there would be other people like themselves thinking the same thoughts or whether the idea of a federal movement existed only in their minds and had no factual relation with reality. Only during the last years of the war, when direct contact among men of the Resistance from various countries was established through Switzerland, did it become evident that under different circumstances and starting from different political premises men from different nations, unknown to one another, had elaborated the same thoughts and reached the same conclusions. At a meeting held clandestinely in Geneva in May 1944, and in the first public meeting in Paris of March 1945, the first stones were laid of what was to become the federalist movement in all democratic countries and eventually their common association in June 1947, at Montreux in the Union Européenne des Fédéralistes.

In juxtaposition to the advocates of federalism stood what has been called the functional approach. Public officials, politicians and experts in the various European states were not accustomed to thinking of solving European problems along federalist lines. The only supranational experience in their memory was that of the two great world wars, in which the partners in the fight had deemed it opportune to establish some specialized integrated authorities of a military and economic character (unified commands, boards for common procurement and allocation of war material, monetary pools, etc.). The execution of these tasks was entrusted to a supranational authority, while the power of political decisions remained in the hands of national governments. It was natural enough to transfer this line of thinking to the field of European reconstruction, and it was a Rumanian, Mitrany, who became the theoretician of functionalism. Jean Monnet during the war years had elaborated the idea of applying the functional approach first to the coal and steel industries, and it was from this that there emerged the European Coal and Steel Community, the first and until now the only example of a functional supranational authority.

Functionalism, born in the minds of high public officials, seemed to be a much more practical approach than that of political federalism. It did not attack directly the problem of the limitation of national sovereignty. It was based on experiences known to European politicians. It was hoped that by increasing the number of specialized institutions a point would be reached when the setting up of a European supranational power would become natural and effortless.

In contrast to the federalists, the functionalists have never organized themselves, but their ideas have spread everywhere. When European statesmen were faced with the problem of European unification, they espoused the functionalist approach, adopting federalist points of view with hesitation and half-heartedly only when forced by necessity and discarding them when the pressure diminished.

From the end of the war to the Marshall Plan

As the various European countries were being liberated and the end of the war was in sight, and the democratic forces were coming back to life, many political parties in the process of reorganizing themselves made declarations, more or less vague, in favor of European union. In reality these were empty declarations, since the European states were not in a position to influence

European policies, the power of which was in the hands of the victors who, at Yalta and at Potsdam, had decided to divide the Continent into two spheres of influence.

The Russians and Anglo-Americans alone made decisions regarding boundaries, political institutions, economic life and relations with neighboring countries. Germany ceased to control its own affairs. Russians and Anglo-Americans made solemn promises to re-establish liberty, democracy and independence in Europe and even to reunite Germany, but actually theirs was an attempt to set up a new kind of Holy Alliance of great world powers with the task of maintaining order in the world and particularly in Europe. The Europeans were in such a state of weakness and desperation as to applaud, with a few rare exceptions, the magniloquent declarations of the great powers, and to hope that among them there would prevail the same cooperation that had existed during the war.

If it had been possible for the United States and the Soviet Union to remain good friends, European history would have ended in 1945. The old Continent would have been divided between the two powers, as had happened in Africa in the preceding century, when that continent was parceled out into spheres of influence of the European powers.

As long as the Americans and Russians attempted, in spite of the growing rivalry, to maintain the basic agreements of Yalta, there was no real European policy. The ideals of European unity remained vague utopias without any following and federalist movements remained small and limited in scope.

Fortunately for Europe a real agreement between Russia and America was not possible. The USSR looked at the Yalta agreements as a transitional phase in the development of its own imperialism. While on one hand increasing its control over Eastern Europe and taking the first steps to transform these weak democracies into Communist dictatorships and Soviet satellites, Russia on the other hand was unfolding a complex policy which had as its aim the final conquest of the rest of Europe.

The Americans realized that by continuing the Yalta policy they would be playing straight into Soviet hands and sanctioning the expansion of Soviet imperialism. Western European states were in such complete political and economic confusion that it was relatively easy for the Communists, who represented the only totalitarian force to survive the war, to rout the democratic forces and set up police-states.

In order to remedy this ill-fated and dangerous situation, the United States decided, after much hesitation, to put an end to this new Holy Alliance policy and to consider the Soviet Union as a dangerous enemy whose expansionistic aims had to be stopped. Consequently, the Americans began to view democratic Europe as a political whole, to be aided as such and to be helped to unite, so that it could become an effective force able to resist by itself the advance of Soviet imperialism.

The problem was not yet viewed in military terms. It was a matter of reorganizing European economies so as to provide solid ground for the reborn democracies. With the announcement of the Marshall Plan there was a profound change in the European situation. The Russians stepped up their control of Eastern Europe, cutting out for these countries any hope for autonomous action. In Western Europe the Russo-American impasse was the determining factor in foreign policy. It was obvious that Western Europe had to choose siding with the Americans and welcoming their protection. But since America offered them economic aid and asked them to devise the best way to utilize it, the Europeans were suddenly confronted with a problem of international policy, since it was up to them to elaborate a common way to share this aid. Here was a purely European situation which could be resolved only through a union of the interested states. Churchill, in his famous speeches at Zurich and at Fulton, was the first statesman to proclaim that European states should reciprocate the new American policy by showing a desire to unite, and he thus gave the first impulse to the creation of the European movement.

Churchill's initiative had been conditioned by English policy. Great Britain had abandoned every prospect of taking part in some kind of European union, and in fact was in the midst of the great Socialist experience inaugurated by the Labour Party. The British, by tradition, opposed any kind of political consolidation of Europe, since it could mean the creation of a great Continental power. But the presence of Russian imperialistic policy prevented Great Britain from taking a position openly against European integration, which would have meant against the United States and indirectly in favor of Russia.

To get out of this diplomatic entanglement, Churchill came up with an idea both clever and cynical. The British would take over the role of guardian of the European movement, which they would guide so as to make sure that a real union never would be achieved. There was no talk of federation, transfer of sovereignty, supranational institutions, or for that matter of creating a real European political framework, but instead an abundance of platitudes and generalities concerning a generic 'union', the heritage of a common civilization, solidarity against communism, a permanent resolution of the Franco-German question, and so on.

It was thus at a moment when the problem of European unity had become alive that there began also the erosive action of the various national conservatisms. This was exemplified by the fact that the most prominent European statesman, Churchill, and the most powerful European state, England, were sabotaging the process of unification which was about to take the first steps.

Unfortunately, the prestige of the man was so great that the still young and poorly organized federalist movements which had been formed between 1945 and 1947 were completely deceived by the Churchillian rhetoric and became founding members of the European movement. Important people gave their support, and a great European congress gathered at The Hague in 1948. There were only a few federalists who, unheeded, denounced the falsity of this propaganda.

Parallel to the propaganda activities of Churchill and of the European movement came the British government's official sponsorship of leadership in European action. To the Marshall Plan the British government responded, backed by European governments, with the Organization for European Economic Co-operation and, somewhat later, with the Council of Europe, that is, with the creation of international institutions which, while giving the impression of unity, were only consultative organs, and thus by-passed completely the problem of national sovereignty.

The Marshall Plan represented the one chance for Europe to unite. If the American government had seen through the false European spirit of the British and had granted the aids contingent on the creation of political federal institutions on the Continent, we would now have European union, since no serious opposition could have been given by the forces favoring maintenance of sovereignty, except, of course, by Great Britain. It is to be regretted that the Americans, on this score, were duped by Great Britain in one of the greatest deceptions in modern European history, and so instead of a political union we have witnessed the maintenance and the strengthening of the national particularisms, vaguely disguised in European terms, which for some time have deceived both American and European public opinion.

The money which the Americans thought they were giving to help the Europeans to overcome economic nationalism served only to reconstitute the old national economies, instead of creating one market and one European economy.

From the Schuman Plan to the Korean War

The uproar raised by the birth of the OEEC and the Council of Europe among those who favored European integration did overshadow for a while the real issues at hand, but it could not obliterate them completely.

With the advent of the Marshall Plan there reappeared also the German problem. West Germany, included in the project of economic rehabilitation, could no longer be treated as an occupied country deprived of political rights. The United States, Great Britain and France had to take a hand in the reorganization of the country by restoring its currency and economy, and by setting it up as a political entity. Little by little the conquerors were giving back to Germany some attributes of its sovereignty. If this came relatively easy for America and England, the same was not true for France, where it seemed obvious that this procedure would once again make possible the resurrection of a powerful German state on the Rhine frontier.

The apparent pro-European attitudes of the English succeeded in part in deceiving French public opinion and political leaders, creating the impression that the British, deeply involved in the reconstruction of Europe, would never again leave them alone to face the Germans. This British attitude, however, did raise some doubts in the minds of Frenchmen, since it did not answer any of the questions which, for them, had been raised by the rebirth of a German state.

France's weak position was rendered more precarious by an economy in a state of disorder and a political life in decay. Attacked by Communists and by the supporters of de Gaulle, the democratic elements in France sought a way out in the European idea. Frenchmen did not know for sure what the making of Europe meant; they had a vague notion that it would imply a union with yesterday's enemies, the Germans and the Italians. It was not a situation which aroused emotions and enthusiasm, and thus the policy issuing from it had of necessity to be methodical, cold, rational and calculated. The politicians who occupied policy-making positions in the Fourth Republic were considerably devoid of any of these qualities. Federalist thinking and the federalist movement were weaker and less influential in France than elsewhere. At a moment when French politicians were forced to tackle the problem of a European political community, the best that French federalists could offer, out of their confused perspective, was a rhetorical exposition of what a perfect federal society should be at the municipal, regional, French, European and world level.

It so happened that the first concrete suggestion made in France on the problem was along functional lines. For France, the central problem was still that of the sovereignty of Germany, but the aspects of this problem which were of importance at that moment were neither political nor military, but stemmed from the rebirth of the heavy industry in the Ruhr. Jean Monnet pulled out of his drawer the project which he had elaborated during the war years of a Franco-German coal and steel pool, and prevailed upon Schuman, then Foreign Minister, to promote it. Schuman showed a great deal of courage in taking up the project, which aimed at setting up a common market for coal and steel under the control of a supranational authority, because he knew that Great Britain would never accede to it; he even declared that France was ready to proceed alone with Germany on this road.

With the conference on the Schuman Plan, composed of representatives from six countries, there began a real attempt at a policy of European unity. With willfulness and clarity, Monnet, presiding over the conference, persuaded the six participating states to accept the creation of a specialized community with a supranational High Authority which, rather than the individual states, would control the common coal and steel market.

The limitations of the European Coal and Steel Community were serious. The common market for these two important raw materials could not be completely divorced from the various economies of the member states, which continued as national economies subject to the control of their respective governments and parliaments. The executive functions of the High Authority were strongly restricted by the ministers of member states, who sat in a special council and alone were empowered to pass on those measures involving the various national economic policies without which the Coal and Steel Community would remain but a pious hope. The Common Assembly of the European Coal and Steel Community, moreover, had no legislative power whatever; this was retained by the respective national parliaments. The birth of this first functional-type community was made possible partly by the French desire not to give back to Germany full control over the Ruhr, and partly by the German maneuver to escape, as much as possible, the limitations which the victors had forced upon her. At the time of ratification by the six parliaments, the founders of the community, Monnet, Schuman and the delegates from the other states, declared publicly that the European Coal and Steel Community would be long-lived only if European unification proceeded along other roads. The European Coal and Steel Community was only a breach in the walls of sovereignty to let Europe pass through, and unless it grew wider, there was the danger of its being closed again.

The elaboration of the Schuman Plan gave important impetus to the federalist movements, which at that time were beginning to rebel against the false position of the European movement and to assume definite political aspects. Starting from the premise that European unification implied essentially integration of the six countries which made up the Schuman Plan, during the period from 1949 to 1951, the federalists, in opposition to the functional thesis then accepted by the governments, championed the idea that the six countries, instead of proceeding toward the formulation of additional pools and markets, should bind themselves with a federal union pact and with a common constitution and political organs. As a procedure to be followed for the drafting and approval of such a pact, the federalists suggested that instead fo proceeding through normal diplomatic channels, the parliaments of the member states elect representatives to a European constituent assembly, which in turn would submit to the national parliaments for ratification the constitution that had been elaborated.

These suggestions made no impression on the European governments at a time when the Marshall Plan and the Schuman Plan seemed to indicate the right road to European reconstruction.

Actually the Marshall Plan was restoring the national economies to a normal state, but it was not creating a European economy. The first visible results of the Marshall Plan were the halting of the Communist menace and the reappearance of big sectional monopolistic business concerns intent on preserving and defending the national economic systems with the privileges inherent in them.

On its part the Schuman Plan had instilled a conviction that the functional approach was the answer to European integration and that what was needed were more attempts along this road.

While Europe and America were emphasizing economic reconstruction, the Korean War broke out in 1950, underlining the fact that Western Europe, the most important industrial force in the world besides America, would not be capable of defending itself in the event of a Russian invasion.

From the Korean War to the ad hoc assembly

The Korean War highlighted in a dramatic fashion the problem of the defence of Western Europe. Under the Atlantic pact the United States was bound to help Europe in case of aggression. It was American military protection, following economic assistance, which saved Western Europe, and the prospect of American intervention served as a deterrent to Soviet encroachment. But in spite of this protection, the fact remained that Germany was still disarmed and the other countries were poorly armed, which meant that Europe could not be defended.

Now the Americans began to supply military aid and to contribute to European rearmament. In the same spirit with which they had backed German economic rebirth within the framework of the Marshall Plan, they now called for the rebirth of German military power, without which the defence of Europe would have been impossible.

The reaction to this in Europe was similar to that which had characterized the formulation of the Marshall Plan. Churchill spoke of a European army, which, of course, would not include Great Britain; the French government, shocked by the prospect of a resurrected German army, proposed also the formation of a European army, but following the functional approach in vogue. When the conference for a European army opened, the only states present were the members of the European Coal and Steel Community.

But to apply the functional approach to the problem of military organization bordered on the absurd. For months and months the delegates of the six countries tried to come up with some sensible scheme for the multinational army, but were constantly rebuffed by insurmountable obstacles of a political nature. To whom would the European army have belonged? Certainly neither to the national states nor to a central European political power, which did not exist. Could it have been made dependent on SHAPE? But SHAPE was only a military command of the Atlantic Council within which the guiding principle was that of a coalition of sovereign states. The European army was a necessity, but it was impossible to create it.

The criticism of the federalists, which at the time of the Marshall and Schuman Plans had been dismissed, began now to take hold on the minds of the politicians. It was inescapable any longer that a unification of the armed forces implied the relinquishing of some sovereign attributes on the part of national states. It was absolutely necessary to create a European political entity to which the individual states would relinquish their sovereignty in military matters.

The first government to give consideration to this request of the federalists was that of Italy, whose delegation at the conference for a European army requested from the beginning that the community be given its own parliament and fiscal powers. When it became evident that the other delegations were not disposed to intepret their mandate so broadly as to mean the preparation of a real constitution, the Italians proposed that at least the assembly which was envisaged as the organ of the EDC be charged with the formulation of a political constitution for the whole community.

This request was accepted and incorporated, in complicated and unsatisfactory language, in article 38 of the proposed EDC Treaty, and with a limitation so serious that it would have caused the failure of the whole effort. The assembly of the EDC was, in fact, not charged with the preparation of a constitution to be ratified by the respective parliaments, but of a preliminary study to be sent to the member governments, which in turn, would have convened an intergovernmental conference to discuss it. What the diplomats granted with one hand, they retrieved with the other.

The federalist campaign, in spite of this, was scoring other successes in the course of 1951. In July, General Eisenhower acknowledged the fact that, without a federation of Europe, the Atlantic Pact could not function properly. In November, Spaak, who up to this time had remained on the unsteady ground of the European movement, of which he was President, recognized the necessity of making a formal request for a supranational constitution. He dramatically resigned as President of the Consultative Assembly of the Council of Europe and allied himself with the federalist movements setting up an Action Committee for a European Constituent Assembly. The problem was now coming into focus. Even the governments represented at the conference for the European army had realized that the EDC could at best be a provisional arrangement, and were inclined to agree that the EDC Assembly should prepare the final statute for the defense community. Since this assembly would be the same as that of the European Coal and Steel Community with the addition of nine members, there was no need to await the ratification of the EDC in order to start working on it. The European Coal and Steel Community Assembly was convened on 10 September 1952, for the first time, since the treaty had now been ratified. The situation was clear-cut; all there was to do was to take article 38 of the projected EDC Treaty as a basis upon which to elaborate the first outline of a political constitution.

The absurd manner in which the problem of a European army had been approached highlighted serious difficulties of a constitutional and political nature, and finally induced the ministers of the six countries to abandon the functional in favor of the constitutional approach. The request of the action committee was accepted. On 10 September, at its inaugural session, the Assembly of the European Coal and Steel Community was charged by the six ministers with the mission of organizing itself as the assembly of the EDC as well, and of drawing up within six months a constitutional project for the European political community.

The assembly modestly turned itself into an ad hoc assembly under the leadership of Spaak, and on 10 March 1954, with conscientious punctuality, presented a constitutional project. It was still a rather weak step, since after calling for a European government and a freely elected parliament endowed with fiscal powers, the organs of which were also given the tasks of assimilating the Coal and Steel Community and the proposed EDC, and of legislating on matters pertaining to the common market, it placed at the side of these institutions a council of ministers from the member states who had to approve unanimously every act of the community. This free federal construction, restricted at every move by the ministers of national state, was the best that the parliamentarians of the ad hoc assembly could do.

When the proposed plan was sent to the six ministers, that phase of European and world politics favorable to European action was coming to an end.

The failure

The train of events which had forced the leaders of six countries to attempt a policy of supranational integration began to slow down with the death of Stalin. From the very beginning it became evident that his successors did not wish to continue the hard policy of the Cold War and, perhaps, lacked the ability to do so. Facing a difficult period of internal readjustments, they inaugurated the policy of distension. And with the lessening of the danger of war, the enthusiasm of many for European unification also diminished. American military and economic aid, if it had failed to bring about European unification, had helped European states to strengthen their administrations, their armed forces, and their national economies. Those forces interested in the preservation of national sovereignty were strong again and made their weight felt. In addition, the general economic situation was rather good, and this contributed to the spread of a general feeling favorable to the maintenance of the *status quo* in Europe.

These circumstances explain why attempts at a European unification on the part of the six nations failed.

The project of the ad hoc assembly was passed by the ministers to a committee of experts and diplomats and, within a few months, nothing more was heard of it.

Four parliaments wearily ratified the EDC Treaty. The Italian Parliament, now incapable of following them, awaited leisurely the decision of France. The French National Assembly, in a sudden surge of national pride for its own army, declared the treaty unconstitutional, while a few months later it approved the rebirth of a German national army. With this act another important factor in European politics was eliminated; Germany was again a fully sovereign state. Here ended in failure the attempts of European governments to create a new level of sovereignty and to abandon the road of particularism and nationalism.

The relaxation in international relations, together with the economic boom, and the revival in all countries of conservative forces interested in the maintenance of national sovereignty, carried in its wake a new equilibrium in world and especially European politics. Europe had not solved any of its problems, but was able to keep alive by accepting this state of affairs. With the passing of the great fear of war, single countries gained greater freedom in the conduct of foreign affairs, even permitting themselves the luxury of acting with more independence with respect to American policy. This new freedom of action did not generate any greater sense of responsibility with regard to the establishment and maintenance of world peace; in fact, because of their division, the European states constituted an element of imbalance. They had become the new Balkans in the world politics and seemed pleased with their accomplishments.

Germany had long believed that she had to choose between national unity and a European community. Now it was obvious that both prospects had vanished. Similarly, France had thought the choice for her lay between French union and European unity. But here again events were taking care of the situation, making no choice necessary.

European revival and the new federalist approach

In spite of all this, the governments of the six countries had not completely lost sight of the question of European unity, although the force of events had confused the problem. And so, partly because of the general listlessness and partly in order to hang on to a political formula that might be useful some day, on 2 June 1955, at Messina, the six countries decided to set up a commission of experts, under the leadership of Spaak, in order to carry out the so-called European Revival and, more precisely, in order to promote the creation of a common European market and of an atomic pool.

Monnet, who by then had resigned from the presidency of the High Authority, together with the secretaries of democratic parties and of the non-Communist unions of the six countries, formed an Action Committee for the United States of Europe. This committee, in spite of its ambitious name, is concerned only with the rapid promotion of an atomic pool. The functional approach is riding high again. Toward the end of last April the experts of the Spaak Commission presented to the interested governments a long report which tries to resolve the impossible. They propose a merging of the various national economies into a common market without, however, touching national sovereignty.

It is probable that the government will discuss at length this report and its proposals, but it is certain that, with the present lack of interest in the problem of European unification, a river of words will flow, but no action will be taken.

The defeat of the efforts for European union has had profound repercussions in the ranks of the supporters of the federalist idea. Many of them insist on believing that the governments are genuinely interested in formulating a realistic European policy; and in order not to embarrass them the federalists refrain from criticizing the erroneous steps which are being taken. Others have come to the conclusion, based on past experience, that nothing can be expected from national governments and from national political forces and that the problem of European integration will be seriously taken up again only if and when a new crisis faces Europe. They plan to form small nuclei of nonconformists seeking to point out that the national states have lost their proper rights, since they cannot guarantee the political and economic safety of their citizens.

They also insist that European union should be brought about by the European populations, and not by diplomats, by directly electing a European constituent assembly, and by the approval, through a referendum, of the constitution that this assembly would prepare.

This is the point now reached by the movement for European integration which grew out of the last war. Whether this is the passing of an experience or the beginning of a new cycle, in the words of Socrates, 'is known to no one but God'.

3 European Commission

Declaration on the Occasion of the Achievement of the Customs Union on 1 July 1968

Declaration by the European Commission on the Occasion of the Achievement of the Customs Union on 1 July 1968.

What is the significance of 1 July 1968?

1 July 1968 will certainly go down as a milestone in the history of Europe.

On that day the first and the major stage on the road to the economic unification of the European continent will be complete. The Customs Union which is one of the first aims of the Treaty of Rome will have been brought into being. Eighteen months ahead of the Treaty schedule, customs duties will have disappeared within the Common Market. Simultaneously, on the same date, the separate customs tariffs of our six countries will have given way to a single tariff, the external customs tariff of the Community. Finally, the first tariff reductions negotiated last year in Geneva in the major discussions known as the Kennedy Round will be implemented.

By beginning the unification of the European territory in this first form, the Six are taking a decisive step in the economic history of the continent.

But Europe is not only customs tariffs. Europe does not belong only to the manufacturers, the farmers or the technocrats. Nor is Europe only the Europe of 180 million Europeans living in the Community. Europe is not only the Europe of the Governments, of the Parliaments or of the administrations. It must also be the Europe of the peoples, of the workers, of youth, of man himself. All – or nearly all – still remains to be done.

The objectives

The Europeans face immense tasks.

The economic union

The Customs Union being complete, work on the achievement of economic union must be continued. This means that the common economic policies designed to transform the customs territory into an economically organized continent must be built up or completed. We must put the finishing touches to the common agricultural policy, much of which is already in place, and finish work on policies for harmonization or unification in the commercial, fiscal, social, transport and other fields, as provided for in the Treaties. We must gradually replace the old national policies with Community policies, changing the European area into an organized European society, with a general economic policy thought out and built up to the scale of the continent.

Three of these policies deserve special mention. In the first place, after having abolished the customs frontiers within the Community, the tax frontiers must also be gradually eliminated so that men and goods can move freely without formalities or controls at the frontiers. In addition, we must make progress in the field of monetary union, first by harmonizing the monetary policies of our six Member States, and then by creating between them a degree of monetary solidarity which will lead stage by stage to the coping-stone of the economic edifice – a common currency superseding the old national currencies. Lastly, Europe must be led to make decisive progress in the field of research and technology, so that it can stand on an equal footing with the other great world economic areas.

Political union

A political Europe – the aim of Robert Schuman, Konrad Adenauer and de Gasperi – must be built up in the same way as our large countries, Germany, France and Italy, were gradually unified by major political decisions. Europe must have institutions enabling it to become a politically organized continent, having not only its economic institutions – which are already well on the road to completion – but also political institutions enabling it to act and become what the declaration of 9 May 1950 called the European Federation.

If this is to be done, Europe must not only have genuine federal institutions; it must also be unified and the other countries of Europe which are willing to accept the same rights and the same duties must gather around the nucleus formed by the Europe of the Six. At the same time political integration must facilitate a détente and cooperation between the East and the West, thus making an essential contribution to the establishment of a pacific order in Europe.

Europe and the rest of the world

Europe bears major international responsibilities. The Europe of the Six, inferior to the United States in military, industrial and financial power, is already its equal in the field of trade. It is the world's leading importer of manufactures and agricultural produce. It is the leading importer of products from the countries of the third world. Today, in its present form, it already has major responsibilities to the developing countries – and these will be even more important tomorrow when Europe is a larger entity.

In addition, at a time when the organization of the world on the scale of the old sovereign nations is yielding place to organization at the level of continents, it is important that the errors of the past should not be repeated at this higher level, that the clash of nations should not give way to the clash of entire continents. Consequently, it is Europe's duty to organize cooperation and association with the other main groups in the world.

Human problems

Lastly, the great social changes in a world dominated by technology and speed raise immense questions for our generation: the transformation of society, the organization of social life, the environment and the destiny of man, his liberty, his security, his health, his life itself.

None of all this, none of these fundamental political, economic, social and human problems can be solved by our old States imprisoned within their narrow frontiers. It is just as impossible to solve them without breaking through the old structures inherited from the past and without creating the European structures which are vital to the work of renewal as it is necessary to retain the old cultures, traditions, languages, originality, everything which gives the States their personalities and which constitutes the beauty, the diversity, the charm and the immanent value of Europe, and in place of which nobody could possibly desire to set up colourless and impersonal machinery.

The means

What is the right approach to these tasks and how are they to be carried out? This is work on a grand scale which will keep a whole generation busy – but there has to be a beginning. Starting from what has already been done, starting from the 1 July deadline, and without looking too far ahead, let us inquire what we can, what we must, do in the next five years.

1. We must take a step forward in the field of political union. A single Treaty, enabling a new stage forward to be begun must take the place of the Treaty of Paris (1951) and the two Treaties of Rome (1957), which created our three European Communities. The Council of Ministers of the Community must be re-established in its normal functioning as a body which can take majority decisions. The out-of-date system of the right of veto, which paralyses action, must be done away with. The single Commission must be given the implementing powers enabling it not only to take the initiative in Community progress but genuinely to manage the Community, with the task of management growing as the new Community policies gradually enter into force.

At the same time, the authority entrusted to European institutions must be steadily given a wider democratic basis – and this must be done more rapidly. The European Parliament must be given greater budgetary and legislative powers. The European peoples must participate increasingly, through direct elections and all other appropriate methods, in Community life at the European level.

2. In coming years we must work through the stages in the construction of the economic union. Stimulated by the results already obtained, particularly in agriculture (here it has made an enormous effort) the European Commission intends to speed up and multiply its proposals to the Council of Ministers, so that the Community may make early and decisive progress in working out the economic, monetary, fiscal, social and other policies, which, in the five coming years, will need to have achieved most of their objectives.

3. The efforts to enlarge the Community and unify the European continent must be resumed. The profound economic and social crisis in some of our countries, both within and without the Community, has shown how far the destinies of the European States have become intermingled. The moment has come to face the implications of this fact.

4. The major economic, social and intellectual forces of Europe must be persuaded to take part more fully in the construction of the European continent.

It would be wrong to wait until the European people as a whole is officially consulted and takes part constitutionally and organically in the political life of the European continent. The major social groups in the Community must be called upon more urgently to help here and now.

This is why the Commission has decided to propose to the Economic and Social Committee that the Committee and the Commission should embark in the autumn on a far-reaching examination of the Community situation considered as a whole. For the same reason, the Commission also proposes to convene next winter three symposia in which the qualified representatives of the main organizations would take part. The first will bring together representatives of employers and workers, the second organizations of the farming community, the third qualified representatives of youth organizations. In each symposium the Commission will endeavour to organize both an overall examination of the European situation and a dialogue on detailed short- and medium-term action programmes. The Commission intends to devote special attention to the problems of keen interest to young people in the European universities – university teaching, training of young people, university exchanges, etc. – and to consider with the qualified representatives of the students what could be done to induce young people of today to look forward more confidently to their future and the part they will have to play in shaping it.

On completing this statement, which is at once an act of faith, an expression of hope and an action programme, the Commission calls on all Europeans not to ignore or underestimate the importance of what is now happening and to appreciate the value of what has been done so far.

Two great spiritual developments dominate this second half of the twentieth century: the reconciliation of the churches and the reconciliation of the peoples. The first is not a political matter, but the second is our affair. The reconciliation of peoples has been first and foremost the reconciliation of European nations, ravaged by the two World Wars of 1914–18 and 1939–45, both born in Europe of the clash of nationalisms: for the peoples of Europe these were genuine civil wars.

That time is now past. The moment has come to call the young and creative forces of Europe to union, action and hope.

4 Ralf Dahrendorf

A New Goal for Europe

Excerpt from 'Wieland Europa', 'A new goal for Europe', *Die Zeit*, no. 28 9 July 1971, p. 3; no. 29, 16 July 1971, p. 3. Translated from German.

Decline of the First Europe

Economic Union is the first large-scale gamble of the European Community that also in substance goes way beyond the Treaties of Rome. That this gamble was undertaken with such great earnestness and emphasis shows the intention of the member states to develop the concept of Europe. That it has not so far succeeded shows the limitations, either of the treaties themselves, or of the ways in which they have been applied.

And just here I am convinced that economic unity is possible, but not in the way in which it is being carried out. It can be achieved but not with the means that are at present at Europe's disposal. And perhaps it is here that the conflict over institutions 'which should be adapted to this purpose' (the last stage of Economic and Monetary Union) does have a definite meaning.

For the institutions of the First Europe have not remained immune from First Europe's decline and fall. In the last few years it has been much discussed in many places, that the Commission of the European Community has experienced an inexorable decline in power from the Hallstein to the Rey era and into the era of Malfatti. At least there is no longer any talk of starting a European government, and there are occasions in which this opinion of the founders of the Rome Treaties' central plan more readily arouses pity than respect.

That may among other things be due to intangible reasons; it may even be exaggerated from time to time. In so far as it is true, there seems to me to be one reason which at the first glance seems paradoxical. As Europe gains in importance so the Commission proportionally seems to decline in stature. The fiction of an uncontrolled European government free from national direction as well as parliamentary doubts was bearable to the member states as long as only very little was to be decided at a European level. As European matters became proportionately more important to member states, so they proportionately withdrew these matters from the Commission or immediately dealt with them elsewhere. More or less subtle evidence for these views is appearing.

One of the places where European decisions are increasingly being agreed (or blocked), is in the least controllable, least authorized and – I may be forgiven for saying this – also least qualified European Institution, namely the so-called Committee of Permanent Representatives. These ambassadors of the member states have dealt conclusively in Brussels with nine out of ten of the questions that have cropped up in these last years, without their ministers ever hearing of these questions.

If there are technocrats in Brussels – those famous objects of de Gaulle's and also of Pompidou's scorn – then they are here: civil servants (*Beamte*) *de facto* as well as even *de jure* responsible to no Parliament, administrators of European matters – however, and herein lies a small consolation, of those matters which concern trade in frozen sides of beef, the labelling of mayonnaise jars and the freedom of movement of midwives. To this extent the permanent representatives embody the First Europe or what still remains of it.

For it accords with the thesis developed here that the weakening of the European Commission has not necessarily led to a strengthening of the Council of Ministers. Even the Council of Ministers has increasingly lost its political function.

I am inclined to point this out: if the negotiations for entry with Great Britain had had as their object the actual political problems of entry – sovereignty, common foreign policy, other political objectives, institutions – then the Council of Ministers of the European Community could never have led these negotiations to a successful conclusion. It could only successfully conclude them because only those matters that concerned the First Europe were discussed – namely, butter and sugar, lamb and fish, parabolically rising financial percentages (*Finanzprozenten*) and the possibilities of a period of transition in agriculture. In these matters the Council was in its own element and the foreign ministers of the six European states were once again allowed to be ministers of agriculture to their heart's content.

And what of Parliament? A democrat can only be ashamed when he sees mature and, in their home countries, honestly elected deputies playing at that farce which they have to go through in Strasbourg or Luxembourg ten times a year for a whole week. Either they are allowed to talk of matters which are of little or no interest to them or they take an interest in problems and are not allowed to talk about them; on no account can they actually make any decisions.

But this is not the main point of my analysis. I am much more concerned about the following. With the treaties of Rome and Paris a development of *European Integration* started which has achieved much. But this development has today exhausted itself. For this there would seem to be many reasons.

1. Technically we have exhausted the possibilities of the treaties.

2. The contradiction between the political aims and the daily reality of the European Community has become all too apparent.

3. The supranational illusions of the European beginnings have constricted rather than spurred on genuine political cooperation.

4. Above all the illogical way towards Europe, which some have wanted to follow, has led us into a cul-de-sac: there is no material necessity (*Sachgesetzlichkeit*), which could force the nations of Europe to save a problematical agricultural policy through a currency union, or a problematical economic union by means of a comprehensive, concerted political approach.

Instead, this nonsensical approach leads to the exclusion of a common political approach and the economic and currency union is already destroyed in its infancy, leaving the farmers alone to find out that a Europe really does exist.

This illogical First Europe has led itself to its own frontiers. Thereby a number of things for which it stood have disintegrated. Much has certainly also remained. But the energy with which those matters are solved, which the European states of today and tomorrow, the member states of the European Community and those who will newly join in 1973 will expect, the First Europe is no longer capable of producing this drive. Here, instead, a new beginning must be made alongside what remains of the old achievements.

The beginnings of the Second Europe

The contradiction is evident. Seldom, possibly as never before, has the political urge towards a European Community been so explicit as it has been since the Summit Conference of The Hague. The Benelux countries are traditional carriers of this urge. Equally, in Colombo's Italy Europe has been discovered as a hope for the future in the face of a less hopeful internal political situation. The Federal Republic of Willy Brandt seeks to show that it means business with the balance of *Ost* – and *West-politik*. The France of Pompidou is slowly moving away from the nightmare of de Gaulle and meanwhile seeks, in clinging to Europe, protection from its increasingly unpredictable partner, the Federal Republic.

Whatever the motives may be, interests are running together in the urge to strengthen and extend the European Community.

The enlargement of the Community seems to have succeeded, but this does not yet imply consolidation. In fact the First Europe proves to be incapable of taking account of this new political urge and turning it into a political reality. This contradiction must be solved if the political urge is not to wither away and only leave behind it the splinters of the First Europe. But how? Where are the beginnings of new opportunities of European development?

The controversial clause of the concluding communiqué from the Hague in December 1969 is without doubt clause 15 on political cooperation. Herein the Heads of State and of government instructed the foreign ministers to examine the question 'how, within the context of extension, advances in the field of political unification can best be achieved'.

That does not seem to be much; and according to the views of some, the Committee, which under the leadership of the general director of the Belgian foreign ministry, Davignon, submitted a report on the basis of the clause, did not produce anything that led that much further.

The Davignon report envisages that the foreign ministers of the member states of the European Community meet regularly for consultations outside the institutions of the Community. Twice so far such meetings have taken place, in November 1970 in Munich and in June 1971 in Paris. The report further envisages that the political directors of the foreign ministries of the Six come together for regular talks. And this has also happened. The Directors have among other things agreed that on specific questions common instructions be given to the ambassadors of the Six in the outside world. Since then in an increasing number of capital cities the diplomatic representatives of the member states of the European Community are meeting to discuss common action.

All this has been especially criticized by the Commission, the European parliament, the pro-European press and by individual prominent politicians. They all regret the intergovernmental character of the Davignon consultations, also the avoidance of existing institutions and above all the seeming retreat from community to concerted action. This, I think, is unjust criticism. The Davignon formula is, as yet, the most important beginning towards a Second Europe. It can become the starting point of a significant new development.

The secret of the success of this formula is simple. The foreign ministers can once again meet in their political consultations as foreign ministers. They can talk about a common European stand to the Middle-East conflict or to the European security conference. And since these are subjects which interest them more than frozen sides of beef, labels on mayonnaise jars and free-moving midwives, the talks are more serious. The political directors are for the first time ever brought into the process of European co-ordination. They begin to appreciate the attraction and significance of the political cooperation of states with similar points of interest. That applies even more strongly for the ambassadors of the Six in the world at large who also soon notice that they are taken more seriously than previously as the spokesmen of a Community of States.

The Davignon formula has three characteristics, all three anathema in the eyes of the Common Market Europeans of the first round, which I would regard as guarantees of success and the beginnings of a new European future:

1. The Davignon formula is not supranational but international. It brings the governments of the involved countries together as representatives of fundamentally sovereign states. That limits the temptation to play off community against national interests or to hide behind European phrases. Even if at first it may sound irrational, the international formula does in fact move the participants towards stronger participation than does the supranational fiction.

2. The Davignon formula means the change from indirect to direct political discussion, the change from the Euro-gibberish (*Euro-chinesisch*) of the Council of Ministers to the normal, somewhat more lively language of politics, in which one names some matters by their name and also defines one's own position on them. The Davignon formula thus stands diametrically opposed to the European Community's terrible habit of raising important matters in a devious way, when it is to be reckoned a success if the others do not realize what one is really after – a

habit which quite justifiably has made third parties uncomfortable in their membership negotiations, as, above all, in relation to the guarantees for sugar imports.

3. The Davignon formula allows one to escape the thematic limits of the treaties and their interpretation. No one can here forbid arguments which are constructive by appealing to the treaties; the substantive issues take precedence over the semantic issues. That opens chances of development which are unknown to the Council of Ministers; above all it gives a new openness to political co-operation, free of the meaningless burden of over-interpreted texts. Here the Davignon formula has played its part in weighing the anchor that has held the ship of Europe berthed for far too long.

A formula has been found for foreign political cooperation; but this formula is without doubt transferable to other fields. The numerous bilateral meetings – much more numerous and above all much more European since The Hague (Summit) – of Minis-ters, heads of state and of government belong to this. The meet-ings of Ministers of Labour and Welfare, of Ministers of Justice, of Ministers of Education which have either taken place or have been arranged, come under similar rules of procedure and aims. Even the Ministers of Agriculture only really moved forward when they met on the basis of the Davignon formula; and in order to seriously draft a common structural policy they would have to even move a few paces further away from the aims and actions of the Council. Above all in the Davignon formula there lies the only possibility of creating a European Economic Union.

The Economic Union takes a key place on the road towards the Second Europe. Next to the growing field of common foreign policy negotiation it is the second leg on which Europe of the future can stand and hopefully also walk. And just as a common foreign policy can be latched onto a common trade policy, so also can an economic union be got under way starting from middle-term coordination, inner harmonization and even also from currency union.

A warning clause when changing over to the second stage is no substitute for the need of a fundamental political basis at the outset – and furthermore a decision that goes beyond the pleas-antly casual talk about 'stability and growth'. The members of an economic union with their knowledge of currency, budgetary and regional politics, and whatever other consequences, must be clearly united in their minds over what they mean by stability and how much growth they want, if their ventures are to have any success.

The logical Europe – or better perhaps: the political Europe – which will then arise, will deal with currency questions on the basis of a common economic policy and agrarian questions on the basis of a currency policy. But such a political union will only be established according to the principle of a Davignon formula: international, direct and without any attempts at over-interpreting the meaning of any text.

The Davignon formula is indeed not the only beginning for a Second Europe. The European Community has occasionally played a role which is worth continuing, for example in the Kennedy Round or in development policy, in the attempt to fight inflation and in the increase in agricultural productivity. But the Davignon formula could mark the beginning of an important new development. For the formula has one evident weakness. Certainly voluntary agreement on important matters is at least more valuable than technically binding agreement on insignificant ones. Herein lies the advantage of the Davignon formula as against the First Europe. But only when this formula is made into a doctrine for Europe can its full effect be realized; and it will only become a doctrine when to the three elements already mentioned a fourth is added: binding commitment (*Verbindlichkeit*).

The Ministers of Finance of the European Community have freely adopted this principle. They meet each other at the invitation of the representatives of the host country, and when their talks are to reach a decision they briefly notify the Council of Ministers whether that is in Hamburg, Brussels or Paris. But even this method also leaves much to chance. International, direct and open political cooperation will only become binding when it can fulfil more conditions:

1. Meetings of those responsible must take place regularly and relate to decisions on substantive issues.
2. A mechanism must be developed to turn the talks into decisions.
3. A framework must be found for the execution of common decisions.
4. Talks and decisions, but especially decisions, must be subject to effective control.

These conditions are the starting point for the institutions of the Second Europe. Institutions which fulfil these conditions admittedly create no patent way. But such institutions lead further. It is therefore worth asking: where do they lead? And how do they make progress a reality?

The European Europe

What shall the Second Europe look like? How can it be realistically visualized over a time-span, up to the most, of ten years?

Let us begin with the inner framework of the European community. One of the big weaknesses of the First Europe lies in its craze for harmonization. Whereever there was a possibility of common regulation or even only the proposal for a regulation, then these regulations were established – irrespective of whether they dealt with bottle shapes, units of account, credit-insurance systems or methods for the production of ice-cream, working hours for lorry drivers or the size of agricultural estates. Fortunately it often got no further than the mere wish to be in harmony. For the good wish to harmonize, which above all seems to have animated the Commission (and made it into a bureaucratic Leviathan), has indeed a few inescapable weaknesses.

Whoever tries to look for a similar if not exactly identical solution, wherever this is possible, for the member states of the European Community, gets into the dangerous position of generalizing the solution which accords with the highest degree of state regulation. That France will make its central bank independent of the government is much more unlikely than that the German Federal Bank will become more dependent. That Italy will abolish its system of supporting exports is less likely than that Belgium will take this system over. Anyway the system of harmonizing is already in itself an adjusting operation (*regelnder Eingriff*). Thus Europe becomes increasingly bureaucratic, and less and less liberal in the best sense of the word. The First Europe is not only an illogical but also an illiberal bureaucratic Europe.

That is one thing. Rather more problematical is another consequence of this craze for harmonization. Whoever tries to look wherever possible, for similar solutions, that is, whoever already regards harmonization as of value in itself, very rapidly loses the ability to distinguish between important and unimportant, necessary and superfluous matters. More than that, he interferes with the power of differentiating between regions and countries and runs into the danger of creating a uniform (*gleichgeschaltet*)

Europe. True, we are still far away from that; diversity is surely more powerful than the power of those in the First Europe; but the search for European solutions for their own sake is already recognizable as incipient ideology – and it is dangerous.

Not everything in Europe is lovely because it happens to be European. A European Europe is also a much more differentiated, colourful, multiple Europe. It is a Europe in which those matters are dealt with and regulated in common which could perhaps only be sensibly dealt with in this way. The transition from the First to the Second Europe demands a move away from the dogma of harmonization towards the principle of functional utility (*Subsidiarität*).

There is no necessary European interest in having farms the same size, nor even perhaps in a common agricultural policy; there is a necessary European interest in a common trade policy. There is no necessary interest in an identical regional structural policy for the whole of Europe; there is an interest in overcoming excessive drops in the standard of living in individual regions. There is no European interest in creating an identical banking system in all European countries; there is an interest in producing favourable development conditions for multinational corporations (*Gesellschaften*). There is a common interest in the freedom of movement of employees, of technological cooperation; opening of the inner frontiers to people and goods. There is an indispensable common interest in democratic forms of government and their control, even when parliamentary democracies and presidential democracies, republics and monarchies, one and two chamber systems are effortlessly reconcilable with this interest.

Even with the strictest interpretation of the principle of functional utility (*Subsidiaritat*) there remains an elementary European interest in the growing coordination of national politics *vis-à-vis* the outside world. The middle and smaller states of today even when they are highly developed are on their own too weak to withstand the pull of the super powers. They are far too weak to play their own role in the world as vehicles for the progress of humanity in peace and freedom. Here possibly lies the real task for a European Europe – and a task at which the First Europe often failed deplorably. And it is just here that it is necessary to speak internationally, directly and openly but at the same time also with the intention of taking binding decisions.

Constitution of the Second Europe

The aims of a European Community are not new; but it is useful to formulate them once more. The institutions through which these aims are to be achieved are also so little of an innovation that now it is necessary to revise them. But there are even fewer solutions than is usual which may be found rapidly and can be maintained over a long period of time. But there are one or two standard perspectives and strategic decisions which can soon be made in the light of these perspectives.

The European Community is keen to go into the lack of democracy of others; those that are enthusiastic in this respect would do well to stop and look at their own house and above all repair it. The construction of First Europe does not measure up well to any great democratic standard. Without urgent support on this point First Europe will not remain and Second Europe will not come into being.

The First Europe was defined by a certain institutional dogmatism. Decisions had to be taken according to what the treaties said and in no other way. That they occurred in other ways after all led to an expensive institutional hypocrisy, among other things to invention of the Committee of Permanent Representatives (including the representatives of representatives and other anomalies). A period of institutional flexibility, with different institutions existing alongside each other would do Europe good.

But the most important perspective is quite different. The Germans especially have participated in the theological struggle over supranationality and renunciation of sovereignty with great dedication. Here the traditional even official German position was almost recognizable by its pleasure in renouncing sovereignty. As substitute for the unlikely reunification of the country, as reparation for a rampaging nationalism of the past, out of embarrassment for a non-existent foreign policy – whatever the motive, the Federal Republic has systematically weakened itself and Europe through supranational illusions. Presumably many Germans still think that the Luxembourg Agreement, acceptance of the rule of unanimous council decisions, has decisively weakened Europe. But that only applies to a Europe of fantasies and professors.

This is of immediate concern to the Federal Republic: so much self-denial must one day produce its own revenge. He who wishes to prevent the reappearance of nationalism will do well to defend national interests especially carefully; otherwise he remains seated on the terrible pendulum that swings between the extremes. It is not a question of subjecting oneself to the wishes of the others, but instead combining one's own interests with those of the others.

What concerns Europe: it will in the end be a reality to the extent that it is supported by its members. A majority decision over agricultural prices, not to speak of economic union, can only imply that those who have been overruled will go their own way. In the middle-term perspective, which we are talking about here, the majority principle can only find a limited use.

For in a future Europe – to walk for a moment on the slippery ice of conflict over meanings – it is neither a matter of supra-national fictions, nor of mere multiplication of nations; neither of a totally new third structure alongside and above the member states, nor of its isolated continuance; neither of renunciation of sovereignty, nor of unchanged exercise of sovereignty. It is a matter of trying to achieve the common exercise of the sovereignty of the European nations.

This expression which is developed in the Europe papers of Giscard d'Estaing's independent republicans, is impressive. The European states in fact decide an increasing range of questions which they could decide independently in a common way. The decision binds them to attempt to find common solutions, but not to accept solutions which they regard as irreconcilable with their own interests. The Davignon formula is less than this; the history of the economic union can be taken as a lesson of the possibilities that lie in the common exercise of sovereignty.

Europe is thus strongest where national interests correspond to common aims (but also vice-versa: where national aims meet common interests). On this basis institutions can be built which will be lasting. Strategic considerations along these lines would be: Ministers of Europe – Commission – Parliament.

Not by mere chance does the old idea of appointing one's own member state ministers of Europe always reappear. The advantages are obvious. In the Council, Ministers of Europe will replace the factually incompetent (as they are busy with other matters) foreign ministers but also the politically incompetent (as they are civil servants) permanent representatives; in the member states, the Ministers of Europe can take better responsi-bility for the coordination of subjects than can ad hoc institutions (like the German Committee of European State Secretaries). The Ministers of Europe need no ministry of their own that goes beyond a small staff of workers. They could be members of their Cabinets but would meet more often with their own European colleagues. They will be present at Davignon consultations just as much as at all the other common activities of the member states, even though they would not necessarily take a leading part. They can develop a common secretariat on the basis of the present-day Council-secretariat, possibly by taking over the services of the Commission. Whether there is a European government or not – the council of Ministers of Europe will be the characteristic institution of the Second Europe, in the way in which the Commission was for the First Europe.

The prospect is hardly attractive, that after the extension of the European community from six to ten members, a commission will be created of fourteen equally deciding members (in theory according to the principle of collegiality). Inefficiency can hardly be organized in a more costly way. The Commission has important functions, even if President Pompidou finds it hard to grasp this:

1. It conducts the everyday business of common (or at least communal) activity.
2. It develops proposals on the basis of previous political decisions.
3. It liaises and moderates in critical council discussions.
4. It represents and watches as guardian of treaties over what has been arrived at in common.

But in order that it can do all this without false claims and thereby supposedly do things better, the traces of its character as a government *in spe* must disappear. One president and two or three vice-presidents (with responsibility to start with e.g. for home and foreign affairs and agriculture) would be fully adequate. The national proportion, that is the conscientious division of fourteen or even twenty-eight persons among the member states can take place at the next level, at that of the general directors. In the actual jobs (*Diensten*) every doubling up with the Council should be avoided; a gradual fusion of both jobs (*beide Diensten*) would not only be rational but also sensible. That can all start soon, and whoever is unwilling to part with his dreams should remember that the future of Europe is much more important than that of the European Commission.

There remains the democratic deficit, the overcoming of which, if only because of the political demands in the economic union, is a necessary condition for the Second Europe. Here also it is not a question of wiping away the tears (*Augenwischerei*). Direct elections to a European Parliament do not change anything; this luxury one can at least avoid. This Parliament needs political issues as its present President Behrendt has righty pointed out; its members are in any case already all elected. The constitutional game whereby a powerless parliament controls the sham government of the Commission must stop. The counterpart to Parliament would in the first instance be the Council of Ministers of Europe (for whom one could in any case in principle gradually substitute the European for the national parliamentary responsibility).

Today's European community has no accounting centre (*Rechnungshof*): anyone who wants to spend money, very often audits it himself. A small borrowing from future member Great Britain could lead to the establishment of a permanent committee of parliament with responsibility for accounts. The seat of parliament must be there where the rest of the institutions are, in order that serious and regular contacts are created. Parliament must automatically be responsible for every new activity of the Community, that is, its competence must not be hemmed in by the limitation of treaties. A separate treaty of the member states concerning the European Parliament is thus desirable. Its preparation could start at once.

These suggestions are indeed not exhaustive. The above is not even a list of the institutions. Within the framework of the Davignon formula it is already possible to create new or to revive former arrangements. Despite the tired last session of its Council of Ministers the West European Union could one day as equally earn a shot-in-the-arm as the worthy OECD has recently experienced for quite different reasons. What a large European free-trade area, of which the European Community is only a part, means institutionally should be tested out just as openly as the future of the Council of Europe.

In any case it is feasible that there can be several equally ranking 'Commissions', that is initiating and executing secretariats for European affairs. The EEC Commission can without doubt exist alongside a Commission of the governors of the central banks and a Davignon secretariat.

The Second Europe is not yet ready. Let us take heed of the failures of the First Europe and avoid saddling it with a perfectionist constitution.

A reminder seems to be of use. Our European aims must not be so distant from the national interest as it was perceived to be by the Common Market Europeans of the first hour; on the other hand, our national aims must not move so far away from our European interests as the Union of Farmers would wish. The political gain to be had from common dealing among the European states is very important. We can have this today in return for a tolerable pledging of national interests. The bitter-sweet weeks can become sweet if we know what we want – and want what we can know.

Part Two
European Integration : Theoretical Perspectives

A major problem in dealing with developments in European integration is to gain some sense of perspective when attempting to relate developments in economic, social and political fields to each other, in order to understand the dynamics of the integration process. Ernst Haas, in a classic statement of the neofunctionalist approach, outlines the way in which converging individual interests lead to a decision to cooperate in one functional task, and the process whereby this limited integration spills over into other fields as it becomes necessary to solve new problems arising from that initial decision. Karl Deutsch summarizes those conditions which seem to be necessary if the attempted integration is to succeed, and discusses some of the philosophic issues which advocates of integration frequently take for granted.

As John Pinder makes plain, it is not possible to divorce economic integration from political integration, in that abolition of such discriminatory devices as customs tariffs may cause problems which can only be solved by major common policies at the Community level if the benefits flowing from the establishment of a common market are to be preserved. Nils Lundgren's analysis of customs union theory takes a different view, namely that the gains from international trade and division of labour are only marginally affected by abolition of tariffs, but may be enormous if the institutional and social differences between countries are understood and in the long term harmonized.

Roger Hansen argues that students of European integration should pay more attention to the international environment in which the process takes place, and recognize that the member governments of the Six were quite capable of establishing a common market without surrendering control over their vital interests to an ever more powerful supranational authority.

5 Ernst Haas

International Integration: The European and the Universal Process[1]

Excerpt from E. Haas, *International Political Communities*, Anchor Books, 1966, pp. 93–110.

European and universal integration

The established nation-state is in full retreat in Europe while it is advancing voraciously in Africa and Asia. Integration among discrete political units is a historical fact in Europe, but disintegration seems to be the dominant *motif* elsewhere. Cannot the example of successful integration in Europe be imitated? Could not the techniques of international and supranational cooperation developed in Luxembourg, Paris and Brussels be put to use in Accra, Bangkok and Cairo, as well as on the East River in New York? Or, in a different perspective, will not the progress of unity in Europe inevitably have its integrating repercussions in other regions and at the level of the United Nations even without efforts at conscious imitation?

Such a development would be most satisfying. Presumably it would contribute to world peace by creating ever-expanding islands of practical cooperation, eventually spilling over into the controversy-laden fields which threaten us directly with thermonuclear destruction. The functionalist theory of international peace might be put to work by a generalization of the European mode of post-1945 international cooperation. Further, those who hope to contribute to the peaceful solution of conflict could take much solace from such a development, for the post-1945 European mode of resolving conflicts among states has demonstrated that 'there often comes a moment when there is a simultaneous revolution of interests on both sides and unity precipitates itself', to quote Mary Follett (1940, p. 40).

Before abandoning ourselves to such pleasant speculation, however, we would do well to state systematically what we have learned about the causes of European integration and then to investigate where else these causes might be operative. This effort calls for some definitions.

1. This article has been altered slightly by the author. It is reprinted from *International Organization*, vol. 15, no. 4, Autumn 1961.

We are interested in tracing progress toward a terminal condition called *political community*. Successful nation-states constitute such communities and subsequent amalgamations of several such states may also form communities. A variety of constitutional and structural factors are compatible with this notion; political community exists when there is likelihood of internal peaceful change in a setting of contending groups with mutually antagonistic claims. The process of attaining this condition among nation-states we call *integration*, the process whereby political actors in several distinct national settings are persuaded to shift their loyalties, expectations and political activities toward a new and larger center, whose institutions possess or demand jurisdiction over the pre-existing national states. It should be noted that the objective economic, social and communications 'factors' often identified with 'integration', in my scheme, are conditions typical of an ongoing political community. At best they may serve as indicators to help us assess the progress of integration.

This focus precludes attention to what may be called the 'immanent myth' of European unity which owes its inspiration to cultural-historical antecedents considered equally relevant to the contemporary process of integration. It appears to me that European unity under the Roman, Frankish and medieval Roman-German imperial realms has no more analytical importance than the unity of all Islam in the eighth century, the domains of the Ming Empire in the fifteenth or the Guptas in the fifth. The mere fact that specific regions were unified politically and culturally at one time seems not to prevent them from subsequently dividing into warring nations denying in their conduct the cultural unity the historian wishes to impute to them: they do not then constitute any kind of political community. If this is so we cannot use some previous historical experience which involved the notion of community as an argument for assuming the natural and inevitable re-emergence of this happy state of affairs. It may indeed emerge, but in response to the factors we shall discuss. Naturally, in the political advocacy of integration by some specific movement, the 'memory' of a historical community may play its part in the construction of a myth; but this does not make the past an active causative agent. On the other hand, a series of traumatic events vividly remembered by a generation subjected to integration may launch and then spur the process. The role of two world wars of unprecedented destructiveness and the threat of the victory of a revolutionary totalitarian movement at the end of the second of these wars were undoubtedly primary among the specific stimuli which, in western Europe, made people receptive to the historical-cultural arguments of the mythmakers. This combination of circumstances does not easily permit repetition elsewhere.

Conflict resolution is a particularly interesting indicator for judging progress along the path of integration. A close study of negotiating processes in international relations suggests the prevalence of three types of compromise, each indicative of a certain measure of integration.

1. The least demanding we may call accommodation on the basis of the minimum common denominator. Equal bargaining partners gradually reduce their antagonistic demands by exchanging concessions of roughly equal value. Gains and losses are easily identified, but the impact of the transaction never goes beyond what the *least* cooperative bargaining partner wishes to concede. This mode of compromise is typical of classic diplomatic negotiations.

2. Accommodation by 'splitting the difference' carries us a little farther along the path of integration. As before, demands are reduced and concessions of roughly equal value exchanged among autonomous bargaining units. But in this mode of compromise the mediatory services of a secretary-general or *ad hoc* international expert study group may be admitted by the parties. Conflict is resolved, not on the basis of the will of the least cooperative, but somewhere between the final bargaining positions. This type of negotiation is prevalent in international economic organizations and in other dealings permitting financial identification of gains or losses, such as the formulation of a scale of assessments for Members of the United Nations.

3. Finally, accommodation on the basis of deliberately or inadvertently upgrading the common interests of the parties takes us closest to the peaceful change procedures typical of a political community with its full legislative and judicial jurisdictions, lacking in international relations. To confuse matters further, this mode of conflict resolution is often identified as 'integration', as by Mary Follett, who wrote that it, unlike mere compromise, signified 'that a solution has been found in which both desires have found a place, that neither side has had to sacrifice anything' (1940, p. 32). If this is so it must mean that the parties succeeded in redefining their conflict so as to work out a solution at a higher

Summary of integration experience of European organizations

Organization	Institutions	Mode of accommodation and functions		Ideological-social environment
OEEC-EPU Age: 12 years	inter-governmental; weak secretariat; strong autonomous expert bodies	upgrading common interests	remove trade barriers	mixed ideologically, economically, social structure
		splitting difference	divide US aid; emergency distribution of goods	
		minimum common denominator	planning for long- range economic growth	
Council of Europe Age: 12 years	inter-governmental; interparliamentary; weak secretariat; rudimentary judicial institution	minimum common denominator	European integration in general	mixed ideologically, economically, social structure, though united on democracy
		minimum common denominator plus parliamentary diplomacy	European legislation	
		splitting difference and parliamentary diplomacy	solution of specific short-range problems	
NATO Age: 13 years	inter-governmental; interparliamentary; strong secretariat; strong autonomous expert bodies	minimum common denominator	integrated defence policy	mixed ideologically, economically, social structure, and in military power
		splitting difference	coordinated foreign policy; joint defence economics	
		upgrading common interests	planning for new weapons and strategy	

Organization / Age	Type	Decision mode	Goal	Homogeneity
Nordic Council Age: 8 years	inter-governmental; interparliamentary	parliamentary diplomacy plus minimum common denominator	economic integration; legal standardization; social security harmonization	homogeneous ideologically, but mixed in social structure and economic development
Benelux Age: 17 years	inter-governmental; interparliamentary	minimum common denominator	economic integration	homogeneous on all counts, except role of agriculture
EEC ECSC Euratom Age: 9 and 4 years	supranational	upgrading common interests splitting difference minimum common denominator	economic integration in long run solution of short-run economic problems; labor mobility; nuclear planning	homogeneous on all counts (except in southern Italy)
Western European Union Age: 6 years	inter-governmental; interparliamentary; weak secretariat; strong autonomous expert bodies	parliamentary diplomacy plus minimum common denominator upgrading common interests	foreign policy coordination arms control	homogeneous on all counts except separate UK ideological position and special German military position
EFTA Age: 3 years	inter-governmental; weak secretariat	splitting difference	remove trade barriers	mixed on all counts

level, which almost invariably implies the expansion of the mandate or task of an international or national governmental agency. In terms of results, this mode of accommodation maximizes what I have elsewhere called the 'spill-over' effect of international decisions: policies made pursuant to an initial task and grant of power can be made real only if the task itself is expanded, as reflected in the compromises among the states interested in the task. In terms of method, the upgrading of the parties' common interests relies heavily on the services of an institutionalized mediator, whether a single person or a board of experts, with an autonomous range of powers. It thus combines intergovernmental negotiation with the participation of independent experts and spokesmen for interest groups, parliaments and political parties. It is this combination of interests and institutions which we shall identify as 'supranational'. The initial creation of such an agency, of course, demands a creative compromise among the states parties to the effort, based on the realization that certain common interests cannot be attained in any other way. This in turn presupposes that identical and converging policy aims, rather than antagonistic ones, predominated at the moment when the supranational organization was set up.

Each of these modes of accommodation, in addition to specifying a type of outcome relating to intensities of integration, also is typified by appropriate institutional mechanisms. There exists, moreover, a fourth prominent procedural device – parliamentary diplomacy – which is capable of producing any of the three outcomes. Parliamentary diplomacy, as Dean Rusk defined it, implies the existence of a continuing organization with a broad frame of reference, public debate, rules of procedure governing the debate, and the statement of conclusions in a formal resolution arrived at by some kind of majority vote (1955). When bodies like the UN or the Council of Europe define a conflict situation by filtering discussion through this machinery they may also be setting the limits within which eventual settlement comes about, though parliamentary diplomacy rarely defines the actual terms of the settlement. Instead it mobilizes political mediatory forces – the uncommitted states, parties, groups or persons – whose voice in the settlement process is given volume by the reluctance of the parties to the dispute to annoy the mediating forces. Since the institutional context in which parliamentary diplomacy can be practised maximizes the representation of a variety of interests emanating from the same nation, it opens up areas of maneuver which are foreclosed in negotiations exclusively conducted by carefully instructed single agents of foreign ministries. To that extent it facilitates a greater amount of integration even though it does not necessarily produce outcomes which upgrade common interests.

Where can these modes of accommodation be identified in the history and institutions of European integration?

The lesson of European integration

Clearly all these modes of accommodation are part of the European pattern of international adjustment. While they do not provide the only indicators of degrees of integration, they appear to be particularly strategic ones in that they focus on decision-making, thereby acting as a summary of, and an abstraction upon, other factors which could also be used as indicators. Broadly speaking, international institutions maximizing decision-making by means of the second and third modes yield the greatest amount of progress toward the goal of political community.

Parliamentary diplomacy is the chief contribution to European unity which can be credited to the various parliamentary assemblies. They have not meaningfully controlled their various executives nor have they legislated in any real sense, though they have attempted and partially exercised powers in both these fields. But they have acted as a spur to the formation of new voluntary elite groups across national boundaries – the European political groups – and the interplay among these has produced a type of diplomatic problem-solving which takes its inspiration from parliamentary resolutions and is able to upgrade common interests. As examples we may cite the work of the Council of Europe in relation to the Saar, in refugee relief and resettlement, and in the relaxation of frontier formalities. We may add the work of the Nordic Council in the negotiation of the now superseded Nordic Common Market Agreement. But let it be admitted at the same time that the total contribution of parliamentary diplomacy is not very great. It found no institutional outlet at all in the Organization for European Economic Cooperation (OEEC); yet that organization's contribution to integration was substantial even though it operated primarily on the level of accommodation by 'splitting the difference'.

The most successful institutions in Europe are the 'Communities' of the Six, constitutional hybrids which once caused nightmares to the public lawyer. They facilitate the resolution of conflict by virtue of all three modes, but the upgrading of common interests is their true contribution to the art of political integration. All fundamental decisions are made by the Councils of Ministers. But they are decisions based on continuous compromise, constantly informed by generally respected expert bodies with constitutional powers of their own and in constant contact with supranational voluntary associations and interest groups. The character of decision-making stimulates interest groups to make themselves heard; it spurs political parties in Strasbourg and Luxembourg to work out common positions; it creates an enormous pressure on high national civil servants to get to know and establish rapport with their opposite numbers; and it sharpens the sensitivities of the legal profession to European norms and political processes in preparation for the inevitable flood of litigation before the Court of Justice. In short, many of the decisions are integrative in their immediate economic consequences *as well as* in the new expectations and political processes which they imply. It is this indirect result which is maximized by the mixture of institutions which usually achieves accommodation at a higher level of agreement as compared to the initial bargaining positions of the parties. Earlier decisions, including the ones constituting the Communities, spill over into new functional contexts, involve more and more people, call for more and more interbureaucratic contact and consultation, thereby creating their own logic in favor of later decisions, meeting, in a pro-community direction, the new problems which grow out of the earlier compromises.

Intergovernmental institutions of the classic variety, even when assisted by respected international civil servants and advisory boards, have not been able to match this performance. The North Atlantic Treaty Organization (NATO) and OEEC, for reasons to be explored, have continued to make their contribution to integration by means of compromises based on techniques found also in the United Nations. They have transcended these only in relation to certain tasks hinging around the direct implications of the welfare state.

This brings us face to face with the key question of which organizational *functions*, or tasks, have contributed most to the process of integration in Europe. The superficial answer clearly points to the field of economics; but by no means all organizations with an economic competence have performed equally well and few of them solve their problems on the basis of upgrading common interests. Parliamentary diplomacy has apparently been of importance in advancing economic integration only in the Nordic Council; OEEC functioned on the basis of 'splitting the difference' or compromising on the level of the minimum common denominator in all areas except those relating to currency convertibility and the removal of quotas (in which common interests were indeed upgraded). The European Free Trade Association (EFTA) has not taken strides comparable to those of the European Economic Community (EEC) and the European Coal and Steel Community (ECSC).

Not merely economic tasks, therefore, but the degree of functional specificity of the economic task is casually related to the intensity of integration. The more specific the task, the more likely important progress toward political community. It is not enough to be concerned with the reduction of trade barriers or the forecasting of industrial productivity. Specificity of task is essential, with respect to such assignments as creating a common market for narrowly defined products, unifying railway rates, removing restrictive practices in certain branches of industry, removing import quotas by fixed percentage points during fixed periods, and the like. Functional specificity, however, may be so trivial as to remain outside the stream of human expectations and actions vital for integration. This would seem to be the case with the standardization of railway rolling stock, for example, or the installation of uniform road signs. The task, in short, must be both specific and economically important in the sense of containing the potential for spilling over from one vital area of welfare policy into others.

Non-economic tasks have shown themselves much more barren. The cultural activities of the Council of Europe lack a focus on intensely experienced human wants. Its emergency-aid measures have been short range and its contributions to the solution of political tensions non-repetitive. The 'European review' function is much too vague to yield observable results. The standardization efforts of the Nordic Council lack the stimulus of controversy and debate: they are so deeply rooted in the Scandinavian setting that one suspects integration of proceeding even without the Council. Continuous contact among civil servants and ministers is capable of contributing to integration in narrowly defined areas even without the participation of parliamentarians. The only functionally specific assignment of the Western European Union (WEU) is the supervision of the arms aspects of the Paris and London

Agreements (1954). This function is being carried out in a supranational manner, but the reason is in the non-controversial and non-recurrent aspect of German rearmament, at least at the intergovernmental level. The other activities of WEU are unlikely to be remembered by history.

What about the field of European conventions? Surely these are specific in content and many of them relate to economics and welfare policy. The fact remains, however, that their very content reflects merely the minimum common denominator among the existing practices and policies of the member states, and that the Council had to resort to the device of 'partial agreements' to get beyond this level. Conventions which depart from this denominator tend not to be ratified by the country whose standards are below the norms fixed in Strasbourg.[2] Integration, therefore, is advanced by the European conventions only to the extent that their content calls for a new – a supranational – political process which can generate new expectations and policies. This, probably, is the case only with reference to the field of human rights, a very significant field indeed. Moreover, there recently evolved in the Council the practice, among the members of the Committee of Ministers, of reporting annually on the willingness and speed of ratifying conventions. While this practice falls short of supranationality it nevertheless exposes the reporting country to the possibility of criticism and pressure.

Military and defence questions have not displayed a close affinity to integration unless the issue involves the related question of saving and allocating resources for welfare measures. NATO's experience in the financing of infrastructure programs, weapons research, integration of air warning systems, and the switch to centrally-controlled nuclear deterrents indicates that the upgrading of common interests does take place – not without obstacles and delays – when the economic burdens of defence for small countries are considered incompatible with their welfare commitments. But the other activities of the Atlantic Alliance make plain that more primitive modes of accommodation continue to flourish and that integration is more pronounced on paper than in the command post, the procurement center and the council chamber.

This survey of the functional lessons of European integration

2. The conventions dealing with the equivalence of university degrees and the movement of persons are exceptions to this generalization. Both of them involved some measure of upgrading common interests.

leads to the inevitable conclusion that functional contexts are autonomous. Integrative forces which flow from one kind of activity do not necessarily infect other activities, even if carried out by the same organization. OEEC could not repeat in the field of tariff bargaining the results it obtained on questions of convertibility. NATO cannot transfer its success in planning strategy for new weapons systems to the standardization of the enlistment period; and ECSC has shown itself more adept in negotiating cumulative compromises on the creation of a common market than on short-run solutions for the coal crisis. Decisions made by identical officials, in organizations with a stable membership, in a non-revolutionary socio-ideological setting with similar institutional characteristics nevertheless vary sharply, in terms of their integrative impact, depending on the functional context. If this is true even in the European setting, how much more true is it likely to be in the United Nations. But the converse proposition is equally important: the autonomy of functional contexts means that disintegration in one range of relations among certain states does not necessarily imply parallel disintegration in other relations among the same states. Thus the breakdown of the Free Trade Area (EFTA) negotiations did not entail a retreat from monetary convertibility; NATO's work on unifying air raid warning systems was not interrupted by the split between the Six of EEC and the Seven of EFTA.

The attempt to compare the European experience with efforts elsewhere compels attention to the environment in which the process of integration is taking place, what some scholars call the 'background' factors. This investigation will show that while 'Europe' – in the largest sense of the nineteen countries west of the Iron Curtain – possesses no completely common factors at all, significant islands of almost identical environmental factors exist among certain of them.

Social structure provides one set of factors. With the exception of Greece, Turkey, Portugal, parts of Spain and southern Italy, the western European social scene is dominated by pluralism. Articulate voluntary groups, led by bureaucratized but accessible elites, compete with each other more or less rationally for political power and social status. The population is mobilized and participates in this process through affiliation with mass organizations. In the countries mentioned, however, effective and functionally diffuse social relations prevail.

Economic and industrial development furnishes a second set of factors. With the exception of the same countries plus Ireland, we are dealing with a very high level of economic development – including that of the countries in which the dominant products are agricultural – from the point of view of productivity, investment and consumption. Significantly correlated with industrialization we find the usual high degree of urbanization and ever-growing demands for government services and durable consumer goods. We also find increasing demands on limited natural resources and greater dependence on foreign (or regional) trade. But note some partial exceptions: Norway's industrial weakness compared to that of Sweden, Belgium's agricultural inefficiency compared to that of the Netherlands.

Ideological patterns provide the final set of factors. Since policies of integration are, in the first instance, advanced or blocked by the activities of political parties and their ministers, parties may be used as an index of ideological homogeneity. A given cluster of countries is ideologically 'homogeneous' if the divisions among the parties are, very roughly, the same among all the countries in the cluster, when the principles professed and the concrete socio-economic interests represented by the parties are roughly analogous on both sides of a frontier. Given this definition, the Scandinavian countries emerge as ideologically homogeneous among themselves (with the partial exception of Iceland) but quite dissimilar from the rest of Europe. The Benelux countries, West Germany, Switzerland and Austria seem homogeneous and seem to have considerable affinity for Italy and France. But a disturbing element is introduced here by the large anti-parliamentary minorities in France and Italy. Portugal, Greece, Spain and Turkey lack the typical European socio-economic structure and therefore the appropriate party systems; they do not fit into any neat ideological package. The British and Irish parties show some affinity for their continental colleagues, especially the socialists, but the patterns of interest aggregation and political style differ sufficiently to prevent the positing of a homogeneous pattern. We therefore have two large ideological clusters: (1) Scandinavia, and (2) the Six (plus Switzerland and Austria), as well as a number of single national systems whose characteristics seem *sui generis*.

Let us relate these environmental patterns to the integration process . Integration proceeds most rapidly and drastically when it responds to socio-economic demands emanating from an industrial-urban environment, when it is an adaptation to cries for increasing welfare benefits and security born by the growth of a new type of society. In the words of two European scholars:

For decades industrialism has been revising the workways and consuming habits of people everywhere. It has enabled cities to grow and the urban way of life to spread. Urbanism is the great outreaching dynamic, breaking down isolation and encroaching upon tradition. Modern industrial urbanism is innately inimical to any isolation. It demands access and stimulates mobility. As earlier it resisted being confined to city walls, now it resists being confined to limited political areas. This resistance to confinement is greater than the resistance against the encroachments. In the measure that industrial urbanism has gained in this contest against the rooted barriers – in that measure integration is needed. The effort toward European integration reflects this need of industrial urbanism for wider organization. (Schokking and Anderson, 1960).

I reject the teleological aspects of this statement. In terms of a social process based on rational human perceptions and motives, no mere concept 'calls for' or 'needs' anything: a discrete set of group motives, converging with motives of cognate groups from across the border, results in a certain pattern of policy; the aims and the policy reflect demands born from the environment, and the later policies may well change the environment in a wholly unintended fashion. Only in this sense, then, does industrial urbanism favor integration. Because the modern 'industrial-political' actor fears that his way of life cannot be safeguarded without structural adaptation, he turns to integration; but by the same token, political actors who are neither industrial, nor urban, nor modern in their outlook usually do not favor this kind of adaptation, for they seek refuge instead in national exclusiveness.

Thus, countries dominated by a non-pluralistic social structure are poor candidates for participation in the integration process. Even if their governments do partake at the official level, the consequences of their participation are unlikely to be felt elsewhere in the social structure. Hence the impact of European integration, in all its aspects, has been minimal in Portugal, Turkey and Greece. Finally, sufficient ideological homogeneity for value-sharing among important national elite groups is essential for rapid integration. The implications for Europe are obvious as reflected in the differential rates of progress toward political community which have been made within Scandinavia, within the Six and within Benelux compared to the all-European level represented by OEEC, NATO and the Council of Europe.

In addition to these environmental considerations, which relate to the internal characteristics of the region undergoing integration, there are often external environmental factors of importance. Fear of a common enemy is an absolutely necessary precondition for integration in military organizations: without the Soviet Union there would have been no NATO. But the common enemy may be a more subtle manifestation, such as fear of external groupings of culturally and economically suspect forces: such considerations were not irrelevant to the 'third-force' argument which entered the integration process among the Six and is apparent in the convergence of interests which resulted in the Organization for Economic Cooperation and Development (OECD). While external environments produce motives favoring integration, they are never sufficient in themselves to explain the rate and intensity of the process.

Institutions, functions and environments provide useful categories for arranging the human data among which our various modes of accommodation made themselves felt; but they do not exhaust the list of crucial given factors of which we are all aware and without which the process of integration simply cannot be discussed. Variations in national policy, for instance, are fundamental to the life of international organizations, especially in agencies which do not possess the institutional power to influence significantly the policy aims of their member states. However, this truism should not be rendered in the all too common form which asserts that differences in *power* among members determine organizational behavior and the speed and direction of organizational response. Variations in national policy provide a power determinant, not in absolute terms, but only with respect to the functional strength of particular states in relation to the specific task of the organization. The military and economic power of the United States in NATO, for instance, is a meaningful ingredient in the life of that organization only when it is brought to bear on infrastructure or procurement negotiations. The fact remains, none the less, that changes in the policy needs experienced by member states, reflecting as they do the pressures of the home and of the international environments, create definite phases in the life of international organizations.

Therefore, lessons about integrative processes associated with one phase do not generally carry over into the next because the specific policy context – often short range – determines what is desired by governments and tolerated by them in terms of integrative accommodations. This, in turn, forces us to the conclusion that types of accommodation, and the associated procedural norms of an organization, developed in one phase of its life do not necessarily carry over into the next. There is no dependable, cumulative process of precedent formation leading to ever more community-oriented organizational behavior, unless the task assigned to the institutions is inherently expansive, thus capable of overcoming the built-in autonomy of functional contexts and of surviving changes in the policy aims of member states.

The importance of this lesson must be illustrated from the experience of one of the more successful European organizations, OEEC, with multilateral accommodation in liberalizing trade and payments – the aspect of OEEC which contributed most to integration in Europe.[3] The typical OEEC procedure included confrontation, collection of detailed information, mediation in closed sessions and the working out of specific solutions to crises by autonomous bodies of national experts. The procedures were perfected during the period (1948–51) when the chief task of OEEC was the distribution of United States aid, assistance which was conditional on trade and payments liberalization. During the next phase (1952–6) the procedure continued and was remarkably successful in further removing obstacles to intraregional commerce, despite the cessation of United States aid. Why? Largely because the major national policies continued to be oriented toward liberalization, and the recurrent French and British payments crises could therefore not successfully challenge the multilateral decision-making process; continuing French and British demands for a relaxation of the OEEC Code resulted in successive compromises along the principle of 'splitting the difference', but involving the upgrading of common interests in the system of review and accountability which accompanied the relaxation. Since 1956, all this has changed. Further economic integration has become enmeshed in the political issue of the Six against the Seven, with the result that the procedures which had apparently been institutionalized successfully in an earlier phase of OEEC's life have stagnated with disuse. Fundamental changes in national policies provide the crucial explanatory variable.

This process went on in a setting of intergovernmentalism. More than in the supranational setting, an environment of intergovernmentalism permits great freedom to states strongly en-

3. My discussion of OEEC benefited greatly from the advice and criticism of William Diebold, Jr and Robert Triffin.

dowed in a specific functional context. Let us use monetary cooperation as an example. The history of OEEC suggests – as that of ECSC and EEC does not – that certain types of states can use their special bargaining power more readily to get their way. Thus, economically weak countries whose trade is not crucial to the system are readily exempted from the governing norms and play little part in decision-making; but economically strong countries, in terms of total foreign trade *and* credit capacity, possess a *de facto* veto power. Structural creditors whose role in regional trade is secondary occasionally assert a veto power and delay decisions, but their influence is never dominant. Structural or occasional debtors (France and the United Kingdom) with a very important stake in regional trade are able to exercise a constant blackmail power and to succeed in obtaining exemptions from regional rules, since they are immune to the threat of retaliation and responsive only to the techniques of discreet mediation and confrontation.

The lesson of European integration can be summarized as follows:

1. Institutionally, supranational bodies most readily lend themselves to accommodation on the basis of upgrading common interests. This is equally true of intergovernmental bodies which permit certain of their expert commissions the role usually associated with the Communities of the Six, such as the OEEC Steering Board for Trade, the Council of Europe's Commissioner for Refugees and WEU's Armaments Control Agency. These institutions are least susceptible to the alternation of phases and most likely to develop cumulative decision-making precedents.

2. Functionally, specific economic tasks resolving policy differences emerging from previous imperfect compromises on welfare questions, but involving large mass interests, are most intimately related to rapid integration. Conflicts may be resolved by all the usual methods, but upgrading common interests predominates. The tendency toward autonomy of tasks can be overcome only by building into the institutions specific assignments which maximize the spill-over process.

3. Environmentally, integration fares best in situations controlled by social groupings representing the rational interests of urban-industrial society, groups seeking to maximize their economic benefits and dividing along regionally homogeneous ideological-political lines. Changing national policy inhibits integration unless compensated by strong central institutions maximizing the spill-over process.

Obviously, integration may take place and has taken place among nations which have few of these characteristics and through international organizations which depart little from the classic intergovernmental pattern. But the pace and intensity of such integration is pallid in such a context as compared to the situation in which all optimal conditions are met. Hence it should come as no surprise that the Communities of the Six represent the most, and the Council of Europe the least, successful organizations in a European spectrum in which all organizations make some contribution to some aspect of the integration process.

References

FOLLETT, M. (1940) in Metcalf and Urwick (eds.), *Dynamic Administration*, Harper & Row.

RUSK, D. (1955), 'Parliamentary diplomacy: debate *v.* negotiation', *World Affairs Interpreter*, vol. 26, no. 2, pp. 121–2.

SCHOKKING, J. J., and ANDERSON, N. (1960). 'Observations on the European integration process', *J. Conflict Resolution*, vol. 4, no. 4, p. 407.

6 Karl W. Deutsch

Attaining and Maintaining Integration

Excerpt from K. W. Deutsch, *The Analysis of International Relations*
Prentice-Hall, 1968, pp. 191–202.

International organizations have often been seen as the best
pathway for leading mankind out of the era of the nation-state.
Beyond the actual international organizations which now exist,
or have existed, there are the great projects for Atlantic Union or
for Federal World Government which still promise much for
supranational integration, if they could only get started. Against
these visions of the future, it is worthwhile to put the experiences
of the past. What have been some of the actual cases of political
integration, and what can be learned from them?

There are, perhaps, four dozen cases of political integration in
the world from which something could be learned fairly directly
that might help us better to deal with our similar present-day
problems. Fourteen of these cases – ten from earlier history and
four relatively recent ones – have been studied for the explicit
purpose of making such comparisons to our contemporary problems, and some of the findings of these studies are worth summarizing here.[1]

The main *tasks of integration* can be conveniently recalled
under four headings: (1) maintaining peace; (2) attaining greater
multipurpose capabilities; (3) accomplishing some specific task;
and (4) gaining a new self-image and role identity.

All these tasks are operationally testable. Whether stable
expectations of *peace* are being maintained within a community
can be tested by the absence or paucity of specific preparation for
war among the political units, regions and populations within it.

1 The historical studies dealt with the cases of successful integration of
England; England and Wales; England and Scotland; the United States;
Germany; Italy; and Switzerland; and with the failures of integration of
Norway and Sweden; England and Ireland; and the Austro-Hungarian
monarchy. The recent cases studied included the successes of the Nordic
Council and of the European Economic Community, and the failures of
the Federation of the West Indies and of the United Arab Republic. For
details see Deutsch *et al.* (1957), and Etzioni (1965).

Evidence can be found in data on the deployment of troops, weapons and military installations; in diplomatic records and in budgetary data; and in opinion data on the elite and mass levels. Whether a community has achieved greater *multipurpose capabilities* would be indicated at least roughly by its total gross national product, its per capita GNP, and the scope and diversity of its current undertakings. Whether the community was fulfilling *specific tasks* would be indicated by the existence, and perhaps by the growth, of appropriate joint functions, joint institutions, and joint resources and sacrifices devoted to these specific ends. Finally, whether the members of the community had attained a new *role identity*, or were in the process of attaining it, would be shown by the frequency of use of common symbols, and by the creation and wide adoption of new ones; by data on relevant elite and mass attitudes; and by relevant aggregate data on the actual behavior of the population, including popular acceptance of unrequited transfers within the community, and of some degree of sharing benefits and burdens within it.

Whether the tasks envisaged for integration can in fact be fulfilled, and whether integration will succeed or fail, depends in part on the *background conditions* prevailing within and among the political units to be integrated. The conditions of integration can again be stated under four headings: (1) mutual relevance of the units to one another; (2) compatibility of values and some actual joint rewards; (3) mutual responsiveness; and (4) some degree of generalized common identity or loyalty. These four conditions interact and may strengthen one another, but in principle each can be verified separately.

Mutual relevance among the units is indicated by the relative volume and weight of transactions among them, such as trade, travel and mail and other communications; by the extent to which such transactions exceed the levels which could be expected from mere chance and the size of the participating units; and by the extent of covariance between their efforts on any two different participating political units.

The existence and extent of *joint rewards* for the partners in the prospective larger community can be attested to by the extent of the *positive* covariance of rewards for two or more of them, so that a reward for one is associated with the significant probability of a reward for the other.

The conditions for *mutual responsiveness* include the ascertainable presence of significant capabilities and resources for communication, perception and self-steering; and a separate source of evidence consists in the actual performance in terms of speed, adequacy and probability of responsive behavior.

Finally, *common generalized loyalty* can be indicated by the frequency and saliency of perceptions of joint interests, both in terms of similar distributions of attention and of parallel expectations of reward, as shown by survey data and by the content analysis of mass media and government communications. Another indication would be the objective compatibility or consonance of the major values of the participating populations, permitting cooperation among them to be perceived as legitimate; and this could be supplemented by indications of common subjective feelings of the legitimacy of the integrated community, making loyalty to it also a matter of internalized psychic compulsion.

The goals and conditions of integration go far to determine the *processes and instruments* by which integration is approached. Once more, we can organize these instruments under four headings, as processes and techniques of: (1) value production; (2) value allocation; (3) coercion; and (4) identification. *Value production* and *value allocation* refer, respectively, to the production (or acquisition) and the allocation of goods, services, or relationships valued by the populations concerned. *Coercion* means primarily military or other enforcement; and *identification* means the deliberate promotion of processes and sentiments of mutual identification, loyalties and 'we' feelings.

Types of communities: amalgamation *v*. pluralism
The process of establishing an amalgamated security community

If the main goal of integration is not only the preservation of peace among the integrated political units, but also – or even more urgently – the acquisition of greater power for general purposes, or the attainment of some specific task, or the acquisition of some common role identity, or some combination of all these, then a so-called *amalgamated political community* with a common government is likely to seem most attractive. If, on the other hand, the main aim is the preservation of peace, then a *pluralistic security community* may suffice, and in fact may be easier to attain and to preserve.

An amalgamated community may also be, of course, an *amalgamated security community*, within which dependable expectations of peace and peaceful change prevail, as attested by the absence of any substantial specific preparations for any large-scale warfare within it. Any well-integrated nation-state, such as were Britain and the United States in 1967, is such an amalgamated security community. But neither a common government nor common laws and institutions can ensure such internal peace and security to a country on the verge of civil war, such as was the United States in 1860–61, India–Pakistan in 1946–7 and Nigeria in 1967. Indeed, the very effort to maintain the amalgamated community or political union by force may bring on exactly that large-scale warfare which a security community was intended to prevent. The possible relationships between amalgamated communities and security communities are shown in Table 1.

Table 1 **Political amalgamation, pluralism and security: for possible patterns of political community**

	Non-amalgamation		Amalgamation
Integration	Pluralistic Security-Community *Example* (Norway-Sweden today)	*threshold*	Amalgamated Security-Community *Example* (USA today)
	———— *Integration*	*threshold* ————	
Non-integration	Not Amalgamated Not Security-Community *Example* (USA-USSR, today)	*Amalgamation*	Amalgamated but not Security-Community *Example* (Hapsburg Empire, 1914)

Note: All four cases involve a high degree of mutual relevance and, therefore, some degree of political unity. In each case, the countries, peoples, and governments concerned must take into account each other's behavior in making their own political decisions.
Source: Deutsch *et al.* (1957).

The significance of these relationships is changing. Whereas large-scale civil wars and bloodshed could in the past be survived by the bulk of the warring population because they were waged with weapons of rather limited destructive potential, today the masses of those involved (and perhaps all mankind) could be wiped out in a nuclear civil war fought on a fairly small scale. Accordingly, as the power of weapons has increased, the preserving of peace, and peaceful change and adjustment of conflicts, have become more important; unification for general-purpose power, or for a sense of greater group prestige and identity, has become less important; the legal distinction between international war and civil war has become less relevant; and amalgamated but not integrated political communities have become more dangerous.

Though now more dangerous in case of failure, an amalgamated security community still will continue to look more desirable than its alternates, for if it succeeds, it will not only preserve peace but will provide greater strength for accomplishing both general and specific governmental services and purposes, and possibly a larger sense of identity and psychic reassurance for the elites and masses of its population. But though more desirable, like all better things it will be harder to attain and keep.

Essential background conditions. One study lists twelve social and economic background conditions, within and among the participating units, which seem to be necessary (though perhaps not sufficient) if an amalgamated security community is to succeed:

1. Mutual compatibility of the main values relevant for political behavior.
2. A distinctive and attractive way of life.
3. Expectations of stronger and rewarding economic ties or joint rewards.
4. A marked increase in the political and administrative capabilities of at least some of the participating units.
5. Superior economic growth of at least some participating units (as compared to neighboring territories outside the area of prospective integration).
6. Some substantial unbroken links of social communication across the mutual boundaries of the territories to be integrated, and across the barriers of some of the major social strata within them.
7. A broadening of the political elite within at least some political units, and for the emerging larger community as a whole.
8. Relatively high geographic and social mobility of persons, at least among the politically relevant strata.
9. Multiplicity of the scope of the flow of mutual communications and transactions.
10. Some overall compensation of rewards in the flows of communications and transactions among the units to be integrated.

11. A significant frequency of some interchange in group roles (such as being in a majority or a minority) among the political units.

12. Considerable mutual predictability of behavior.

Together, these background conditions provide much of the indispensable social, economic and psychological environment for the more well-known political conditions for an amalgamated security community, which consist mainly in the willingness and ability of the preponderance of the politically relevant strata in all participating political units to:

1. Accept and support common governmental institutions.

2. Extend generalized political loyalty to them and to the preservation of the amalgamated community.

3. Operate these common institutions with adequate mutual attention and responsiveness to the messages and needs of all participating units.

Even if it has been established, an amalgamated security community, such as a federation or an empire, often is highly vulnerable to civil conflict or secession. Any one of half-a-dozen conditions is likely to make for its disintegration:

1. Any steep increase in economic, military or political burdens on the community or on any participating unit (particularly if this increase in burdens comes at an early stage, before integration has become consolidated by the learning of deep political loyalties and habits).

2. A rapid increase in social mobilization and political participation, faster than the process of civic assimilation to the common political culture of the community.

3. A rapid increase in regional, economic, cultural, social, linguistic or ethnic differentiation, faster and stronger than any compensating integrative process.

4. A serious decline in the political or administrative capabilities of the government and the political elite, relative to the current tasks and burdens with which they have to cope.

5. A relative closure of the political elite, slowing drastically the entry of new members and ideas, and giving rise to hostile counter-elites of frustrated potential elite members.

6. A failure of the government and the elite to carry out in time needed reforms and adjustments wanted or expected by the

population (and perhaps already demonstrated in some salient areas abroad); or failure to adjust in time to the imminent decline or loss of some privileged or dominant minority position (such as the position of the white minority in the former Federation of Rhodesia and Nyasaland).

Pluralistic security communities are easier to establish and to maintain, and hence often are a more effective means to keep the peace among their members. They seem to require only three major conditions for their existence:

1. Compatibility of major political values.
2. Capacity of the governments and politically relevant strata of the participating countries to respond to one another's messages, needs, and actions quickly, adequately, and without resort to violence.
3. Mutual predictability of the relevant aspects of one another's political, economic and social behavior (but these relevant aspects are far fewer in the case of a pluralistic security community than they would be in its much more tightly-knit amalgamated counterpart).

The process of integration. Amalgamated security communities, such as nation-states or federations, are not like organisms. They do not come into existence by a process of growth through a fixed sequence of stages, similar to the way in which a tadpole develops into a frog, or a kitten grows to be a cat. Rather, integration resembles an *assembly-line process.* Integrated communities are assembled in all their essential elements and aspects in the course of history, somewhat as an automobile is put together. It matters little for the performance of the finished car in what sequence each part is added, so long as all its necessary elements eventually are incorporated. Certain characteristics of the process of integration, however, have been observed in many past cases; and they will be worth watching for in present and future ones.

The process of integration often begins around a *core area* consisting of one or a few political units which are stronger, more highly developed, and in some significant respects more advanced and attractive than the rest. The governments and political elites of such potential core areas take the role of active leader, unifier, or (in Etzioni's term) 'elite' for the emerging integrated political system. England played this role in the British Isles; Piedmont did so in the unification of Italy, and Prussia in that of Germany; and Massachusetts, Virginia, Pennsylvania, and New York did so jointly in the integration of the thirteen American colonies into the United States.

Early in the course of the integrative process, a psychological 'no war' community often also develops. War among the prospective partners comes to be considered as illegitimate; serious preparations for it no longer command popular support; and even if some of the prospective partner countries find themselves on opposite sides in some larger international conflict, they conduct themselves so as to keep actual mutual hostilities and damage to a minimum – or else refuse to fight each other altogether. A virtual 'no-serious-war' community of this kind emerged among the Swiss Cantons in the sixteenth century; among the Italian states since the mid-eighteenth century; among the American States since 1775; and among the German states since the mid-nineteenth century; and it may have emerged since 1950 among the EEC countries, despite many memories of past wars among them.

Often also the most salient political divisions within the emerging amalgamated security community become weaker, and – still more important – they shift away from the boundaries of the participating units. Political life then becomes dominated by divisions cutting across the original political units and regions. The more varied and salient these mutually *cross-cutting divisions* are, the better for the acceptability of the emerging union. The history of such cross-cutting alignments of political parties, religions and economic interests (all supplementing, modifying and partly overriding the old ties to the original units and regions) can be traced in the history of the unification of Britain, Switzerland, Italy, Germany and the United States.

Conversely, where cleavages among regions and political units are paralleled and reinforced by old or new cleavages of language, religion, ideology, economic interest and social class, there integration is likely to be halted or reversed. This happened between Britain and most of Ireland; among the various parts of the Austro-Hungarian monarchy; and temporarily between the North and South in the United States. In each case, the amalgamated security community collapsed – only temporarily in the United States, but (so far) permanently in the other cases.

Finally, in the successful cases of integration by political amalgamation, the main cross-regional political factions or parties stood for something new. They were identified with one or several *major cross-regional innovations* which were both important and attractive at that place and time. The Reformation and the reforms of the Tudor kings both played a major part in the integration of England and Wales, and so did the reforms of the Whigs (and their substantial acceptance by the Tories) in the unification of England and Scotland. Liberals and Liberalism played a similar part in the unifications of Switzerland, Italy and Germany in the nineteenth century, often aided by the acceptance and sponsorship of important reforms and innovations by enlightened conservatives such as Cavour and Bismarck. The United States were unified with the aid of the American Revolution, and both Hamilton's Federalists and Jefferson's Democratic Republicans stood for major (and in part unprecedented) innovations. By contrast, this element of major cross-regional innovation was weaker in the English-Irish Union of 1801; in the Hapsburg monarchy after 1810; and in the Norwegian-Swedish Union after 1814; and all these unions eventually were dissolved.

The issue of functionalism as a path to integration. In contrast to these major aspects of the process, the much-debated issue of *functionalism* turns out to be much less important. Functionalism, we recall, means partial amalgamation. It works in this way: some specific tasks are handed over by the participating governments to some common agency. But these tasks are not very important, and so usually do not transfer enough general-purpose power to the new agency to allow it to be, even 'in effect', capable of any act requiring overall amalgamation. Thus, most of the time, it must settle for partial, or functional amalgamation. Such functional amalgamation sometimes *has* led step-by-step to overall amalgamation. This happened, for instance, in such cases as those of the German Customs Union in the nineteenth century, the common administration of the Western lands by the United States under the Articles of Confederation (1781–91), and the Swiss Cantons since the late fourteenth and early fifteenth centuries; and between England and Wales and England and Scotland preceding full amalgamation in each case.

On the other hand, Italy was unified without any significant preceding functional amalgamation; and the presence of functional amalgamation did not keep the Norwegian-Swedish Union from dissolving. Moreover, although a period of functional amalgamation preceded full amalgamation in the cases of England and Ireland, and of Austria, Bohemia and Hungary, these amalgamated communities ultimately failed.

Functionalism and functional arrangements, we may conclude, have little effect by themselves upon the eventual success or failure of efforts to establish amalgamated security communities. The outcome in each case is most likely to depend on other conditions and processes, particularly on how rewarding or unrewarding were the experiences associated with functional arrangements. The most that can be said for functionalism is that it avoids the perils of premature overall amalgamation, and that it gives the participating governments, elites, and peoples more time gradually to learn the habits and skills of more far-reaching, stable, and rewarding integration.

The politics of integration: leaders and issues. As a political process, integration has a *takeoff point* in time, when it is no longer a matter of a few prophets or scattered and powerless supporters, but turns into a larger and more coordinated movement with some significant power behind it. Before takeoff a proposal for integration is a theory; after takeoff it is a force.

Such larger unification movements may aim mainly at peace, and hence at integration based upon consent to peaceful change and conflict management; or they may aim mainly at power for specific ends, or for general purposes, and hence at amalgamation which may also be accomplished by conquest or coercion. Often, indeed, political unification movements have been broad coalitions, some of whose supporters have chiefly cared for internal peace while others have wanted most of all collective power through this larger union; and still others have wanted both.

To become acute, the basic issue of integration must become salient to substantial interest-groups and to large numbers of people. In the historic cases studied, this happened usually in the course of a threefold process of habit-breaking. First and most important, a new and attractive way of life had to emerge, with common expectations for more good things to come and with enough experiences of recent improvements over the past, or over the standards of neighboring areas, so as to make these common expectations credible and to give the populations and political elites concerned at least some latent sense of unity of outlook and interests. Second, this latent sense of unity had to be aroused by some external challenge which clearly required some new and joint response. And third, a new generation had to arrive on the political scene, taking the earlier degree of common interest and outlook for granted, and ready to treat it as the starting point for new political actions. The third of these events, the arrival of a new generation in politics, is highly probable, since it occurs roughly every fifteen years. The second, the impact of some external challenge, is also rather probable, since fairly substantial political and economic challenges are likely to occur in a fast-changing world at least every twenty to twenty-five years, if not more often. Only the first process is improbable. It is the emergence of a rewarding new way of life, and with it, of a latent sense of unity and common interest in defending or extending it; and in most parts of the world this happens at most once in several generations.

Once this improbable combination of events occurs, political leadership toward unification usually is provided not by a single social class but by a cross-class coalition. Typically, such a coalition in our historical cases linked some marginal or partly alienated members and groups among the elite ('the most outside of the insiders') to some of the strongest and most vigorous groups among the non-elite ('the most inside of the outsiders') who were beginning to press for a larger share of political power.

From the outset, major *political compromises* will be needed to hold together these integrated movements and broad cross-class coalitions whose members are apt to be quite diverse in background, interests and outlook. But they are likely to be special kinds of compromises. They will be designed not to frustrate all parties by giving each much less than what it wants most, but on the contrary to reward each by conceding it much or all of that demand which is most salient to it, in return for its concessions on other matters which are less urgent to it but more salient to other partners in the coalition. Such compromises imply political 'log-rolling' instead of mutual obstruction; instead of frustrating one another, the partners must discover a way to exchange political favors and to dovetail genuine and substantial concessions to one another's vital interests.

This work of discovering and establishing viable patterns of mutual political accommodation often will take considerable time. Accordingly, many integration movements show a succession of three stages. At first, there is a stage of *leadership by intellectuals*, during which the movement is mainly supported by intellectuals (and not necessarily by a majority of these) and by relatively few and limited groups from other strata. Later on, there comes the stage of the *great politicians*, when broader interest-groups begin to swing behind the integration movement, and mutually rewarding political compromises are worked out. Finally, this stage shades over into the stage of *mass movements* and/or *large-scale elite politics*, when the issue of political unification becomes intensely practical. Even so, the movement is likely to have setbacks and failures. As Richard Merritt's study of the unification of the American colonies suggests, integrative activities and popular support for them are likely to rise and then decline again in a manner somewhat resembling a learning curve. If the social learning process is successful, however, each peak and each trough on this curve will be higher than its corresponding predecessor, until the process crosses some critical threshold and some major step toward an amalgamated security community has been accomplished.

Appeals and methods. In the course of this social learning process, the relevant elites and populations have to learn to connect all or most of their important political concerns and issues with the issue of unification, and they must come to perceive this issue clearly as a single and relatively simple decision, uncluttered by too many competing alternative proposals. Most effective among the political appeals and interests to be harnessed to the cause of integration are appeals for new or greater rights and liberties for individuals or groups. Next in effectiveness to the appeals for greater liberty rank the appeals for more equality – political, social and/or economic. Close to these two, there ranks the appeal of a rewarding way of life, often including some experience and/ or promise of prosperity and material well-being. In contrast to these three effective appeals, the appeals of seeking greater collective power for its own sake, or of defending and preserving some special minority privileges of group or class, seem to have had little or no effect in deciding the outcome of an integrative process: in one historical study, these last two types of appeal occurred about as often in cases of failure of integration as in cases of success.

To promote political amalgamation, all the usual political methods have been used, but not all have been equally effective. By far the most effective method, in terms of the relative frequency with which it was followed by success, was the enlistment of broad popular participation and support. Among the cases studied, every amalgamation movement that won such popular participation was eventually successful. The second most effective method was the acceptance of pluralism, and hence of the autonomy and sovereignty of the participating political units for substantial transition periods. Next in terms of effectiveness ranked the large-scale use of propaganda; the promise to abolish specific items of unpopular legislation; and the promotion of political or administrative autonomy for the participating units.

By contrast, some methods had little or no effect in making amalgamation come about: they occurred about as often in cases of success as they did in cases of failure. Such relatively ineffective methods included the promotion of specific political institutions, the use of symbols and the use of patronage for the appointment of purposefully selected individuals to political or administrative office. All these methods may have been necessary, but by themselves they seem to have contributed little or nothing to make success more likely.

Three methods turned out to be counterproductive – that is, they were significantly more often associated with the failure of amalgamation than with its success. These counterproductive methods were early insistence on overall amalgamation, early efforts to establish a monopoly of violence, and outright military conquest.

Opposition to amalgamation most often came from peasants, farmers and other rural groups; and in the second place, from privileged groups or regions which feared to lose something from amalgamation. Peasant opposition seems to have made no significant difference to the success or failure of amalgamation movements, but active peasant support, though rare, was invariably associated with success. Privileged groups seem to have made no difference to the eventual success or failure of integration, neither by their opposition nor by their support, but they almost always gained some substantial concessions to their interest; and as far as the amalgamation movement in each case was concerned, the making of such concessions to the privileged groups seems to have had a low but distinct effect in favor of success.

In the end, amalgamation movements often succeeded through a combination of closure and creativity. They usually succeeded by closing out all competing proposals and alternatives, so as to eventually channel all political attention and action toward the single paramount issue and policy of amalgamation. But they often succeeded in doing so, and in maintaining and broadening their political coalition, only by means of the originality and resourcefulness with which the proponents of amalgamations invented and formulated specific plans for union and specific institutions to make it work. Often this element of political invention and innovation seems to have been critical. Many of the central institutions of successfully amalgamated security communities were original and relatively improbable at the time and place at which they were adopted. Conversely, several amalgamated security communities were wrecked by routine policies and views, and by obvious decisions, all of which were highly probable but inadequate at the time and place they occurred. In the politics of amalgamation, too, genius often consisted in discovering an improbable but highly relevant solution, or a sequence of solutions of this kind, and in turning them into reality.

The process of establishing a pluralistic security community. Just as a pluralistic security community requires fewer favorable background conditions for its success, so it requires simpler, though perhaps subtler, processes in order to come into existence.

The main process required seems to be an increasing unattractiveness and improbability of war among the political units of the emerging pluralistic security community, as perceived by their governments, elites, and (eventually) populations. A second process, similar to that favoring the rise of amalgamated security communities, is the spread of intellectual movements and traditions favoring integration, and preparing the political climate for it. A third process, perhaps, is the development and practice of habits and skills of mutual attention, communication and responsiveness, so as to make possible the preservation of the autonomy and substantial sovereignty of the participating units, and the preservation of stable expectations of peace and peaceful change among them. The difficulties in the way of these three processes are by no means trivial; but they are less than the difficulties in the path of outright amalgamation among almost any group of sovereign nation-states in today's world.

Some emerging issues of integration and world politics

Three broad philosophic issues emerge from our survey of the conditions and processes of integration. The first is the issue of the primary goal to be adopted. Is it to be *peace* within the integrated area, *or* is it to be some form of corporate *power*, perhaps for its defence against outsiders, or for some variety of other purposes? Or if both peace and power are emphasized as long-run goals, which is to be sought first, and what time-path toward the ultimate attainment of both goals is to be envisaged?

The second issue is that of the possible *hegemony* of one political unit (such as the most powerful nation-state) within the emerging security community, as against the substantial equality or near-equality of its more-or-less sovereign members. Related to this question is that of majority voting, as against negotiations and special concessions. Though majority voting looks like – and sometimes is – an equalitarian device, it also can be used to establish the hegemony of one great power, or of a few of them, with the help of the easily influenced or controlled votes of some lesser powers.

The result could be a pattern resembling a pyramid of holding companies. A power with great but limited resources could secure for itself a practically paramount role in the decisions of a small group of countries. This group – let us call it alliance A – could jointly command paramount influence within some larger alliance B. Alliance B, in turn, could be used to control alliance C; and so forth, until some alliance finally would lead to formal majority control of the United Nations, and to substantive control of much (and ideally all) of the world. Nothing quite like this has ever happened, but the possibility is there; and the almost instinctive resistance of many countries to far-reaching majority voting in international or supranational bodies, and their preference for mutual negotiations and responsiveness among sovereign units, may be related to these considerations.

The third issue is related to the second. It is this: can larger organizations be built up best by downgrading their components, so as to make them easier to control and cheaper to replace? Specifically, are federations to be built up by weakening their member states, and international organizations by weakening the nations of which they are composed?

For the near future, some tentative answers can be indicated. Keeping an uneasy but tolerable peace is likely to appear more urgent to most governments than creating large supranational organizations with vast powers for more or less general purposes. Sovereignty with only a few limitations will seem more attractive to most governments than submission to the hegemony of any great power or partial coalition of great powers. And the up-grading, rather than the downgrading, of the capabilities and the prestige of nation-states will look both more practical and more desirable to most of their governments and peoples.

All this means that an era of pluralism and, at best, of pluralistic security communities, may well characterize the near future. In the long term, however, the search for integrated political communities that command both peace and power, and that entail a good deal of amalgamation, is likely to continue until it succeeds. To succeed, not only good will and sustained effort, but political creativity and inventiveness will be needed, together with a political culture of greater international openness, understanding and compassion.

Without such a new political climate and new political efforts, mankind is unlikely to survive for long. But the fact that so many people in so many countries are becoming aware of the problem, and of the need for increasing intellectual, moral, and political efforts to deal with it, makes it likely that it will be solved.

References

DEUTSCH, K. W. *et al.* (1957), *Political Community and the North Atlantic Area*, Princeton University Press.
ETZIONI, A. (1965), *Political Unification*, Holt, Rinehart & Winston.

7 John Pinder

Positive Integration and Negative Integration:
Some Problems of Economic Union in the EEC

J. Pinder, 'Positive integration and negative integration: some problems
of economic union in the EEC', *World Today*, vol. 24, 1968, pp. 88–110.

When we talk about economic integration, the intelligent listener
usually assumes that we are talking about the European Economic
Community and perhaps its two sister Communities, and the
intelligent listener is usually right. But when we try to analyse the
problems of integration with some precision, we shall find ourselves in trouble unless we have a more precise definition. We
shall probably find ourselves in trouble anyway, because the
most important problems are largely uncharted; but a precise
definition at least removes an unnecessary source of difficulty.
(Those who prefer such difficulties to definitions may wish to
turn straight to the next section, which starts on p. 127.)

According to the Concise Oxford English Dictionary, integration is the combination of parts into a whole, and union is a
whole resulting from the combination of parts or members. Thus
integration is the process of reaching the state of union. The
important choice now lies in the definition of union: in other
words, in deciding when a combination of economic parts or
members, in this case national economies, is to be regarded as a
'whole'. Balassa says that a state of economic union has been
reached when there is not only free movement of products and
factors of production between a group of countries, but also
'some degree of harmonization of national economic policies in
order to remove discrimination that was due to disparities in
these policies' (1961, p. 2).

It often happens that the whole character of an argument is
governed by the definitions of the key words that are used, and in
my view there is a danger that the problems of economic integration in the European Communities will be misunderstood if
discussion is based on this definition of economic union. As I will
argue later, once the member countries of the Community have
removed from the economic transactions between their citizens
most of the discrimination that was formerly caused by the fact

that those citizens were subject to different national laws and regulations, it is essential for them to go further. If they are to deal with the problems that result from this freedom of transactions, and to make the most of the opportunities for increasing welfare that are offered by the larger market, they must coordinate their national policies and form common policies in many ways that go beyond the mere removal of discrimination. Balassa recognizes that this may be desired, and therefore goes on to define 'total economic integration' which 'presupposes the unification of monetary, fiscal, social and counter-cyclical policies and requires the setting-up of a supranational authority whose decisions are binding for the member states' (1961, p. 2). But there are two main objections to Balassa's definitions.

First, economic union is the term used, in contemporary discussions in the Community, for the economic destination of the EEC; and if economic union is defined as the removal of discrimination, it may be implicitly assumed that this represents the limit of the process of integration in the Community. According to what may be called 'free-trade ideology' this would indeed be the best result; but I do not think it is a sensible result in an age when economic policies are required to stabilize both prices and balances of payments, to secure both full employment and rapid economic growth, and to aim at a number of other objectives designed to maximize welfare, and in circumstances where the removal of instruments for acting unilaterally on the balance of payments reduces the possibility for the government of each member country to attain these objectives by means of its own policies.

The second objection to Balassa's definitions is that 'total economic integration' sounds as if the economy of the union is going to become a replica of an existing national economy (and the word total implies a tightly centralized one, at that), with the national governments being reduced, for economic purposes, to the role of, say, a state government in the United States. This may eventually happen. But one of the most interesting questions that can be asked about economic integration (and indeed about political integration) is whether it does have to go as far as that, or whether there is an intermediate position between national independence and the role of the state in the American federal system, where the member countries of a union can act jointly with enough decision to satisfy their main objectives. If this is found to be possible, the pattern of regional organization in existing nation-states might move in the direction shown by the experience of the Community, not the other way about. It would be a great pity if the definitions of economic integration and economic union made this question more difficult to ask.

I will therefore define economic integration as both the removal of discrimination as between the economic agents of the member countries, and the formation and application of coordinated and common policies on a sufficient scale to ensure that major economic and welfare objectives are fulfilled. It follows that economic union is a state in which discrimination has been largely removed, and coordinated and common policies have been, and are being, applied on a sufficient scale.

For a clear discussion about the European Communities, it is necessary further to have a word for the removal of discrimination by itself, without the other elements of economic integration. Here I will use two terms that have been used by Tinbergen, although again it seems necessary to change his definitions so as to make the terms as useful as possible, in the light of the experience of the Community as it has evolved. The terms are negative integration and positive integration, and I will use negative integration for that part of economic integration that consists of the removal of discrimination, and positive integration as the formation and application of coordinated and common policies in order to fulfil economic and welfare objectives other than the removal of discrimination (Tinbergen, 1954, p. 122).[1]

Negative and positive integration together comprise economic integration, whose end is economic union. The end of negative integration unaccompanied by positive integration may be called a common market, although it may be objected that the Rome Treaty, and still more current usage, employs the term common market ambiguously, sometimes including and sometimes excluding some of the fruits of positive integration. I know of no case where it has been proposed to unite a group of countries by

1. Tinbergen defines negative integration as 'the elimination of certain instruments of international economic policy', and a 'positive policy of integration' as 'supplementary measures in order to remove inconsistencies that may exist between the duties and taxes of different countries', plus 'positive action in the field of production' in order to put through a 're-organization programme', i.e. to deal with the problems of transition. Thus Tinbergen bases his distinction between the two terms on whether policy instruments are to be eliminated or new policies formed, whereas I base mine on whether the purpose is to remove discrimination or to maximize welfare in other ways.

means of positive integration without negative integration. But this is by no means inconceivable, nor indeed would the result have to be very different from a national economy with a regional policy that discriminates powerfully in favour of that nation's less-favoured regions. This is, admittedly, normally done with instruments such as tax allowances, subsidies, cheap loans, low transport rates, government buying policies, etc., and not by means of import and exchange controls on transactions between the region and the rest of the country. The Rome Treaty foresees that member governments will wish to pursue such policies for their development regions, and expressly allows them to be pursued, subject to the Commission's agreement that the aid, or discrimination in favour of the region, is not excessive. To this extent the EEC, like many national economies, intentionally falls short of complete negative integration. It is thus possible that positive integration will be undertaken by a group of countries without complete negative integration, and this may indeed, in an age when regional policies are prevalent, become the normal form of economic integration. Whether the discrimination in favour of regions will always be confined to 'non-tariff barriers', or whether regional import and exchange controls might sometimes be found to be a useful device, is another question that need not be dealt with here.

For what Balassa calls an 'all-out liberalist' (1961, p. 7), a common market and an economic union are the same thing, because for him negative integration constitutes common policies on a sufficient scale to ensure that major economic and welfare objectives are fulfilled. For me, a common market is a far lesser thing than an economic union, and without economic union will prove to be unviable.

Trade creation and trade diversion: the static effects of customs unions

The movement towards economic integration in the last two decades has evoked a considerable quantity of economic literature, much of which has been concerned with the immediate effects on trade, and hence on welfare, of the establishment of a free-trade area or a customs union. This part of the literature has, on the whole, been based on the analytical apparatus bequeathed to us by the classical economists and thus on static equilibrium assumptions, i.e. on the assumptions that resources, including the stock of capital, are given, and that if the existing equilibrium is upset by any change, for example by the removal of a tariff, forces will come into play that will cause it to be replaced by a new equilibrium position.

The first landmark for the post-war debates on customs unions and free-trade areas was Viner's famous work (1950). Viner challenged the assumption, hitherto accepted by liberal economists, that any customs union, being a step in the direction of free trade, would increase the sum total of welfare in the world. As is well known, he divided the changes in trade that would result from a customs union into trade creation, where new trade between members of the customs union would replace higher-cost production in the importing member, and trade diversion, where existing imports from a non-member would be replaced by imports from a member. The trade creation would cause an increase in welfare because higher-cost production would be replaced by lower-cost; the diversion would reduce welfare because the old imports from a non-member were, since they had been bought by the importing country when the same tariff had faced the member and the non-member, clearly lower-cost than the new imports which replaced them because of the tariff preference. Thus any proposal for a customs union should be examined to discover how much trade creation and how much trade diversion there would be, before any judgement could be formed as to whether welfare would be enlarged or reduced.

After Viner had shown that the changes in trade caused by the establishment of a customs union could be the subject of an interesting analysis, other economists pursued his line of thought and, from Viner's small beginnings, evolved a theory of customs unions of considerable refinement. Meade in particular lent his mind to this exercise (1955). He showed that, in order to calculate the changes in trade that would follow directly from the mutual reduction of tariffs on the trade between a group of countries, it would be necessary to take account of a number of factors including the initial heights of the tariffs and the sizes of the cuts (assuming a preferential area was possible as well as a free-trade area or customs union), the competitiveness or complementarity of the economies taking part, the elasticities of demand and supply, the change in the amount of consumer surplus, the effect on the terms of trade, and the relative incomes of those from whom, and in favour of whom, trade was diverted. The theory as it has been developed by Meade and others is pretty tough fare and serves to sharpen the intellectual teeth. It is therefore a good instrument of education. But there are two major reasons why it is not a useful guide for practical policy: the 'static' effects of trade creation and trade diversion are probably much less important than the 'dynamic' effects on economic growth via influences on competition, investment and the balance of payments; and customs unions tend to be set up for 'political' reasons rather than because of econometricians' forecasts of changes in trade, from which it follows that economic analysis would be more fruitfully focused on the implications for economic policy of the existence of customs unions than on the justification of customs unions in terms of forecast changes in the flows of trade.

The dynamic effects of free trade

During the last decade the view has gained ground that the static analysis indicated by Viner's approach is in any case relatively unimportant,[2] even if this approach can be subjected to an elegant theoretical analysis and to quantitative forecasts of greater or lesser plausibility. Lipsey, reviewing the estimates made by Verdoorn[3] and by Johnson (1958), on the basis of the forecasts made by the Economist Intelligence Unit (1957), as well as making his own 'common-sense check' based on feasible savings in costs due to the freeing of trade, accepted that the best estimates gave 'figures of the net gain from trade amounting to something less than 1 per cent of the national income'. The reason for this small order of magnitude is that the 'static gain' to welfare due to increases in trade is equal, not to the increment in trade itself, but to that increment multiplied by the reduction in cost due to the change in the source of production (Johnson based his estimates on the percentage rates of the tariffs that would be removed). Thus large forecasts of trade increases, such as those made by the Economist Intelligence Unit for a wide European free-trade area or by Stamp and Cowie (1967) for a North Atlantic free-trade area comprising Britain, Canada and the United States, turn out to imply very small, once-for-all increases in GNP. It clearly

2. See, for example, Scitovsky (1958, pp. 72, 73): 'In the literature of the subject much importance is attached to the question whether or not the cost reduction renders production within the union cheaper than it is in the outside world. In the long run, however, this seems irrelevant, from the point of view either of the union or of the world as a whole.' See also Balassa, *op. cit.*, p. 14; 'In evaluating the effects of economic integration, we shall take dynamic efficiency as the primary success indicator' (see also Lipsey, 1960).

3. An unpublished paper quoted by Scitovsky (1958, pp. 64–7).

needs only a small dynamic effect on the rate of growth of GNP, say an increment of 0·1 per cent a year compound for twenty years, to far outweigh effects of this order of magnitude due to direct trade creation and trade diversion.

It can of course be argued that gains from trade creation or trade diversion will themselves have a very important dynamic effect if, for example, they replace a balance-of-payments deficit by a surplus and thus remove the external constraint from an economy whose growth is checked by that constraint, or conversely if they cause or intensify an external deficit that checks growth. Thus a net gain of $550–$650 m such as Stamp and Cowie forecast for Britain within a NAFTA might, by solving the balance-of-payments problem, allow the British economy a substantially faster rate of growth; or a £600 m worsening of the UK deficit, forecast by *The Times Business News* (1 May 1967) if Britain were to join the European Communities, could prevent such growth as the British economy might otherwise achieve. But these once-for-all trade effects can be achieved/countered, according as they are favourable/unfavourable, by once-for-all measures, such as devaluation (which in the case of the British devaluation of November 1967 is forecast to improve the balance of payments by £500 m); and the dynamic effects of customs unions on, for example, investment remain of very much greater potential importance than the effects through the immediate impact on trade. An act of policy such as the creation of a free-trade area, customs union or economic union, which is likely to take some years to establish and then to have over a long period profound economic and perhaps political effects going far beyond the immediate impact on the balance of payments, would indeed be a strange instrument to use in order to rectify a current payments deficit.

The work that has been done so far on the economies of scale and the extent to which they can be derived in markets of various size has been reviewed by Balassa (1961, pt. 2) and by Swann and McLachlan (1967, pp. 7–31). They conclude that the gains for Britain from a market larger than that of the UK could be significant. The most interesting analysis of the possible gains from production for a wider market remains, however, that of Scitovsky (1958, pt. 3), who makes some points that appear to be important, particularly in relation to Britain's circumstances, but that do not seem to have been further developed theoretically, let alone tested by empirical research.

Scitovsky suggests that the crucial factor in a firm's decision whether to invest in new and optimum plant is whether the firm will (expect to?) be able to increase its sales by the amount that such plant will produce. This depends on the annual increment in the total market, on the market share of the firm in question, on the speed and extent to which customers will switch their allegiance towards a cheaper or better product, and on the energy with which the firm will seek to encroach on its competitors' market shares: in fact on the size of the market, its expected rate of growth, the size of firm, and the competitiveness of consumers' and producers' behaviour. In Britain's case, the change in these factors resulting from membership of the EEC (or of a NAFTA) would be such as to make British firms a great deal more prone to invest in optimum equipment. The size of market to which the manufacturer of the average product would be confident of having free access would be greatly increased. Even if the growth performance in the EEC is not what it was, the expectation would still probably, and reasonably enough, be that the rate of growth of the total market will continue to be faster and certainly less liable to sudden interruptions in the EEC (or the US) than in Britain on her own. Customers in Britain, whether consumers or those who purchase on behalf of firms, are thought to be more conservative and slower than those on the Continent (or in the US) to switch their suppliers. And many British businessmen seem to have been inclined to base their attitudes on their competitors' markets on those of a country gentleman towards his neighbour's property: poaching has been widely held to break the rules of the game. This ethic seems less widespread on the Continent and in the US; and more important, businessmen are less likely to have such fine feelings for the welfare of their competitors where these are industrialists from another member country, rather than from their own country and thus more likely to be known personally.

It is possible that these factors would have a great effect on the investment decisions of firms whose environment has hitherto been the relatively small, slow-growing, and uncompetitive British market. Scitovsky's analysis certainly failed to take account of the greater opportunity for a firm to invest in optimum plant when it is possible for it to write off existing plant (the capacity of the plant to be written off being added to the expected increment to sales); but even so the opportunities for investment in optimum plant would surely be greatly increased. The same argument applies to modernization through reorganized production, e.g. as part of a productivity bargain, because the gains would be larger and more certain and would thus more readily outweigh the inconveniences of change.

Thus the dynamic gains due to considerations of 'scale' and the 'climate of competition' seem likely to be far more important than the static gains or losses due to trade creation and trade diversion, at least for a country the size of Britain and in the economic circumstances of contemporary Britain. The other main dynamic factor introduces a more doubtful element as far as Britain is concerned, however, particularly in relation to the NAFTA proposal.

The protection of industries that are weak because they are new has long been justified by the infant-industries exception to the classical free-trade theory. More recently this exception has been generalized so as to apply to the whole of industry in a less-developed economy. The idea that the dynamic effects of free trade may be such as to wither the growth of a weaker economy has been but little supported by economic theory, chiefly no doubt because the theory of growth is still underdeveloped in relation to equilibrium theory, and because growth theory, such as it is, has concentrated on the problems of growth within a single national economy (and without much attention, either, to the problems of regions within a national economy, which are analogous to the problems of growth and balance of payments of the member countries of a free-trade area, customs union, or economic union). But Prebisch has provided some theoretical justifications of the practice of protection of underdeveloped countries (1950, 1959), and Streeten has discussed the problem with particular reference to economic integration in Europe (1961, pp. 53–67).

The pessimistic view of the impact on a weaker economy (southern Ireland, southern Italy) of free trade with a more dynamic economy (England, northern Italy) is based on the following type of argument. According to the classical equilibrium theory, the weaker area should export those goods in which it has a comparative advantage and, if the exchange rate is such as to allow equilibrium in its balance of payments, it will have a comparative advantage in enough products. If the weaker area is part of the same national economy, moreover, capital will flow there to take advantage of the cheap labour. According to the pessimistic view, however, the trade of the weaker area with the dynamic area will always be running into deficit because the dynamic one will always be developing new and better products or lower-cost methods of production, so as to undermine the comparative advantage of the weaker area at the existing exchange rate. The weaker area therefore has the alternative of continually devaluing its currency or depressing its wages (or reducing its area income by deflating). If the weaker area is part of the same national economy or economic union its case is even worse, because it probably cannot devalue; capital will flow to the dynamic region where, even if wages are higher, the economic and social infrastructure is better and the business environment is such as to lead people to expect higher profits; and the enterprising people will move to the dynamic area, thus continually draining the weaker area of its energy and talent.

This argument may or may not be correct. But the important thing to realize is that, at the present state of the theory and of the evidence on this subject, it is impossible to *know* whether, or in what circumstances, the argument is correct or not. The classical free-trade theory, beautiful though it is, does not deal with this problem and therefore neither confirms nor disproves it. My own judgement is that the prolonged existence of 'regional problems' in many countries shows that the pessimistic view of the effects of free movement of products and, even more, of factors between a weak economy and a dynamic economy is in certain (not rare) circumstances, or with certain (not very restrictive) definitions of weak and dynamic, the correct view; and that for this purpose, the attributes of a weak/dynamic economy are likely to include a low/high income per head, a low/high degree of capital-intensiveness and R & D-intensiveness, and a low/high degree of competitive dynamism (a question-begging attribute, but one that seems to be recognizable if one moves from Tokyo to Bombay). Specifically, I would be pessimistic about the prospects for Britain in a NAFTA *à la* Stamp and Cowie comprising Britain, Canada, and the US, but not about the prospects of Britain in the European Community.

The political motives for establishing free-trade systems or economic unions

As I suggested earlier, the motives for establishing or joining economic groupings such as free-trade areas, customs unions or economic unions usually have more to do with political orientation than with calculations of economic gain. This was certainly the case with the European Communities; and it was also the case with the British application to join the Communities, announced in May 1967, for when the application was made the official forecasts of the net effect on British trade and the British balance of payments had been very discouraging. It is true that the dynamic and longer-term effects were in both cases believed to be beneficial; but these beliefs, depending more on subjective judgements than on scientific deduction, spring from the same part of the mind as the political orientations, and it should not be a cause for surprise that, for most economists, long-term economic judgement and political orientation point in the same direction (nor is there any evidence that the economic judgement usually precedes the political orientation).

Meade himself wrote that, if he were a citizen of a Benelux country, he would be 'an ardent proponent and supporter of the building of Benelux' for basically political reasons, even if his calculations showed that it was likely to reduce economic welfare (1955, pp. 114, 115). Surely we need no further encouragement to turn from the subject of the economic pros and cons of establishing or joining customs unions, which has occupied so much of economists' attention to date, to that of the problems that arise for economic policy when a customs union is in fact created.

**Policies in the European Communities:
the bias against economic union**

We can now draw upon ten years' experience of the creation of a customs union and of moves towards economic union consisting of a group of advanced Western economies, and we can therefore take a significant step away from pure speculation and towards the analysis of evidence – although, as we shall see, the most interesting and important questions remain unanswered by the experience so far.

Let us consider two main aspects of the problems of the European Economic Community and of the policies that have been or could be designed by the Community to deal with them. The problems can be divided into those that arise in the process of trying to eliminate discrimination between the economic agents in the different member states (the problems of negative integration, or of establishing a common market, as defined on p. 126), and those that arise in a collective attempt by the member countries to maximize welfare in the customs union (the problems of positive integration, or of establishing an economic union). The policies can be divided into those that have a strong chance of being implemented (strong political motives, strong provision in the Treaty and/or in the Community's institutional procedures) and those that have a weak chance.

There is a one-sided relationship between these two dichotomies, which is very important in understanding what has been achieved so far in the Communities and what problems are likely to arise in the future. This is that the policies which have a strong chance of being implemented are those that deal with negative integration, while those with a weaker chance are those concerned with positive integration. 'Free-trade ideology' is firmly built into the system, but the 'planning ethic' is no more than a possibility for the future.

There are four main reasons for this. First, the one thing on which almost everyone concerned with the foundation of the Communities was agreed was that they were inaugurating a new deal for Europe in which war between the member countries would become unthinkable, and that they should therefore as far as possible cease to treat the citizens of other members as foreigners by discriminating against them. Non-discrimination has become a deep-rooted reflex among those who run the Communities. Second, it is not difficult to provide in a treaty for the removal of discrimination, which is relatively simple to define and to enforce. But it is much harder to ensure by means of a treaty that an effective common policy will be formed; for a policy might take any one of a thousand forms, and it will usually be hard to attribute to any individual or government responsibility for failure to define a common policy, and still more for failure to define an effective one. In short, a treaty can more easily make effective the 'thou shalt not' commandments than the 'thou shalt' ones.

Third, the neo-liberals who were until recently in sole control of the German Government adhered to an economic ideology that stressed free trade and rather strictly circumscribed the role of economic policy. Dr Erhard, in particular, was opposed to the idea that Brussels should become a policy-making power-house. Given the importance of Germany in the Community, this placed a severe limit on the extent of common policy-making. Fourth, General de Gaulle, who is also at present an important element in the Community, adheres to a political ideology that violently rejects the idea of any authority above or outside the nation-state, and the French Government has therefore ferociously resisted the institutional procedures by which common or coordinated policies on the complex issues of positive integration are likely to be brought about. More passively, there is a natural tendency for other national bureaucracies and government machines to resist any loss of their power of unilateral decision and action, which is inevitably implied in an effective procedure for taking decisions in common.

Apart from General de Gaulle, who was in temporary retirement when the Rome Treaty establishing the EEC was negotiated and signed, all these factors influenced the content of the Treaty, which is therefore in its detail strongly biased in the direction of negative integration and away from positive integration. This is illustrated in Article 3, which outlines the activities of the Community, as well as in later articles where some details are filled in. Thus Article 3 speaks of 'the elimination, as between member states, of customs duties and of quantitative restrictions . . . as well as of other measures with equivalent effect'; and 'the establishment of a common customs tariff': very precise objectives, which are specified in detail in later articles. Then there is 'the abolition as between member states of the obstacles to the free movement of persons, services and capital' and 'the establishment of a system ensuring that competition shall not be distorted in the Common Market': equally unequivocal objectives of negative integration, whose implementation is, however, more complicated than is the establishment of the customs union, and is therefore less precisely provided for later in the Treaty.

Article 3 also specifies a common commercial policy, a common agricultural policy, and a common transport policy: these sound definite enough, but, as has already been noted, it is much easier for the member governments to default on their obligation to form an undefined common policy than it is for them to evade their promises to remove discrimination and distortions.

When Article 3 comes to such crucial elements of positive integration as economic policies and balance-of-payments problems it becomes extremely vague and permissive instead of definite and mandatory. It merely writes of 'the application of procedures which shall make it possible to coordinate the economic policies of Member States and to remedy disequilibria in their balances of payments'. In the body of the Treaty there is only one article, and a pretty feeble one at that, dealing with 'policy relating to economic trends', and six articles dealing with balance-of-payments problems, compared with twenty-nine on the establishment of the customs union.

The remaining items listed in Article 3 are the 'approximation' of laws, which concerns mainly the removal of discrimination and distortions; the creation of the Social Fund and the Investment Bank, which are certainly elements of economic union but which, with their present resources, can have only a small influence; and the association of overseas countries and territories.

Article 3 accurately reflects the emphasis of the Treaty on the removal of discrimination and distortions, i.e. on negative integration and the consequent establishment of a common market. The next article refers to the Community's institutions – Assembly, Council, Commission and Court – which constitute the other main concrete achievement of the Treaty itself. As will be seen from the following section, however, the only other big steps towards the economic union of the member countries have resulted from the political bargain between France and Germany over the agricultural policy and the Kennedy Round.

Policies in the European Communities:
the five major achievements

The first great policy achievement of the European Community has, of course, been the establishment of the customs union. The programme for this was laid down in detail in the Rome Treaty, and by 1 July 1968 it will have been virtually completed sooner than was originally planned.

The Community's second major policy achievement has been the creation of the agricultural common market. Free trade is harder to establish for products in relation to which the member countries have managed markets, because the cheaper product is as likely to be the more-subsidized as it is to be the lower-cost, and member countries would rightly refuse to accept the 'unfair competition' represented by a flood of imports of some foodstuffs from another member country that were cheaper than the domestic product solely because they were more subsidized by the other member country's government. It follows that the only alternatives are to stop managing the markets for such products or to manage them in common. The Community chose the latter course with respect to agricultural products, and it was clear from the amount of attention given in the Rome Treaty to the agricultural policy that a high priority was attached to it.

The reason for this was simple. French industry was weak in relation to German industry, but French agriculture, based on very favourable natural conditions, was in a strong competitive position, with excellent prospects for the future. Economically, the European Community has been for France a bargain in which a risk was taken for French industry in exchange for a great and certain gain for French agriculture. If this bargain had not been kept, General de Gaulle would have broken the Community by withdrawing France from it. The Germans as well as the other members knew this, and therefore agreed, after long, difficult, and repeated sessions in the Council of Ministers, to a 'common agricultural policy', which consists of a system for the fixing of prices on a common Community basis, and for supporting these price levels, notably with the help of import levies and subsidies to producers.[4] The achievement of this most thorny task was a notable triumph for the Community system in general and the Commission in particular. It is probably true to say that never before had an international organization succeeded in shaping a common policy with respect to which such sensitive national interests were so deeply involved.

Notable though the achievement was, however, its importance and contribution to positive integration should not be exaggerated. In effect the 'policy' at present is almost entirely centred on the fixing of a common price (and an uneconomically high one at that), which is the only way of removing discrimination as between the member States: the system has been called 'merely a complicated kind of customs union'. The 'guidance' part of the Guidance and Guarantee Fund (FEOGA)[5] provides a basis for a positive policy aimed at the structural improvement of agriculture and of the predominantly agricultural regions of the Community. But the Council of Ministers has recently decided that only half of this amount should be spent jointly, and that the other half is to be returned to the national governments to be spent in their own agricultural programmes.

In the other main managed-market sectors, energy and transport, the Community has made relatively little progress towards an effective common policy. A coordinated common policy for the main types of energy, hampered hitherto by the division of responsibility between the three separate Communities, has not even begun to materialize. Even in the several energy markets the experience has been disappointing. The European Coal and Steel Community successfully inaugurated free trade in coal during

4. The system is described in Warley (1967). See also articles by Trevor Parfitt in the *World Today* of July 1965 and January 1968.
5. Fonds Européens d'Orientation et Garantie Agricole.

the mid-1950s, when there was a sellers' market; but since the coal mines have been up against it, the national governments have largely taken responsibility for defending their interests and the role of the Community's common policy has been minimized. Euratom, too, got off to a good start, with a very active research programme initiated at a time when it was expected that a large output of nuclear power would be wanted fairly quickly. Since then, however, the timetable for nuclear power generation has been put back and member governments, with the French Government in the lead, have stressed their national programmes at the expense of Euratom. Now the Euratom budget, which has been running at approximately $100 million a year, is to be halved.

In the field of transport, there has been some progress with the removal of discrimination, but a common policy for the development of the Community's transport is still a distant and shadowy prospect, while a pricing policy, based on a 'fork' of maximum and minimum rates, is still hanging fire.

There was, when the ECSC was established, provision for a managed market in steel at times of severe under- or over-production, to be based likewise on a fork of maximum and minimum prices. But although there has been critical over-production, particularly in 1963-4, the High Authority of the ECSC has been politically too weak in relation to the member governments to make use of these possibilities, and the only effective action it could take was to get the member states to increase their protection against imports (and this was done by a constitutional sleight of hand, showing how the institutional procedures can affect the outcome even when the member governments are not willing to cooperate in framing a common policy) (Forsyth, 1964, pp. 348–59).

The experience of the Community is, then, that with respect to managed markets a common policy that is at all effective has been formed and applied only where there was a political motive powerful enough to override the very tough national interests that exist in these sectors; and even where, as in agriculture, an effective common policy has been formed, it has tended to be based on the sum of the member countries' protectionisms rather than on a rational conception of the welfare of the Community as a whole. It must be added that this weakness in forming policies of positive integration has been due, to an extent that we cannot measure but may suppose to have been considerable, to the presence of General de Gaulle at the head of the French Government during the whole period of the EEC's existence, which has added an element of abnormal activism to the passive resistance to the reduction of their national powers that may be expected from most national governments most of the time.

The third major policy achievement of the Community has been the successful negotiation of the Kennedy Round. This was partly thanks to the bargain between France and Germany, whereby France got the common agricultural policy while Germany got satisfaction for her industrial interests, who were very keen on freer trade. To some extent, perhaps, the common external tariff is the Community's international status symbol, and the ability to negotiate a major tariff agreement was felt to be a test of its international standing. Whatever the reasons, however, the conclusion of the Kennedy Round remains as a massive exception to the theory that the Community, as it stands, is unable to pursue policies of positive integration.

Some other aspects of the Community's performance in its attempts to evolve a common commercial policy have been more reassuring to the proponents of this pessimistic theory. In relation to the less-developed countries in general and to Eastern Europe, the Community has made no recognizable progress towards a common policy, although the Rome Treaty stipulates that a common commercial policy is to be formed by 1970. On the other hand, the treaties of association with Greece and Turkey were of some importance, and the system of association for former colonies represents a not inconsiderable achievement. But the original association arrangements for former colonies, enshrined in the Treaty of Rome, were accepted by the other members with great reluctance as part of a bargain with France. The French Government was in a strong position because France was essential to the creation of the Community (Germany plus the other four being too unbalanced a group to be politically viable); and late in the negotiations on the Treaty the French insisted on the inclusion of the association system for their former colonies, and the others accepted this in order to get France to sign. This association was formally renewed in the Yaounde Convention, when a certain reduction in preferences was traded for a certain increase in aid, at the same time as the system was endowed with institutions that recognize the sovereign status that almost all the associated countries had by then acquired. The lessons of this association system, which may be regarded as a case of positive integration, are that it came into existence because of a strong manifestation of political will on the part of France (securing the agreement of the others by threatening that there would be no Community if they failed to agree), and that it then became a fairly stable factor in the Community system.

The fourth major policy achievement has been the cartel policy. This started with the ECSC, where the High Authority was given sharp teeth to prevent the formation of concentrations of economic power caused by mergers of big steel companies. Recently, however, the need for larger units has been accepted, and mergers that would formerly have been prevented are being allowed. The EEC in turn adopted a system of cartel policy that gives the Commission considerable power to decide what kind of cartel agreements affecting intra-Community trade shall be allowed, subject to appeal to the European Court of Justice. Although the Commission does not yet seem to have used this power in such a way as to have any great influence on industry in the Community, the system is an instrument of no small potential importance.

The cartel policy is, however, yet another aspect of negative integration, designed mainly to remove discrimination as between firms in the different member countries. The other side of this coin, representing an important aspect of positive integration, is industrial policy, which is still almost entirely at the stage of discussion rather than action at Community level. The European patent is fairly far advanced, but the plans for a European company and the unification of the capital markets are still at an earlier stage, and science policy (and *pro tanto* a technological community) is virtually virgin territory (apart from Euratom, which has now been raped).

The fifth major achievement in Community policy is the agreement to adopt a uniform system of tax on value added (TVA). But here again the motive and implementation lie in the realm of negative integration: the TVA is to remove competitive distortions and, when the rate is made uniform in each country, to enable the member countries to abolish 'fiscal frontiers' between them (Dosser and Han, 1968). There is so far no element of positive integration – of the use of tax policy or tax revenue for ends other than the removal of discrimination or of economic frontiers between the member states.

The ECSC has its own taxing power in the form of a levy on the turnover of the enterprises in the coal and steel sectors, and this has been used for policies of positive integration such as the finance of research and of retraining; but the High Authority's political weakness has inhibited it from exploiting more than a fraction of the tax power given it by the Treaty establishing the ECSC, and it has operated on a correspondingly limited scale. The import levies on agricultural imports into the EEC are a major revenue-raiser, but this revenue is tied to the subsidization of agriculture, so that this turns out to be a distorted and unfair fiscal system, involving large transfers to the farmers and to them alone from the consumers of imported foodstuffs and from them alone (the Corn Laws in reverse).

Thus the emphasis of the Community has been, in practice as much as in the letter of the Treaty establishing the EEC (which is by far the most important of the three Communities), on negative rather than positive integration. There is no intention on my part to underrate the Community's achievement of implementing enough measures of negative integration to come within striking distance of the establishment of a full common market, in which discrimination as between the economic agents in the member countries has been virtually removed, with respect to numerous non-tariff discriminations as well as to import and exchange controls. This was a great task, not only technically and economically but also politically and morally; and it is astonishing that it has been so nearly accomplished. But I do intend to emphasize that this achievement will be incomplete, and may even be found to have created worse problems than it has solved, unless equivalent progress is made in the field of positive integration, resulting in the creation of a full economic union.

The case for economic union

There are a number of varieties of positive integration that may be held to be necessary if a reasonable effort is to be made to maximize welfare within a common market. Among these are industrial policies, including the creation of large enough firms; science and technology policies, including the financing of research and development on the vast scale required in some high technology industries; policies towards investments in the common market by firms originating in third countries; the development of a modern transport network for the common market as a whole; rational policies in the sectors such as agriculture, energy and transport, where goods or services traded between the members of the common market are subject to managed markets; policies of aid and assistance for development regions within the common market; common external policies relating to trade, aid and currencies, calculated to advance the interests of the common market as a whole and to create a satisfactory world economic environment. But here I will concentrate on one aspect of positive integration, which I believe may be found to be the most important: policies to deal with the member countries' balance-of-payments problems.

A country that is not a member of a common market or free-trade system may use import controls, export subsidies, exchange controls, or adjustments of exchange rates to help solve its balance-of-payments problems. These weapons are in principle denied to a member country of a common market. But such a country may well find itself in balance-of-payments trouble. Cost push or lax monetary or budgetary policies may drive its costs above those of other countries, particularly of other member countries; the world market may evolve in such a way that the structure of its exports becomes ill-adapted to their growth at a satisfactory rate; its consumers' propensity to import may grow at a rate which its foreign exchange earnings cannot rival; or it may suffer from an endemic lack of dynamism of the type discussed earlier (pp. 131–3). If these things happen, the country has little alternative to deflation to rectify its deficit, if it is not allowed to impose trade or exchange controls and if the common market lacks a common policy adequate to deal with the problem. (Symmetrically, a country can suffer from balance-of-payments surpluses which are aggravated by its membership of a common market, but for simplicity the argument is confined to the problem of deficits.)

Deflation may be an acceptable instrument if it rectifies the trouble in a fairly short time – say inside a year. But suppose that a deflation is applied that is severe enough to stop economic growth and the deficit nevertheless persists; or the brakes are kept on sufficiently for payments to be in balance but growth is in consequence very slow for a long period. What can the country do, if it holds economic growth to be an important objective?

There are two broad alternatives. One is for the country to be allowed to contract out of the common market for a period by imposing trade or exchange controls, or to 'distort the conditions of competition' by devaluing. These contingencies are allowed for in the Rome Treaty, but the Community system would be severely shaken if they were applied; and the knowledge that their use would be a major issue would certainly stand in the way of a quick and efficient solution to the problem by means such as this.

The other alternative is for the common market to have joint policies, in the actual case operated by the institutions of the European Community, to deal with problems of this type. An examination of the way in which problems of interregional balance of payments and disparities in regional growth rates are dealt with in national economic systems may indicate the nature of the policies that would be required. It seems likely that these would include:

1. A large joint programme of aid for the growth of less-developed or ailing regions. In countries where economic growth of the various regions is accepted as a major objective, aid for the improvement of infrastructure and for industrial development is an important arm of policy, which at the same time counters the structural deficits that such regions are likely to have in their balances of payments when they are enjoying economic growth. Aid provided jointly for such regions in a common market would make a big contribution to solving problems of balance of payments and inadequate growth in those member countries where such regions were important (or where indeed the whole country might constitute such a region or a group of such regions). The EEC can at present provide collective finance only at bankable rates of interest and through the modest resources of the Investment Bank. Without substantial powers to raise taxes and loans, the Community will not be able to perform these functions on the scale required to solve substantial balance-of-payments and growth problems of the member countries.

2. Development of transport facilities, and the granting of favourable transport rates, that will encourage the economic growth of the less-favoured regions, and in particular of any region whose lack of dynamism is proving to be a drag on the balance of payments of a member country.

3. Unemployment and retraining assistance on a joint basis. The flow of unemployment and retraining assistance within a national economy is an important equilibrator of both short-term and long-term regional deficits. The same would apply in a common market if unemployment assistance were collectively financed. The Social Fund of the EEC is empowered to finance half the cost of unemployment pay and of retraining for workers made redundant because of the establishment of the Common Market.

If its scope were extended to cover unemployment and retraining in general it could become a substantial equilibrator, particularly of short-term deficits that are being met by deflation in the deficit country.

4. Fiscal and budgetary powers. The strong budgetary role of a national government gives it powerful instruments for dealing with, among other things, problems of regional growth and balance of payments. In the European Community, fiscal powers could be used not only as already indicated for regional development and for unemployment assistance, but also for purposes such as industrial policy, including financing of R and D and of structural improvements in declining industries, for social policy, and for aid to less-developed countries, as well as for the agricultural subsidies that are the main object of expenditure in the EEC at present. Such budgetary powers give the official institutions scope for an influential role in the short-term capital market (in the course of financing leads and lags in expenditure and tax collection), as well as for applying regional policies in the form of tax remissions or in certain cases public purchasing arrangements that discriminate in favour of development regions.

5. The facilitating of labour migration. Labour migration is one of the means of resolving the problem of disparities between regions in a national economy. Cultural differences will generally make this a less promising solution in a common market. It is, however, desirable at least that unnecessary barriers in the way of labour mobility should be removed and the EEC, true to its practice of emphasizing negative integration, has done much in this direction.

6. A free flow of capital. An efficient unified market for both long-term and short-term capital plays a major role in the inter-regional balance of payments of advanced countries. This role *may* be a disequilibrating one (cf. the argument about cumulative deficit problems for weak areas such as southern Italy), but equally it is hard to envisage an adequate equilibrating system that does *not* include a unified capital market. The EEC has made a good deal of progress in removing the legal and administrative barriers to the flow of capital between the member countries, but the capital market at Community level remains relatively weak and ineffective, and a stronger system is essential for balance-of-payments reasons (in addition to being an important element in a positive industrial policy). This implies a monetary union and eventually a common currency. A powerful role for the Community institutions in the raising of loans from the market to finance Community expenditure of a capital nature and to cover the Community's short-term financial requirements could make a major contribution to the evolution of an adequate capital market. Meade has pointed out that an integrated banking system can also be very helpful as an equilibrator in relation to the flow of short-term capital.[6]

7. *Coordination of member countries' monetary, budgetary and incomes policies.* Since tendencies towards inflation or deflation in one member country will have a direct impact on the other members, and they have renounced the main weapons with which they could formerly defend themselves, coordination of national monetary and budgetary policies may be required in order to ensure that member countries do not export their problems to each other. (Tinbergen makes a useful division of national policy instruments into 'supporting instruments', that act in the same direction on the well-being of all the countries concerned – e.g. public spending in a time of economic depression in all member countries; and 'conflicting instruments', whose use by one country conflicts with the objectives of other countries' policies – e.g. devaluation at a time of depression in all member countries. Supporting instruments are suitable for decentralized, or national, use and conflicting instruments for centralized, or coordinated use (1954, pp. 98, 99).)

The first six of these areas of policy would seem to be the main elements in the equilibrating of inter-regional balance-of-payments deficits (or surpluses) in advanced national economies, without harmful effects on the growth of the regions that have structural deficits and indeed while stimulating their growth. The seventh item belongs to an economic union, where the separate monetary, budgetary (and perhaps incomes) policies of the member countries remain important. Taken together, the seven items offer a framework in which one could be fairly certain that both short-term and long-term balance-of-payments problems of member countries would be met without unnecessary or prolonged restriction of the economic growth of a country or of important regions within it.

6. See Meade (1953, pp. 40, 41). Part 2 of this book contains a useful general discussion of the balance-of-payments problem in an economic union, as does chapter 1 of Meade (1955). Part 2 of Scitovsky (1958) and chapter 12 of Balassa (1961).

The fact must be faced that this would imply a high degree of positive integration. The common market in question, in our case the European Community, would have to develop its own major policies on a wide range of subjects: regional, transport, social, capital market (including the raising of public loans), monetary, fiscal (including the raising of money for community purposes), industrial and technological. It would also have to coordinate the monetary, budgetary and incomes policies of the member countries. These represent most of the elements of economic union.

The failure of the Community to achieve much in this direction so far has been attributed earlier to the relative ease in general, in post-war Europe, of securing agreement upon and implementing negative integration, and to the hostility of General de Gaulle, combined with the passivity of most member governments, to the strong institutional system that is necessary if substantial positive integration is to be brought about. I also mentioned the doctrinal reservations of the German neo-liberals, and of Dr Erhard in particular, about some of the aspects of positive integration. The latter is a special case of a general problem that constitutes one of the greatest obstacles to positive integration. This is the problem of agreement upon the objectives of policy and also, in so far as the instruments are not only technical means but also have implications with respect to ends, upon the use of instruments to secure the objectives.

The general problem is briefly considered by Tinbergen (1954, pp. 101–3). In relation to the Community in particular, Denton has analysed the main differences between the French 'planning school' and the German neo-liberals, that have been a part of the context for policy discussions and decisions (or failures to decide). Recognizing the fundamental importance of this problem in the long run, the Community has set up the Medium-Term Policy Committee, which produced the first Medium-Term Economic Policy Programme that was approved by the Council of Ministers in 1967 (Denton, 1967, pp. 9–21). This is a promising start, and it is encouraging that in the midst of all its current difficulties the Community has been capable of doing something about its basic long-term problems. But it is only a small beginning along what must certainly be a long and uphill road.

In the face of difficulties as great as these, the reader may ask himself why one should bother to try to overcome them. Some of the arguments for negative integration were considered earlier in this article and need not be repeated here; it may be enough to say that it is hard to envisage a return to national autarchy. My argument for positive integration has been largely confined to one objective – balance-of-payments equilibrium without unnecessary restriction of growth – and, although there are powerful arguments in relation to other objectives, it seems to me that this alone shows that negative integration is unsatisfactory, and may well prove to be objectionable, unless it is accompanied by a substantial measure of positive integration. This view, and the failure of the Community to undertake the necessary positive integration, was recently confirmed by Uri in an assessment of contemporary experience in the Community:

The course of the Common Market is something of a disappointment. . . . Stagnation now prevails in all member countries except Italy. . . . The peril of a pure and simple liberalization of trade – the propagation of deflation – was fully realized (by those who conceived the idea of the Community), hence the importance attached to common economic policy. . . . The freer trade is, the more serious the effect . . . [but] coordination is hardly more than a word. . . . The Brussels Commission, more often than not, is content to advise each country to do no more than it is prepared to accept – which will normally be what it intended to do anyway. To request member states to pay attention to the impact of their policies on their partners is generally wishful thinking (Uri, 1967).

Conclusion

The European Community has virtually completed its customs union and has gone far towards the removal of non-tariff discrimination also and hence towards the establishment of the common market. It has formed a common agricultural policy, an unsatisfactory but nevertheless an effective one, and it has, with the conclusion of the Kennedy Round, carried out a major trade negotiation. It has institutions and a capable civil service that could be effective if member governments had the will to let them work, though this condition may imply that, in order to be effective, the central institutions need to be strengthened. It has blueprints, more or less far advanced, for policies that comprise many of the aspects of positive integration.

But the Community so far has, apart from the agricultural policy and the Kennedy Round, no major achievements of positive integration, that is, of policies that go beyond the removal of discrimination. Positive integration, particularly to solve the balance-of-payments problems of member countries now that their national economic defences have been removed, may be necessary to the success and even the survival of the Community. This may require (i) major common policies at Community level over a wide range of key subjects, including regional, social, monetary and fiscal policies with the corresponding fiscal and loan-raising powers, and (ii) the coordination of the monetary, budgetary and incomes policies of the member states.

My contention is that the Community, having for good reasons made negative integration effective, will find itself compelled to swallow this large dose of positive integration or seriously to water down the Common Market that has been achieved. If this is so, two basic questions remain: 'Will the Community regain the political momentum, and find the economic means, to establish these essential elements of economic union?' and 'Would Britain, if she became a member, contribute to or impede this process?'

References

BALASSA, B. (1961), *The Theory of Economic Integration*, Allen & Unwin.
DENTON, G. (1967), *Planning in the EEC: The Medium-Term Economic Policy Programme of the European Economic Community*, PEP European Series, no. 5.
DOSSER, D., and HAN, S. S. (1968), *Taxes in the EEC and Britain: The Problem of Harmonization*, PEP European Series, no. 6.
Economist Intelligence Unit (1957), *Britain and Europe*, London.
FORSYTH, A. (1964), *Steel Pricing Policies*, PEP.
JOHNSON, J. G. (1958), 'The gains from full trade with Europe: an estimate', *Manchester School*.
LIPSEY, R. G. (1960), 'The theory of customs unions: a general survey', *Econ. J.*, vol. 71, no. 4, pp. 511–13.
MEADE, J. E. (1953), *Problems of Economic Union*, Allen & Unwin.
MEADE, J. E. (1955), *The Theory of Customs Unions*, North Holland.
PREBISCH, R. (1950), *The Economic Development of Latin America and its Principal Problems*, United Nations.
PREBISCH, R. (1959), 'Commercial policy in the underdeveloped countries', *Amer. Econ. Rev.*
SCITOVSKY, T. (1958), *Economic Theory and Western European Integration*, Stanford University Press.
STAMP, M., and COWIE, H. (1967), *The Free Trade Area Option*, Maxwell Stamp Associates.
STREETEN, P. (1961), *Economic Integration: Aspects and Problems*, Sythoff.
SWANN, D., and McLACHLAN, D. L. (1967), *Concentration or Competition: A European Dilemma*, PEP European Series, no. 1.
TINBERGEN, J. (1954), *International Economic Integration*, Elsevier.

URI, P. (1967), 'Stagnation threatens the Common Market', *The Times*, 29 September.

VINER, J. (1950), *The Customs Union Issue*, Carnegie Endowment for International Peace.

WARLEY, T. K. (1967), *Agriculture: The Cost of Joining the Common Market*, PEP European Studies, no. 3.

8 Nils Lundgren

Customs Unions of Industrialized West European Countries

N. Lundgren, 'Customs unions of industrialized West European countries', in G. R. Denton (ed.), *Economic Integration in Europe*, Weidenfeld & Nicolson, 1969, pp. 25–54.

The drive for regional economic integration during the last two decades has stimulated a good deal of research into the mechanisms of such processes. It is curious, however, that while the main setting for integration policies has been the European continent (Benelux customs union, ECSC, EEC, EFTA, Comecon) the theory has been developed mainly in the Anglo-Saxon countries. This fact may have had important consequences for the relevance of existing theory for the most conspicuous of the economic integration projects, the European Economic Community. The EEC was largely the result of a political enthusiasm for a united Europe and it represented to its proponents a necessary first step on the road towards political integration after the failure of that directly political project, the European Defence Community. The EEC is intended to be an economic community including a customs union, a common market for labour and capital, harmonized economic legislation and a high degree of cooperation in economic policy. The motives for this and other projects were, among others, to improve the international division of labour, increase competition, make possible the exploitation of large-scale economies, and to gain increased bargaining strength in trade policy.

In contrast, the theoretical framework for studying the economics of integration has its roots in the classical English theory of foreign trade and is in fact restricted to a theory of customs unions. The main contributions to this body of theory have been the work of Professors Viner (1950b), Meade (1955b) and Lipsey (1961) and may be described as an adaptation of that traditional foreign-trade theory which studies the effects on welfare following a change from protection to free trade. The ordinary assumptions for the pure theory of foreign trade are accepted, such as market economies working under perfect competition, productive factors immobile between countries, undifferentiated products, technically efficient production methods, no transport costs, no monetary aspects, etc. The problem is whether abolishing duties on imports from some countries and retaining them against the rest of the world is a move towards higher welfare for the country studied, for the members of the union and/or the whole world. It is, fundamentally, an application of the theory of second best within the neo-classical framework.

However, in the interdependent system that a modern industrialized economy constitutes, the formation of a customs union will obviously affect most economic variables to greater or lesser degrees, and the extension of the theory may therefore be said to be limited in two dimensions. First, there are several variables that could be made the object of study in customs union theory, for instance, employment level, balance of payments, industrial structure, distribution of income, bargaining strength in trade negotiations. Second, there are many channels in this interdependent system through which a customs union may manifest its effects on the variable selected for study. Traditional theory is focused on the effect on national product or welfare, which is rational for an approach that has its roots in classical foreign-trade theory. There is now in the literature the germ of a new approach to customs union theory with an altogether different starting point. The best representation of this new line is found in the recent work by Harry G. Johnson (1965), where the basic assumption is that governments have introduced tariffs for reasons of economic balance, to offset divergencies between private and social costs or benefits, etc. The work of Becker (1957), Breton (1964) and Downs (1957) has broken the path for this kind of approach, which is also found in two recent articles by Cooper and Massel (1965).

The two latter asked why a customs union would ever be resorted to in the pursuit of higher real income, as a non-preferential tariff policy could always do the same job in this theoretical framework. They point out that if a country wants the benefits of free trade, it should go the whole way and not stop halfway at a customs union. If, on the other hand, it is willing to forgo some real income, because protection brings a compensating advantage, why should it agree to give up part of that by joining a customs union.

This criticism is in fact directed against the limitation of the theory in this first dimension. Cooper and Massel work with the hypothesis that the objective of protection is a diversified industrial structure and work out a theory of how a customs union may retain enough protection for non-competitive industries, while at the same time some market-swapping with union partners makes it possible to increase the degree of specialization and thereby keep down the cost of this diversification.

Their point seems valid and their contribution is an interesting extension of the theory, but not a replacement of the traditional approach with focus on national product. For while it is true that we need a theory that can tell us the effect of a customs union on all variables that are included in the welfare function of the decision-makers, it remains a fundamental task of the economist to express the loss or gain of a customs union in terms of national product.

The limitation of the theory in this first dimension may not be too contentious either, in an age when levels and rates of growth of national products are at the centre of interest of both economists and politicians. Criticism against the scope of the theory has been mainly concerned with the second type of limitation referring to *the mechanisms* through which a customs union may affect national products. Lipsey (1961) made a list of such mechanisms which we will make our starting point:

1. Further specialization of production according to comparative advantage.
2. Improvement in the terms of trade.
3. Improved utilization of economies of scale.
4. Improved productive efficiency due to fiercer competition.
5. Acceleration in the rate of economic growth.

The mechanisms are cast in a positive form here, assuming that the customs union is effective in achieving a higher national product.

The established theory of customs unions is formally limited to the first two mechanisms, of which the terms of trade effect will be neglected here as it is a distribution problem, not one of improved use of resources. The conclusions obtained by this approach would therefore refer to the effects of further specialization according to comparative advantage.

Assuming that the basic structure of this theory is generally known I shall limit myself to an analysis of some of its basic propositions and a review of the available empirical evidence.

A full-scale analysis of the last three mechanisms still remains to be done, but I shall attempt to introduce, even at this stage, some general viewpoints in order to sketch out the background for the static specialization argument. This is because there is such a strong tendency to point to the last three mechanisms asserting that there are immense gains to be expected from them in customs unions while traditional theory adds negligibly to our understanding of the problem. I shall argue that potential gains from (3) and (4) *that are conditional upon the present tariffs* must be fairly limited.

Comments on the traditional theory of customs unions
Trade creation and trade diversion

The concepts of trade creation and trade diversion have penetrated the customs-union debate both at the theoretical and the political level and are very often abused or misunderstood, because they were introduced by Viner (1950) in a model based on even more simplified assumptions than those prevailing in the subsequent literature.

As Viner worked with constant costs and fixed patterns of demand, consumption of a good would, in any country, be satisfied either out of domestic production *or* from imports, but never from both sources simultaneously. If country A consumes 100 units of a commodity which are imported from C and joins a customs union with B which makes B's product excluding tariff cheaper in A than C's with tariff, then A will switch all her imports to B. The volume of trade has not changed in this three-country world, but has been diverted from one supplier to another. Viner logically called this *trade diversion*. If consumption came from domestic production and the elimination of the tariff makes B's product cheaper than the domestic imports from B will substitute domestic production and 100 units of foreign trade have been created. This is Viner's *trade creation*.

The trouble with this terminology is that it is not applicable outside Viner's model and therefore invites a slipshod use of the term *trade creation*. In journalese the rise of intra-trade in a customs union or free-trade area is usually referred to as trade creation. However, in most other models and usually in the real world, a commodity is produced in all countries under rising costs and some are exporters and others importers. Normally, trade creation and trade diversion will therefore appear together. A will switch some of her imports from C to B *and* will increase her imports from B at the expense of falling purchases from domestic producers. A registered increase in intra-union trade is therefore partly offset by a fall in member countries' trade with the outside world.

The fruitful approach would seem to be a use of terms that indicate *whether the rise in intra-trade is a substitute for trade with third countries or for domestic production.* We have a gross creation of intra-trade which must be balanced against a loss of member countries' trade with third countries. To Viner this problem did not occur as his model did not permit simultaneous production and imports so that imports from member countries due to the formation of the customs union would have to be substitution for *either* domestic production *or* imports from third countries, but never both at the same time.

Introducing price-sensitive demand patterns we get another mechanism through which a customs union may affect trade flows. In addition to trade created and/or diverted because demand is satisfied from supplies from other countries than previously, the price changes may lead to higher or lower consumption, which will also give rise to changes in trade flows. We have a consumption effect in addition to the *production effect* just described.

We can now get a rise in imports from member countries which is a substitute neither for imports from third countries nor for domestic production of the same good. It may be a substitute for consumption of another good which has not become cheaper to the same extent, i.e. presumably a good bought from third countries or domestic suppliers. It may also be the result of new expenditure made possible by higher real income achieved through resources saved by the institution of a customs union. (The argument can be reasoned in a similar way with a negative sign for a fall.) Meade labelled those effects trade expansion and trade contraction (1955a).

We are landed accordingly with a substitution effect between producers, a substitution effect between goods and an income effect, all operating on trade flows in a neo-classical system.

A quest for policy criteria

It is not altogether unfounded to assert that within the neo-classical framework there is no need for a particular theory of customs unions, as the technique of analysing the effect of changes in certain levies on the allocation of resources is already well known. The justification of a particular theory is the need to establish general criteria for when customs unions should be formed. The implication for the traditional customs union theory is that the step from analysis of trade changes to analysis of changes in national products must be taken.

The founder of the school, Viner, worked with constant costs and fixed patterns of demand. He was therefore able to say that any increase in trade volume due to the formation of a customs union involved a switch of resources from less to more efficient occupations, while a diversion of trade represented the opposite. Viner does not develop his ideas on this point, but apparently he meant that trade creation therefore saved resources that could be used to increase real income, while trade diversion again had the opposite effect. An increase in overall real income of a society is unambiguously good, a fall unambiguously bad, whatever the simultaneous changes in income distribution. Clearly, the policy criterion here is of a simple kind which is reasonably easy to apply in principle. A rise in real GNP is good, a fall bad. As a welfare concept it may be defended by the use of one of the compensation principles invented by Scitovsky, Hicks or Samuelson. As we are here studying international economics the principle would have to be extended to apply also between countries. Viner does not deal with the problem that a rise in GNP in one country must offset a somewhat smaller fall in another country's GNP.

Even in Viner's simple world it is not enough to calculate the net effect of trade creation and trade diversion, as the expansions and contractions of trade flows may save and waste resources in very different degrees and would therefore have to be weighted. Meade pointed this out, and working with rising costs and infinitesimal changes in tariffs he showed that the change in every trade flow should be weighted by the height of the tariff in the importing country. It would then measure the difference between the amount of resources freed in the importing country and the additional amount of resources employed in the exporting country as the changes would be marginal.

However, Meade also introduced a price-elastic demand side to gain increased realism. As a result he had to use some kind of utility concept as there could now be desirable or undesirable effects of changes in consumption even if production could not be reallocated. Meade, who already in his earlier work (1955b) had decided that a theory of international economic policy must work with a demand utility concept, had no inhibitions. He therefore established his theory of customs unions with a welfare measure based on a cardinal interpersonally comparable, utility concept of the Marshallian type.

By assuming in addition that marginal utility of income is

constant (another heroic assumption of long standing in neo-classical theory), he could use price as an expression for utility and disutility per unit. An infinitesimal tariff cut will then lead to a net increase in world utility, which arises from the fact that price and accordingly utility was one plus the *ad valorem* tariff times higher in the importing country. Meade concluded that the way to weight the changes in trade flows to get a welfare measure of reallocation effects is to multiply the money values of the trade created and diverted by the tariffs of the importing countries and then take the net value as a measure of the welfare created.

Gehrels (1956–7) and Lipsey (1957) both avoided this Marshallian approach to consumption effects by using community indifference curves, which may or may not be a more acceptable tool than consumer surpluses. Michaely (1965) finally showed that the same result could be obtained with the aid of modern gains-from-trade theory as presented by Kemp (1962) and Samuelson (1962). All three make the point that a diversion of imports from a lower to a higher cost country may raise welfare in the importing country, 'due to the elimination of formerly existing discrepancies between domestic and international relative prices'.

The trouble with this method is that we are then stuck with a proposition that is not open to empirical testing. As customs unions by their nature combine welfare-increasing and welfare-decreasing aspects it is, however, necessary to quantify in order to get a net result. While accepting the well-known criticism of the Marshallian welfare concepts used by Meade and Johnson, the present writer therefore would still be inclined to accept Meade's result that trade diversions and trade creation should be weighted by the height of the tariffs, though for somewhat different reasons. One argument for this is that for trade changes arising out of shifts in production the method gives an indication of resources saved. If we assume with Spraos that 'broad patterns of demand' are pretty independent of the minor price differences caused by tariffs it would be perfectly justifiable; and even if we know that changes in consumption have caused some of the trade creation or diversion, there still remains a part about which it can be maintained that it should be weighted in this way (1964).

But surely, for the demand-induced changes also it could be maintained that the higher the tariff the better that it should be removed, because the more it disturbs consumers. Even if one is not prepared to swallow his arguments in utility terms, there may still, therefore, be a case for accepting Meade's way of weighting changes in trade flows by tariffs, in order to get closer to a generally acceptable measure of the reallocation effects of customs unions.

I have in my unpublished thesis attempted an algebraic model along Meade's lines, where I worked with full-scale tariff changes instead of infinitesimal ones. The main conclusions were that an increase of intra-trade in a customs union must be balanced against the killing off of trade with third countries, that it should be weighted by something less than the *ad valorem* tariff and that trade creation and trade diversion are not at all uniquely correlated with improved or worsened resource allocation. Once this link is broken, the reaction of trade cannot be made the policy criterion. As we have postulated here that the *raison d'être* of a particular theory of customs unions is the search for policy criteria, we must conclude that such a theory has to go beyond the analysis of changes in the volume of international trade.

Height of tariffs

All approaches to customs unions result in the conclusion that the higher the intra-tariff eliminated and the lower the common union tariff instituted the larger the gains. This is a very natural outcome. The traditional neo-classical foreign trade theory gives the result that free trade is better than protection. It is in fact the theoretical foundation of the free-trade doctrine and it seems logical that an adaptation of the same theory to the problem of customs unions should render the same basic result.

The reason why the elimination of high tariffs is more profitable than that of low tariffs is, of course, that the tariff is an expression of the difference in marginal cost between the exporter and the importer. It is now a widespread belief that high-tariff countries have more to gain from customs unions than low-tariff countries. This is basically true as long as we have *ceteris paribus* assumptions about other aspects, size of union, etc. and *including the height of the common-tariff wall*. However, if there is reason to believe that there is a correlation between initial-tariff levels in the individual countries and the union-tariff level that will be agreed upon, it is no longer possible to say that high-tariff countries generally have more to gain. This is an important qualification.

It is often asserted that a customs union of low-tariff countries will lead to trade diversion on balance. However, this depends on the level of the common-tariff wall instituted. A union with high tariffs might also result in trade diversion, if the common-tariff wall were to be set too high.

It seems to be the tacit assumption of many economists that political constellations are such that generally a protectionist, trade-diverting customs union will be desired by decision-makers, but will be the more difficult to obtain the higher the initial-tariff walls of the union, which is true. It should be remembered, however, that a union of low-tariff countries created by politicians who honestly want trade creation can always be made to produce that result by selecting a liberal customs policy.

Size of union

The size of union aspect is probably the best known by the public at large. By the size of the union here is not meant the number of countries. What we have to do is to imagine what the pattern of trade between economic subjects would be if there were no restrictions on trade. The size of a customs union depends on what proportion of the trade that the member countries would carry on under a universal free-trade system takes place inside the union. Sweden could form a customs union with the other Nordic countries or with Australia and New Zealand. In both cases Sweden would then be in a market of some twenty million people with a joint GNP of some thirty to forty million dollars, but it is obvious to everyone that functionally the second union would be much smaller in the sense that much less of potential Swedish trade with abroad would be freed in that case.

If we can assume that existing barriers to trade are fairly neutral between countries in their effects, we can use the share of foreign trade accounted for by the potential union under the present restrictions as a measure, and this is a measure commonly used. Finally, if the actual or potential members are at roughly the same level of economic development and geographically close, it is also possible to add up the population or total income as a measure of functional size, but only then. It should be noted, however, that these measures are only approximations of the ideal functional concept. According to the first, EFTA is considerably bigger than EEC to Denmark, while applying the second the reverse is true.

Now, assuming that the customs union comprises the whole world, we have universal free trade, which in a neo-classical model would be ideal. Excluding Iceland from this union would obviously not affect this optimum situation much but it seems intuitively plausible that we are moving further away from maximum efficiency as the size is reduced. Put in another way, traditional theory shows that the beneficial effects of a customs union are achieved in intra-trade, where a more efficient division of labour always results, while the negative effects occur in trade with third countries. However, the smaller the union in the functional sense, the larger the volume of trade between members and third countries in relation to intra-union trade and the greater, accordingly, the risks that the losses incurred will outweigh the gains in terms of resource allocation.

There is an interesting corollary to the conclusion that a small customs union might *ceteris paribus* lead to a worse allocation of resources. If the Benelux customs union was too small so that the three countries were better off on their own, must it not follow that a country such as Germany, if it could not join a bigger customs union, might instead gain from introducing tariff walls between the *Länder*, i.e. from dissolving the *Zollverein*. The answer to this may according to the current customs-union models well be in the positive. That this result seems contrary to common sense is because common sense takes into account economies of scale, administrative economies, effects on competition, etc., which do not appear in conventional customs-union theory.

Here we must instead draw upon the results of the theory of the second best. We could put it in the way that there are two ways of moving from the present situation of tariff-protected national economies towards universal free (geographically undiscriminated) trade by the use of changes in the geographical pattern of discrimination. One is the creation of successively bigger customs unions until all the economies have merged into one single union. This is the model of development we normally think of. There is, however, in principle another way, namely, that of splitting every economy into successively smaller units with uniform tariffs on imports, until each productive unit is a customs area of its own. To all economic subjects all goods will bear the correct price relations to each other with the exception of their own product. Given a tax equal to the tariff on that produce and neutral distribution of the tariff revenue we have attained the benefits of universal free trade.

It is not my intention to attach any other value than the purely pedagogical to the second procedure, but the conclusion is that in traditional customs-union theory it is natural that there should exist a pessimum, a maximum loss of world income, connected with a certain degree of division of the world into customs areas from which changes towards smaller or larger units both represent more efficient allocations of resources. There is therefore nothing surprising in the result that the merging of some countries into a customs union may lead to a less efficient situation or in its reflection that the splitting of any economy into several customs areas may be beneficial. It is the necessary conclusion of the prevalent theory of customs unions and scepticism against those results therefore hit the theory as a whole. It is interesting to see that Lipsey does in fact apply this kind of reasoning for another purpose, namely that of establishing criteria for which countries should form customs unions (1961, pp. 507–9).

Competitiveness and complementarity
The question which type of economies can most profit from forming customs unions has a long standing. It should be remembered that early advocates of customs unions included people like Friedrich List, who was by no means a free trader but nevertheless a supporter of the German *Zollverein*. This is because his nationalism led him to want protection for the new-born German industry on the basis of the infant-industry argument, while at the same time he wanted free trade between the German states to increase productivity through the division of labour. In particular, the agricultural and the industrial German states would complement each other. The desire to integrate economically complementary regions to achieve a greater degree of autarchy and its corollary, greater political independence, has often been present in political arguments for customs unions.

Free traders, however, also used to come down in favour of customs unions of complementary countries (see, for instance, Haberler, 1936). Viner maintained the opposite, that the more competitive the economies of the member countries the greater the beneficial effects of a customs union and this is now embodied in the accepted theory of customs unions. However, there is still considerable confusion as to the definitions of the terms complementarity and competitiveness, which makes it difficult to get to grips with this problem.

Haberler's definition appears from the following:

The fact that two countries are, so to speak, economically complementary, means only that the nature of their respective resources and there fore of their production possibilities, the conditions governing the location of industry, and so on, make an extensive exchange of goods between them especially favourable since differences in comparative costs between them are especially great and, possibly, transport costs between them relatively low. The criterion for this is the intensity of their mutual trade relations, provided that these are not artificially disturbed by interventions, such as differential duties (1936, pp. 389–91).

This quotation shows that when Haberler thinks that tariff integration is most profitable for complementary countries he does not mean anything in addition to what has already been said above on size of union (share of total trade carried on with members) and height of tariffs (reflecting differences in comparative costs).

Viner's opinion concerning this problem is clear from the following quotation of two factors that are said to promote gains from a customs union: 'the greater correspondence in kind of products of the range of high-cost industries as between different parts of the customs union which were protected by tariffs in both of the member countries before customs union was established, i.e. the *less* the degree of complementarity – or the *greater* the degree of rivalry – of the member countries with respect to *protected* industries, prior to customs union'; and 'the greater the differences in unit-costs for protected industries of the same kind as between the different parts of the customs union, and therefore the greater the economies to be derived from free trade with respect to these industries within the customs union area' (1950, p. 51).

The second quotation contains the view found in most writings, namely the obvious truth that the greater the cost differences in goods, where intra-trade is going to increase, the better. If we assume rising costs this is simply equivalent to the result that the higher the tariffs abolished in intra-trade the better. The first quotation is not very clearly expressed and it is interesting to read Lipsey's reformulation: 'A precise way of making the point is to say that the customs union is more likely to bring gain, the greater the degree of overlapping between the class of commodities produced under tariff protection in the two countries' (1961).

It seems impossible to avoid interpreting these statements as both saying that a customs union is better the larger the volume of member countries' imports that come from third countries only.

This cannot be correct, however, as the outcome in this case has been shown to be wholly dependent on at what level the common-union tariff is fixed (Spraos, 1964). The constellation that must prevail should instead be the one where a commodity that is protected by a member should have been supplied by another member before union. The tariffs that are abolished should mainly have had the effect of protecting domestic industry against competition from other member countries, because then intra-trade creation will prevail over diversion of trade from third countries.

To be fair to Viner we must take into account, however, that he assumed constant costs. Production and imports are therefore mutually exclusive so that if there is production under protection in the potential member countries there are no imports from third countries to divert. On the other hand, when intra-union tariffs are removed the lowest cost producer inside the union will capture the whole union market, i.e. there will certainly be trade creation. As we find the risks of trade diversion excluded and the possibilities of trade creation assured, we must agree with Viner that this is an advantageous case for customs unions. Accepting his definition of rivalry as one where a wide range of goods is produced by both (or all) union members before the union, we must therefore agree with Viner's conclusion that 'the *less* the degree of complementarity – or the *greater* the degree of rivalry – of the member countries with respect to protected industries, prior to customs union', the more beneficial the effects of it.

There are two important qualifications to add, however. Even inside Viner's model it seems obvious that the best situation is when all member countries were producers before union and *one of them was doing so without protection*, i.e. was the exporter in Viner's world. Secondly, with rising costs protected industries would normally be competing with imports from other member countries *and* from third countries. Trade diversion will then occur when a union is formed. If all member countries protect the same industry we have Spraos's case, which as already mentioned, is not a particularly good situation for achieving a more efficient resource allocation.

It seems curious that both Viner and Lipsey should have concluded that overlapping of protected industries is the criterion when obviously it is the existence of production in both member countries and of *protection in at least one country* that is the exact formulation. It seems probable that the reason is that with constant costs there would be no union tariff on the commodity in the latter case and that they both feel that such a case is less interesting. This may be true in their model, but if we work with the more realistic assumption of rising costs we cannot draw the same conclusion.

Our conclusion must instead be the following. The ideal for a customs union is that before union a maximum range of products is produced in both member countries, with maximum differences in marginal cost, one country being an exporter of each commodity. The best thing is accordingly that large differences in comparative advantage exist, which through very high protection are prevented from leading to an efficient division of labour prior to union. The economies should be complementary as far as basic productive conditions are concerned, but competitive in the range of products actually produced due to protection *against each other*. They should not, as Viner and Lipsey assert, have many industries in common that they protect against third countries. This is a result that is wholly dependent on a model based on the extreme assumption of constant costs.[1]

The protectionist is interested in merging in a customs union two countries which are basically complementary and have not tried to build up industries protected against competition from the potential partner country. They can then form a customs union without becoming exposed to more competition from inside the union, but can get a tariff discrimination in their favour in the partner country for its own export industry. If the two countries finally are competitive in the sense that they export and import the same goods before union the gains from a customs union will be small. A more concise formulation would be that customs unions should be formed by countries which are fundamentally complementary but actually made competitive in their range of production through protection. If they are fundamentally *and actually* complementary the customs union would be mainly protectionist (trade-diverting) in its effects. If they are fundamentally and actually competitive the effect of the customs union would be small.

In fact the introduction of terms such as complementarity, rivalry, competitiveness, seems unnecessary, the more so as it has

1. Lipsey has a footnote saying that if one country in the union should be an efficient producer there would be *a fortiori* a gain. This has probably been added as an afterthought and the main conclusion on competitiveness and complementarity is allowed to stand unchanged.

led to considerable confusion. The basic condition is that it is better the more a customs union results in the dismantling of tariffs that were mainly protecting domestic industries against partner countries' exports and the less it is directed against imports from a third country. Whether we term the relation between the economies one thing or the other depends on the angle of observation.

This is the result of customs union theory as it is presented by Viner, Meade, Lipsey *et consortes*. If we take into account the existence of economies of scale and differentiated products the results may become different, but this is another story.

The empirical evidence

The solution of the traditional general equilibrium model in price theory is Pareto optimal, and is looked upon as a desirable situation by most economists though they often make reservations about the resulting income distribution. The policy conclusions then become arguments against interference with market prices, but for legislation that helps to ensure the behaviour of economic subjects according to the rules of the game. The conventional wisdom is for free trade and against monopoly. The contribution of the theory of second best is to demonstrate that this is not necessarily equivalent to advocating *freer* trade and *less* monopoly. If all interferences cannot be abolished, the removal of one or a few may on balance lead to either a better or a worse situation.

When traditional trade theory deals with the case of introducing free trade in an otherwise ideal neo-classical world, i.e. of removing the only disturbances in the system, a qualitative result is sufficient for policy decisions if social costs of adjustment and politically undesirable specialization are disregarded. However, with a second best problem, such as the outcome of a customs union, the qualitative result cannot be determined until the effects in both directions have been balanced against each other on a quantitative basis. It is, therefore, natural that while there has been little interest in quantifying the gains from establishing universal free trade in terms of GNP, attempts to do this for customs unions have been quite frequent in recent years.

There is a basic distinction here between what Balassa calls *ex ante* and *ex post* approaches. The *ex ante* approach implies building a model with parameters (tariffs), behaviour equations (foreign-trade elasticities) and some equilibrium conditions (exports = imports, etc.). By introducing known or assumed values of parameters and variables and simulating the tariff changes a given customs union would entail, a new trade pattern is established and trade creation and trade diversion can be calculated. This is a test of traditional customs union theory. Applying the weighting procedure suggested by Scitovsky or Meade or the one derived in my thesis, we can quantify the effect on economic welfare as defined by the same authors.

The *ex post* method is to look at changes in international-trade patterns over a given period within which a customs union came into existence and try to identify the changes which are due to the formation of the union. This procedure is not really a test of traditional customs-union theory. Even if it is successful in weeding out all changes that have nothing to do with the union, it will present a hotch potch of customs-union effects which may also be due to, for example, increased or decreased monopoly elements, increased spread of know-how, or widened economic horizons in business. While these may be very important, they will corrupt the results as tests of traditional theory.

Both types of approaches have mainly been concentrated on the effects of customs unions on foreign trade, while the second step involving a calculation of the gains in terms of saved resources (or the opposite) has received less attention.

The investigations that come closest to being tests of traditional customs-union theory are the *ex ante* estimates, which are based on knowledge of trade structure in a given base year, the tariff changes connected with the union and a set of estimated foreign-trade elasticities. Such calculations have been made by two Dutch economists, Verdoorn (1954) and Janssen (1961), who both worked with variants of a general equilibrium approach. In the case of Verdoorn this only means that he calculated the exchange-rate corrections that would be necessary to restore the balance of trade of each member country to its pre-union state, while Janssen also brings in resources and total expenditure in a simple manner.

The difficulty in all *ex ante* studies is, of course, to get information on how export supply and import demand would react to the parameter shifts, i.e. the tariff changes. Verdoorn assumed that export supply elasticities were infinite and that elasticities of substitution were uniform in all countries. Substitution elasticity was set at $-\frac{1}{2}$ between domestic production and imports and at -2 between imports from different countries. The investigation covered manufactured products except iron and steel at SITC three-digit level and the elasticities were assumed uniform over all these commodity groups as well. An average of the west European tariffs weighted by imports was assumed to be the external tariff of the customs union.

Verdoorn reached the result that the volume of intra-west European trade would rise by 19 per cent while imports from outsiders would fall by 6 per cent. If exchange revisions were to be undertaken to restore the balance-of-payments positions prior to union, the net result would be an increase in intra-trade of 14 per cent, imports from outsiders would hardly change and exports to outsiders would fall by about 5 per cent.

Janssen's results, which refer to the customs union of the Six, are less easily summarized as he worked with several alternative values of elasticities and with the cases of complete and incomplete specialization. Furthermore, he did not give aggregated results for the whole customs union. However, I have calculated such aggregates for the case of incomplete specialization from his material in order to make possible a comparison with Verdoorn. Janssen worked with two values of the elasticities of substitution of demand ($Q = 1$ and $Q = 4$), which he regards as a very low and a very high value respectively. It appears that the effect on EEC's trade with third countries would be a reduction by 3–5 per cent under either elasticity assumption, while intra-trade would increase by 64 per cent in the first case and by 161 per cent in the second case. The equilibrium in the balance of payments is here produced by the model itself.

In a recent study of the NAFTA proposals Balassa has calculated how the trade pattern in industrial goods between industrialized market economies would change as compared to 1960 (1967b). This year was selected as base year on the assumption that EFTA and EEC had not yet changed the trade structure too much. As Balassa assumed that the group accounted for virtually all exports of industrial goods he could work with import demand elasticities only and avoid substitution problems. Export supply elasticities were assumed infinite in the variant referred to here.[2] The conclusion was that free trade in industrial

2. An alternative where West European countries were assumed to raise their export prices by a third of the tariff cut did not produce a too different result for the total. Neither does it seem to matter much if the new concept of effective tariff rate is utilized. The discussion of effective tariff rate seems to be heading for the conclusion that it is to the underdeveloped countries that the distinction between nominal and effective rates is important.

goods would increase the volume of trade of the industrialized market economies in such goods by 21 per cent. Total trade would rise by about 10 per cent.

Finally, the Economist Intelligence Unit made a forecast of the effect a European Free Trade Area would have on British trade with Western Europe (1957). These estimates are less suitable for the purpose of testing customs-union theory, as they deal exclusively with the effect on British trade, but the results cast a certain light on the quantitative aspects of customs unions. British exports of manufactures to Western Europe were estimated to increase by 160 per cent and imports by 75 per cent over the fifteen-year period 1955–70. These are high figures, higher than the two Dutch estimates, but it seems reasonable that this should be the case, as trade with Western Europe accounts for a rather low share of total British foreign trade and British foreign trade in its turn accounts for a relatively low share of British output and expenditure. It is difficult to know how much of this assumed change would be due to increased British participation in the international division of labour (trade creation) and how much would just be the result of the discrimination between Britain's trade partners in favour of Western European countries (trade diversion). The Economist Intelligence Unit does not say anything on this for British exports while imports from third countries are said to be rather unaffected by British membership of a West European free trade area.

Now, all these four estimates of the effects of tariff dismantling on foreign trade can be and have been criticized for various deficiencies. Balassa goes as far as declaring Verdoorn's results useless as forecasts of the changes in West European trade patterns following the formation of a customs union. He points, in particular, to the possibility that elasticities may be much higher in the long run than they are in the short run (1961). Janssen obtained larger effects on trade mainly because he assumed higher values for the elasticity of substitution of imports, and there is little to stop us from asserting that they would be even higher in the very long run. The calculation of the effects on Britain of free trade with Western Europe are based on informed guesses by experts in various branches of industry and are not open to detailed criticism of methods. Another set of experts, more optimistic or pessimistic, might have reached completely different results.

As a Western European customs union or free-trade area has

not been created it is not possible to test either Verdoorn's or the Economist Intelligence Unit's estimates against *ex post* data. Janssen's forecast, however, referring to the Six, can be compared to a large number of attempts to identify the tariff effect on EEC trade. It is true that Janssen assumes the full tariff effect to be seen only after fifteen to twenty years, while the empirical studies refer to such a short period that the tariff integration was not even completed, but the comparison is nevertheless interesting.

We will limit ourselves here to three of the most recent studies by economists who have had material available at least up to 1963; namely, Trappeniers (1965), Duquesne de la Vinelle (1965) and Balassa (1967a). All these three studies try to weed out the tendency towards regionalization of the foreign trade of the Six that was present already before 1958. The Trappeniers study, which is methodologically by far the simplest, assumes that the acceleration since 1958 in the growth of the share of intra-trade in the total trade of the Six is due to the Common Market. Trappeniers concludes that over the period 1957/8–1962/3 intra-trade rose by 65 per cent due to the Common Market. How much of this is trade creation in the true sense and how much is trade diversion is not discussed and Trappeniers furthermore believes that only half of this increase is due to the customs union part of the EEC. Duquesne de la Vinelle has taken up an ingenious method invented by Verdoorn and Meyer zu Schlochtern (1964) which is based on a comparison of the development of import and export shares. Bringing in other commodities than manufactures, and introducing 1964 figures, Duquesne de la Vinelle found that according to this method trade creation had amounted to $4000 million in 1956–64 or to 22 per cent. (Verdoorn and Schlochtern had estimated 26 per cent on manufactures, excluding semi-manufactured metals, for the period 1956–62.) This is the total common-market effect, however, and the pure tariff effect is likely to have been lower. Verdoorn and Schlochtern estimated the tariff effect in their study at about two-thirds of the total. Also, the element of trade diversion is uncertain.

Balassa, finally, takes his starting point in the tendencies to regionalization of intra-West European trade that were discernible already in the 1950s. He therefore calculates the income elasticity of imports from various countries for the period 1953–9 and assumes that in the absence of the Common Market these would have remained unchanged. By applying these income elasticities to the realized growth rates in the Six in 1959–65 and comparing with the actual development, which displays higher income elasticities, he gets a difference in trade patterns in 1965 which can be attributed to the creation of the Common Market. The trade creation in intra-trade would then be about 13 per cent and the increase[3] in imports from third countries due to the Common Market would be about 1 per cent, calculated at current prices.

In addition to the attempts to identify the effect on trade patterns of the customs union of the Six there are some other recent studies of the effect of tariff dismantling that contribute to our knowledge of the quantitative aspects. Verdoorn has made a study of the patterns of intra-bloc trade of Benelux in 1955, when intra-Benelux tariffs and all qualitative restrictions on manufactures had been abolished for six to seven years, as compared with trade patterns in 1938 and in 1928 (1960). He then found that the Benelux shares of the three countries' exports and imports added together had increased from about 11 per cent in 1928 and 1938 to over 16 per cent in 1955. At the same time the share of OEEC trade in total trade of OEEC members had remained about the same. It would be tempting to conclude that Benelux has led to trade creation of considerable importance. However, making the same calculation for five other small OEEC countries, Denmark, Italy, Norway, Sweden and Switzerland, he finds that their mutual trade as a share of their total trade (exports plus imports) rose from 9 per cent in 1928 to 11·3 per cent in 1938 and to 13·6 per cent in 1955.

Percentage increase in share of mutual trade

	Benelux	Five countries
1928–55	42	51
1938–55	50	20

It is undeniable that in the latter period intra-Benelux trade shows a very rapid increase, but it appears that the tendency for all small developed West European countries to enter into more intensive trade relations with each other is an important part of the explanation. Making a regression analysis on manufactured exports from the Netherlands to BLEU, Verdoorn estimates that

3. The increase is due to the behaviour of oil and machinery, where special explanations apply. For other commodity groups a trade diversion effect was registered.

the increase of its share in Belgian imports in 1938–55 was around 125 per cent of which, at most, around 65 per cent could be assumed to be due to the customs union. The material is not presented in such a way that an increase of intra-trade due to the union can be quoted in dollars or percentage increase of intra-trade, but seeing that manufactures probably did not account for more than half of Dutch exports and BLEU did not receive more than some 15 per cent of total Dutch exports the figures involved cannot be all that large.

Wemelsfelder has made a study of the effect on German imports of the unilateral tariff reductions undertaken by that country in 1956 as counter-inflationary measures (1960). On finished industrial goods these cuts amounted to nearly half of the original tariff level, while duties on semi-manufactures were cut by considerably less. Wemelsfelder made a correlation analysis of national income with imports and with domestic production minus exports for the years 1950–58 (after the reduction). For finished industrial goods the result was quite impressive, with very clear-cut trend changes in the expected directions. Comparing actual figures registered for 1958 with what they would have been according to the trends from the earlier 1950s he found that imports were twice as high as would have been expected, an increase by 2500 million DM. At the same time production for the home market was 3200 million DM lower than the earlier trend; while total production increased due to increased exports. Wemelsfelder points out that even if Germany's terms of trade did not deteriorate, the import price elasticity would be as high as 8–10, since the tariff changes corresponded to price cuts of 10–12 per cent while imports doubled. For semi-manufactures a similar correlation analysis gave a weaker reaction but in the right direction.

The two obvious objections that worsening price competitiveness or some exogenous shift in demand preference may have happened to occur around the mid-1950s are shown to be invalid and Wemelsfelder's results may therefore seem to be fairly water-tight. Nevertheless, a comparison with the less dramatic results obtained in studies already referred to inevitably creates some suspicion, and I would venture the following suggestion as to why the effect of those German tariff reductions may have been smaller than this analysis appears to imply.

Wemelsfelder's approach is based on the implicit assumption that no other change in German economic conditions was taking place simultaneously. Two such propositions, just referred to, are disproved. However, if one reflects upon the reasons for these tariff reductions one realizes that the German economy was in a rather interesting plight in the mid-1950s. Its low-valued currency had resulted in strongly export-led growth after the currency reform in 1948. As long as supply could expand rapidly enough this did not cause an upward adjustment of the German price level in relation to its trade partners, through imported inflation. The European boom in 1955–8 coupled with full use of German industrial capacity created fears, however, that inflation abroad would spread to Germany. More precisely, it was desirable that the largely export-induced excess demand in Germany should be satisfied through imports, but it was undesirable that this should be brought about by an upward adjustment in the German price level. As Germany could not expect foreign price levels to fall, the alternative was to affect the terms at which German and foreign goods exchanged in Germany, and so the government resorted to tariff cuts.[4]

If this is a correct analysis of the German situation in 1955–7, Wemelsfelder's correlation results do not prove what he contends. It seems likely that he is generalizing from a too special case. If one opens the dam gates in a flood rather than have them broken, it does not follow that one will obtain the same magnificent spectacle whenever they are opened. On the other hand, it would then follow that unilateral tariff reductions may be an efficient means to meet inflationary pressures. However, it could be that high supply elasticities abroad and in Germany coupled with high elasticity of substitution of demand in Germany did most of the job so that much the same result on imports and price levels would have been obtained also without the tariff reductions. It seems safe to conclude, anyway, that there is a considerable degree of exaggeration in Wemelsfelder's estimates of the tariff sensitivity of German imports.

A more recent study with a similar objective by Kreinin (1961) uses the fact that the United States has granted important tariff concessions over wide ranges of commodities in the 1950s, for a study of the quantitative effect of tariff cuts on imports. As the concessions were not all-inclusive Kreinin is able to establish control groups of similar composition that had not been subject

4. Other possibilities open to the German government would have been revaluation, which was resorted to in 1961 under similar conditions, and export duties, which Finland used, in a sense, when she devalued in 1957.

to tariff concessions. Kreinin's most significant result is that in the period 1955–9, the volume of imports on which tariffs had been cut by 15 per cent in 1956 (implying a decrease by 2·5 per cent in price) increased by 66 per cent, while the control group increased by 54 per cent. Taken at face value this would mean that the reduced group was 12 per cent higher than it would have been without the tariff concessions. As export prices rose by 3·9 per cent in the reduced group and by 2·4 per cent in the control group, it could be assumed that the difference (1·5 per cent) was the exporter's share, and that the remaining 1 per cent went to American buyers. The import price elasticity would then be 8 per cent: 1 per cent = 8, which is virtually identical with Wemelsfelder's very high elasticity for Germany.

Again, the risk of overestimation is present. Kreinin does himself point out that the control group is likely to have been affected negatively since it contains substitutes. We would put it in the terms that we do not know the extent of intercommodity trade diversion just as we often do not know the extent of international-trade diversion. The fact that imports in general account for a very small share of the American market is another reason why one would expect the import increase to be very high as a percentage of imports. If imports accounted for about 5 per cent of American purchases of these goods a shift to foreign sources of an additional 1 per cent would leave us with a 20 per cent increase in imports.

There are many aspects to criticize in both the *ex ante* and the *ex post* estimates. In particular both the elasticity estimates in the *ex ante* approaches and the assumption in the *ex post* approaches that the 1950s were 'normal' in the sense of being unaffected by geographically biased trade liberalization are doubtful. Also, the goods that have had their tariffs lowered are not random samples, but are the result of political decisions according to certain criteria. For the present purpose, however, it should suffice to conclude that calculation methods hitherto used point to the conclusion that the direct quantitative effect on trade of a customs union consisting of Western European countries is surprisingly small, and that, in general, the effect of tariff cuts on trade between industrialized countries is not large. It appears from the following schedule that really high figures have been recorded only for the individual countries, Britain, the Netherlands, the USA and Germany. We have already pointed out that rather small shares of trade and consumption are involved in the first three cases, and that the result for Germany is likely to be a vast exaggeration of the tariff sensitivity of imports.

Empirical investigations

Author	Location		Tariff change	Percentage increase in intra-trade in goods covered by study
	Geographic	Historic		
Verdoorn	Western Europe	1952	to nil	+19
Janssen	EEC	1956	to nil	+64 or +161
Balassa	NAFTA	1960	to nil	+21
Economist Intelligence Unit	Britain with Western Europe	1955–70	to nil	Exports +160 Imports +75
Trappeniers	EEC	1957/8– 1962/3	by 50%	+30–+35
Duquesne de la Vinelle	EEC	1956–64	by 60%	max. +22
Balassa	EEC	1959–65	by 70%	+13
Verdoorn	Dutch exports to BLEU	1938–55	to nil	max. +65
Wemelsfelder	German imports	1955–8	by 50%	+100
Kreinin	US imports	1955–9	by 15%	+8

Janssen's *ex ante* estimates are higher than Verdoorn's simply because he assumes higher elasticities than Verdoorn and at least for the elasticity of substitution of imports his reason for doing so appears unwarranted. The three tests of Common Market tariff reductions all give unexpectedly low percentage increases and the highest, Trappeniers's, does not attempt to identify the diversion effect. On the other hand we have to keep in mind that they studied the result of a construction only half way on its road to completion. If lags rather than anticipation mark the behaviour of the traders[5] future developments may be more dramatic.

To estimate the gains in terms of GNP or some other welfare measure of a customs union, is, of course, an even more difficult thing to do than to try to estimate the effect on trade flows. Nevertheless, such attempts have been made by a number of authors who have felt that this is necessary, if results of use for the policy discussions are to be obtained.

5. Some choose an early year such as 1956 for base year, referring to anticipation as an explanation of a rise in intra-trade before the implementation of the customs union. Duquesne de la Vinelle does this and remarks that an extrapolation of the observed trend over a generation will give a very impressive result.

Utilizing Verdoorn's material for Western Europe and weighting the trade changes with tariffs roughly in the Marshallian way, Scitovsky concluded that Western Europe would gain an increase in GNP of 0·05 per cent. Johnson (1958) performed a similar operation on the *Economist* Intelligence Unit's material and concluded that the gain in the British GNP from free trade with Europe would then be about 1 per cent, though he thought this an excessive figure. Janssen, on his own material, obtained a maximum gain of $\frac{1}{2}$ per cent in the combined GNP of the Six using a different general equilibrium method of calculation of his own.

The Wemelsfelder study indicated that manufactures worth 2500 million 1954 DM were produced with about 5 per cent less resource input after the tariff cuts; a gain of 125 million DM compared to a German GNP in 1958 of about 200,000 million DM, i.e. a gain of about 0·05 per cent. Reasons have been given why this is likely to be an exaggeration.

Finally, Balassa's NAFTA study showed that the trade increase would amount to 0·9 per cent of the combined gross domestic products of the industrialized countries. As tariffs are in the interval 10–15 per cent on average, it seems that about 1 per cent of total resources would be moved from occupations where their productivity is 10–15 per cent lower than normal to occupations where they would be 10–15 per cent more productive. According to this crude estimate the gain to the industrialized world in terms of their total output would be something like one or two thousandths.

These examples will suffice to demonstrate the order of magnitude involved, if one is prepared to apply the ordinary textbook theory of trade in its customs union version to real world quantities. As both Scitovsky and Johnson have pointed out, it does not matter if we find reasons for revising the underlying figures upwards. As long as the basic approach is accepted, the quantitative results will remain extremely small. So small that they would not be measurable in the present systems of national accounts and so small that it would hardly seem worth while to devote so much of the attention of economists, statisticians, politicians and newspaper editors to the problem of removing tariffs between industrialized countries.

The case for a reappraisal

The inconspicuous results obtained in all empirical tests of traditional customs-union theory have led eager proponents of

West European integration to stress the other mechanisms through which a customs union may affect productive efficiency. It has become increasingly common to maintain that traditional theory has little to tell us and that three factors – the exploitation of economies of scale, increased competition and faster economic growth – are the important benefits of customs unions. When these are taken into account, the qualitative effects of customs unions become enormous, if we are to believe this school.

It is, of course, impossible to analyse these contentions in any depth within the present context, but even the following very fundamental observations make the possibility of an *Ehrenrettung* along those lines unlikely.

The existence of economies of scale is undeniable and it seems obvious that their effect on industrial structure and productivity is fundamental. It does not follow, however, that existing tariffs are an important obstacle to the exploitation of such economies. Where the fall in unit costs from a production increase based on sales in foreign markets is larger than the import duties levied in those markets the exploitation of economies of scale is not prevented by tariff walls. If one reflects on the structure of world trade one realizes that such economies are already being exploited to a large extent. Tariffs change the distribution of income rather than the pattern of trade in these cases. At the same time the existence of several firms competing in identical products even in small protected markets must imply that unexploited economies of scale either are not present or remain unexploited for other reasons than existing tariff walls.

Strictly speaking, the economies of scale argument in customs union theory applies only in the case where unit costs of a monopoly firm would fall by less than the average tariff abroad even at a considerable increase in the scale production. The frequency of this situation seems doubtful. My hypothesis, which will be the starting point for a future study of customs unions, is that, while the existence of economies of scale is a very important feature in industrial economies, they are either already being exploited or, when not, their exploitation is not generally conditional upon the removal of national tariff barriers, but rather upon the removal of political risks and imperfect knowledge in business. Certain aspects of international economic integration may contribute to such a development, but this is then not a problem of customs union theory.

The second mechanism, stressed by Scitovsky, can be dealt with in a similar way. The effect of weak competition can appear at several levels. The first is the textbook case of restricted production and higher sales price, which is rational behaviour if short-run profit maximization governs the behaviour of business. Secondly, entrepreneurs may be using inefficient methods of production in a less competitive climate, because to change them requires a psychological exertion that is uncomfortable. In both cases increased competition would bring about a change implying improved utilization of resources.

Again there is a limit to the extent to which this inefficiency can be conditional upon the level of protection. We would venture the hypothesis that important gains can be reaped from fiercer competition, but that imperfect knowledge and political risks are again the obstacles rather than national tariffs. Hardening competition since the 1950s in Western Europe does not appear to have been very closely correlated with the establishment of EFTA and EEC, and it is typical that Scitovsky puts more faith in American business behaviour spreading from the US to Europe than in the independent nascence of a more competitive spirit inside a Western European customs union.

As for the third argument, its vagueness makes it virtually impossible to treat it in the general manner used for the other two. 'The dynamic argument' is obviously a hotch potch, containing all sorts of dynamic variants of what has been said above. To begin with we have to weed out the increase in economic growth that the adjustment processes predicted by the other mechanisms would entail, as these would be once-for-all gains, only spread out over an historic period. They are not additive to the gains calculated in the other static mechanisms, they are the same.

Moreover, it seems likely that permanent increases in growth rates arising from tariff changes would have their mirror images among the other types of reactions in a static world, so that the previous comments would apply there, too. Take the following example: assume that petrochemicals is an industry in which the prospects of technological progress are much more promising than for industry on average. Assume further that no West European country is a big enough market to allow the exploitation of economies of scale in that industry. The United States will get this kind of industry, but not Western Europe and this will, *ceteris paribus*, make the rate of economic growth permanently higher in America. Only with West Europe as one market will the area get its share of such growth industries.[6]

Our point is that the validity of this dynamic argument will depend on the validity of the static economies-of-scale argument: the economies of scale must be very important and yet too small to outweigh the tariff costs on exports to Western Europe.

Obviously, this discussion cannot lead us much further without the development of a more rigid theoretical framework. We have only wanted to explain here why there are good reasons to expect that the results of the traditional theory of customs unions may be of greater relevance than one would believe after having been told about all the economies of scale, increased competition and economic growth arguments that it does not deal with. First, if the traditional theory does not lead to a positive judgement on a customs-union project, it seems unlikely that the other two static arguments would tilt the balance the other way. If traditional theory shows that a certain customs union would lead to less specialization according to comparative advantage, it is hard to believe that the loss would be made up for by fiercer competition and/or more specialization to exploit existing economies of scale.[7]

Secondly, dynamic effects are likely to have a static counterpart which can be analysed with the traditional tools. And thirdly, we have made the point that national tariff barriers, at least in Western Europe, may have little to do with the prevailing degree of competition or the extent of utilization of economies of scale.

While these observations may indicate that our traditional approach contains more of the truth about customs unions than is currently believed, it does not follow that the theory must produce very drastic effects of customs unions. We have reached

6. If this case is to assume some kind of generality, we have to introduce a further assumption: rapid growth of demand and fast technological progress are typical for the science-based industries and such industries display important economies of scale due to large overheads in research and development and in fixed investment. This assumption seems to be realistic enough.

7. We are referring here to the directly economic effect of the tariff changes. It is not at all unlikely that even a strongly protectionist customs union as a political manifestation might widen the economic horizon of business and reduce the risks of intra-union trade. This could lead to fiercer competition and the exploitation of existing economies of scale to the extent that production might rise on balance.

a number of conclusions about heights of tariffs, price sensitivities, size of union, complementarity and competitiveness of affected countries, etc. The analysis, conducted in traditional terms, casts a certain light on some of the policy conclusions commonly drawn from customs union theory. Nevertheless, the investigation of the empirical work undertaken shows that the quantitative effect of customs unions is likely to be very small and these statistical tests conform roughly to traditional theory. If my hypothesis holds, that the other arguments for customs unions are not likely to lead to very different judgements from those obtained in traditional theory, we are left with the conclusion that existing tariffs do not in themselves seriously disturb the division of labour in the industrialized world.

This may be a surprising conclusion after all the fuss about customs unions, free trade areas and Kennedy Round negotiations, but there are in fact good reasons why this should be true. The most obvious is that, after all, a rather small part of the total production result is traded internationally. Services, the public sector, building and construction are not affected by tariffs. But there is probably another explanation which is generally overlooked. If the removal of protection is to make a real difference it is because the previous protection was really costly to the economy and such instances are very difficult to find, because there has been no political support for such wasteful protection. The most extreme cases are, of course, raw materials, where domestic production may be physically impossible or possible only at astronomic costs. Raw materials are normally duty-free. The same is true about the most specialized commodities, ships, aircraft, computers, machine tools, heavy printing equipment, nuclear reactors, hydroelectric turbines, etc. In fact, most countries allow exemptions from import duty on all investment goods which the importer can prove to be unavailable from domestic producers. This rule may have quite important effects in small countries with less diversified industrial production. For the same reason small countries normally have lower tariffs than big countries. It would be too costly for them to forgo the gains from specialization.

In fact, the gains from international trade are enormous because natural resources and specialized skills are so unevenly distributed geographically. It does not follow, however, that the removal of existing tariffs would be of great importance. On the contrary, no industrialized country has been able to, or willing to, accept the cost of disturbing seriously the international division of labour by high tariffs. This is the reason why we find that proposed customs unions and even Atlantic free trade would bring such small gains. The gains from trade are either already being reaped or, if not, their exploitation is not conditional upon duty-free imports, but on closer international contact and better knowledge of foreign markets on the part of business.

This view is supported also by the experience of regional liberalization of trade inside the Common Market, which has not led to the close-down of industries or an increased rate of bankruptcies. On the other hand, the anxiety expressed by particular industries or companies about the effects of tariff discrimination are not incompatible with the notion that effects from across--the-board tariff cuts are minor. First, there may, of course, be individual cases where existing protection really implies quantitatively important waste. Agricultural production in Sweden is an outstanding example. It seems that the Swedish people may be using twice the amount of resources they need (Gulbrandsen and Lindbeck, 1966), but the following should be noted:

(a) that this is partly seen as a defence cost;
(b) that this is seen as a temporary arrangement necessary because moving labour out of agriculture to industry is a much more complicated process than intra-industry reallocation;
(c) that the cost is only a few per cent of GNP;
(d) that in spite of (a)–(c) this agricultural policy is an important political issue.

Secondly, even if a whole industry would have to close down when its protection was removed, the alternative use of the freed resources may be only slightly more productive. This is in fact likely, as seen from the previous discussion. Thirdly, the position of industries threatened by loss of tariff protection may be over-dramatized because they do not take into account the exchange rate revision (downwards) that a high tariff country would have to undertake simultaneously with an extensive dismantling of tariffs.

In summary my general conclusions from the analysis conducted so far would be the following. The traditional foreign-trade theory in its customs-union application may have a higher explanatory value than is often assumed. The extent to which such factors as economies of scale, degree of competition and dynamic relationships may change its results remains to be investigated. I have, however, presented some general reasons why it is likely that their influence on economic life, though considerable, may be only marginally affected by the existing tariffs and by changes in those tariffs.

Our second general conclusion is that the inconspicuous results of empirical customs-union studies are explained by the fact that existing tariffs between industrialized countries are, on the average, not important obstacles to the international division of labour. The reason is that the general interest has prevailed over the particular interest in the vast majority of cases. Protection that is really costly in terms of national product does in fact not exist, at least not outside agriculture.

This does not imply that the gains from international trade are small. On the contrary, they are enormous. The implication is that the gains from trade are already being exploited and when they are not, the reason is usually not tariff walls. Our hypothesis is that uncertainty about future international relations, ignorance of conditions in foreign countries and the accumulated effect of thousands of big and small differences between countries in institutional and social respects are the real obstacles to a further extension of the international division of labour. The tariffs levied are only a minor part of this.

We end up by a remark on what the conclusions for trade policy would be. It seems that a customs union, even if it is proved to be beneficial, is not a very important thing. On the other hand, economic integration in the widest sense of the concept is progress along all the three frontiers, reducing uncertainty, ignorance and cultural heterogeneity. This process is to a large extent an historical process which takes place rather independently of deliberate attempts such as EEC or EFTA. Nevertheless, this integration process must involve a number of political decisions about international cooperation, each of which may add very little to the whole. It does not follow that they can all be turned down on the basis of their unimportance taken separately.

References

BALASSA, B. (1961), *The Theory of Economic Integration*, Allen & Unwin.
BALASSA, B. (1967a), 'Trade creation and trade diversion in the European Common Market', *Econ. J.*, vol. 77.
BALASSA, B. (1967b), *Trade Liberalization among Industrial Countries: Objectives and Alternatives*, McGraw Hill.

BECKER, G. (1957), *The Economics of Discrimination*, University of Chicago Press.

COOPER, C. A., and MASSEL, B. F. (1965), 'A new look at customs-union theory', *Econ. J.*, vol. 75.

DOWNS, A. J. (1957), *An Economic Theory of Democracy*, Harper & Row.

DUQUESNE DE LA VINELLE (1965), *La Création du commerce attribuable au Marché Commun et son incidence sur le volume du produit national de la communauté*, Informations statistiques, no. 4.

ECONOMIST INTELLIGENCE UNIT (1957), *Britain and Europe*.

GEHRELS, F. (1965–7), 'Customs unions from a single country viewpoint', *Rev. Econ. Studies*, vol. 24, no. 63.

GULBRANDSEN, O., and LINDBECK, A. (1966), 'Svensk jordbrukspoiltik mot internationell bakgrund', *Skandinaviska Banken Kvartalsskrift*, vol. 4.

HABERLER, G. (1936), *The Theory of International Trade*, Hodge.

JANSSEN, L. H. (1961), *Free Trade, Protection and Customs Union*, Stenfert Kroese.

JOHNSON, H. G. (1958), 'The gains from freer trade with Europe: an estimate', *Manchester School of Economic and Social Studies*, vol. 26, no. 3.

JOHNSON, H. G. (1960), 'The economic theory of customs unions', *Pakistan Econ. J.*, vol. 10.

JOHNSON, H. G. (1965), 'An economic theory of protectionism, tariff bargaining and the formation of customs unions', *J. Polit. Econ.*, vol. 73.

KEMP, M. C. (1962), 'The gains from international trade', *Econ. J.*, vol. 72.

KREININ, M. E. (1961), 'Effect of tariff changes on the prices and volume of imports', *Amer. Econ. Rev.*, vol. 51, June.

LIPSEY, R. J. (1957), 'The theory of customs unions: trade diversion and welfare', *Economica*, vol. 24.

LIPSEY, R. J. (1961), 'The theory of customs unions: a general survey', *Econ. J.*, vol. 71.

MEADE, J. E. (1955a), *The Theory of Customs Unions*, North Holland.

MEADE, J. E. (1955b), *The Theory of International Economic Policy*, vol. 2, *Trade and Welfare*, Oxford University Press, ch. 5–7.

MEYER ZU SCHLOCHTERN, F., and VERDOORN, P. J. (1964), 'Trade creation and trade diversion in the Common Market', in *Intégration Européenne et Réalité Economique*, Bruges.

MICHAELY, M. (1965), 'On customs unions and the gains from trade', *Econ. J.*, vol. 75, September.

SAMUELSON, P. (1962), 'The gains from international trade once again', *Econ. J.*, vol. 72.

SCITOVSKY, T. (1958), *Economic Theory and Western European Integration*, Allen & Unwin.

SPRAOS, J. (1964), 'The conditions for a trade-creating customs union' *Econ. J.*, vol. 74.

TRAPPENIERS, F. (1965), *L'Economie de marché dans l'intégration de l'Europe Occidentale*, Louvain.

VERDOORN, P. J. (1954), 'A customs union for Western Europe – advantages and feasibility', *World Politics*, vol. 6.

VERDOORN, P. J. (1960), 'The intra-bloc trade of Benelux', in E. A. G. Robinson (ed.), *Economic Consequences of the Size of Nations*, Macmillan.

VINER, J. (1950), *The Customs Union Issue*, Carnegie Endowment, New York.

WEMELSFELDER, J. (1960), 'The short-term effect of the lowering of import duties in Germany', *Econ. J.*, vol. 70.

9 Roger Hansen

Regional Integration: Reflections on a
Decade of Theoretical Efforts

R. Hansen, 'Regional integration; reflections on a decade of theoretical
efforts', *World Politics*, vol. 21, no. 2, 1969, pp. 242–56.

The appearance of major studies by Karl Deutsch and Ernst
Haas in the late 1950s won for integration theory a prominent
position among the contemporary approaches to the study of
international relations (Deutsch *et al.*, 1957; Haas, 1958). A
decade later its achievements are very much a matter of debate.
While many students of integration theory have been led, by disappointment with results, to focus their attention on smaller and
more manageable units, such as local communities and city-
suburb relations, others continue investigations at the international level.[1]

Among the latter group the so-called 'neo-functionalists' have
been particularly prominent, largely because of the favorable
reception accorded to Haas's *The Uniting of Europe*. For some
time Europe remained the focal point for most of the works on
regional integration, but in the past several years the application
of integration theory to Latin America, Africa and Asia has
become increasingly fashionable. During the course of these
endeavors Haas and Philippe Schmitter have developed a conceptual framework that they suggest will illuminate the process
of regional integration in the European environment and in less
developed areas of the world as well. Since Haas has studied
integration efforts in both industrial and non-industrial settings
and has attempted to devise a conceptual approach applicable
to both, an investigation of some of the limitations it entails
provides a fairly accurate assessment of the present neo-functional
contribution to regional integration theory. This is true for two
reasons: Haas is one of the most thoughtful and sophisticated
theorists of regional integration; and most, though not all, of his

1. For some of the recent trends in the literature on political integration,
see Jacob and Toscano (1964).

major concepts and conclusions complement and confirm those of other leading students in the field.[2]

A model of regional integration

'Does the economic integration of a group of nations automatically trigger political unity? Or are the two processes quite distinct, requiring deliberate political steps because purely economic arrangements are generally inadequate for ushering in political unity?' (Haas and Schmitter, 1966). The Haas–Schmitter model is specifically addressed to the question of the automaticity of the link between economic and political integration; and their thesis is that 'under modern conditions the relationship between economic and political union had best be treated as a continuum' (p. 261). Why? In order to portray the Haas–Schmitter views most fully and fairly, their answer is presented with no intervening interpretation:

Linkages between economic objectives and policies, on the one hand, and political consequences of a disintegrative or integrative nature, on the other, are of a 'functional' character: they rest very often on indirection, on unplanned and accidental convergence in outlook and aspiration among the actors, on dialectical relations between antagonistic purposes. They also frequently contain elements of creative personal action by administrators who seize upon crises, the solution of which upgrades common interests among the actors; hence they include an organizational component which may, depending on the organization, be of dominant significance. Integration can be conceived as involving the *gradual politicization* of the actors' purposes which were initially considered 'technical' or 'non-controversial'. Politicization implies that the actors, in response to the initial purposes, agree to widen the spectrum of means considered appropriate to attain them. This tends to increase the controversial component, i.e. those additional fields of action which require political choices concerning how much national autonomy to delegate to the union. Politicization implies that the actors seek to resolve their problems so as to upgrade common interests and, in the process, delegate more authority to the center. It constitutes one of the properties of integration – the intervening variable between economic and political union – along with the development of new expectations and loyalties on the part of organized interests in the member nations (p. 261–2, italics added).

The authors define a successful political union as a regional entity upon which actors bestow a 'significant portion of their

2. See, for example, the various writings by Deutsch, including his several essays in Jacob and Toscano (1964); by Amitai Etzioni (1964); and essays collected in Davison (1966).

loyalties'. They posit that a successful union implies an end to threats of revolt or secession even though the scope of central control continues to be extended. 'In other words, a political union can be said to exist when the politicized decision-making process has acquired legitimacy and authority' (pp. 265–6).

Having developed the dynamic of *politicization*, Haas and Schmitter construct three sets of observable variables 'which seem to intervene more or less consistently between the act of economic union and the possible end product we label political union' (p. 266). They consist of *background variables* (size of member-units, rates of interunit transactions, extent of social pluralism within the units, and elite complementarity), *variables at the moment of economic union* (degree of shared government purposes, and powers delegated to the union), and *process variables* (decision-making style, post-integration rates of transactions, and the adaptability of governments in situations of disappointment and crisis). High, mixed, or low ratings are to be determined for each set of variables as they are applied to the study of any regional grouping. The higher the scores, the more likely it is that an economic union will automatically be transformed into a form of political union.

Because a spillover is likely to occur in these cases [i.e. cases of high scores for all three sets of variables], the functional adaptation to its implications is likely to be 'automatic' in the sense that the participating actors will make the kinds of decisions which will safeguard their collective economic welfare (p. 274).

The lower the scores, the less the automaticity and the more difficult the move from economic to political union.

With the exception of the final variable – adaptability in crises – all are familiar in the literature of regional integration and need not be discussed here. A further word should be said about the adaptability measurement, however, because it involves an issue of some importance to our following analysis of the Haas–Schmitter scheme and Haas's original theoretical observations upon the course of European integration. Haas has consistently maintained that economic integration will have more spillover into a broad range of political issues than will any other functional approach – i.e. that economic issues and policies are less 'autonomous' than others. The process of spillover from economic integration will not only lead to *gradual politicization*, but also to occasional *crises*. 'Crisis is the creative opportunity for realizing [the] potential to redefine aims at a higher level of consensus' (p. 273). Thus, a low degree of autonomy characterizing modern industrialized economic sectors and the propensity for economic integration involving such economies to engender crises are crucial assumptions in Haas's 'expansive logic of economic integration', and will be analysed below.

A final element in the Haas–Schmitter model should be noted – the concept of the 'functional equivalent'. The authors argue that in Western Europe

the element of automaticity to which we have called attention is provided by the internal logic of industrialism, pluralism and democracy. . . . Industrial society is *the* setting in which supranationality and a lively spillover process are able to flourish. . . . [However,] specific regions may well possess unique cultural or stylistic attributes which are able to serve as *functional equivalents* for important traits isolated in [Western Europe] (pp. 284–5, italics added).

Much of the article in which this model appears is devoted to a study of the functional equivalents in the Latin American scene which may help to overcome the otherwise low scores that the authors attribute to their integration variables in the case of the Latin American Free Trade Association (LAFTA).

A critique

The theoretical and empirical weaknesses in the model may best be illustrated by applying it to the process of integration first in Western Europe, and then in less developed regions of the world. The Haas treatment of European integration might be sketched thus: within the European economy limited sectoral agreements so increase trade flows and ensuing common problems that a supranational bureaucracy develops to deal with them, and an ever-broadening number of economic activities are touched by growing supranational jurisdiction. Industrial groups also organize at the new regional level in order to influence the emerging power centers. Over time these centers of jurisdiction are granted increasing powers; political loyalties, following in the wake of economic interests, gradually attach themselves to the new supranational entities. As Haas recently summarized his early views,

The superiority of step-by-step economic decisions over crucial political choices is assumed as permanent; the determinism implicit in the picture of the European social and economic structure is almost absolute. Given all these conditions, we said, the progression from a politically inspired common market to an economic union, and finally to a political union among states, is automatic (1967).

The major question that has arisen over the Haas analysis (and prognosis) is the necessary extent of the political ramifications of economic union in the Western European case. As Etzioni suggests, 'how far [spillover] carries unification before it is exhausted is a question whose answer is as yet largely unknown' (1964, p. 54). Much recent criticism of the dialectic of spillover simply points to the obvious fact that the pace of European integration has diminished.[3] To the extent that the 'logic of economic integration' as expounded by Haas and other functionalists suggested an inevitability about the eventual political unification of Europe of the Six, this type of criticism appears to have at least temporary validity. Most of it, however, analyses *what* has happened rather than *why* it has happened, thereby contributing little to a better understanding of the integration process in industrially and politically developed regions. Of much greater importance, and therefore considered in some detail below, is a theoretical critique developed by Stanley Hoffmann and others. In addition, economic theory and economic events in the Western European setting suggest some limitations to the spillover thesis that heretofore have been ignored or overlooked.

Economic analysis, both theoretical and empirical, is most helpful, however, in calling into question the relevance of the Haas–Schmitter model to the understanding of the connections between economic and political integration in Latin America and other semi-industrial and non-industrial regions. One perceptive student of regional integration in African and Latin American settings has suggested that in many underdeveloped areas 'much that in the European context would be simple welfare politics becomes tinged with emotive and symbolic content that is usually associated with national security politics. One consequence . . . is that there is less opportunity for autonomous bureaucrats

3. For contrasting views on the present pace of and prospects for Western European integration, see Inglehart (1967); Deutsch (1966); and Deutsch *et al.* (1967). Whereas Deutsch and his collaborators believe that the integration movement 'has stopped or reached a plateau since 1957–8,' Inglehart argues that the political socialization of Western Europe's post-war youth in a setting of European cooperation has produced an orientation favorable to continued moves toward political integration. These studies provide interesting examples of differing methodological approaches to the study of regional integration, including the use of transactions flow measurements, elite and mass-opinion survey techniques, and content analysis.

to go quietly about the business of integration in "non-controversial" spheres. . . . If the problem in most underdeveloped areas is one of premature "overpoliticization", then it is not helpful for comparative study to conceive of the integration process as "gradual politicization" ' (Nye, 1965). A discussion of the theory and practice of economic integration in such unions as the Central American and East African common markets will both substantiate the objection raised by Nye and suggest the necessity of some major revisions in present neofunctional approaches as applied to economically less developed regions.

Western Europe: 'high' politics and the international system

Stanley Hoffmann recently wrote of Europe of the Six that 'the failure (so far) of an experiment tried in apparently ideal conditions tells us a great deal about contemporary world politics, about the chances of unification movements elsewhere, and about the functional approach to unification. For it shows that the movement can fail not only when there is a surge of nationalism in one important part, but also when there are differences in assessments of the national interest that rule out agreement on the shape and on the world role of the new, supranational whole' (Hoffmann, 1966, p. 867). He argued that 'functional integration's gamble could be won only if the method had sufficient potency to promise a permanent excess of gains over losses, and of hopes over frustrations. Theoretically, this might be true of economic integration. It is not true of political integration (in the sense of "high politics")' (p. 882).

In treating the distinction between 'high politics' and economic welfare issues in this manner, Hoffmann's analysis contrasts sharply with the Haas–Schmitter model, which insists that 'economic and political union had best be treated as a continuum', and Haas's view that 'the advent of supranationality [within the EEC institutions] symbolizes the victory of economics over politics, over that familiar ethnocentric nationalism which used to subordinate butter to guns, reason to passion, statistical bargaining to excited demands' (1963). It is one of two major elements in the Hoffmann approach to the study of regional integration that both differentiates it from that of the neo-functionalists and produces some markedly dissimilar theoretical and empirical observations. Hoffmann, Liska and other 'traditionalists' have consistently argued the validity of the distinction between 'high' and 'low' – or welfare – politics. They view the latter as concerned with interests that are both calculable and representative of only a negligible fraction of a nation's resources. In contrast, high politics has as its core 'the vital interests of national diplomacy and strategy' (Hoffmann, 1968, p. 404). When dealing with these major issues of foreign policy and defence, 'nations prefer the certainty, or the self-controlled uncertainty, of national self-reliance' (Hoffmann, 1966, p. 882) to any commitment to supranational mechanisms. Viewed in this context, the Haas approach to regional integration appears to omit a significant set of variables, and has led Hoffmann to argue that 'as long as the process is not completed, we must analyse the building of the political community as an incipient instance of "interest-group politics", of "domestic politics of the community", and as a continuing example of traditional interstate politics' (Hoffmann, 1963, p. 11).

The second major element in the Hoffmann approach to Western European integration that clearly distinguishes it from that of the neofunctionalists is its emphasis upon the international setting in which the European integration experiment has been undertaken. Hoffmann argues that the failure of the unification movement among the Six to progress into high politics via economic spillover can be traced to the interaction of three elements in the present international system – 'one of which characterizes every international system, and the other two only the present system' (Hoffmann, 1966, p. 864). The universalistic factor is 'the *diversity* of domestic determinants, geo-historical situations, and outside aims among its units; any international system based on fragmentation tends, through the dynamic of unevenness . . . to reproduce diversity' (p. 864). Of the two unique features, one is that today's is 'the first truly *global* international system; the regional subsystems have only a reduced autonomy; the "relationships of major tension" blanket the whole planet' (p. 864).

The inevitable result of the combination of these two international system features, Hoffmann argues, is that intra-Six relations have become 'subordinated to their divergencies about the outside world; the "regional subsystem" becomes a stake in the rivalry of its members about the system as a whole' (p. 865). And he offers as evidence of this dynamic the mounting disagreements among the units of the Six – between France and Germany in particular – over the world role of Europe and its relationship with the United States. The third-system feature – the nuclear age and the present 'stability of a bipolar world' –

supports and expands the operations of national diversity. 'Damocles' sword has become a boomerang, the ideological legitimacy of the nationstate is protected by the relative and forced tameness of the world jungle' (p. 865).

One might add that the legitimacy of the European states of the Six in recent years has been supported not only by the operation of nuclear deterrence, but also by their effectiveness in the areas of economics and welfare. Experiencing some of the world's most rapid growth rates, the Six emerged from their weakened national situations of the immediate post-war years with a renewed capacity to attract popular support. Paradoxically enough, economic integration played a major role in strengthening these national capacities for independent action in other policy areas. Thus the very effectiveness of economic cooperation in stimulating economic growth within the EEC expanded the margins for political conflict among its members on a broad range of foreign and defence policy issues. One of the reasons for the contradictory outcome of the functional approach to regional integration is that the spillover from economics into politics has been to date far more limited than that which Haas had projected, a point which will be developed below.

The Hoffmann analysis thus raises two major issues with regard to the present neofunctional literature on regional integration. The first involves the interaction between what we might label the endogenous and the exogenous variables – between the region engaged in integration schemes on the one hand, and the international environment on the other. The second involves the distinction between high and low politics. Is the traditional view of a discontinuity between the two preferable to the continuum proposed by Haas and Schmitter? The answer to both questions will of course be conditioned as much by one's particular interest in and approach to the study of international relations as by the inherent merits and demerits of present regional integration theory itself. There is evidence to suggest, however, that the neofunctionalist approach should be significantly modified if it is to deal effectively with the range of issues raised by Hoffmann and others.

We shall argue below that the Haas–Schmitter model suffers from a serious theoretical inadequacy in its dealing with regional integration schemes in less developed areas: it does not attempt to isolate and measure those exogenous factors in the international environment that affect the integration *process*. Moreover, its theory is so constructed that questions about the inter-action between subsystem and macro-system do not generally appear relevant to the outcome of integration efforts beyond the initial analysis of 'elite complementarity'. It makes no systematic attempt to locate and measure the effects of international en-vironment changes on elite perceptions within the regional union over time. In the European case, those who approach the study of integration from a different conceptual viewpoint – e.g. that of historical sociology and systems analysis – also raise the same general issue. Hoffmann, as we have seen, traces much of the failure of spillover to the diversity of national situations in Western Europe and the intimate connection between the region and the bipolar relationship of major tension that has structured the international system since the end of the Second World War.[4] These interacting variables engendered Hoffmann's 'logic of diversity', which soon challenged Haas's 'logic of integration' (i.e. spillover) in the race for Europe's future. While much empiri-cal work remains to be done in order to test the relevance of the variables suggested by Hoffmann and others who employ some-what similar modes of conceptualization, the limitations inherent in the neo-functionalist approach should encourage further efforts in that direction.

Haas himself has recently recognized that 'something is missing' in his exploration of the integration process in Western Europe (Haas, 1958, p. 327). But he does not view the inadequacy of his original theory as a product of its disregard for the inter-action between exogenous and endogenous variables. Rather he continues to focus exclusively on aspects internal to regional integration experiments, and concludes that he underestimated the 'built-in limits' of pragmatic interest politics concerned with economic welfare.

Pragmatic interests, simply because they are pragmatic and not reinforced with deep ideological or philosophical commitment, are ephemeral. . . . And a political process which is built and projected from pragmatic interests, therefore, is bound to be a frail process, susceptible to reversal. And so integration can once more develop into disintegration (pp. 327–8).

The halting of the gradual move towards political union in Western Europe followed the rejection by de Gaulle's EEC

4. A nation's 'situation,' in Hoffmann's terms, is 'made up altogether of its internal features – what, in an individual, would be called heredity and character – and of its position in the world' (p. 868).

partners of his bid for a common foreign and defence policy, and his subsequent failure to lure the Bonn government away from its Washington moorings. It appears that at this point the General was unwilling to allow the Community to pass into its third stage, which would have instituted a process of decision-making by a majority-vote method in the Council of Ministers. Although not all of his reasons are yet known, the outcome of his stand during the 1965 crisis was to restrain effectively the movement toward supranationality within the Six.[5] Thus the integration movement, based on 'pragmatic politics', was stalled by the opposition of one member state whose government viewed increased supranationality as detrimental to its own conception of a proper European foreign policy and defence posture.

Haas develops the following matrix to encompass his amended views of regional integration:

Aims of non-governmental elites

		Dramatic-political	*Incremental-economic*
Aims of Statesmen	Dramatic-Political	Integration either direct and smooth; or impossible	Integration erratic and reversible
	Incremental-Economic	Integration erratic and reversible	Integration gradual but automatic

The trouble with Haas's amended approach is that it offers many possibilities without suggesting how we are to account for any of them. What situations, events, pressures are conducive to the dramatic-political integrative leadership of a Bismarck, a Cavour? When will similarly motivated elites appear? To say, as Haas does, that 'reliance on high politics demands either a statesman of this calibre or a widely shared normative elite consensus' (1958, p. 328) and that 'in most actual situations in which regional integration is desired, neither ingredient is present in sufficient quantity' (p. 328) may indicate something about the general distribution of an integration effort's basic ingredients. However,

5. All discussions of these events are conjectural, though some are undoubtedly better reasoned than others. Leon Lindberg argues that de Gaulle's efforts were an attempt not so much to halt the process of integration as to restructure the EEC so as to provide France a maximum leverage within the Community (see Lindberg, 1966).

such static observations are of limited value in explaining, for any given case, either the initial 'mix' of the variables or the dynamic process itself.

The appearance of a de Gaulle remains a mystery within the context of the Haas approach, and Haas still refers to France as the 'deviant case' within the Six (p. 319). In terms of the contrasting Hoffmann paradigm, the interaction of international-system characteristics and the process of European integration suggests the inevitability of such 'deviance' as perceptions change on the part of one actor or another. Thus, while Haas's amended theory is surely strengthened by his recognition that 'integration and disintegration as two rival social processes are simultaneously at work' (p. 315) it still seems too isolated from external variables that may well help to account for the variety of outcomes observed. In some cases, as will be suggested below, certain 'compelling' international environmental pressures may trigger and sustain integration efforts; in others, the minimum degree of interaction between system and regional subsystem may enhance the prospects for success.[6]

The fact that Haas now agrees with his critics that the distinction between high and low politics is a valid one[7] still leaves integration theorists of whatever persuasion with an unresolved methodological problem. We must agree with Karl Kaiser that the traditional distinction between high and low politics makes sense only if it refers to attitudes, and not to fixed objects of politics. 'The same issue may shift on the spectrum between "low" and "high" (a) according to specific circumstances, (b) within time, and (c) between different countries. Hence no clear lines can be drawn either according to issues or attitudes alone' (1967).

Kaiser's own view of the neofunctionalist approach to regional integration in Western Europe is that its concepts

remain valid in a large area, but they do not help us to understand various issues of 'high' politics or defence that have come to plague the Community, nor do they provide an answer to the interconnection

6. It may not be accidental that most successful instances of African integration occurred under colonial rule, which imposed a type of sub-system autonomy, and that the United States' experiment in federation was undertaken during a period when the Atlantic Ocean implied extended periods of isolation from – rather than involvement at – the center of world politics.

7. 'The results of our surmises add up to a rebirth of nationalism and anti-functional high politics as far as France is concerned' (Haas, 1958, p. 325).

between the two. Similarly, the body of systematic knowledge developed by a more Hobbesian outlook on a world of conflict and tension does not provide the tools, let alone the explanation, for examining the impact of functional integration within the EEC (pp. 404–5).

Stressing the necessity of incorporating the insights of the thus far 'partial' theoretical approaches to the study of regional integration in the European Community, Kaiser proposes an empirical systems-analysis approach expanded from Stanley Hoffmann's initial suggestions of a decade ago (1959). Patterns of interaction among the basic units of international politics are to be studied in terms of structure (including dimensions of influence and form), tasks performed in common, transnational forces operating across the frontier of the major units, unit objectives and means, and unit determinants (both ecological and socio-political). Within this framework ' "unification", "community building", "sector integration", or "functional integration" can be researched as part of manifestations of system change' (Kaiser, 1967, p. 410).

Western Europe: the economic limitations on spillover

The increasingly comprehensive paradigms for the study of regional integration – witness Kaiser's approach, among others – clearly suggest that the neo-functionalist approach has failed to comprehend some major relevant variables. Another weakness of the Haas model is that it has overweighted one of its own primary concepts, that of spillover from the economic to the political sector. An analysis of the economic achievements of the EEC to date reveals two characteristics that have helped to weaken the logic of spillover. The first is that the Common Market can operate so as to produce major economic gains without moving from customs union to political union. The second is that the benefits of economic integration in the Common Market have been equitably spread among the member units, thus avoiding to a considerable extent a series of 'distribution crises' that might well have aided the spillover process.

Expanding the size of the market open to producers within the EEC has permitted the achieving of economies of scale resulting from mass production and product specialization; it has also induced greater competition. Further, increased rates of regional investment, both domestic and foreign, have been engendered by the move toward free trade within the Six and the establishment of a common external tariff. A recent Brookings study of the Common Market concludes that its economic achievements have been very substantial.

The conditions requisite for a successful customs union are all present: the members are advanced countries at an almost equivalent level of industrialization; they have long been major trading partners and have common geographical borders; they are all heavily engaged in international trade and some of them had high tariffs originally, allowing much scope for rationalization. Furthermore, the EEC began during a period of economic prosperity, which made the required economic adjustments easier. In turn, because the EEC was successful, economic prosperity was prolonged and enhanced. Thus there has occurred an interaction between income growth and international trade in a 'virtuous circle' often sought but seldom achieved (Krause, 1967, p. 20).

Intra-EEC trade 'grew at a truly remarkable compound annual rate of 17 per cent between 1958–9 and 1965' (p. 21). Investment rates rose substantially in each country, as did GNP growth rates and the inflow of foreign capital.

Of vital importance in understanding the limitations to the logic of spillover in this setting is the recognition that these very substantial benefits have been achieved without much movement toward greater supranational jurisdiction. Economists have long recognized that customs unions among developed countries can deliver a substantial economic payoff for a very limited price in terms of the surrender of national sovereignty. In a theoretical work written in 1960, Bela Balassa concluded that 'an intergovernmental approach appears to be sufficient to ensure satisfactory operation of an economic union without a unification of the institutional structure' (1961, p. 272). Krause, in his new study of the EEC, confirms the Balassa view:

Economic integration requires coordination of many economic policies and this involves essentially political decisions, but formal political institutions may not be needed to bring this about. Governments do not need to be told, for instance, that excessive inflation in an open economy quickly leads to difficulties for themselves and their trading partners. They can see for themselves the rapidly deteriorating balance of payments, and pressures immediately arise for corrective actions. A 'hidden hand' toward policy coordination is directed by the market mechanism and it has proven to be very effective with the EEC (1967, p. 24).

And Krause's analysis of the workings of the Common Market led him to the following conclusion: 'What is certain is that political integration will occur only as a result of a positive political decision to bring it about, not as a result of economic pressures alone' (p. 24).

The final observation to be made with reference to the workings of the EEC and the process of spillover is that the gains from economic integration were spread among the Six in such a way that no major 'distribution crises' arose, thus depriving the spillover process of opportunities in which to 'redefine aims at a higher level of consensus'. While the bitter contest over a common agricultural policy might be characterized as a problem of distribution of benefits – French agricultural gains balanced against German manufacturing gains – this particular issue had its origin in the Messina negotiations. It *did not arise* as an unexpected crisis resulting from integration: rather, like the ghost of Hamlet's father, it appeared in the first act and never ventured far from the stage. The other major crisis faced among the Six, involving various British bids for membership in the EEC, has had little to do with economic issues.[8]

Economic theory suggests why the 'hidden hand' of the marketplace helped to minimize the problem of an equitable distribution of economic gains from free trade among the EEC countries. It is worth investigating because it also provides us with a frame of reference for understanding the quite different experience with economic integration among less developed countries.

Economists have noted that economic integration efforts are often accompanied by two contrasting types of results; Myrdal has labeled one set 'spread effects', and the other 'backwash effects' (1957, ch. 3). *Spread effects* are those that tend to minimize income disparities within a market area; they include such factors as increased demand in more developed centers for the products of the less developed periphery and the transmission to the latter of technological knowledge, improved skills and capital. *Backwash effects* include the movement of capital and skilled labor toward the more advanced centers, and the concentration in them of new industries, thus tending to increase regional disparities in levels of economic development.

For the purpose of this essay, the relevant point of these theoretical observations is that spread effects, which are likely to reduce regional disparities on the average, predominate in a

8. The crisis over agriculture, for that matter, was an issue less of economics than of politics. All commentators on the 1965 confrontation concur that the moment was chosen by de Gaulle to press the issues of structure in and direction of the Community.

union of developed economies (Balassa, 1961, p. 204). Highly developed price systems permit the exploitation of cost differences; existing industrial structures in each country allow all to benefit from the effects of increasing intra-industry specialization; infrastructure similarities discourage the concentration of foreign investments in any single member-unit; and the existence of highly developed transport and communications facilities promotes intraregional exchange. Factors such as these have often been cited as contributing, for example, to the decline of disparities in income among various regions of the United States. They have undoubtedly helped to minimize both the number and the magnitude of crises in the EEC and, in doing so, to limit the opportunities for an active spillover process.

In contrast, backwash effects play a far greater role in unions of underdeveloped countries; the more marked the initial disparities in such a union, the more the backwash effects tend to predominate.

With an imperfect price system, primitive transportation facilities, and an uneven distribution of social and economic overhead in these areas, *agglomerative tendencies* assume importance. These are related to the availability of overhead capital, skilled labor and linked industrial processes, when the latter not only provide ready markets and low-cost inputs but also contribute to future improvements through the exchange of technological information and induced technical change (Balassa, 1965, p. 123, italics added).

In retrospect, we may tentatively suggest that three factors led to an overestimation of the expansiveness of functional integration in Europe of the Six. They were, first, a failure to relate the process of regional integration closely enough to relevant international system factors; second, a tendency to deny rather than to investigate the discontinuity between high and welfare politics proclaimed by traditionalists; and third, a failure to recognize that sizeable (and equitably distributed) economic gains would result from a common market *coordinated* by sovereign states rather than managed by ceaselessly expanding supranational authorities.

References

BALASSA, B. (1965), *Economic Development and Integration*, Mexico.
DAVISON, W. P. (ed.) (1966), *International Political Communities*, Praeger.
DEUTSCH, K. W. (1966), 'Integration and arms control in the European political environment', *Amer. polit. sci. Rev.*, vol. 60.

DEUTSCH, K. W. *et al.* (1957), *Political Community and the North Atlantic Area*, Princeton University Press.

DEUTSCH, K. W. *et al.* (1967), *France, Germany and the Western Alliance*, Scribner.

ETZIONI, A. (1964), *Political Unification: A Comparative Study of Leaders and Forces*, Holt, Rinehart & Winston.

HAAS, E. (1958), *The Uniting of Europe*, Stanford University Press.

HAAS, E. (1963), 'Technocracy, pluralism and the new Europe', in S. Graubard (ed.), *A New Europe*, Beacon Press.

HAAS, E. (1967), 'The "uniting of Europe" and the uniting of Latin America', *J. Common Market Stud.*, vol. 5, no. 4.

HAAS, E. and SCHMITTER, P. (1966), 'Economics and differential patterns of political integration: projects about unity in Latin America', in W. P. Davison (ed.), *International Political Communities*, Praeger.

HOFFMANN, S. (1959), 'International relations: the long road to theory', *World Politics*, vol. 11.

HOFFMANN, S. (1963), 'Discord in community: the North Atlantic area as a partial system', in F. O. Wilcox and H. F. Haviland (eds.), *The Atlantic Community: Progress and Prospects*, Praeger.

HOFFMANN, S. (1966), 'The fate of the nation state', *Daedalus*, Summer.

HOFFMANN, S. (1968), '*Gulliver's Travels*', *or the Selling of American Foreign Policy*, McGraw Hill.

INGLEHART, R. (1967), 'An end to European integration?', *Amer. Polit. Sci. Rev.*, vol. 61.

JACOB, P. E., and TOSCANO, J. V. (eds.) (1964), *The Integration of Political Communities*, Lippincott.

KAISER, K. (1967), 'The US and the EEC in the Atlantic system: the problem of theory', *J. Common Market Studies*, vol. 5, pp. 401–2.

KRAUSE, L. B. (1967), *European Integration and the United States*, Brookings Institution.

LINDBERG, L. (1966), 'Integration as a source of stress on the European community system', *International Organization*, vol. 20.

MYRDAL, G. (1957), *Economic Theory and Underdeveloped Regions*, Duckworth.

NYE, J. S. Jr (1965), 'Patterns and catalysts in regional integration', *International Organization*, vol. 19, pp. 870–84.

Part Three
The Dynamics of European Decision-Making

The transfer of decision-making power and legitimacy from the nation state to the institutions of the European Community lies at the heart of the political integration process. As Paul Taylor makes clear, the European Commission is faced with a paradox when it seeks to increase its competence *vis-à-vis* the member governments of the Community. Without real power to act decisively in a situation, the Commission is unlikely to attract popular support; without popular support, there is no compulsion for member governments to cede real power to the Commission. David Coombes finds that the Commission's dual role, as the bureaucracy and the political conscience of the Community, has severely limited its ability to undertake effective political initiatives in areas where no consensus exists among the member-governments.

In those areas where a consensus does exist, effective action by the Commission depends upon full cooperation from the national governments. Giancarlo Olmi's analysis of the implementation of the Common Agricultural Policy (CAP) illustrates the complexity of such Community ventures, and indicates why they are difficult to change once they have been finalized. Leon Lindberg and Stuart Scheingold suggest that the success of CAP lay in the perception of some governments and national interest groups that integration in this field would produce benefits which would not be available in a purely national context. The attempt to establish a common transport policy failed because no such advantage was apparent, and the Commission was unable to generate support at the national level.

Helen Wallace points out that European issues have in general been treated as foreign-policy matters by national governments,

and have thus tended to remain insulated from the domestic
political process. Although the impact of the European
Community at the national level has therefore been limited,
L. J. Brinkhorst sees in the development of Community law a
means of involving the individual citizen with European
integration, since the legal regulations have force in domestic law
and affect not only member governments but also all those
engaged in economic activity.

10 Paul Taylor

The Concept of Community and the European
Integration Process[1]

P. Taylor, 'The concept of community and the European integration
process', *Journal of Common Market Studies*, vol. 7, no. 2, 1968,
pp. 83–101.

Among the problems which face the student of international integration processes, such as that between the six members of the
European Communities, is that of finding a way among the
various theoretical approaches to the subject. The theoretical
approach which one adopts is certain to affect one's understanding
of the integration process, and each approach has its own implications for the kind of strategy which is thought to be appropriate in seeking further integration. This essay seeks both to
illustrate these points and to clarify some aspects of integration.

I distinguish between two possible approaches to understanding the problems of the Europe of the Six. Each approach
has its own implications for the kind of strategy which is thought
to be appropriate in seeking further integration. The first approach involves the attempt to use the analogy of national
government in interpreting the existing structure and process of
European institutions and in suggesting possible ways of
furthering integration; it employs national governmental institutions and methods of control as a model for understanding
and improving the institutions of the Six. The second, which
might be termed a Functionalist approach, in the style of the
older Functionalists (such as David Mitrany), draws a distinction between the desirable end-situation and the methods of
achieving it, between the conditions of the stable state which
should result from integration, and the requirements of the
strategy for achieving those conditions.[2] It suggests that the

1. This essay was first presented as a contribution to the Political Studies
Association Conference held at the University of Sussex in April 1968. I
should like to acknowledge with gratitude the helpful comments of colleagues, which have suggested to me certain revisions and alterations. In
particular, the first section has been amended and expanded.

2. Mitrany (1966). The volume reprints the original essay, under the same
title, of 1943 with additional new essays and an Introduction by Hans
Morgenthau.

analogy of the national government might not be appropriate at present, and indeed, that its use might suggest courses of action which would lessen the chances of its being appropriate later on.

In presenting these two broad approaches to European integration, I first discuss some of the traditional concepts of political science and the way that these are viewed in different theoretical approaches to the integration process; secondly, I consider the community method of policy-making in the Europe of the Six; and, thirdly, I discuss the present stage of integration in Europe and the possibilities for future development.

Some observers, particularly the neo-functionalists and the federalists, have seen in the Europe of the Six an emerging bipolarity of power and authority.[3] On the one side there is the community method, centred upon the Commission, which has competence and takes decisions in its appropriate sphere; and on the other side, the residue of power and authority is left in the hands of the national governments. An important part of the integration process in this analysis is the transfer of decision-making powers from the national governments to the European institution, that is, to the Commission; the Court sustains the Commission's decision-making by establishing and protecting the supremacy of Community Law over National Law in the integrated areas. The progress of integration in this case lies in the expanding competence of the international institutions, particularly the Commission. In a recent article Professor Lindberg detected the beginnings of a European political system; and, in doing so, he counted those decisions which the European institutions now take and those which remain the preserve of governments (1967). His analysis is highly illuminating on many aspects, but it accepts implicitly certain assumptions about the nature of sovereignty and authority which would be challenged by those who take a different theoretical approach to the subject.

There are, of course, several different views on the nature of sovereignty. One view – the older one – lays primary stress upon the legal aspects: that power is sovereign which has the legal right to act and 'whose acts are not subject to the legal control of another, so that they cannot be rendered void by the act

3 The term neo-functionalist is normally applied to those writers who since the mid-1950s have criticized and developed the older Functionalist propositions (see Karl Kaiser's use of the term in his article, 1967). The neo-functionalists include Ernst B. Haas, Leon L. Lindberg, J. S. Nye, Lawrence Scheinman, J. P. Sewell and others.

of another human will' (Grotius, quoted in Herz, 1962, p. 50). In this case it is the possession of the legal right to undertake certain activities, such as the defence of the realm, which is the most important aspect of sovereignty. Another view, however, goes beyond this to demand as a condition of sovereignty that the power should be based on a popular consensus, upon a community or nation; the power of government should receive the sanction of popular approval and support before that government can be said to be sovereign. And the same general distinction can be made about authority: authority of governments can be based upon a recognition of competence expressed, for instance, in treaties or in the general principles of law; or it can be viewed as conditional upon a process of legitimization expressed through the approval of the mass of the citizens. Authority in this second case derives from a general agreement that the government should have the right to act; in the first case it comes from a legal dispensation.

I should indicate at this point the sense in which I use the word community in this paper. Where I am not talking specifically about the European Community, in the sense of the institutions and methods of the Six, I mean community in the sense of a community of beliefs, values, attitudes and loyalties. I call this a socio-psychological community, and would distinguish it from, for instance, the political community of Amitai Etzioni[4] (1965, p. 4), or the system of co-existing but differing interests which Professor Haas discusses (1958, pp. 30–35). The socio-psychological community is very similar to the community with which Professor Deutsch is concerned in his discussion of the nation and in his discussion of the amalgamated security community (1966). This type of community is, of course, similar to that detected by Tönnies when he made his distinction between *Gemeinschaft* and *Gessellschaft* at the end of the nineteenth century (1940). *Gemeinschaft* is translated as community, and *Gesellschaft* as society. Society, Tönnies suggested, is characterized by competitiveness and the transactions within it are based on contract. Community, on the other hand, describes a sense among the individuals forming it of belonging together, of having common loyalties and values, of kinship; and tasks performed within a community are not performed because of reciprocal arrangements such as contracts, but because of a feeling of duty, a sense of contributing

4. Etzioni's political community possesses three kinds of integration: it has a monopoly on the control of force; it has a single centre for decision-making; and it is the dominant focus of identification for members.

something worthwhile to the good of the whole. An example of society in Tönnies's sense is the firm; an example of community is the family, the church or the nation.

It is interesting that the Gaullist view of sovereignty is similar in many respects to that of the older functionalist theorists such as David Mitrany. The functionalist argument seems to be that sovereignty is vitally dependent upon the loyalties of citizens; that institution is sovereign which attracts popular loyalties. The dynamic of integration for the functionalists is the learning process of citizens who are gradually drawn into the cooperative ethos created by functionally specific international institutions devoted to the satisfaction of real welfare needs; the latter are distinguished from those which are created artificially by the state. For instance, the existence of the state both creates and satisfies the need for security, and it encourages the search for national prestige and influence at the expense of a range of more important needs such as increasing the level of incomes, setting up efficient transport systems, and developing satisfactory welfare schemes. Functionally specific international institutions which escaped from the bonds of national frontiers could satisfy these needs more efficiently; and in doing so they could attract the loyalties of citizens by convincing them of the advantages of cooperation. Citizens would learn to cooperate from their experience that cooperation brought them the greatest benefits.

This very brief discussion of the integrative dynamic of the older functionalists is sufficient to bring out two major aspects of their attitude towards sovereignty; first, sovereignty is in their view conditional upon the appearance of popular loyalties which are focused upon the sovereign body; and secondly, the functionally specific institution attracts loyalties by efficiently carrying out its task of satisfying real welfare needs. A number of successful international institutions can gradually erode the loyalties of citizens towards national governments and refocus loyalties upon themselves: there is an 'accumulation of partial transfers' which brings about a 'translation of the true seat of authority' (Mitrany, 1966, p. 31). This in turn leads to a 'sharing of sovereignty' and to the imposing of restraints upon national governments. But, most importantly, the transfer of the function is but the beginning of the process of transferring sovereignty, and creating a new basis for the authority of international institutions (Haas, 1964, ch. 1); the process is one of building a sociopsychological community which transcends the nation state.

Similarly, writers such as Rosenstiel, who might be said to represent a Gaullist position, argue that sovereignty is vitally linked with its sociological base (1963). They argue that at present in Europe the Six national governments attract the overwhelming loyalty of the majority of their citizens. The Six nations continue to provide the sovereign basis of the Six national governments; and in the consequential absence of a European nation European institutions cannot be sovereign; the term supranational is a misnomer. They must be viewed as an extension of the juridical and administrative arm of the national governments. As to the older functionalists, sovereignty to the Gaullists is vitally dependent upon a community of values, beliefs and attitudes which sustains it. Similarly, in their view, institutions cannot be said to possess authority unless they have been legitimized by receiving the support and reflecting the values, attitudes and beliefs of citizens.

It hardly needs pointing out that the Gaullists and the functionalists have drawn very different conclusions from these similar assumptions about the relationship between community and sovereignty. The Gaullists see the continued vitality of the different European nations as a reason for resisting the encroachment of Europe. The functionalists' argument, when applied to Europe, suggests a strategy for creating the conditions under which sovereignty can be transferred.

The neo-functionalists and the federalists, on the other hand, share a suspicion of the Tönnian view of community, and accept a pluralist model of society.[5] Professor Haas rejects *Gemeinschaft* and substitutes for it a pluralist model of society, a kind of community of competing interests which co-exist because of an agreement about the rules of the game within a constitutional system. He rejects the older functionalists' idea of an emerging consensus on social questions: there is no common good 'other than that perceived through the interest-tinted lenses worn by the actors' (Haas, 1964, p. 35). And, because social life is dominated by competition among interests, 'integration is conceptualized as resulting from an *institutionalized pattern* of interest politics, played out within existing international institutions' (p. 35).

5. It would, however, be inaccurate to say that Professor Haas is for all practical purposes a federalist: I hope that my argument does not suggest this. But I am concerned to show that in some important areas their ideas are mutually reinforcing, and that the common ground is strong enough to distinguish both clearly from the older functionalists.

It is the 'institutionalized pattern' which is significant to the neofunctionalists, and not the development of a socio-psychological community. Institutional spillover and the learning process of bureaucrats is substituted for the older functionalists' integrative dynamic of the learning and experience of citizens (pp. 47–50). And, as they concentrate on institutional developments and not upon the emergence of socio-psychological community, they implicitly accept the view that sovereignty is strengthened by an expanding legal competence. The strengthening of the sovereignty of the international institutions follows upon the granting of a legal competence by national governmental institutions, and the existence of a socio-psychological community is not immediately relevant; community is not viewed as the essential base of sovereignty, although, of course, it is hoped that a community of competing interests will follow from the transfer of sovereignty. Similarly the authority of the international institution in this analysis derives from the recognition by national governments of an institutional competence, which in Europe might reside in the Commission or even in an Assembly; it does not depend upon the prior appearance of *Gemeinschaft* which could sustain the international institutions.

These two differing views of community, and their relationship with sovereignty and authority, profoundly affect attitudes on the status of the decisions of the existing European institutions. If socio-psychological community is accepted as the essential basis of sovereignty and authority, and if there is no European community, even the decisions of institutions which have been granted a significant range of formal powers are each, in effect, dependent upon the decision of national governments to allow implementation. This continues to be the case no matter how long the international institutions exercise their formal powers; the decisions of the European institutions are thus of a different and lower kind when compared with those of national governments. On the other hand, if the granting of formal powers by the governmental institutions itself represents a transfer of sovereignty, then the decisions of the international institutions (the Commission and associated institutions) have the same status as those of national governments. They may be compared on a like-to-like basis. Although they are not explicitly stated, the latter assumptions seem to form one of the starting points of Professor Lindberg's analysis.

In their acceptance of the pluralist model of society the neo-functionalists agree with the European federalists. Federalism can be viewed either as providing a political solution, a way of managing different interests within a single political framework; or it can be viewed as an administrative convenience, a method of governing a homogeneous society within which there is a high degree of consensus. The neo-functionalists seem to fall squarely into that American tradition which sees federalism as providing a political solution; it is not necessary to the stability of the political system that it should be coextensive with a socio-psychological community. The federalists, in the absence of a European socio-psychological community, also find this argument plausible, and it reinforces their determination to place a high priority upon developments at the institutional level and upon finding a political solution (Duclos, 1961).

The older functionalists, on the other hand, are suspicious of federalism; David Mitrany has written about the dangers of seeking solutions to societal conflict in formulas such as federalism (1966, p. 31). It cannot provide a political solution to the problem of divisive interests, and might in the absence of socio-psychological community add to the divisions in society. A suspicion of federalism as a political solution is also to be found in Rosenstiel's argument (1963).

I will return to these different approaches to the fundamental problems of the integration process in the other sections of this essay. But, in preparing to do this, I must first consider the relationship between the *capacity* of international institutions and the level of community feeling. Capacity has been defined as the ability to receive, understand and act upon the demands fed into an organization from its environment; it is an indicator of performance.[6] Low capacity indicates that the organization is not able to satisfy all the demands made upon it; a high capacity suggests the ability to respond quickly and adequately.

The level of capacity required in a stable state has been thought to vary with the strength of the community within it. If there is only one community in the state, a government needs only moderate capacity in order to maintain the stability of that state. A failure of response does not generate the belief in individuals and groups that their interest cannot be satisfied at some future time by that government. If capacity is consistently low, however,

6. The older functionalists would view power, also, as an indicator of legal competence and would distinguish this from power legitimized by a socio-psychological community; it then becomes 'authority'.

the community might disintegrate into a number of communities. On the other hand, where an institution has the task of responding to the demands of several different communities, only a high level of capacity can maintain stability. Different communities remain together in a single-state framework when their different interests are recognized and satisfied quickly by the government. If a government maintains a high level of capacity, however, it is likely that the various communities in the state will slowly integrate into a single community. Professor Deutsch mentions that many existing nation states contain remnants of older nations (1966, p. 105); the British government in general maintained a high level of capacity and contributed to the appearance of a relatively homogeneous community. The government of Austro-Hungary, on the other hand, lacked adequate capacity and was unable to prevent the various nations from eventually breaking away.

The older functionalists were deeply concerned with the problem of capacity; the success of their approach depended crucially upon the performance of the institutions: they were required to perform their tasks efficiently in order to attract the loyalties of citizens, and without a high degree of capacity the approach would fail. It was for this reason too that the older functionalists were concerned that experts should play a leading role in the international institutions. The experts could often formulate the technical arguments for increasing the scope and level of integration; and their researches could lead to the discovery of new areas where integration would increase the prosperity and strengthen the economic and social security of citizens. Within the framework of functional institutions experts could play a leading part in the creation of a socio-psychological community which would transcend the framework of the nation state. Indeed, as part of a strategy for international integration – the traditional forms of government only being appropriate when socio-psychological community had appeared – the old functionalists envisaged something which is surprisingly similar to what we now call technocracy (Mitrany, 1966, pp. 121–8).

I hope that this brief discussion has brought out some of the general characteristics of the various theoretical approaches to international integration; I have not attempted a detailed discussion (I intend to compare the older functionalists' and the neo-functionalists' ideas in greater detail elsewhere). But enough has been said, I hope, to clarify two broad approaches to the subject. The neo-functionalists have distinctive views on the relationship between community, and sovereignty and authority, and they are mainly concerned with developments at the institutional level. And the neo-functionalists' acceptance of the pluralist model of society fits easily with the federalists' belief that a unified Europe can provide a political solution. The older functionalists, on the other hand, insist upon the development of socio-psychological community as an essential precondition of sovereignty; and they believe that without such a community federalism cannot work.

In the following two sections I consider the implications of these two approaches as they apply to a full understanding of the problems of the European communities, and hence to the choice of an appropriate strategy for furthering European integration.

The Community method

The differing views on relationships between community and sovereignty affect views on the nature of the community method in the Europe of the Six. When first examined the method may seem like a very haphazard series of interactions between international civil servants (the Commission), national governments, and a variety of more or less organized interested groups. But functionalist theory on the one hand, and neo-functionalist and federalist theory on the other hand, would each make a different kind of sense of the method; and this affects views on strategies which are available to the Commission in working towards further European integration.

Unlike earlier techniques used in international institutions – even the more advanced ones – the methods of work of the EEC involve a two-pronged attack upon the integrity of national decision-taking structures. The confrontation of policy technique of the OEEC, whatever its successes in establishing agreement between governments, served to consolidate the national interest. The technique was highly successful in harmonizing governments' plans for the distribution of Marshall Aid and in reducing trade and payment barriers; but it was nevertheless concerned with the plans of governments.[7] It recognized the differences between governments and it stressed the position of governments in representing and interpreting the interest of the state as a

7. For a good report on the methods of work of the OEEC see Political and Economic Planning (1959).

whole. The status of governments as guardians and conductors of the national interest was, if anything, emphasized by the confrontation of policy.

The method of work of the EEC, on the other hand, tends to fragment the national interest. National governments are certainly still able to resist proposals for further integration which are made by the Commission; but in doing this, it is becoming more difficult for them to present their views as if they represented a generally agreed national position. The Commission, by its existence, sharpens the awareness of alternative courses of action among groups within the state; and when it enters into relationships directly with these groups, the Commission effectively highlights the extent to which the views of governments and the views of some internal groups differ. Governments are on the defensive in so far as they now have to make a deliberate effort to preserve an appearance of state interest in the face of the Community. The integrity of national decision-taking structures is challenged by attack from without and erosion from within.

The Commission's ability to generate pressures upon governments derives to a great extent from its concern with three kinds of Community interest. First, it is involved with the harmonization and coordination of the interests of governments. It puts forward proposals on integrative measures for the attention of governments and attempts to obtain the community interest of seven sets of harmonized objectives: those of the Six member governments and its own. Secondly, as I have mentioned, in consulting with a wide variety of interest groups and organizations it makes itself aware of the Community interest of these groups; it prompts the articulation of these interests. And, thirdly, its character as a technocracy in which experts and highly skilled and professional administrators are brought together, makes it aware of a technocratic interest. It develops on the basis of this expertise an awareness of a preferred solution which it thinks would be the best method of obtaining the objectives entrusted to it.

The Commission's concern with three kinds of Community interest is an important part of its strength; both the older functionalist and Gaullist thinkers, and the neo-functionalists and federalists would agree on that. But differences arise in views on the relationship between these three types of interests. The following question is the pertinent one: 'In the community method – a dynamic on-going process – which interests are dominant and which interests are subordinate?' The different views on the community method involve quite different views on the place of the three interests in the integration process.

In explaining the community method the neo-functionalists and federalists concentrate upon relationships between governments and the Commission.[8] The Commission proposes; governments are persuaded, sometimes by direct consultation on particular problems and sometimes by the use of a peculiar kind of diplomatic technique which relies for its success upon the self-interest of governments, namely the Commission's presentation to the Council of a package of proposals. And the whole process is lubricated by the interpenetration between national bureaucracies and the Commission – the process which involves national civil servants in the Community – and by the logic that holds that partial integration produces problems which can best be solved by further integration. The European interest which is being worked for in this case is a common interest of governments modified by the technocratic interest of the Commission: the community interest of groups is subordinate to this interest.

From the process of interaction with governments, the neo-functionalist argument runs, the Commission increases the range of its formal powers; and it increases its capacity to act in areas affecting the interests of groups within the state. It is worth repeating that, in this analysis, the main dynamic of integration lies in the interrelationship between governments and Commission. The transfer of formal powers enables the Commission to increase its capacity and the emergence of a European focus for group interests is expected to follow from this. The community method viewed from this vantage point can be summarized diagrammatically as follows:

The theoretical approach of the older functionalists stresses different aspects of the method. And President de Gaulle's

8. This analysis of the community method is not based on any single neo-functionalist or federalist writing; the same is true of the functionalist one which follows. Each is a projection and interpretation of a range of ideas which are contained in a number of writings.

opinions and actions would suggest that he is more concerned with the likely effects of this method. The community method from this perspective is much more of a circular set of inter-actions; its main dynamic is the growth of a socio-psychological community among citizens. The process may be broken into at any point, but if I start with the role of the Commission the resulting steps are as follows:

1. The Commission, having been allocated areas of competence and some formal powers by the agreement of governments, maxi-mizes its capacity to act in these areas.

2. As a result of the Commission's activities the group interests are activated and attracted to the Commission. A change of interest in favour of further integration is generated and directed at national governments; at this stage a re-focusing of loyalties away from national government towards the European institu-tions takes place.

3. National governments, subject to a series of influences and pressures from within the state, are persuaded to allow the Com-mission greater powers; the possibilities for independent action by national governments are reduced by the weakening of internal loyalties and citizens' changing expectations.

4. The Commissioner's greater powers allow it to increase its capacity; and the circle begins again.

The view of the community method may be represented as follows:

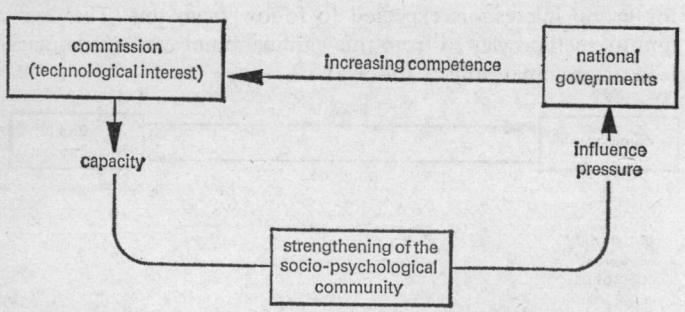

In this analysis the most important relationship in the com-munity method is that between the Commission and the citizens within states. The dynamic of the process of integration is the development of a European-wide socio-psychological community through the exercise of the Commission's capacity; the exercise and increase of capacity follows from the granting of formal powers by the governments. And in this case the European interest which is being worked for is a harmonization of the technocratic interest of the Commission with the community interest of groups. The community interest of governments emerges and is modified in accordance with the development of this interest.

President de Gaulle, as one might expect from his views on the nation and its importance to sovereignty, is aware of the dangers of this method. Hence his attempts to restrict the Commission's public relations activities and his insistence on restricting inter-actions at the Community level to those between the Commission and national governments. He is probably more frightened by the possibility of the erosion of the French system from within than by direct attack on it by the Commission. He sees the danger to French sovereignty of a coming together of the community interest of groups and the technological interest of the Community.

The neo-functionalist, federalist and older functionalist tenden-cies in thought each lead to a characteristic interpretation of the community method; the two tendencies also lead to the use of characteristic models in interpreting the problems of Europe and in selecting strategies for the further integration of Europe. Professor Haas clearly puts primary stress upon changes in behaviour among the institutional elites; but neo-functionalists and federalists have their institutional concern in common. The view which emerges from a merging of the neo-functionalist and federalist positions is that institutional change is the more im-portant aspect of integration.[9] The nature of the links between neo-functionalism and federalism could itself form the subject of a paper, and I hope I may be forgiven for passing very briefly over these problems. But the institutional stress of the two ap-proaches tends to lead to the attempt to apply analogies drawn from theories of national governmental institutions to the existing structure of Europe; and guidelines for action are sought in these analogies. It leads to the putting of less stress upon the problems of the European interest and upon the appearance of socio-psychological community as a condition of further integration. This tendency in thought is associated with the first view of the community method.

The older functionalist ideas when applied to Europe lead to a

9. Monsieur Monnet is himself an excellent example of the merging of federalism and neo-functionalism.

different position. They lead to the view that the analogy of national institutions is highly inappropriate at present precisely because of the absence of a European interest. Institutional changes would not be useful because the new institutions could only increase the existing differences in interest rather than bring them together; and to create new institutions, such as a more powerful and representative assembly now, would discourage the later emergence of a European interest. A further criticism which the older functionalists might make of the institutional approach is that the traditional theory of national government, such as that of democratic control, is becoming less appropriate even within states. The federalists are trying to introduce democratic control into the Community precisely at a time when it is becoming increasingly difficult at the national level, if only because of the enormous complexity of the modern technological state.

The different strategies for furthering the integration process in Europe which derive from these assumptions are considered in the next part of this paper.

The evolving European system

The preceding brief discussion of the two views on the community method and of the various ways of viewing the problems of Europe suggests that two main strategies for furthering the European integration process are conceivable: one can be deduced from the neo-functionalist/federalist propositions, the second from the ideas of the older functionalists. Perhaps I should add here that I am to some extent deliberately misapplying some of the ideas of the older functionalists. I consider their view of the dynamics of integration and the relationship between sovereignty and the loyalties of citizens in order to illustrate and clarify one possible line of argument about Europe; but the end-situation to which I relate their dynamic, a united Europe, is not one which they would welcome. Their ideas, however, do point to one possible way of obtaining that goal.

The first strategy is dominated by the federalist ideas and strongly influenced by those of the neo-functionalists. It holds that as a matter of immediate concern the Commission should seek to increase the range of formal powers allowed to it by national governments, and this should be accompanied by the development of closer links with the Assembly. After increasing the Commission's formal powers, the problem of control and responsibility should be overcome by making it responsible to a directly elected Assembly. The latter should have the power to appoint and to dismiss the members of the Commission, and as a result of these changes the Commission would greatly strengthen its bargaining position in relation to the national governments. It will be able to accelerate the process of spill-over between functional areas and persuade an increasing number of national bureaucrats to adopt a community perspective. The focus of this first strategy seems to be upon increasing the political involvement of the Commission – a neo-functionalist proposition – and intensifying engagement between itself and the national governments.

Because this line of thought puts primary stress in the integration process on relationships between the Commission and governments, the latter should centralize within their individual governmental structures the handling of contacts with the European institutions. This would increase the chances of harmonizing the interests of governments and Commission in an efficient way, and would lead to the easier and more rapid taking of decisions. In general this strategy reflects a concern with changes in institutions and the behaviour of elites rather than a concern with the nature of the different community interests. Sovereignty is separable from the socio-psychological base; it can be transferred from governments to international institutions by the formal granting of the rights of sovereignty; a community of competing interests will come into being at some future date after the Commission has thus strengthened its position.

The second strategy, which follows the tradition of the ideas of the older functionalists, is different in many aspects, although it regards a similar end-situation as desirable. The transfer of sovereignty, in this analysis, can only follow from the appearance of a socio-psychological community; and, in helping to create this, stress should be placed for the present upon maintaining and developing the capacity of the Commission – not necessarily its formal powers. Capacity is best maintained and developed by stressing the technocratic aspects of the Commission's activities and by persuading citizens of the greater usefulness of the technocratic approach. The Commission should for the present seek to strengthen popular beliefs in the technocratic method by increasing its efficiency, both in administration and in research; and, in the absence of a community base of interests and attitudes it should not, at this stage in the development of Europe, seek to take on any of the character of the national governments.

The stress in the development of capacity should be on the efficient performance of those tasks which already involve groups and interests within the state. A greater involvement with such groups should be sought, so that tasks are not only in fact performed efficiently but are seen to be so performed. And wherever possible careful documentation on the nature and purpose of the task should be produced. By this method pressures are built up in the interest groups themselves towards the gradual expansion of those task areas which are entrusted to the Commission.

Relations with governments are one of the highly sensitive aspects of the expansion of task areas. It is, of course, necessary that expansion should be acknowledged by the granting of an increasing area of competence by governments to the Commission. But the technocratic-functionalist analysis sees the expansion as being a gradual one, and competence as being granted piecemeal as a result of the careful expansion and strengthening of the sociological base. Certainly, any head-on collision with governments in the attempt to obtain an increase in formal powers is to be avoided. The tensions which result from such collisions would result in governments being put on their guard against the expansion of the Commission's responsibilities in particular task areas. There is a constant danger of reactivating the older nationalist prejudices; this, it is argued, was one of the unfortunate consequences of the 1965 crisis. The Commission moved too soon; it sought to obtain formal powers from governments without regard for the socio-psychological community, the essential popular European interest, and it made the mistake of appearing to contaminate its technological status with political ambition. This crisis upset the process of bringing together the technological community interest and the community interest of groups.

Indeed, a strategy for integration which was based on the ideas of the older functionalists would require that the Commission be isolated as far as possible from political influence and involvement at this stage. The responsibility of the Commission is not defined in terms of the power over it of an elected assembly, as with the neo-functionalist/federalist approach, but essentially in terms of the strength of its own interest in the continuing process of integration. Responsibility results from the awareness of the technocratic interest, from the need to maintain links and strengthened contacts with groups within the states, from the necessity of avoiding as far as possible any head-on collision with governments, and from the requirement of maintaining an appearance of impartial efficiency. The restraints imposed by the Treaty of Rome and the guiding hand of the Court also serve as parameters of the responsibility of the Commission in this functionalist analysis. The functionalist argument suggests that if we define responsibility in this way for the present we may improve the chance of creating a popular European interest and of the Commission's obtaining real sovereignty and authority in the future. It reflects a concern with pragmatic operational requirements rather than an institutional formalism.

This strategy sees serious dangers in political involvement at this stage. Responsibility to a directly elected Assembly, far from helping the Commission, would tend to reduce its efficiency; it might, for instance, result in a lowering of the calibre of the members of the Commission, on whom so much of its reputation depends. Elected officials or officials responsible to an assembly, tend to lose their reputation for impartial efficiency; they tend to be successful in maintaining their position more through political machination than technical skill and expertise. Furthermore the idea of the representation of particular interests is anathema to the technocracy; it tends to detract from its impartiality and to drag it into the area of politics. And, anyway, in the absence of a community of interest what kind of interest could be represented? On what kind of consensus could a Commission which was responsible in the traditional sense base its decisions?

The relationship between socio-psychological community and these two broad strategies for the integration of Europe is an interesting one. Neither strategy denies the importance of community to the stability of the integrated state; but the first, the federalist neo-functionalist, sees its emergence as one of the possible results of the transfer of formal powers and of 'sovereignty' from national governments to the Commission; and it is not to be a community of common loyalties and values but, rather, a community of competing interests contained within an accepted constitutional framework. Integration results from the Commission's ability to convince national governments that it is capable of attaining those objectives which they prefer, or come to prefer, as a result of the spill-over between functional areas. (Part of the neo-functionalist rationale for creating a technological community is that success here would produce pressures upon governments to harmonize – and integrate – their defence policies.) The technocratic/functionalist strategy, on the other hand, sees socio-psychological community as the essential *con-*

dition of the transfer of real power and sovereignty to the international institution. Until that stage is reached any transfer of formal power is likely to be misleading; it will continue to be the governments who are expected to act in crisis situations and they will continue to attract new tasks to themselves. In this case the main dynamic of integration lies in the development and strengthening of identitive relationships between the Commission and citizens and groups within the state. The bringing together of the technocratic interest and the interest of citizens and groups, rather than the harmonization of the interests of the Six governments and the Commission, is the main task of the Commission. One of the essential differences between the neo-functionalist/federalist and the functionalist approaches is this: the functionalist strategy sees integration as a process which passes through several stages which are different from the end-situation, but which it must pass through in order to reach the end-situation; the neo-functionalist/federalist approach, on the other hand, seeks to involve the end-situation as far as possible in the present one.

I have discussed two broad approaches to the problem of integrating Europe; yet I am unable to come to any clear conclusions as to which is the more useful of the two, or, indeed, whether they could not be used together in some way despite their mutual contradictions. The federalist/neo-functionalist argument can be supported by pointing to the multiplicity of institutions in Europe, and the undoubted expansion of the Commission's area of competence. On the other hand, the problems which result from direct confrontation with governments are also becoming increasingly apparent. The effectiveness of the Functionalist approach is more difficult to demonstrate because the factors with which it is concerned are far less tangible and dramatic.

Yet there is some evidence to suggest that socio-psychological community is developing in Europe and that governments are at least beginning to feel its influence. Many European citizens attribute the increase in their standard of living to the EEC (Etzioni, 1965, p. 251) and many interest groups and businessmen are beginning to feel that they have a lot to lose if integration does not proceed. (The question of whether they would in fact lose is strictly speaking irrelevant.) Further, despite at least three major crises, the 1963 and 1967 French vetoes on British entry and the 1965 crisis over the Commission's powers, it is noticeable that almost everywhere a belief in the future of the EEC remains. Once the crisis is past the general feeling seems to be that integration will continue. Perhaps part of the explanation lies in the development of a primitive interest unit (after the July 1965 crisis French farmers calculated that the abandonment of the CAP would cost them about 2500–5000 million new francs per year);[10] and another part – and one which is more relevant to the functionalist argument – might lie in the development of common values and sympathies among some sections of society, such as young people (Inglehart, 1967).[11] Such developments are bound to impose some restraints upon governments and to push their policies in a Community direction.

But how far can socio-psychological community develop? Can governments still command national loyalties as effectively as General de Gaulle would have us believe? Professor Haas has recently amended the theory of integration which appeared in his book *The Uniting of Europe* (1958; 1967). His earlier stress upon the value of incremental decision-making was revised to cover the possibility of its being halted by *High Politics*, such as those of General de Gaulle. His revisions may be entirely in the interest of accuracy; on the other hand the possibility exists that the observers might themselves be deceived by the sound and fury of high politics. One of the characteristics of incremental decision-making is that its effects upon interests are not dramatic and easily noticed; it involves a gradualist, quiet, piecemeal approach which, nevertheless, could be as effective as the more flamboyant one in creating a community of interest. Of course, the General's occasional opposition has caused problems from the point of view of the European institutions. But his position might be much more an attempt to halt forces which he feels he will soon be unable to control than the reassertion of an obviously greater strength. His methods could be a symptom of weakening of national governments in the face of an emerging European-wide socio-psychological community, rather than a demonstration of their power. Tests of functionalist theory are to be discovered as much in the development of restraints upon governmental action as in positive acts of integration.

10. *Agence Europe*, September, 1965.

11. Inglehart concludes (p. 91) that 'far from finding a stagnation of integration processes since 1958, I would argue that, in some aspects, European integration may have moved into full gear since 1958'. From extensive public opinion surveys he shows that 'those whose outlook has been undergoing formation since the end of the Second World War (i.e. young people) are increasingly European' and that this attitude 'seems to persist under rather adverse conditions' (p. 105).

But the problem is that it is very difficult to test these views; perhaps the real test will only come during a period of crisis some time in the future. If national governments are still those who are expected to act then this suggests that loyalties have not been transferred to the international institution. On the other hand, if it is the Commission which is popularly expected to act, then it could be argued that national governments have in practice yielded up some of their sovereignty. In the USA the separation of powers and the division of internal sovereignty between the Federal Government and the separate states were challenged during the economic difficulties of the 1930s. It was the Federal Government which was expected to act; it did so when it took steps such as the setting up of the Tennessee Valley Authority. From then on the argument that the states only exercised powers in their allotted spheres with the consent of the Federal Government seemed a more plausible one.

I have set out a number of speculations about the place of community in the European integration process and have distinguished between two major approaches to the problems of understanding and furthering the integration process. Some of them, I know, are very speculative indeed; but I hope that they may have clarified some aspects of integration theory and that they may have added to our understanding of the strategies which are available to those who now wish to further integration in Europe.

References

DEUTSCH, K. W. (1966), *Nationalism and Social Communication*, MIT Press.
DUCLOS, P. (1961), 'La politification: trois essais', *Politique*, April–June.
ETZIONI, A. (1965), *Political Unification*, Holt, Rinehart & Winston.
HAAS, E. B. (1958), *The Uniting of Europe*, Stanford University Press.
HAAS, E. B. (1964), *Beyond the Nation State*, Stanford University Press.
HAAS, E. B. (1967), 'The uniting of Europe and the Uniting of Latin America', *J. Common Market Studies*, vol. 5, pp. 315–43.
HERZ, J. (1962), *International Politics in the Atomic Age*, Columbia.
INGLEHART, R. (1967), 'An end to European integration?', *Amer. Polit. Sci. Rev.*, vol. 61.
KAISER, K. (1967), 'The US and the EEC in the Atlantic System: the problem of theory', *J. Common Market Studies*.
LINDBERG, L. L. (1967), 'The European community as a political system', *J. Common Market Studies*.
MITRANY, D. (1966), *A Working Peace System*, Quadrangle Books.

POLITICAL and ECONOMIC PLANNING (1959), *European Organizations*, Allen & Unwin.

ROSENSTEIL, J. (1963), 'Some reflections on the notion of supranationality', *J. Common Market Studies*, vol, 1, pp. 127–39.

TÖNNIES, F. (1940), *Fundamental Concepts of Sociology: Gemeinschaft and Gesellschaft*, New York.

11 David Coombes

The Organization of the Commission

Excerpts from D. Coombes, *Politics and Bureaucracy in the European Community*, Allen & Unwin, 1970, pp. 234–40, 307–13, 326–31.

The contemporary historian, with only clumsy conceptual tools at hand and relying on superficial comparisons with the formal powers of other existing bodies such as international secretariats and federal governments, is unable to fit the Commission into any meaningful classification. The Commission seems to have been assigned formal powers and characteristics in an unprecedented way. It certainly is the case, as we shall argue in the first section of this chapter, that the Commission performs a variety of functions in the political system of the Community. Roughly speaking in some aspects the Commission is expected to act as a bureaucracy and to have the essential characteristics of an implementative, 'goal-seeking' organization, while in others it must behave as if it constituted the political leadership of the Community, acting as an initiating, 'goal-setting' body. We shall suggest here that the Commission has in practice attempted to meet both these broad criteria and that its organization reflects both political and bureaucratic characteristics. This assumption fits with our earlier empirical investigation of actual decisions and is compatible with the conflict between political and legal obligations which we found to underlie the administration of personnel within the Commission. Our immediate purpose is to elaborate upon this assumption by providing a *vue d'ensemble* of the Commission's role in the Community process and of its internal organization. We hope that this will enable us to reach some conclusion as to the conditions upon which the Commission depends for performing its role as a political leadership.

The functions of the Commission

The Commission can be described as performing a number of functions of a substantially different nature. The first of these is that of Initiative. This function derives from some of the Commission's most important legal powers, particularly that to initiate Community legislation. It also has the power to make recommendations on any matter it thinks fit within the framework of the Treaty. It is generally maintained that the Commission's practical initiatives are a key factor in providing the dynamic of the Community and serve as milestones in its development – for example, the 'Acceleration' decision of May 1960, the various major steps towards the achievement of a common agricultural policy, and the setting up of the various economic policy committees. Such initiatives have been backed up by the now familiar techniques of canvassing support among interest groups and public opinion in the member states, speeches in the European Parliament, and so on. At the same time the Commission has kept up a consistent stream of publications setting objectives for the future work of the Community and interpreting past achievements. It is important to note that our use of 'initiative' here must not be confused with the notion of discretion. The exercise of discretion is not necessarily related to the function of initiative as treated here, which involves essentially the elaboration and formulation of new programmes of action. Officials exercise discretion even in carrying out existing programmes of action, as we shall see below. Initiation requires a degree of innovative activity which is not normally found in a bureaucracy, which is designed essentially for the execution of existing programmes.

Closely allied to this function of initiative is another best described as normative. We have already referred to the fact that the Commission has a number of formal powers as 'guardian of the Treaty' and 'conscience of the Community'. The way in which the Commission regards itself as having the right to interpret the Rome Treaty and to determine the Community interest is just as famous as its acts of initiative. This is illustrated by its role as honest broker in the Council of Ministers during the legislative process, in that the Commission will amend its proposals in order to find a majority on the Council only if the amendment is justified in the Community interest. Numerous examples of the Community's normative function could be cited from the history of the Community so far, but one or two will suffice here, such as its condemnation of the French Government for going outside the Council of Ministers to veto British entry in 1963, its disapproval of the Franco-German Treaty, and its representation of the Community in the Kennedy Round negotiations. In all these cases the Commission took upon itself the duty of laying down the Community interest, rather as a national government interprets the public interest. The Commission has not been afraid to invoke this right against the Council of Ministers. For example, in 1964 the Council of Ministers rejected a proposal of the Commission for a new Community quota for goods transport by road and produced instead its own draft for an alternative system. The Commission thundered in its Annual Report that it 'could not see its way to accepting this solution', which diverged 'appreciably from the Commission's initial proposal, which was more in keeping with the Community spirit' (EEC Commission, 1965, p. 267).

This normative function is quite different from the regulatory function exercised by a number of public, official bodies when they interpret the meaning of statutes in individual cases. The Commission's normative function extends to 'filling out' the provisions of the Treaty of Rome and also to having the right to react to unforeseen situations (such as the French veto of British membership). Indeed, the initiative and normative functions of the Commission are interdependent and together give it the role of political leader and promoter of the Community interest. It is quite evident that without this role the Community would turn into an inter-governmental organization like OECD or the Council of Europe. It is a role, however, which may well be fully effective only under certain conditions. For example, the institution which performs it may well need to be autonomous and to derive its authority from some source which is independent, in the case of the Community, of the member states and the Council of Ministers. It must wield enough power over other actors in the system to support its initiatives by getting its own norms accepted. Again, it would almost certainly have to be capable of identifying with a particular set of values, for otherwise it would be unable to derive these norms of action in the Community. Thus, the Commission should be able to hold consistently to some body of European doctrine. Thirdly, however, such an institution must be inventive and creative, for it has to interpret values in the context of changing circumstances.

The Commission has also come to acquire an increasingly important administrative function. We mean by this not simply the technical tasks of preparing for decisions, producing data and keeping records, but also the taking of the vast number of regulatory decisions arising under the Community legislation concerning the customs union, the common policy on competition between enterprises and the common agricultural policy. At the same time, as 'guardian of the Treaty' the Commission regularly has to decide on a number of purported infringements of the Treaty. These are basically mechanical activities in that they involve the implementation of existing policies and programmes. This does not exclude the exercise of discretion. For example, the making of such administrative decisions may involve deciding whether or not to enforce particular regulations on the basis of the facts of a case, applying policy to particular circumstances, or interpreting a policy which is expressed only in very general terms. Nevertheless, students of organization normally draw a fundamental distinction between this kind of reproductive decision-making according to settled policies and the taking of critical, innovative decisions needed to initiate new policies. Moreover, regulatory activity unlike the setting of norms is based on delegated authority (March and Simon, 1958, p. 177–8).

It may well be that the initiative and administrative functions each call for completely different kinds of organization. As we have seen above, recent research suggests that, in the industrial context at least, the 'mechanistic', bureaucratic type of organization, designed to produce accurate and efficient performance of routine tasks, is not suited to unstable conditions where innovation and reaction to change are at a premium. Indeed, since few organizations exist in completely stable conditions, the difference is probably best expressed as a problem of management, a challenge to the organization's leaders to make special provision for innovative decision-making. This can be done by deliberately attracting resources to unprogrammed activity (for example, setting up special planning teams, or setting deadlines for the settlement of particular detailed questions which cannot be settled before decisions have been taken on wider issues of principle). However, the initiating role of an organization is under constant threat from its administrative responsibilities:

If all the resources of an organization are busily employed in carrying out existing programs, the process of initiating new programs will be slow and halting at best. Frequently, when a new program is to be developed, a new organizational unit is created and charged with the task first of elaborating the new program and then carrying it on when it has been elaborated. This procedure provides for a spurt of innovative, program-developing activity – a spurt that automatically diminishes as the program is elaborated and the task shifts gradually from one of planning to one of execution (March and Simon, 1958, pp. 186–7).

Finally, the Commission has a mediative function, which arises from its duty to bring about agreement between the member states in the Council of Ministers. This is the normal function of the secretariat of an inter-governmental organization (like that of GATT, for example). Such a body tries to reconcile the proposals of different member countries, usually by drafting solutions of its own which seek to chart a middle path, or by devising formulae which compensate for the losses and gains of the various parties. The Commission often seems to be doing this in its work in the Committee of Permanent Representatives and its sub-committees and in the Council of Ministers itself, changing its own proposals in response to particular national objections. It is because of the presence of a mediative function that the Commission involves itself in such complex and multiple contacts with representatives of member states at various stages of the decision-making process. Lindberg describes how the Commission skilfully performed such a function of mediation during the discussions on the proposed 'Acceleration' decision of 1960: 'a decision could not have been achieved without the Commission. The inability of the governments to agree on a precise formula forced them to delegate the task of formulation to the Commission. No one was willing to accept the possibility of a deadlock' (Lindberg, 1963, p. 193).

The Commission also seemed to be performing this function when it was preparing a Community position before the final stages of the Kennedy Round Negotiations.

In theory the Commission is meant to exercise its mediative function in conjunction with its initiative and normative functions, so that any settlement in the Council of Ministers will 'upgrade the common interest'. We have already noted that this is extremely difficult to do. Certainly, we would expect mediative activity to be usually incompatible with normative activity and even contradictory to it, in that the former calls for flexibility, objectivity and impartiality and the latter for commitment to certain values and even zeal in defence of them. We might assume, therefore, that the Commission is generally faced with a choice between acting as an independent, uncommitted secretariat and as a zealous band of Europeans. We might also assume that the effective performance of the mediative function does not necessitate the exercise of a great deal of power over those between or among whom one mediates. Far more important are qualities such as impartiality and detachment and a reputation for fair-mindedness combined with negotiating skill and a full technical knowledge of the issues involves. The mediator may well be frequently called on to innovate and to invent new courses of action, although the proposals he makes may not get beyond the drafting stage without the support of at least some of the agents of his mediation. Indeed, the initiative and mediative functions are often combined in existing international secretariats, and this probably explains why such bodies spend much of their time in a crisis concerning the proper extent of their powers (witness the United Nations' General Secretariat's hesitation about intervening in military situations). Basically, however, the two functions are on opposite sides of the organizational spectrum. The mediator who initiates too frequently runs the risk of seeming partisan or at least of making enemies by accident. The initiator in his turn must have the backing of some legitimizing, norm-setting authority, whether this be a representative assembly, or a mass political movement, or whether the authority is in some way vested in himself (as in the case of the Commission). The mediator does not require such authority and may well find it an embarrassment, for his role depends on his unimpeachable independence and impartiality. In this sense, while the administrator lacks the creativity and inventiveness required by the mediator, there is a certain complementarity between the two. (This is, perhaps, why, although diplomats are usually civil servants, the diplomatic service of most countries is generally regarded as showing more initiative, and as being less anonymous, than the home Civil Service.)

In the decision-making process of the Community it must be a great temptation for the Commission to stick to the role of mediator and to 'split the difference' between various national positions, rather than go to the lengths of asserting a distinct Community point of view. Similarly, it is a great temptation to any organization to administer existing programmes of activity rather than to initiate new policies. There must be a constant strain within the Commission between its normative and initiative functions, on the one hand, and its mediative and administrative ones, on the other. The dichotomy between the two different sets of functions could be described roughly as that between a political or promotive role and a bureaucratic or implementative one. The promotive role exercised by the Commission in performing its initiative and normative functions is usually identified within the national state of Western experience with the political leadership, say, a cabinet of ministers, which is popularly elected, or which is responsible to a representative assembly. This is the way the promotive institution acquires legitimacy and wields the necessary power for its task. The administrative and mediative functions, on the other hand, are in theory performed in the national context by regulatory agencies, government departments, advisory committees, or other sections of the bureaucracy, whose power is essentially based on delegated authority. Parallel to this difference in the amount of power exercised in performing different functions is a difference in type of organization. The highly structured, mechanistic type of organization associated with the performance of routine administrative tasks is not adaptable to the exercise of initiative or to the setting of norms. It may not even be suitable for the mediative function.

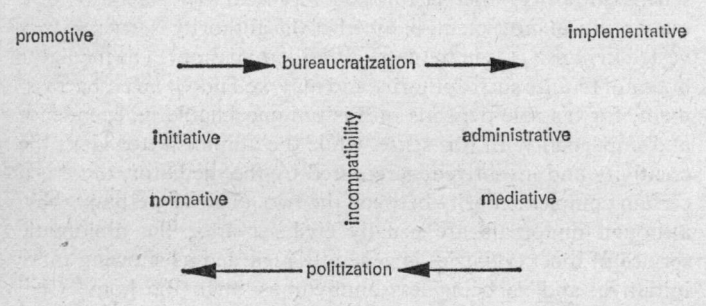

the functions of the commission

The role of political institutions

It has been a central theme of this book that the Community venture cannot succeed unless it is regarded as an essentially political undertaking. Subsidiary to this has been a related theme bearing the warning, increasingly resonant among economists and commentators of all kinds in recent years, that real political unification is not an automatic consequence of agreeing to take certain economic decisions in common. There can be a very real obstacle to unification in the authority and self-consciousness of the governments of nation states. Yet this authority and self-consciousness cannot be undermined simply by a process of paying off tangible short-term interest in exchange for vague long-term commitments, of buying *ad hoc* decisions on immediate economic issues by agreeing to postpone confrontation of one's ultimate goals. Similarly, government officials and the representatives of interest groups do not represent the power of governments. Bureaucratic activity in the Communities may have been re-oriented in many important respects on to a European axis, but this means little or nothing in terms of real political support. Power in all essentials still rests in the national capitals of Europe. It may have to be channelled through Brussels more than before – but this means little to national political leaders who are in the long run aware that their power does not depend on decisions taken by this means.

According to the 'functionalist' view of integration, however, it was a sufficient beginning in the attempt to unite Europe politically to establish a magnet for economic interests. Thus political mobilization within the Community was entrusted primarily to the Commission, which would be expected to gradually increase its own power and scope in economic matters at the expense of the national governments and by this means act as a magnet for political forces in the six countries. In time, when the latter were oriented towards the common economic centre of the Community, the European Parliament would be directly elected and gradually no doubt the Commission would derive its support from this body to which it would become increasingly responsible.

Although it lacked some of the essential features of the government of a nation state (including even a source of popular support or independent means of raising finance), the Commission was expected to perform functions normally associated with the political leaders of a state – initiating policies for the common good and setting and preserving norms of action. The leaders of the Commission were appointed not elected, most of their actual powers were to be delegated not intrinsic, and superficially it looked more like an ordinary international secretariat whose job was to mediate between the claims of national governments and to administer certain common services. However, the Hallstein Commission seems to have performed the promotive role expected of it by developing an *esprit-de-corps* and by behaving like a committed band of partisans, fighting for the European cause. As we have seen, there are still definite traces of such elements in the Commission's organization. However, given the distribution of functions and roles in the institutional system of the Community, and given that the final power of decision rested with the national governments, the Commission had, on the one hand, to perform a mediative function, and, on the other, to acquire administrative tasks of implementing Community legislation. Yet the pursuit of these courses of action demanded a different kind of organization from the partisan type, with the result that, in the first instance the Commissioners themselves became increasingly representative of extraneous interests, and eventually the administrative services were infiltrated by means of a loose, open-ended recruitment policy. This evolution into what we have chosen to call a porous type of organization immediately triggered off a defensive reaction on the part of the Commission in the form of the growth of bureaucratic rules and methods of working. In any event, an organization based on such representative principles is bound to fall prey to rigidities of one sort or another (for example, the need to maintain equilibrium between nationalities in the deployment of posts). Finally, these automatic pressures towards bureaucracy must now be intensified by the growing number of tasks accruing to the Commission of a regulatory, implementative character, calling as they do for a mechanistic system of management suited for the making of routine decisions.

The 'Hallstein' approach was remarkably effective and a number of successes can be attributed to it – the foundation of the Community in the early years in spite of an unfavourable international situation (Lindberg, 1963, pp. 167–205), the achievement of an industrial customs union, agreement on a common policy for competition between enterprises, the establishment of an agricultural common market (pp. 219–82). Of vital importance was the creation of an organizational common culture based mainly on a sense of shared adventure and common commitment to European unity and supported by a relatively loose and open-ended system of personnel administration. This common culture seems to have lasted even after the partisan phase of the Commission had passed and beyond the early years of pioneering, purposive commitment to getting the Community off the ground. The organization came to rely increasingly on seconded national officials rather than on specially selected partisan Europeans and, at the same time, it was becoming far more difficult to maintain unity within the organization without forming 'coalitions' based on different styles of administration and different norms. Nevertheless, the survival of a common culture served to hold this porous organization together and supported such ventures as the Commission's successful negotiation of the Kennedy Round on behalf of the whole Community.

The same approach was also responsible for a number of

initiatives which failed to come off, but which, nevertheless, met the criterion of providing political impulsion and which, in conditions of consensus among the national governments, might have resulted in striking advances towards European unity. In this category one must mention the Commission's reactions to the Gaullist veto of British membership in 1963 and 1964, and the famous proposals for financing the common agricultural policy in the spring of 1965.

If, then, the Commission was initially successful, and if its later failures can largely be explained by severe dissension among the member states which many observers believe to have been a temporary phenomenon lasting only for the tenure of office of President de Gaulle, why are we so sceptical about the present institutional arrangements of the Community? The answer is partly, as we have said, that one cannot depend on the national governments for political leadership of the right kind. Partly, again, the answer is that the Community has not so far made significant steps towards positive integration and, even without Gaullism, such steps are qualitatively different from the achievement of negative integration, involving as they do evaluative decisions of major social and economic importance. Finally, the answer is concerned with the nature of organizations and our conviction that the organization of the Commission must increasingly perform bureaucratic functions, which will disable it from behaving as a partisan body and will eventually change it from its present porous condition.

This part of our argument tends to prejudge another, in that it implies that there was insufficient consensus among the member states to support the partisan Commission. The organization which President Hallstein led in the first few years of the Community, and which left its mark on the institution for many years afterwards, is best typified by making an analogy with a political party or highly organized pressure group rather than with an administrative organization. This organization was held together largely by common loyalty and understanding – there was little demand for mechanical rules and regulations and little stress on hierarchical lines of command and on departmental prerogatives. The values esteemed in this organization were energy, enthusiasm and creativeness. Yet to be effective its initiatives and its authority depended upon the willingness of the member governments to allow themselves to be committed to measures designed in the long run to lead to European integration. The tactics by which this was achieved are significant. In general, the governments were led to accept European measures because of the short-term, selfish advantages they could get from them.[1] This procedure often involved, as we have seen, tortuous bargaining on matters of incredible detail. The main strategy of the Commission was to work through national officials and interest groups and to get the national governments into a position where they had to agree to a Community solution or else have no solution at all.

There is, however, an inherent contradiction in the role of the Commission in this procedure. We have already remarked on this and it is what has led so many observers to puzzle over what sort of political system the Community represents and to describe the system as *sui generis*. On the one hand, the Commission must be European – or as we have now come to call it, partisan. On the other, the fact that Community legislation can be legitimized only by the national governments requires it to be independent, to perform the function of impartial mediator among the various national positions. Of course, in situations where the national governments were so at one over the social and economic questions involved in the Community that the attitude of one coincided with that of all the others, the role of mediator would be very simple, not to say hardly necessary at all except as a purely secretarial, clerical function. However, such situations are most unlikely to occur, even in the absence of General de Gaulle and his supporters. Consensus on short-term goals can certainly be engineered; even General de Gaulle could be convinced that France's interests would be served by an agricultural common market (on certain terms) and that a common system of corporate taxation should be adopted throughout the Community. But engineering such a consensus places the Commission into the position of a bureaucracy, by demanding of it a mediative function requiring impartiality, and resting on delegated authority. The partisan commitment of the early Hallstein Commission was based on organizational principles which were basically unsuited to the role the institution was performing. Ironically enough, its very successes were probably the result of a role which was incompatible with the values the organization held so highly. Its initiatives which failed did so because the Commission had proved too partisan and insufficiently impartial for the member governments. So in time the Commission's leadership and its organiza-

1. This is the interpretation we derive from Lindberg's analysis of the Community Method (see Lindberg, 1963, pp. 284–6).

tion adapted to necessity, by becoming more and more representative. This was the only realistic course for practical men to take – any other action would have grossly overestimated the ability of national governments and socio-economic interests to achieve consensus. Our main point about the bureaucratization of the Commission is that this porous organization is essentially transitional, in that we predict that an automatic, built-in resistance to its open-ended nature is bound to arise. This resistance will result (indeed, has already resulted) in mechanistic devices of personnel administration. At the same time, the present decision-making process of the Community is so inefficient, in that the mediative agency of the Commission can achieve only a limited amount of agreement in a certain amount of time, that more and more decisions will have to be delegated to the Commission. This has already begun to happen in the case of policy on competition, agriculture and so on. These decisions will be of a programmed, routinized variety – though naturally there will be differences of degree – in that it will have been the member governments and not the Commission itself which will have approved the legislation under which the powers are delegated.

Of course, if President Hallstein, along with Vice-Presidents Mansholt and Marjolin and all the other partisan Commissioners, had been able to stand for election, or to gain direct legitimation in the six countries in some other way, their partisan style of leadership would have made considerable sense. This may sound an excessively vague qualification, for we know little enough about processes of legitimation, about the nature of political leadership, and about the way executive leadership should be exercised over bureaucracies. It is a vitally important qualification, however, for, at least, it points us in the right direction so that we know what problems we have to solve in order to build an institutional system capable of promoting European unity. We shall only touch on the subject here. This qualification also places the onus of proof regarding the likelihood of consensus of the member governments on those who argue the 'functionalist' case. It must be remembered that the amount of consensus required is not just a preparedness to agree to some vague, long-term goal such as European unity (which might well be possible after de Gaulle), but sufficient consensus to provide active leadership for the officials and representatives who must make the short-term decisions necessary to make this long-term goal a reality. The governments of national states spend a major proportion of their time drawing on resources of legitimacy acquired from electorates, or parliamentary majorities, or referenda, or party machines, in trying to reconcile the demands of competing groups within their countries with a view to promoting the national interest. How much more difficult it must be for an institution whose leaders are appointed by six different national governments from whom practically all its powers are derived to do the same thing at an international level. [. . .]

Our special study of the role of Commission of the European Communities has already enabled us to point to some general conclusions regarding the role of bureaucracy in relation to politics. Thus we found that the Commission came increasingly to exercise purely delegated, administrative functions and that this was related to its tendency to acquire a more and more bureaucratic organization. Conversely the more it became suited to performing relatively mechanical, routine tasks (even where these needed the exercise of considerable discretion of an administrative kind), the Commission would be able to show less and less of the creativity and initiative demanded of a body capable of promoting political unity in Europe. Similarly, the more it compromised its role as initiator and upholder of the common interest by coopting national officials and permanent representatives into the decision-making process, the less it would be capable of laying down with any efficacy the norms of legitimate behaviour within the Community. This seems to lead us to resuscitate the dichotomy between politics and administration, even though this has become rather disreputable among students of government (Chapman, 1959, pp. 273–95; Friedrich, 1936, pp. 386–410). However, in so far as there does seem to be a marked incompatibility between the Commission's 'political' role as promoter of the common interest and its 'bureaucratic' role as administrator and mediator, our work suggests that the dichotomy does still have some important operational value.

While in its early years the Commission might have seemed to be more like an autonomous, federal executive in embryo than like the administrative, implementative part of the Community's system of institutions, in the course of time the latter has grown to be more and more the true description. Our confidence in regarding the Commission as a bureaucracy was increased when we saw that the character of its internal organization and the behaviour of its members and personnel increasingly came to fit the criteria associated with bureaucracy just as much as did its external relations with other parts of the Community system. What is more, there seemed to be something almost inevitable about this development, for it seemed to be directly related to the delegated nature of the Commission's formal powers and to its need to adopt a mediative function in relation to the real political authorities of the Community (the national governments). The evolution of its organization into a 'mechanistic' type could be directly related to the external relationships of the Commission, in that bureaucratic methods of personnel administration, and a decision-making process that stressed hierarchy and formalism, were developed almost as a defence against infiltration from extraneous groups and influences and against opposition to its own development.

This seems to give an almost tautological theme to our study: a body with essentially delegated functions (a 'bureaucracy') reveals an essentially mechanistic ('bureaucratic') organization.[2] However, although the Commission became more and more like the conventional type of bureaucracy, for a long time it seemed to function quite differently and it was certainly not intended to take such a form by the committed Europeans who founded the Communities. How then, can we classify it in terms of the normal institutions of a political system? It is evidently not the same sort of institution as the typical executive branch of government, whose members lead a political party or parties, or are directly elected into office; nor for that matter is it entirely the same as a purely administrative organ of the state organized and staffed according to classical bureaucratic principles. Indeed, if we attempt to list the main formal characteristics of the Commission in quite general terms, we get an interesting combination of 'political' and 'bureaucratic' qualities:

1. Its members are appointed not elected to office, and the criteria of appointment do not include representation (at least not formally and explicitly). Technical qualifications for membership are not formal and explicit, but are implied and understood (even if only at the level of general technical competence). Appoint-

2. This proposition is incomplete, of course, for it makes no reference to the 'vicious circle' of bureaucracy, whereby the bureaucratic features of the internal organization feed back on its external relationships and keep these at a delegative implementative level. Bureaucrats resist the taking of initiatives and withdraw into routine, programmed activity where they feel more secure.

ment is at the discretion of legitimized political leaders (the national governments acting together).

2. Membership of, or allegiance to, a particular political party is not usually a condition of membership, but the members are not expected to be anonymous or impersonal. Moreover, the members (and also to some extent the staff) of the Commission are expected to show a considerable degree of personal commitment to the aims of the organization, however vaguely these may be expressed and however long the term in which they are to be accomplished. Such commitment is probably a more important factor than salary or other material benefit in motivating participation in the organization at most levels.

3. The members constitute the leaders of the organization and appoint their own staff, largely on the basis of open, competitive examination to test qualifications and merit. There is formal specialization and division of labour, but the members are constituted on a collegial basis and the organization is meant to be bound together by common leadership. Thus, the leaders are separated from the rest of the organization (by being separately appointed and bound by collegiality), and there is no formal way of passing from its lower ranks up to this leadership by promotion according to seniority or merit.

4. The Commission's formal powers are delegated, being derived partly from the Treaty of Rome and partly from regulations passed by the Council of Ministers. (It does, however, also have power to make delegated legislation in consultation with other parties.)

5. The Commission (in the person of its members) is solely responsible for interpreting and exercising its powers, subject only to judicial review, the threat of vote of censure by the European Parliament, and the need to take into account the views of this and other consultative bodies. Such consultation may be used by the members, along with other forms of public exposure, as a means of mobilizing direct support for their aims.

It is clear merely from this listing of formal characteristics that the Commission is a most interesting hybrid kind of body. 'Political' characteristics such as a sense of shared commitment and purpose, relative independence of the national governments, the right to publicize its views and to canvass moral support, a collegial system of leadership which is not bound by the same rules as the rest of the organization, are found alongside bureaucratic traits such as the fact that the members are appointed not elected, that its powers are delegated not intrinsic and that it is not directly accountable to a Parliament or an electorate. However, this is a good point to recall that this juxtaposition of seemingly contradictory formal characteristics is not entirely accidental or irrational. In the circumstances of the Community, as seen particularly by people such as Jean Monnet and others more or less associated with the 'functionalist' approach to integration, the establishment of a supranational institution with these extraordinary features had a special appeal.

In the first place, the Commission was entrusted with protecting and furthering the European idea, to which it had to remain firmly committed, and with acting in strict independence of the governments of member states. It had to have means of mobilizing support for further integration. On the other hand, a directly representative kind of body was undesirable because it would have challenged the sovereignty of the member states. At the same time, some scholars have argued that such a body would have 'over-responded' to elements hostile to further integration. The European idea could be regarded in a sense as being too fragile for that kind of exposure (Etzioni, 1965, p. 75). Finally, the Commission's task was to be an extremely technical one, particularly in the first years, and the service of men, chosen to a large extent for their competence as much as for their conviction, was essential.

As we have seen, a body of this sort did for a time prove to be highly suitable for furthering integration under the circumstances prevailing in the early years of the Economic Community. While the member governments (the real sources of political authority both at a national and at a Community level) did not resist the long-term goal of political unity, then the Commission was able to carry short-term measures designed to lead to that goal (such as the removal of barriers to trade, the free movement of labour and services, and the adoption of a common policy on cartels and restrictive practices). The Commission achieved this by remaining firmly committed to the long-term goal of political unity, interpreting it in technical terms in the present, and thereby 'selling' its short-term implications to social and economic groups. However, in order to continue implementing measures of integration in the present, it had to compromise different national, social and economic differences, and the only way to sustain a short-term consensus was by mediating between these and even coopting their representatives into the decision-making process. We have already traced in detail how this tended to detract from the Commission's political role.

This was not the only cause of discomfort on the Commission's part. Eventually, it was bound to evolve common policies in vital sectors of economic and social activity, and here, too, it was faced with the need to reconcile different ideologies, which were already active at a national level. Thus there was not consensus about the proper role of public authorities in economic management and this made the evolution of common economic and industrial policies more difficult. Even when and if consensus can be found on this fundamental question, the Commission will be faced with the need to take over from member governments the responsibility for defining the public interest in social and economic affairs – a responsibility which strains all the resources of legitimacy and support which political authorities, even at a national level, can muster. In such conditions a body with only hybrid political form is inadequate.

A body like the Commission shares with the conventional type of administrative organization the essential quality of acting within defined fields of action on the basis of an established consensus of values. At the international level, as we have seen, such a basis must be the ideologies and interests of the leaders of nation states, who, in the absence of political leadership mobilized at a federal level, retain real power. A 'supranational' bureaucracy does not seem on the evidence we have collected to have resources enabling it to overcome opposition to its long-term aims from such national political leaders. What is more, it is not even in a position to take their place in mobilizing support for measures in the long-term common interest.

References

CHAPMAN, B. (1959), *The Profession of Government*, Allen & Unwin.
EEC COMMISSION (1965), *Eighth General Report on the Activities of the Community*.
ETZIONI, A. (1965), *Political Unification*, Holt, Rinehart & Winston.
FRIEDRICH, C. J. (1936), *Constitutional Government and Democracy*, Harper & Row.
LINDBERG, L. (1963), *Political Dynamics of European Economic Integration*, Oxford University Press.
MARCH, J. G., and SIMON, H. A. (1958), *Organizations*, Wiley.

12 Giancarlo Olmi

The Role of Community and National Institutions in the Implementation of the Common Agricultural Policy

G. Olmi, 'Le rôle respectif des institutions communautaires et nationales dans la mise en œuvre de la politique agricole commune', *Institutions Nationales dans le Développement des Communautés*, Editions de l'Université de Bruxelles, 1967, pp. 115–37. Translated from French.

Agricultural problems have a prominent place in the preoccupations of the European Economic Community. Repeatedly, during past years, debates on agricultural policy have given rise to controversies between the six partners, even to the extent of causing delays in the building of Europe; repeatedly, these debates have resulted in spectacular agreements, achieved at the price of 'marathons', which have been the springboard for new leaps forward in all spheres. And it is not without significance that even the crisis of 30 June 1965, an eminently political one, arose during discussions relating to agriculture.

It is not surprising, therefore, that at the time of the negotiations which preceded the conclusion of the Treaty of Rome, the question was raised to begin with as to whether agriculture should or should not be included in the Common Market. In actual fact this question immediately received a positive reply. It would have been unthinkable to leave outside the European venture an economic sector so important and so bound up with the main body of the other sectors. But the necessity of providing this positive step with appropriate special measures was realized.

If one compares it with industry, agriculture is much more exposed to difficulties due to unforeseen factors (one has only to think of the influence that meteorological phenomena have on the quantity and quality of the harvest), while it is much less capable of reacting to the effects of these factors with a view to re-establishing the balance of the market. In the short term, the supply of agricultural produce is rigid: it is done at fixed times corresponding to the harvest, for, by virtue of the perishable nature of the produce, it is impossible to delay supply too long. For its own part, the demand for agricultural produce is also rigid and does not increase proportionately to the decrease in prices. With the good news of a rich harvest there follows more often than not the bad news of the collapse of the market.

Long-term development is no more encouraging. The technical progress of these last decades, which ought to have raised the standard of living of the farmers by a lowering of costs, has had the opposite effect in Europe: the large increase in production has in fact resulted, because of the rigidity of demand, in a decrease in the price of agricultural produce. Inversely, their costs of production in machines, motor-fuel, fertilizers and other industrial products have increased. Agricultural revenue has thus become very inferior to industrial revenue: it is estimated, in broad terms, as being one half of the latter.

Another disturbing element: the world market. Cereals, sugar, vegetable oils are all produced in large quantities by non-European countries. It is a matter of agricultural exploitation on a grand scale, with very fertile land and modern machinery. The exploitation of the developing countries has the benefit of cheap labour; richer countries have the benefit of government subsidies, which, in the United States, are annually in the order of hundreds of millions of dollars. These countries throw their surplus on to the world market maintaining a very low price level and, moreover, an extremely fluctuating one.

The European states have thus been led into undertaking a series of measures in favour of agriculture, partly within the framework of the so-called structural policy which aims to lower the cost of production by the reintegration of land units, land improvements, mechanization and the other objectives of the various 'green plans'. But to be effective in the long term, structural policy demands a lot of time and money. In the present state of affairs, it is undeniably easier to effect a market policy and a commercial policy, than it is, say, to act in the short term on the markets, supporting and stabilizing prices.

Thus it is that in different degrees the European states have, on the one hand, intervened in the home market and, on the other, taken protective measures against imports. Intervention takes the form of the purchase of considerable quantities of produce at a minimum guaranteed price: the produce is stocked, to be then released and re-sold on the home market at a more favourable time, or, if that time is long in coming, sold at a loss on the world market. Protection against imports ranges from the classic methods of customs duty and the fixing of quotas to restrictions on quantity, compulsory corporation and import monopolies: in short, a whole arsenal of measures adjusting the degree of protection to the needs of the moment and aiming to achieve the result that, whatever the fluctuations of the world market, imported produce comes on to the home market at a price which does not imperil the national produce.

Thus a national agricultural policy can be carried out effectively only in a closed market which is protected against the outside; protected not only by customs duty and a quota system, but by flexible measures which can allay the fluctuations of the world market.

When the authors of the Treaty decided to include agriculture in the Common Market, they also had to realize that, firstly, an agricultural policy was indispensable in order for European agriculture to survive and flourish, and, secondly, that such a policy could no longer be national, a national policy presupposing a closed national market.

There remained only the solution stipulated in article 39, para. 4 of the Treaty: 'The functioning and development of the Common Market for agricultural produce must be accompanied by the establishment of a common agricultural policy . . .'. The main instrument of this will be, as is foreseen in article 40, para. 2, a common organization of agricultural markets, taking up on a European scale the measures which had hitherto been adopted on a national scale in extended order and along divergent lines.

Legal experts who have made a study of the treaties setting up the European organizations have, following the lines set out by Reuter (1953, p. 96), called attention to two types of restriction on the sovereignty of member states:

1. Limitation of powers, that is the acceptance of certain regulations which set out precisely the conditions to which the member state is subject in the exercise of powers in which it formerly enjoyed complete freedom of action.
2. Transfer of powers, that is the relinquishing of power by the member state to the advantage of an organization to which – as regards transferred powers – it is subordinate.

The European Community differs from preexisting international organizations by the number and importance of transfers of power of a normative, executive and judicial nature.

Articles 39 and 43 of the EEC Treaty require a considerable transfer of powers to the Community in matters concerning the formulation and implementation of the common agricultural policy. This transfer is, however, only potential; it was not automatically achieved on 1 January 1958 with the coming into effect of the Treaty, but is achieved gradually as the Community legislature, by virtue of article 43, makes rulings on various matters which form the subject of a common agricultural policy. As long as these matters are not subject to a Community regulation, they continue to fall within the powers of the member states.

Before the implementation of the common policy we remain in the sphere of simple 'limitation of powers'. The member states remain free to pursue their national agricultural policies provided that they observe certain rules of the Treaty. It is a question first and foremost of rules which impose the progressive establishment of the Common Market: the abolition of barriers preventing the flow of goods between member states and the establishment of a common customs tariff. These general rules are, however, partially replaced by special regulations, such as articles 44 and 46 which allow the setting up of systems of price minimums and compensatory taxes by waiving the ban on creating new obstacles to trading between the member states, and article 45 which permits the continuance of import restrictions where they are an integral part of 'national marketing organizations'.

Even in this intermediate stage – which still exists for produce not yet subject to the common organization of marketing, such as fish, tobacco and non-edible horticultural produce – there exist transfers of power to the Community. It is primarily a matter of the jurisdictional power of the Court of Justice, which particularly includes the power of determining the conformity of acts of the member states with Community law (article 169) and that of interpreting Community law with compulsory effect on national courts of law (article 177). Then there is the control exercised on the activity of member states by the Commission, by virtue of article 155, which instructs the Commission to see that Community law is observed, and also by virtue of article 169, which allows it to call attention to infringements of this law and, if the member state does not take heed of its warning, to refer the matter to the Court of Justice. Apart from this there exist specific powers of decision.[1]

1. These powers consist of: drawing up restrictive clauses in the application of the Treaty, for example the objective criteria for establishing systems of price minimums (art. 44, para. 3); applying sanctions, for example decisions by which the Council could revise price minimums incorrectly fixed by member states (art. 44, paras. 4 & 5); granting authorization, for example in establishing compensatory taxes referred to in article 46.

In this intermediate stage, the member states are thus subjected to a power of control by Community institutions, but we remain essentially within the framework of a limitation of the powers of the state: these powers of legal and statutory bodies and of administrative control have, in general, the sole aim of ensuring the execution of Treaty regulations which impose negative obligations on the member states.

This picture changes entirely with the common agricultural policy which marks a considerable 'transfer of powers'.

This transfer firstly takes place at the stage of conception and definition of the common policy. The Treaty itself is confined to determining, in articles 39 to 42, certain general objectives and principles, but it has assigned to the Community in article 43 the power of laying down all regulations, directives and decisions necessary for 'the formulation and implementation of the common agricultural policy'. Thus article 43 constitutes one of the most important allocations of normative powers to the Community which are made in the Treaty.

The definition of the common agricultural policy has been assigned to the Council which gives judgement, unanimously in the course of the first two stages of the transition period and afterwards by a qualified majority, on proposals from the Commission and after recommendations by the European Parliament (article 43, paras. 2 & 3). Of course, the member states, by participating in the Council, contribute in the formation of the will of the Council; but the Council is a Community institution and the regulations, directives and decisions which it decrees are Community acts which are imposed on the member states with the power of compulsion conferred on them by article 189 and subsequent articles of the Treaty.

Article 43 places no limits on the normative activity of the Community. In practice, however, the Community has not yet made rulings on – and thereby taken charge of – all matters liable to be the subject of a common policy; certain matters continue consequently to be the responsibility of national authorities.

The normative activity exercised in pursuance of article 43 includes, apart from the carrying through of essential provisions, the matter of institutional regulations for the implementation of the common agricultural policy, consisting of:

1. Defining the respective powers of the Community and the member states.

2. Dividing the powers reserved for the Community between Community institutions, particularly between the Council and the Commission.

The Community legislature enjoys considerable latitude in determining these institutional regulations.

As far as 'structural policy' is concerned, the Community, considering 'that the structural deficiencies are found on a local and regional level and that an improvement in agricultural structure is only possible thanks to the active cooperation of those who are immediately affected', has preferred for the moment to limit itself to a task of coordinating policies pursued by member states. It carries out this task by means of the Council, summoned to take measures by virtue of article 43, of the Commission, instructed to examine bills, plans ranging over several years, etc., formulated by member states and, should the occasion arise, to express an opinion on these, and finally by means of a permanent Committee on agricultural structure in which periodically the ideas of the Commission and the member states confront each other.[2]

Moreover, the Community can to a certain extent stimulate and orientate national structural policies through the 'orientation' section of the European Fund for Orientation and Agricultural Guarantees (FEOGA). Credit is annually made available for financing projects dealing with the improvement of agricultural structure which are presented to the Commission by individuals or bodies with the favourable recommendation of the interested member states. These projects must be registered within the framework of 'Community programmes' established according to the procedure set out in article 43.[3]

European integration is inevitably much more advanced in the field of common organization of agricultural markets, which establishes the complex machinery of the 'market policy' and the agricultural 'commercial policy' of the Community. These policies demand in fact a unity of conception and execution. However,

2. Decision of the Council of December 1962 concerning the coordination of policies on agricultural structure (*Journal Officiel de la Communauté Européenne*, 1962, p. 2892).

3. Article 3, para. 1d and 5 para. 2 of regulation no. 25 of 4 April 1962 relating to the financing of the common agricultural policy (*JOCE*, 1962, p. 991) and article 11 and subsequent articles of regulation no. 17/64/EEC of February 1964 relating to the conditions of aid from the European Fund for Orientation and Agricultural Guarantees (*JOCE*, 1964, p. 586).

even in this field, the Community legislature enjoys a certain freedom in dividing powers between Community and national institutions. This results particularly from article 40, para. 2 which stipulates that, according to the produce, common organization can take one of the following forms:

1. Common regulations in matters of competition.
2. Compulsory coordination of various national marketing organizations.
3. A European marketing organization.

Let us leave aside the 'common regulations in matters of competition', in which the normative aspect comes before the constitutional aspect and which do not therefore hold any great interest for our study,[4] and let us examine the other two forms.

The expression 'European marketing organization' expresses an idea of centralization, of administration concentrated in the hands of European institutions. On the other hand, the words 'compulsory coordination of various national marketing organizations' express an idea of decentralization.

One must however emphasize that, even if this second form were chosen, there exists a minimum number of powers which could not be handed over to Community institutions. This is necessitated, categorically, by the terms 'compulsory coordination' and 'common organization', and on a practical basis by the principles laid down in articles 38, para. 1 and Article 40, para. 3. The first of these two arrangements places agriculture and trade in agricultural produce in the 'Common Market', that is a market without internal frontiers between member states. Article 40, para. 3 expressly stipulates that common organization must exclude all discrimination between both producers and consumers within the Community. These two principles are subject to some limitations during the transition period foreseen by the Treaty, but must be brought into full effect by the end of this period. This means that the most important decisions, beginning with those which determine the guaranteed price for the producers, could not possibly be taken – at the single market stage – at a national level. Different prices in different member states would necessitate, for its continuance, the upholding of customs and quota barriers between these states which would

4. The only common organization already established which bears a resemblance to this type of organization is that for fruit and vegetables (such as results from regulation no. 23 of 4 April 1962, p. 965).

be incompatible with the Common Market. They would, more-over, constitute discrimination between both producers and consumers within the Community.

In short, 'compulsory coordination of national organizations' will differ from 'European organization' by its more advanced decentralization, in the sense that its administration will be largely entrusted to national authorities; but the coordination – which must make a synthesis of these various organizations to be worthy of the title 'common organization' – will obviously be the task of Community institutions.

For its own part, 'European organization', in spite of its centralization, certainly admits of assigning powers of execution to national authorities.

The agricultural regulations of 1962 and 1964 proclaim in general terms the establishment of a 'common organization of marketing' without specifying what shape it is to take. There is every reason for observing that the Treaty does not make us dependent on the particular legal consequences of adopting either one form or the other. It is thus of little use not only to specify in the regulation which creates a common organization what form it is intended to give it, or any more, once the organization is established, to try and find out what form it has taken in the sense of para. 2 of article 40.

The importance of this provision is not due to its foreseeing a classification of organizations to be created, but to the fact that it indicates various paths to the Community legislature. We have made here a brief analysis to show that the authors of the Treaty have allowed – within the limits which we have seen – that common organization can, depending on the produce, assume a more or less centralized form, in other words that some reasonably important tasks are entrusted to national institutions.

In order to analyse more effectively the connection between the functions of Community and national institutions in the 'common organization of agricultural markets', it is interesting to take a concrete example and to examine, therefore, in greater detail the common organization established in the field of 'cereals' by regulation no. 19 of 4 April 1962 (*JOCE*, 1962, p. 933).[5]

This regulation, like those already in force for dairy produce and rice (*JOCE*, 1964, pp. 549, 574) and like plans for vegetable

5. For a deeper understanding of the principles of the common organization of agricultural markets, see Brunet (1964); Megret (1964).

oils and sugar which the Council should be dealing with in 1966, establishes a price rate, that is arrangements centred on the political fixing of a price which one will endeavour to make effective, in the interest of farmers, by action taken at the frontier and in the home market.

Regulation no. 19 has established a system of three prices: the target price, the threshold price and the intervention price. These prices are determined for the time being by each member state.

The target price is that which the public powers hope to ensure on the market during the coming year; it is published before the winter sowing in order to give farmers some indication – it is not yet a guarantee – and to allow them to organize their farm planning.

To make sure of a real price on the home market which differs as little as possible from the target price, one must first of all take measures against importation, sheltering the home market from the falls and fluctuations of the world market.

To this end, a rigid protective measure such as customs duty would have been by itself entirely inappropriate; duty of this sort, fixed once and for all as a customs tariff, which it is relatively difficult to modify, will be an insufficient protection and will give rise to an invasion of low-priced produce if the world market collapses. When, on the contrary, the world price rises above a certain level, customs duty can become prohibitive. The European states, therefore, preferred in the past to add to or substitute for the customs duty flexible protective measures such as those which were enumerated at the beginning of this report.

Rejecting the monopoly system, which is a denial of competition, as well as restrictions on quantity, which excessively interferes with trade, the EEC chose the system of the 'variable levy', which consists of exacting, on importation, the payment of the difference between the price which one wants to ensure on the home market and the low, unstable price of the world market. The home market can thus be compared to a dock, connected to the troubled sea of the world market by a lock. This lock allows the maintenance of a constant and relatively high level within the system.

The levy is the result of a subtraction, whose elements are the price which one wants to ensure on the home market and the price on the world market.

The first of these should be identified with the target price.

However, for technical reasons which it would be impossible to go into briefly, regulation no. 19 anticipates for this purpose the fixing of a threshold price which results from adjusting the target price due to certain factors, for example unloading fees, transport charges from the frontier to a particular commercial centre, and which represents the threshold where the application of the levy increases the price of the imported produce when it enters the member state.

The second part of the subtraction is the price on the world market or, more precisely, as the regulation defines it: 'the CIF price established on the basis of the most favourable conditions for purchase on the world market'. It is important that this price is announced each day – the world market in cereals being extremely variable – with the greatest precision, and that this announcement is centralized, otherwise there would no longer be a uniform levy but as many levies as there were offices in charge of this announcement. This job has therefore been entrusted to the Commission. The Commission decides the CIF price of the various cereals every working day in the afternoon, on the basis of data provided by member states and by other sources of information. The decision determining these prices is sent to the six capitals by telex; it is on these prices that the levy applicable the following day is calculated.

The target price must, however, be protected not only against the world market but also against disturbances which originate inside the market such as, for example, the fall in prices due to a bumper harvest. To this end regulation no. 19 anticipates purchase to support the crop to be made by state organizations for intervention. An intervention price, somewhere between 5 per cent and 10 per cent lower than the target price, is fixed annually, in the same way as the latter. The relevant organizations must buy cereals which are offered to them at the intervention price (which in practice happens when the market price has fallen below the intervention price). The produce is then stocked, that is to say that it will be placed in a warehouse to be brought back into circulation only when the market situation allows. For this purpose, the organizations for intervention are forbidden to re-sell the produce below the target price.

It is possible that the situation will not allow the produce in stock to be put back into circulation within a short space of time; it will then be necessary to hold over the stock to the following year which means sustaining considerable storage charges and interest charges. To avoid this, the public powers try to free the market by encouraging exports to outside countries. As exportation must be made at world market prices, one must to this end grant subsidies which, in the language of the Community, are called export 'restitutions', and which constitute, in a certain sense, the opposite of levies.

In the present state of development of common organization, the decision to grant or refuse restitutions to exporters is in the hands of the member states, but the maximum sum which can be granted is fixed by the Commission. In order to take this important decision, as with many others, the Commission must at the outset ask the advice of an 'administrative committee' formed by representatives from the member states.

From 1 July 1967 there will be a genuine single market for cereals. The barriers between member states will disappear; there will be a common price level for the whole Community. Of course, natural price differences will continue to exist from region to region (as has always been the case within each national market), by reason, for example, of the distance between the various consumer areas and production areas and consequently of the difference in transport charges. On the other hand, it will no longer be permissible for a member state to artificially maintain a different price level isolating its own market.

The target price valid for the whole Community will then be fixed annually by the Council. Hand in hand with the common indicative price, the Council will furthermore determine:

1. A threshold price, against which will then be assessed the price of imported produce which comes from outside countries by applying a single levy wherever the point of importation may be.

2. An intervention price, which will govern a single system of interventions on the home market.

The single market has not yet been achieved, but is only in the course of progressive realization. The member states have already had to standardize the mechanics of market organization, and thus, for example, have substituted the single measure of the levy, calculated according to the strict rules of the Community, for the arsenal of duties, restrictions, monopolies and other national measures which hindered the import trade in the past; they have also had to adopt a single rate of intervention on the home market. But one very important power has been left to them: that of fixing the target price as it suits them (although within a 'fork' established by the Council), that is to say, to take a determinating decision of market policy.

First consequence: the fixing of the threshold price and the intervention price and also, therefore, of levies against outside countries, which differ between one member state and another.

Second consequence: as long as prices are at different levels, one must maintain barriers between member states. We are not confronted by one single dock but by a series of docks with different levels provided with locks not only facing the open sea of the world market but also placed between the docks. These locks are formed by 'intra-Community levies', technically similar to levies against outside countries, but calculated as a result of the difference in national prices (the threshold price of the importing state minus the 'free-frontier price' of the exporting state) and decreased by a small lump sum to give trading preference to Community produce.[6]

6. This price rate is not wholly applied to each one of the products within the jurisdiction of regulation no. 19 but only to a certain number of 'basic products'. For 'converted produce' with a cereal base, among which one can also count pork, poultry and eggs given the importance of the feeding costs for cereal fodder, there do not exist target, threshold and intervention prices. Imports are affected by a levy divided into two parts, one which is fixed like the classic customs duty and the other variable, calculated on the price of basic cereals and periodically adapted to the variations in this price. Regulations 20 to 22 establish, however, a 'lock price' calculated by taking account of the world price of fodder cereals and of a normal coefficient of conversion. In the case of imports offered at a lower price than the lock price, abnormally low therefore, the levy must be increased by a supplementary sum equal to the difference between the price offered and the lock price.

One part of the levies and lock prices is fixed by the Council; the others, as well as the supplementary sums, by the Commission after advice from the administrative committee.

A rate analogous to that for cereals and their converted products exists in the spheres of rice and dairy produce and will exist for olive oil and sugar. As for cattle meat, the price rate established by regulation no. 14/64/EEC is centred on a 'price indication' fixed for the moment by the member states and in the future by the Council. This rate is not unlike that for cereals but the normal protective measure is still customs duty, to which a variable 'levy' is added solely in the case of an abnormally low offering price and this is determined each week by the Commission.

There is not yet a price rate for fruit and vegetables. Regulation 23, however, anticipates the fixing by the Commission following advice from the Administrative Committee of a 'compensatory tax' on imports from outside countries if the offering price falls below a 'reference price'.

From this examination of the main elements of a common organization of agricultural markets one can, as a general guide, come to the following conclusions:

1. From the moment of its creation, common organization is machinery run by the Community, whose procedural rules are entirely drawn up by the Community.

2. Among decisions of a political character, only the decisions – even if they are fundamental – concerning the fixing of prices (target, threshold, etc.) of basic produce are still left up to the member states, within the fairly broad limits of Community 'forks'. The rest are the preserve of the Community. The fixing of target prices and others will also revert to the Community when we reach the stage of having a single market.

3. Some important tasks of execution are entrusted to the member states and are likely to remain within their competence once the single market stage is reached.

4. The principle Community decisions are assigned to the Council, the others to the Commission, often assisted by an Administrative Committee formed by representatives of the member states.

The agricultural regulations now in force allow important powers to the member states. It is still their prerogative to determine the target prices of cereals, rice and dairy produce, as well as the 'price indication' for cattle meat. Even when we have passed from the temporary present order of things to the establishment of the single market and when the power of price fixing has been transferred to the Council from the member states, it is probable that wide powers of execution will remain with the member states.

The agricultural policy and the organization of markets will be no less a Community affair. To this end, it is not necessary for powers of execution to be concentrated in the hands of the Community institutions as is the case, for example, with the policy on competition. Agricultural regulations multiply the interesting phenomenon of the intervention of the member state acting as a compulsory relay station for carrying out decisions taken within the framework of the Community.

This phenomenon is open to several interpretations. One could say that in the agricultural regulations, the Community has simply bound the field of action of its own institutions within certain limits, beyond which the member states have retained their original powers previous to the Treaty. At the most, these powers have perhaps been subjected by the regulations to provisions imposing conditions and restrictions. We would then still be in the sphere of mere 'limitation of powers'.

According to another interpretation, by the fact of settling certain matters in the agricultural regulations adopted by reason of article 43, the Community has implemented the transfer of powers announced in article 38 and subsequent articles of the Treaty. These matters are the subject not only of fundamental rules, but of institutional rules which, partly, reserve powers for the institutions – particularly the power to decree provisions which are immediately applicable to the member states – and partly delegate powers to the national authorities. Powers which they exercise under this hypothesis are no longer original but derived.

If one follows this theory, although the powers in question are exercised by the member state, it is a matter of powers transferred to the Community and which are then delegated to the member states. 'If the transfer of powers is particularly striking when acts of the Community institutions have a direct bearing on the nationals of member states, it is no less real and tangible, in substance nor in its consequences, when national public Powers are obliged to take measures of enforcement imposed on them by legal regulations' (Sohier and Megret, 1965, p. 115).

I would not like to take up a position on either one theory or the other. Although the problem can be extremely interesting, the practitioner of law in me prefers to leave the solution to more subtle minds. Hereafter I shall provide the professors and students of law with other factors which will be useful to them if they wish to ponder this problem.

The agricultural regulations refrain from interfering with the division of powers within each member state. They entrust powers and obligations to the member states; it is then up to them to appoint the competent authorities for carrying out the arrangements in question. There is thus a return to national public law. According to the constitutions of most of the member states, in the absence of delegation to the executive, the competent authority will be the national Parliament. In matters governed by agricultural regulations there exist, however, either constitutional or legislative clauses of a general nature or *ad hoc* laws adopted to implement the Treaty or the agricultural regulations which give wide powers to the government, a minister or a para-state organization.[7] From then on the act of execution will take effect by virtue of the constitutional or legislative provision which bestows these powers.

Furthermore, such an act will take the form of a law, a decree, an order or a decision, that is to say act of public authority, with the force of compulsion for those governed which the state possesses in its internal legal system.

However, it is necessary also to consider the act of execution from the angle of Community law. For Community law, what counts is the allocation of power in the acts passed by the Community, by virtue of the Treaty.

This power is more often than not tied; it is completely tied when the state is called upon to carry out a provision which does not leave it any margin for increase as, for example, the one which makes it collect a levy fixed by the Council or the Commission, or a levy which the state will have calculated itself but which is based on the CIF price determined by the Commission.

On the other hand, the member states exercise a completely discretionary power, when they are free to act or not, without being bound by Community rules. More often the power is discretionary only within certain well-defined limits, which means that it is partially tied. There is a whole range of such acts. In the matter of export restitutions, national authorities are free to grant or to refuse such restitutions; if they decide, however, to grant them, they must keep below a ceiling set by the Commission.

In the matter of determining the price of cereals, there is discretionary power in another sense. In the assessment of the amount of the target price great freedom is left to the member states, greater than that which is granted them for export restitutions (certainly they must keep within a 'fork' laid down by the Council, that is to say, to respect a lower and upper limit, but the Council has fixed this double limit very generously). However, the member states are obliged to determine the prices in question; they cannot abstain; and we know that with the coming into effect of regulation no. 19 this price fixing was binding not only for France and Germany who already knew similar measures before 1962, but also for those states who had previously practised nothing of the kind. The discretionary margin becomes more

7. In the German Federal Republic, the Parliament has, however, reserved itself the right of decision over political prices, as well as control, exercised according to the particular case by the Bundestag or the Bundesrat, over a series of decisions of the executive.

narrow for the intervention price which must find a level below the target price with a deviation of 5 per cent minimum and 10 per cent maximum. The states are almost completely tied where it concerns threshold prices which must be equal to the indicative price except for the addition or subtraction of certain elements: national authorities certainly have a technical power of increase of these factors, but do not really have a discretionary power; they could not fix a threshold price higher or lower than that resulting from a precise calculation, with the aim of increasing protection of their national produce or of encouraging imports.

When we reach the stage of the single market, prices, including target prices, will, it must be remembered, be fixed by Community institutions, while national institutions only retain the power of execution.

We have seen that acts by which national institutions exercise their power are presented as acts of public authority. For Community law there are good reasons for making the following remarks in this connection.

As regards the nationals of the member state, the national act of fixing a threshold price or collecting a levy remains, even for Community law, an act of public authority which the state has the right of carrying out by virtue of its territorial sovereignty; but it finds its foundation, or at least its legal framework, in the Community regulation which has assigned to the state the power of action and determined the conditions and methods of exercising this power. From then on, if a national decision does not conform with the Community regulation which constitutes its foundation or framework, or if the national decision conforms with the regulation but the latter is illegal, the injured parties can appeal to the relevant national courts to obtain an annulment of the national decision or payment for their loss (the national courts being able to or having to, according to the case, refer the matter to the Court of Justice under article 177 for interlocutory questions of interpretation of Community law or of assessing its validity).

As regards the Community and the other member states, the national act in question obviously does not present itself as an expression of sovereignty, since the Community and the other states are not, under the legal arrangement of the Community, subordinate to the member state which is the author of the act. It presents itself, on the contrary, as the exercise of a legal power, indeed the carrying out of an obligation, as defined in the Community regulation.

This national act creates, of course, obligations for Community institutions, for other member states and their nationals. Thus the levy assessed by a member state is imposed on imported goods coming from other member states.[8]

In another respect, one must observe that such acts create obligations for the member state which is itself author of that act. Thus the fixing of a target price for one season then forces it to fix by means of this price, according to strict criteria, the intervention price and the threshold price for the same season.

Finally, in the exercise of these powers, the member states are subject to the control of Community institutions. Apart from the powers of the Court and the general task of surveillance entrusted to the Commission by articles 155 and 169, which we called attention to in the second part of our study, it is interesting to note that in several cases power is given to the Commission, after consultation with the Administrative Committee, to revise a national act: that is the case with the threshold price fixed by a member state without conforming to articles 4 or 8 of regulation no. 19; that is also the case with safeguarding measures taken by a member state within the framework of article 22 of regulation no. 19 or of corresponding articles in other agricultural regulations.[9]

By virtue of article 43, acts relating to the implementation of the common agricultural policy are passed by the Council – unanimously during the first two stages of the transition period and subsequently by a qualified majority – on proposals by the Commission and after consultation with the European Parliament.

8. Another example: the choice by a member state of a certain point of entry on its frontier for imported produce forces the Commission to estimate the CIF price of free-frontier price for this point, that is to say, to add to the stated price of certain representative goods from the exporting country the transport charges as far as the chosen point of entry on the frontier.

9. If, through the application of the measures for the common organization of markets and because of imports, the market of a member state undergoes or is in danger of undergoing serious trouble, that member state can, during the transition period, take the necessary safeguarding measures concerning the imports in question. The Commission must be immediately notified concerning these measures and, after consultation with the member states through the Administrative Committee and within four working days, it will decide if these measures must be maintained, modified or annulled. The decision of the Commission is enforceable, but on the request of a member state it can be modified or annulled by the Council on a qualified majority decision.

That is the solemn procedure which the Treaty foresees for most of the important normative acts of the Community; this is the procedure which is nearest, including in its formation, to the legislative procedure in existence in the member states.

The twelve regulations of 4 April 1962 and 5 February 1964 which created common organizations for agricultural markets, were passed according to this procedure. However, if one consults the *Official Journal of the European Communities*, one discovers that in more than a few cases of other texts drawn up by virtue of article 43, several hundreds of regulations, not counting directives and decisions, were passed according to more rapid procedures, for example by the Council on a proposal from the Commission without the recommendation of the Parliament, or indeed simply by the Commission. These acts are not drawn up by virtue of article 43 itself, but in compliance with special allocations of normative powers contained in the basic regulations which were themselves passed by virtue of article 43.

In this connection one must dispel the impression, which reading article 43, para. 2 could give, that every decision concerning common agricultural policy requires the lengthy procedure established by this article. It would be absurd to require the application of this procedure to decisions which must be taken within a specific, brief period of time in order that the system can work. It is true that to this end the Council is allowed in its acts to allocate executive powers to the Commission, by virtue of article 155, the last note in the Treaty. But there are politically important executive measures for example in the matter of fixing indicative prices (which determine the level of guarantee given to farmers and which govern a whole system of protection at the frontier and intervention on the home market) which it was advisable to allocate to the Council.

In reality, the solemn procedure of article 43 must be followed for determining the principles of the common agricultural policy; but the normative acts passed by virtue of article 43 can allocate the power of making decisions 'of application' either to the Commission or – especially when it is a matter of important political options – to the Council.

This interpretation is reinforced when one considers that the procedure of article 43 must be followed, as para. 2 of this article shows, especially when passing acts which have a bearing on the common organization of agricultural markets. Now an 'organization' does not merely consist of a body of provisions but of a body of machinery set up to implement those provisions. Apart from the normative aspect of common organization, it is worth emphasizing also its institutional aspect. To create an organization, does not mean only to formulate a series of basic rules but to go further and set up machinery whose job it is to draw up acts, of specific or general importance, of which the life of the organization consists.

Furthermore, a new consultative body not foreseen in the Treaty, the Administrative Committee, was created for each sector of the Common Market organization.

The basic regulations of 4 April 1962 and 5 February 1964 anticipate three categories of working measures:

1. Measures by the Council making rulings on proposals from the Commission.
2. Measures by the Commission making rulings after consultation with the Administrative Committee.
3. Measures by the Commission on its own.

The powers of the Council are involved in:

1. Completing or specifying basic regulations by working criteria or means of application where a political choice is implied, for example the criteria for fixing the target prices of cereals (article 6); or the regulation of levies or restitutions relating to converted produce with a cereal base (gruels, semolina, starch, etc.) which concern very important economic interests (article 14 of regulation no. 19).

2. Passing certain measures of political interest, for example, at the single market stage, the fixing of indicative and other prices which each year determine the degree of protection vouched to farmers; in the present temporary state of affairs, the fixing of 'forks' between which the member states decide their target prices.[10]

The powers of the Commission on its own have been foreseen only where it concerns executive measures which do not imply the use of discretionary powers or which must be taken urgently, for example all statements about CIF prices and free-frontier prices which act as the basis for calculating levies; they have also

10. In addition, fixing a lock price for pig meats and the factors which the Commission must use as its basis for formulating the lock price for eggs and poultry, which determine the degree of protection for these products against what is judged as abnormally low-priced imports.

been foreseen where it concerns tasks analogous to those which the Treaty entrusts to the Commission alone, for example authorizations for lowering import levies on certain articles, corresponding to the power, allocated to the Commission by article 25, para. 3, authorizing each member state to suspend in whole or in part the collection of common customs duty on agricultural produce.

All other acts foreseen in the basic regulations, working criteria or means of application as well as concrete measures, are decided by the Commission after consultation with the particular administrative committee for that sector.

Each administrative committee is composed of representatives from the member states who meet under the chairmanship of a representative of the Commission. It has no power of decision: it produces advice to the Commission, which then makes any decision. The advice is forwarded on a majority decision and the votes of the member states are weighted in the same degree as foreseen by article 148 of the Treaty for Council debates. The advice is obligatory yet not wholly binding on the Commission. Nevertheless, the Commission's non-acceptance of advice forwarded by the Committee entails a legal consequence, namely that of giving the Council the power to make a new decision on the point of controversy, different from that of the Commission. It is obvious that this procedure represents a compromise between two requirements; on the one hand to allow the member states to cooperate with the Commission in the administration of the Common Market organization and, on the other, to reserve for the Commission, in spite of everything, the real power of decision.

The first plan for establishing these committees, put forward by a national delegation in October 1961, gave the power of decision to the committees themselves. This plan was debated for some time and was finally rejected on this point, above all for reasons of a legalistic nature. It appeared in fact that the wide normative powers assigned to the Community by article 43 in matters concerning the creation of the common organization of markets certainly allows the creation of new *ad hoc* machinery which had not been anticipated by the Treaty, but in respect of what are called the constitutional principles of the Community, that is the fundamental rules written down in the Treaty. Now the Treaty entrusts the power of decision only to the Council and the Commission which is made firm by the passing of compulsory acts (articles 145, 155, 189). The acts of these institutions alone are submitted to the control of the Court of Justice (articles 173 to 176). The creation of new machinery armed with the power of decision would thus have resulted in depriving the Council and the Commission of powers which they alone are entitled to exercise and, moreover, in withdrawing the administration of the common agricultural policy from the legal control of the Court.

It is worth remembering that in two judgements of 13 June 1958 Meroni *v.* High Authority (*Recueil* IV, pp. 11 onwards and 51 onwards), the Court of Justice imposed precise limits in the matter of delegation of power. While not excluding the possibility of delegation regarding the provisions of the ECSC Treaty, the Court judged that such delegation could only apply to 'precisely defined powers of execution' excluding a 'discretionary power implying wide freedom of action'; in addition these powers must be 'entirely controlled in the use which is made of them' by the delegating authority. Now the power which it was hoped to confer on the administrative committees was to a large extent discretionary; moreover, these bodies being collegiate and composed of representatives of member states, nominated and recalled by them, could not be subjected to the control of the delegating institution.

The formula which was found, consisting of allocating the power of decision to the Commission with the one reservation of the power of revision by the Council in the possible case of a conflict between the Commission and the majority of the representatives of the member states in the administrative committee, seems a happy formula and one which conforms to the Treaty.

The experience of three years has shown that collaboration between the Commission and the administrative committees has had excellent results. Real problems are sorted out in these Committees, not without battles, but on an essentially technical basis, without there being a need for the Commission and the Council to engage in a political dialogue. A dispute between an administrative committee and the Commission has only had to be brought before the Council for four regulations or decisions out of about four hundred which have been carried through according to this procedure. This has allowed an impressive amount of work to be carried out in a very short space of time.

What I have just explained can have given an inaccurate idea of political and legal reality. One might think that, since basic agricultural regulations have referred to Community institutions most of the important decisions during the preparatory period and all of them at the single market stage, the member states are progressively ousted from all participation in the definition and important administration of the common agricultural policy.

The reality of the situation is quite different, in the sense that the member states actively participate in drawing up and implementing the common agricultural policy by the fact that they form an integral part of the Council and the committees which assist the Commission.

The Treaty has effected a certain sharing of powers between the Council, the Commission and the European Parliament. For all decisions which deal with the formulation and implementation of the common agricultural policy, article 43 has established a procedure involving the intervention of the three institutions. It is true that the initiative lies with the Commission, an objective, independent, 'supranational' body; it is true that before the decision a political debate must take place in the Parliament which represents, as article 137 says, 'the peoples of the states brought together in the Community'. But it remains none the less that the power of decision belongs to the Council, which by virtue of article 146 represents the states themselves, each government delegating one of its members.

Inside the Council there is a confrontation between the interests of the various member states; here, usually during the course of several successive sittings, much uphill work is carried out with the aim of producing solutions which satisfy at the same time all these interests, or, if that is impossible, solutions which share equally the sacrifices and advantages in the common interest. To this end, the Commission takes part in the sittings of the Council in order to hear the point of view of the national delegations, put forward its own and modify its proposals. But it comes back to the Council, that is to say the representatives of the member states gathered together in this corporate body, to draw conclusions and to make the decision.

The basic agricultural regulations assign to the Council both the job of passing practical regulations as well as concrete measures of political importance.

The other practical decisions are entrusted to the Commission but, apart from those which do not constitute the use of discretionary powers such as the establishment of market prices, they are nearly all made after advice from an administrative committee and subject to a different decision by the Council in the case of a dispute between the Commission and the committee. The main function of this procedure does not appear to be the recording, and submission to the Council's arbitration, of disputes between the Commission and the representatives of national administrations. Rather is it to ensure strict cooperation between the Commission and the member states to achieve maximum efficiency in the common organization of markets. Only in exceptional cases does a dispute between an administrative committee and the Commission have to be brought before the Council. On the other hand one can say that all acts passed by the Commission by means of this procedure are the result of preparatory work carried out together by the representatives of the administrative committee. The representative of the Commission (who chairs the committee but has no voting rights) concerned to win the support of the majority of the votes for the Commission's plan, in fact amends the plan during the session in the course of the debates, with a view to giving the maximum satisfaction to the various delegations, either by retaining the solutions they propose as they stand or by effecting a compromise. This means that the plan which comes out of the meeting and which will be put forward for adoption by the Commission is no longer the plan originally put to the administrative committee by the Commission's representative, but a text reviewed in committee with the collaboration of the member states.

The committees thus carry out in the agricultural field a special form of administrative activity compatible with article 5 of the Treaty which results from the cooperation between national and Community bodies (Monaco, 1961, p. 251). The periodic human contacts which result from this between the civil servants of these various bodies have the further effect of bringing together national ideas about the basic problems and thus give birth in Brussels, which then spreads to the different capitals, a 'European' outlook on these problems.

We can thus conclude that if it is true that in the sphere of the common organization of agricultural markets, the member states, taken individually, are increasingly reduced to simply implementing acts passed by Community institutions, it is none the less true that in the carrying through of these decisions they play an active role by the fact that they are an integral part of the Community machinery or are closely associated with its work.

References

BRUNET, J. P. (1964), *La politique agricole commun de la CEE*, Brussels Institut d'études européenes.

MEGRET, J. (1964), 'Principes du région applicable à l'agriculture dans le marché commun', *Revue du Marché Commun*, p. 267.

MONACO, R. (1961), 'L'organizazzione amministrativa delle comunità europee e la pubblica amministrazione italiana' *Revista di diritto Europeo*, p. 251.

REUTER, P. (1953), *La Communauté Européene du charbon et de l'acier*, Paris.

SOHIER, M., and MEGRET, C. (1965), 'Le rôle de l'executif national et du legislateur national dans la mise en oeuvre du droit communautaire', *Droit communautaire et droit national*, semaine de Bruges.

13 Leon Lindberg and Stuart Scheingold

The Failure of the Common Transport Policy:
A Comparison with the Success of the Common
Agricultural Policy

Excerpt from L. Lindberg and S. Scheingold, *Europe's Would-Be Polity*,
Prentice-Hall, 1970, pp. 163–81.

In sharp contrast to agriculture, up to 1968 almost no progress
was made toward a common transport policy. The picture has
been one of almost total deadlock.[1] One observer went so far
as to write in November of 1967 that: 'In no area of Community
endeavor is progress so completely blocked' (*Common Market*,
no. 7, November 1967, p. 270). It is not that the Commission has
failed to make proposals for action. In April 1961 it issued a
general 'Memorandum on the Main Lines of a Proposed Common Transport Policy'. This was followed a year later by a much
more extensive 'Action Program' and subsequently by a series
of yearly proposals for specific actions to be taken by the Council.
All have been extensively discussed and debated throughout the
Community: by interest groups, by the European Parliament and
the Economic and Social Committee, and by government officials
at all levels, from technical experts to high officials to Cabinet
Ministers. The Commission's proposals were quite ambitious and
far-reaching. A common policy was to be based on five principles:
the freedom of users to choose among different means of transport and of suppliers to charge what they liked; equal treatment
for all forms of transport as regards taxation, social charges and
subsidies; all forms of transport should pay their own way; the
costs of maintaining and developing transport infrastructure
should be shared and paid by users; and there should be a coordination of investments.

The Commission proposed to move toward these goals by

1. At this writing there are some signs of a possible breakthrough in
transport. In July of 1968 the Council of Ministers adopted a number of
specific regulations affecting rates on the road and harmonization of
national laws. It is too early to evaluate the substantive significance of the
limited steps taken: in any case they do not explain away ten years of output
failure between 1958 and 1968. The possibility that a change may be occurring does underscore a significant point, namely that no issue-area is likely
to be forever characterized by any one outcome pattern.

establishing for all forms of inland transportation (for road, rail and inland waterway) a system of 'forked tariffs'. These are:

published upper and lower limits within which haulers would be free to charge whatever they choose. The lower limits would be set so as to prevent cut-throat competition, and the upper limits prevent the exploitation of monopoly positions (Shanks and Lambert, 1962, p. 98).

These 'forked tariffs' represented a sort of compromise among the systems then in force in the different countries, some of them having completely fixed rates, while others complete rate freedom. They were probably intended to be an instrument of transition, such as was the system of variable levies proposed in agriculture (*Common Market*, no. 4, October 1964, p. 195). But they were not neutral in a policy sense: they disadvantaged at least one country, the Netherlands, which had the most efficient and lowest-cost transport industry in the Six.

Given the very different policies and interests of the governments, no agreement has been possible in the Council. After four years of discussion and delay the Council finally adopted in June 1965 a resolution calling on the Commission to change its proposals and to base them not on a uniform system of forked tariffs, but on a complex set of special arrangements for each different category of transport (*Common Market*, no. 7, November 1967, pp. 272–3). The Commission submitted amended proposals in October of 1966. But once again the Council was deadlocked and finally, a year later, decided that 'the system of rates was no longer to be a matter of priority, but . . . that (other) steps should be taken . . . in an endeavour to secure a balanced organization of the market' (Commission, European Community, *Tenth Annual Report*, p. 231). The Council then went on to invite the Commission, in effect, to make much more modest proposals with a view toward a coordination of national policies and harmonization of conditions affecting competition in transport, namely the minimum necessary to prevent discrimination and the abuse of monopoly positions and hence to permit the common market to function. The Commission proceeded to submit a new memorandum on a common transport policy in February 1967 and more specific proposals during the year. These finally led to the initial Council decisions of July 1968.

Ten years of effort in the field of transport have thus produced very little. The Commission presented its blueprint for a common transport policy, but was unable to get the assent of the

Council of Ministers, even to the nature of the policy goals that ought to be collectively pursued. It was not possible to overcome the divergences of interest that will almost inevitably exist among these countries in any specific issue area. As a consequence of deadlock, some governments, as well as other actors, came more and more to question whether, indeed, transport should not be regarded simply as a potential source of distortion to trade,[2] instead of as an integral part of the common market.

In its most extreme form, this view would imply that the common transport policy should limit itself to eliminating discrimination on the basis of national origin or destination and nothing more. . . . It has been argued that there is no need to go beyond the creation of certain rules for international transport, and an elimination of all discrimination against foreign carriers in transport. This would leave the separate states free to organize their internal transport systems as they saw fit (*Common Market*, no. 4, October 1964, pp. 192–3).

Others, especially the German government, have announced that they could no longer await joint action by the Community, but would proceed to implement their own national programs to deal with the problems posed by the development of the common market, among other things. The tenor of these measures is apparently such as to make it even less likely that a common transport policy would ever be achieved.

Its proposals to increase the protection of the national railways by various restrictions on road haulage, and to impose the internal German tariffs on international Rhine shipping are clear signs of a more national-oriented outlook gaining ground (*Common Market*, no. 7, November 1967, p. 271).

Transport is then a case of what we have called *output failure*, that is, the system has been unable to translate a general commitment to participate in a collective decision-making effort into an acceptable set of policies or rules. Ten years of debate and discussion have not enhanced either the scope of the Community, or the capacities of its institutions.[3] Many would argue that the authority of the Commission has even suffered a decline as a result of what has been generally perceived to be a very inept performance in transport.

2. This had been the approach of the ECSC Treaty and had been the view of some governments all along.

3. Some very minimal steps have been taken in the area of the harmonization of legislation, but these have not been important enough to much affect either scope or capacity.

It is apparent that the several mechanisms of coalition formation we have associated with forward linkages (functional spill-over, side payments and log-rolling, actor socialization, and feedback) have not been activated in transport. The potentialities for functional spill-over are seemingly every bit as extensive as with agriculture. Transport policy was clearly perceived to bear an intimate relationship to the successful operation of the common market.

If EEC is to derive the full benefit from tariff and quota liberalization, then it is necessary to prevent their effect on the pattern of trade from being frustrated by countries using transport rates or conditions of carriage to give their own products artificial advantages. . . . Rail charges can be used to fulfill the same functions as tariffs on imports by means of rate discrimination against users conveying products of other countries – charging them a higher rate than would be paid for the conveyance of home-produced goods over the same distance and route. Other practices may restrict trade in general by artificially raising the cost of both exports and imports. . . . Railway rates may also be used to distort the pattern of trade. If they are varied according to the nationality of the consignor, lower rates may be charged for exports to or imports from some countries than others (Political and Economic Planning, 1963, p. 228).

Furthermore, all could recognize that transport capacity in all the countries would have to be increased rapidly and rationally, so as not to hinder the development of trade.

Improvements in the quality and cost of transport services can themselves also help to stimulate production and location in areas of lowest production cost. Thus, policies are required which will ensure not only an adequate volume of investment in transport, but also a satisfactory balance between, for instance, investment in roads and in vehicles (p. 229).

Ample incentives would seem to have been available for the adoption of programs of cost-sharing in the area of infrastructure development and investment coordination. Certainly there were difficult problems to be overcome, but we see no reason to consider them technically or politically more insoluble than those of agriculture.

Nor were side payments and log-rolling much used to try to break deadlocks and advance the process.[4] The Commission held

4. Scheinman points out that the Commission did try in a limited way to make use of log-rolling, but with very minimal results limited to the harmonization field, Scheinman (1966).

to proposals that were adamantly opposed by the Dutch government because they would probably have severely compromised the favorable competitive position the Dutch had achieved in the international road transport market. For example, the Commission proposed a system of Community licences that would replace bilateral quotas, whereby a carrier might offer his services anywhere in the Community. These licences were to be distributed among the six countries on the basis of a quota which would have given the Dutch 19 per cent. Dutch opposition is understandable when one considers that they then supplied 40 per cent of all international road transport in the EEC (*Common Market*, no. 4, October 1964, p. 195).[5]

In short, the Commission did not do as they had done in agriculture, namely shape their policy proposals so as to elicit the active support of the government (or governments) that perceived the greatest positive stake in integration. Instead, their proposals in fact undermined the possibilities of support or leadership from the one government that was the most actively concerned. There were apparently few real efforts made to combine proposals so as to offer compensation to those who might be expected to be disadvantaged. The Commission proceeded in a piecemeal fashion rather than offering a wide package of proposals ranging across transport policy and offering something to everyone. And they began by proposing the introduction of an instrument – the forked-tariff system – which instead of being neutral would have involved sacrifices by some before any collective rewards were assured. Similarly, bargaining among the governments in the Council did not lead to the kind of log-rolling we saw in agriculture. Nor were efforts made to make progress in transport a condition for progress in other fields. By and large, bargaining has been restricted to this one field, and to only a few kinds of proposals within the field.

Since transport has been so disappointing it has received much less attention from commentators and scholars of integration. Consequently we know much less about activities concerning transport than we do about agriculture. We have almost no 'hard data' on actor socialization and feedback processes in transport. The available evidence indicates that the transport negotiations have had much less impact on participants in the

5. Road transport in itself was not the biggest problem faced in transport Of even greater importance to the Dutch, and an even greater cause of intragovernmental impasse, was the problem of inland water transport.

bargaining process, on interest groups, and on the general public than the agricultural negotiations had. This is hardly surprising considering the record of complete frustration and deadlock on transportation. The authority of the Commission has suffered. Interest groups and governments have become more nationally oriented. Transport has been perceived as an agent of disintegration and division rather than of integration.

Explaining the contrasting outcomes in agriculture and transport

It has been argued that differences in the ability of the European Community to produce decisions could be explained in terms of variations in the flow of demands and in the leadership available to process them. Our purpose here is to isolate the factors associated with success in agriculture and with failure in transport in order to illuminate the ways in which demand flow and leadership are related to decisions or outcomes that induce growth, that is, to forward linkages. Specifically, we seek to discover how and why the mechanisms of functional spill-over, side payments and log-rolling, actor socialization and feedback were activated in one case and not in the other. We see this as a first step toward our eventual goal of hypothesizing about the general conditions or causes of forward linkage and output failure.

Demand flow

Was there a clear difference between agriculture and transport in the numbers and types of political actors making or resisting demands on the system, in the nature of their interests in integration, and in the distribution of such interests among the actors?

In agriculture all governments accepted the principle of a common or closely harmonized policy. There was a consensus that national agricultural policies had been generally unsuccessful in dealing either with problems of income maintenance and modernization or with those of providing for a more efficient international division of labor in agricultural production. This consensus started with the interest groups concerned and extended to most technical experts and the responsible government officials. All were receptive to replacing national policies with a Community policy. The often enthusiastic espousal of a common agricultural policy by agricultural interest groups was especially crucial since farmers are politically potent in most Community countries. Several governments manifested such a strong interest in achieving a common agricultural policy, most notably France and the Netherlands, that they were prepared to make it an absolute precondition for progress in other areas. In the case of General de Gaulle, a dramatic-political actor if there ever was one, these interests were sufficiently compelling to induce him to make use of a number of dramatic-political actions (threats, warnings, boycotts) to push the negotiations along.

Although there was reluctance in some circles, notably from German farmers' organizations, it was balanced or neutralized in each country by support from other groups or elites. No major political actor, either at a system or subgroup level, perceived the common agricultural policy to be *ipso facto* a threat to his own basic interests. What opposition there was could be overcome with side payments (as in the Kennedy Round) or by logrolling (as with acceptance of a relatively high agricultural price level and special compensatory payments to German farmers who suffer income losses).

There was thus a high potential for the construction of a coalition of supporters of positive action in agriculture within each Community country and transnationally at the Community level. Both incremental-economic and dramatic-political elites made demands for action on the system based on calculations that their interests were better served in that way than by the national alternatives open to them. Furthermore, the overall distribution or patterning of their interest perceptions was essentially convergent, that is, all anticipated gains from different aspects of the proposed policy and few really expected to suffer irrevocable harm.

In transport the situation was very different. While there has been a rather vague and generalized interest in some kind of common transport policy, no major government or category of political actors (interest groups, for example) has perceived it to be in its vital interests that such a policy be rapidly developed. It is reasonably clear that so far no government has felt itself under real pressure, either from transport interest groups or from other interest groups, including those representing users of transport facilities, to push strongly for positive action. Nor have governmental decision-makers or civil servants themselves taken the initiative to force the pace. Indeed, the government with the largest economic stake in transport, the Netherlands, has been the one most opposed from the very beginning to the proposals made by the Commission. Opposition in the Netherlands has been nearly unanimous, with almost all actors agreeing that no action was to be preferred to what the Commission was proposing. The Commission's proposals have been somewhat more to the liking of the French and German governments, but in neither case has there been very much enthusiasm for the kinds of proposals being made.

A consensus that there must be a common transport policy has simply not emerged. The sense of urgency generated over agriculture has been absent in transport. In short, governments have tended to support the defensive positions taken by the national interest groups most concerned and by civil servants in the transport field. The railroads have been the persistent problem. These are government monopolies in each of the Six, and they have been operated in a variety of uneconomical ways to give preference to favored regions or sectors of the economy. It is not surprising that those with vested interests in the present policy would resist change, especially since the broad outlines of the new policy are not clear.

In retrospect, then, there seems to have been much less potential for forward linkage in transport because of the absence of a strong flow of demands for action into the system. Most interest groups and the civil servants concerned defended the status quo, and interest perspectives of the policies being proposed by the Commission formed a conflictual or divergent pattern rather than a convergent one. What one actor saw as possibly in his interests another saw as diametrically opposed to his.

The availability of leadership

If demand flow is the life blood of the Community system, then leadership must be seen metaphorically as the heart that distributes this vital substance to its cells and organs. Demand flow provides the raw material for activating the mechanisms of spill-over, log-rolling, side payments, actor socialization and feedback. But this raw material must be exploited, combined, balanced, molded. Functional links must be capitalized upon, bargains and exchanges proposed and accepted, socialization and feedback mechanisms nurtured or stimulated. These are the functions of leadership, both national and supranational.

Can the agricultural and transport experiences also be distinguished on the basis of inputs of leadership? Let us first consider national leadership and its potential roles relative to demand formulation, the development of bargaining norms, and the stimulation of support. As we noted in the last chapter, the concepts of demand flow and national leadership tend to overlap. A prime way in which governmental actors lead is by trying to move the system in some desired direction by developing public expectations and making demands on it. To move the system they must try to develop coherent national demands that can be transmitted to the Community. To do this they must simplify or reduce the often divergent interests and demands that may be generated within the national system. In the case of agriculture this has often meant supporting the demands of some (for example, efficient agriculture producers) against others (less efficient producers or consumers). It may also mean neutralizing opposition by making active efforts to subsidize or indemnify those who fear losses from Community policies, as for example when the German government offers special payments to farmers who would suffer because the German wheat price is lowered as a result of the common agricultural policy. We have already seen that in agriculture at least two governments, those of the Netherlands and France, were insistent that an agricultural policy be passed, and they worked hard and persistently to accomplish that end. Although the Dutch and the French are at loggerheads in most other areas of Community policy-making, their interests in agriculture converged and therefore their leadership efforts reinforced each other. The German government saw integration in agriculture as necessary for the continued progress of the Common Market and were hence willing not only to make sacrifices in terms of the bargaining settlement (transfer payments to France in the agricultural budget), but also to absorb domestic discontent with the policy and some of its effects. In transport there was little of this insistence upon action by governing elites and what there was was conflicting and cancelled itself out.

To the extent that governments want something from the system, we may expect them to develop incentives to make the system work, as they did in agriculture. For example, the French under de Gaulle, although obstreperous and unpredictable in many other areas, by and large played the Community game in agriculture. They stressed how important the Community was for them; they accepted and indeed promoted partnership with the Commission in the policy preparation process; they were willing to compromise and take the other countries' interests into account; and they accepted proposals that increased the Commission's powers in agriculture. During their 1965–6 boycott they did not obstruct the functioning of the machinery of agricultural policy that was already in operation. In these ways they have nurtured and activated the socialization mechanisms and all that they imply.[6]

De Gaulle and other governmental leaders have also stimulated public support for the Community's efforts in agriculture, in part by the feedback mechanism and in part by evoking symbols that relate to the affective dimensions of integration. Especially in France, but also in the other Community countries, governmental leaders have given much publicity to the common agricultural policy, and to how it promised to alleviate the problems of the farming population. It has loomed large in parliamentary debates and in electoral campaigns. Governmental action has thus facilitated the communication of information about the outputs, both actual and anticipated, of the Community system to the population at large and to farmers in particular. Although this was done primarily to stimulate support for the national governments ('See how well we defend your interests'), its effect is also to help establish the authority and legitimacy of the Community system.

Governments have not had incentives to give priority to action on transport matters. As far as we can tell from the limited evidence available, log-rolling and side payment exchanges have not been actively sought. Bargaining has not nurtured the Community spirit. Nor have governments publicized transport activity or emphasized it very much, except as a potential threat.

What was the role of supranational leadership in the two cases? We have suggested that for a number of reasons an active Commission is a necessary condition for successful coalition formation, that under some circumstances it can capitalize on disagreements within governments or among them to create consensus for its proposals, and that even when governments have been internally unified, and desire positive outcomes, they are seldom able to activate the Community system without the aid of the Commission.

These assertions seem amply supported by the events in agriculture. Most of the credit for building the coalition and for holding it together must go to the Commission and especially to the Commissioner in charge of agriculture, Sicco Mansholt. This is not to underestimate the significance of national 'leadership' in

6. De Gaulle was not always happy with some of the side-effects of actor socialization and there is evidence of efforts to limit the development of pro-European constituencies in the French government.

the form of pressure from the French and Dutch governments. But Mansholt and his staff have operated with extraordinary skill to make the most of the leadership resources of the Commission, its special perspective, its 'power' of initiative, and its technical expertise. Let us now illustrate how each of these was brought to bear at each stage of the policy process in the agricultural case, to activate coalition formation mechanisms and produce system growth.

As we have said, only the Commission can legitimately claim to be acting solely in the interests of the emerging 'new Europe'. National initiatives and policy proposals must always be somewhat suspect, since they are seldom divorced from individual national interests and ambitions. This gives the Commission the possibility of appealing to all groups who perceive any stake, whether economic, political or symbolic, in integration. To do this it must express and symbolize specific proposals and technical arrangements in terms of the broader goals of integration. The specific arrangements and decisions that make up the daily stuff of integration in any sector are not the sort of thing that fire the imagination, and unless they are cast in a broader context of an emergent European common interest, they will be relevant to only a narrow range of experts and interest group representatives. If the Commission is to help mobilize supporters outside this immediate specialized constituency, which it generally must do if it is to build the broad political coalition required for forward linkages, progress in a particular sector must be made to appear vital to integration *per se*. The common agricultural policy is a staggeringly complex mass of regulations that in and of itself practically defies understanding or even description. Yet Mansholt has succeeded in casting its overall goals in such a way as to keep agriculture at the center of integration politics for ten years. Each successive step has been widely celebrated and acclaimed. Somehow, a great many groups and individuals have taken vicarious satisfaction in the steady advances made in agriculture. Mansholt has become perhaps the best-known of the Commissioners – a real European personality, and indeed, a veritable European Minister of Agriculture.

Besides this broad constituency, the Commission must, of course, be able to appeal to those who are immediately affected by its proposals. In the case of agriculture this means above all the farmers. Commission proposals must be accepted by the Council of Ministers, and hence have to take into account the specific interests and needs of individual countries, and the balance of benefits and costs among them. Mansholt clearly designed his proposals for a common agricultural policy to serve the interests of those Community countries for which agriculture was already an important economic sector and which anticipated maximum gain from a rationalized, Europe-wide agricultural market. He also cast his lot with those in each country who saw the future in terms of a declining agricultural population, larger and more efficient farms, and a major migration from the land to other occupations.

Mansholt not only took 'constituency' interests into account, but he also coopted those interests into the decision-making process so as to give them a maximum sense of *participation* in the great European enterprise. In so doing, he went well beyond the standard consultation procedures usually engaged in by the Commission. He actively stimulated the creation of Community-level farmers' organizations (over a hundred now exist). He consulted them at every stage of the process of preparing for changes of policy, thus forcing them to try to reach common viewpoints, rather than expressing six national ones. Each of the market organization systems provides for official advisory committees representing farm groups, thus giving them a role in the routine decision-making process of the agricultural policy. It is no accident that Mansholt is so well-known among European farmers, or that he has usually been able to count on their support when his proposals have gone to the Council of Ministers.

The Commission's ability to make proposals that will be taken seriously depends in part on its command (or potential command) of a technical expertise that is simply not available to any government. The Commission is at the center of a Community-wide web of communications, giving it the substantive and statistical information necessary to the formulation (and implementation) of Community-wide policies. Capitalizing on this favoured position demands gathering around you a competent and cohesive staff that shares your goals and that understands the technical dynamics of the economic sector in question. Mansholt's success in this area had also been striking (Lindberg, 1966, p. 208).

One use the Commission has made of its resources of perspective and expertise is to incrementally time proposals so as to maximize functional spill-over. For example, in building a common agricultural policy, the Commission began with a proposal for a levy system that provoked little opposition precisely because, in itself, it involved no real policy changes. But once a levy mechanism was in existence, this increased the incentives to take the much more difficult policy decisions that were then implied. In a similar way, Mansholt's first substantive proposals were in the area of price policy, even though he had himself always been generally committed to an agricultural policy that relied on structural policy rather than price policy (that is, on increased efficiency and modernization rather than high prices) as a guarantee of the long-term future of European agriculture. But structural reform ran too much counter to existing policies and would be much harder to get accepted on the European level. It was likely to succeed only if a price and commercial policy already existed. The shortcomings of this approach might then be expected to become apparent to everyone. The Community's butter surplus problem discussed earlier is a case in point.

Besides bringing its resources to bear at the policy initiation and preparation stages, the Commission has also played a vital role at the bargaining and decision stages by acting to facilitate log-rolling and side payments. As we have seen, these are the vital mechanisms of forward linkages, whereby governments seek the bargains and balances that integration inevitably involves. Experience has shown that six governments meeting in the Council, each defending its own interests, find it extraordinarily difficult themselves to come up with that balance of gains and losses that can precipitate final agreement. Because it sits by right in most Council meetings, because it speaks with the voice of the Community interest, and because its formal assent is required if its proposals to the Council are to be amended, it has become almost standard procedure to wait for the Commission to formulate the final package deal. And it is no exaggeration to say that it has been Commissioner Mansholt who has practiced the art most successfully. On the basis of his long acquaintance with agricultural problems (he has been a farmer, a Minister of Agriculture for thirteen years in the Netherlands, and a moving force in the UN Food and Agricultural Organization), his understanding of the positions of each government, acquired through the negotiations and through his extensive travels in the Community, and the respect which all the negotiators hold for him personally, Mansholt has been able time and again to piece together the almost magical compromises that have marked the progress of the common agricultural policy.

If agriculture is a classic case of how much active Commission leadership can accomplish, transport is perhaps a classic case of what happens when leadership resources are not utilized.

In spite of policy differences and the problems inherent to the transport sector that limited possibilities for growth, and in spite of the absence of great pressures for action from the governments, it does appear that there was in transport a sufficient potential for functional and political linkages for the Commission to build a coalition in favor of some sort of common policy (albeit more modest than in agriculture) had it acted with anything like the skill and imagination shown in agriculture.[7]

At the outset, there was more optimism with regard to transport than there was for agriculture. And as late as 1965, Jensen and Walter in their fine study wrote of the manifold pressures for action that existed:

The degree of economic specialization is dependent upon the size of the market, and the size of the market is determined to a considerable extent by the nature and costs of transportation. . . . The many new, expanded needs and requirements brought about by gradual economic integration should be met by favorable rate structures and freedom from undue discrimination (Jensen and Walter, 1965, p. 141).

The delays which have characterized the formulation of the common transport policy during the first years of the EEC seem to have been overcome to some extent. It may reasonably be expected that the Commission's transport program will be fully realized during the remainder of the Transition Period (p. 149).

While we cannot demonstrate conclusively that there would have been more progress had the Commission acted differently, we consider that a persuasive case can be made out of the sharp contrast between its modes of operation in agriculture and in transport.

In the judgement of one commentator, the Commission did not show in transport the kind of 'long-range vision and obvious independence' (*Common Market*, no. 7, November 1967, p. 276) so important in agriculture. Indeed, its original proposals seem not to have been based on the kind of consultation and compromise with client groups and national governments

7. It is significant to note that the apparent progress made in 1968 coincides with the departure of the Commissioner formerly in charge of transport. With the new Commissioner has perhaps come a new set of tactics and strategies that may more closely resemble the agricultural pattern.

necessary if a coalition of supporters is to be built. They have been totally unacceptable to a small but important country and the Commission has shown itself generally unresponsive to criticism, not only from the Dutch, but from the Economic and Social Committee representing interest group opinion, from most private economists, and even from a committee of five independent experts consulted by the Commission itself. German and French official opinion tended to shift in favor of a different approach as action on the Commission's proposals seemed blocked. But the Commission was seemingly insensitive to all this and instead of taking the initiative and reshaping its own proposals, it was the Council that finally 'suggested' that it make new proposals to accommodate to the balance of interests that existed in the Community.

There are some who argue that it is the Commission's whole approach to transport policy that is at fault. Having decided to go beyond a minimalist approach of simply trying to assure that discrimination in transport did not unduly distort competition in the Common Market, the Commission failed to cast its net widely enough. Its Action Program envisaged an entirely new set of balances in the transport market.

The overall philosophy . . . is that the distribution of traffic between different forms of transport should be effected by the price mechanism, and controls on capacity and other institutional forms of protection . . . should play a less important part. . . . At the same time, the pressures which have artificially boosted or lowered costs of providing one or other types of transport services, are to be removed. Thus, the policy relies on two simultaneous adjustments: first, prices charged are to be brought more into line with actual costs of provision, and, secondly, financial costs incurred . . . are to be brought more into line with the true economic costs of their operations (Political and Economic Planning, 1963, pp. 243–4).

But the Commission's initial specific proposals were in one policy area only and would have affected only one kind of transport, namely road transport. As such, they demanded, as we have seen, a sacrifice on the part of one of the bargaining partners long before compensation could be provided in other types of transport or in other policy areas, or before the outlines of the overall policy and its balanced benefits and compensations would become visible.

Whether or not the programme as a whole is a desirable one, implementing it piecemeal may have dangers. There is a logic in all the proposals taken together, while some of them in isolation could have effects which are opposite to those desired. . . . The precedence of some measures over others can so affect the present transport market that some undertakings may lose traffic because they have lost some institutional burden on their costs. . . . There is also a long-term danger of proceeding to implement some of the measures on the assumption that the others, which completed the 'balance' will follow, and finding that agreement on these cannot be reached (p. 244).

Thus, in contrast to its practice in agriculture under the leadership of Sicco Mansholt, the Commission failed to articulate the general goals of a common transport policy in such a way as to create a general expectation of long-term gain that could compensate individual short-term sacrifices. In its specific proposals for action, it has persistently failed to discover the limits of the possible so that a coalition of supporters at the national level could be built. For example, Scheinman argues that the Commission had ample possibilities to mobilize users associations in the transport field who presumably had more of a stake in getting a common policy than suppliers, but that no real effort was made to do so (1966).

As we have seen, side payments and log-rolling have been strikingly absent from the transport negotiations. The Commission did not respond in a creative manner to the objections of governments and groups to its initial plans, and it failed to play the role of broker by modifying and broadening its proposals so as to facilitate the construction of package deals.

Conclusions

In this chapter we have compared two sequences of decisions that led to contrasting outcome patterns. The general purpose of the comparison was to learn something about the conditions and requirements of incremental growth in the European Community system. Our most general finding was that a forward linkage outcome requires the formation of a supportive coalition among groups at the national level, so as to cause governments to act, and among governments at the Community level, in order for the Council to act.

Forming such a coalition in favor of extending the policy scope of the Community or the authority and decision-making capabilities of its institutions, is itself a process of accumulating or generating a variety of pressures or demands for governments to act. It depends ultimately on the extent to which political actors see, or can be made to see, their present or future aspirations served by integration. Such pressures or demands can arise in a number of different ways. First, political actors may respond to particular perceived relationships between a current problem and a task or obligation already assumed by the system, as in *functional spill-over*. Second, political actors may respond to the need or desire to maintain a balance of benefits gained and losses incurred from integrative action, as in *side payments* and *log-rolling*. And finally, political actors may respond to changes in the perspectives, loyalties or identifications of decision-makers (as in *actor socialization*), and of broader publics (as in *feedback*), which provide procedural and substantive legitimation for the initiation of Community decision processes.

In the case of agriculture all of these things occurred. The result was a supportive coalition based on a convergent interest pattern that was strong enough to initiate a process of incremental growth that survived serious crises which appear to have frustrated progress in other areas. A supportive coalition did not appear in transport. We tried to document the differences between the two cases: the kinds of actors mobilized, their perceptions of the values of integration, the availability of national and supranational leadership.

But why were forward linkage mechanisms activated in agriculture and not in transport? Are there any general lessons to be learned here? Can we derive hypotheses from these contrasting experiences that might be useful in predicting the chances of future growth in other areas? Two things seem to stand out. First, that forward linkages are most likely to take place where increased Community activity holds out the promise of a redistribution of benefits in a particular sector. Only this is likely to stimulate the needed demand flow. And, second, that even then forward linkages are unlikely to take place unless very special leadership skills are brought to bear.

If integration in a particular area of decision is expected to lead only to a reordering that leaves existing interests more or less intact, then political actors or interest groups are unlikely to develop a real stake in integration. Only if some actors come to anticipate that integration will involve a redistribution of benefits will they be likely to generate the political pressures needed to overcome opposition and to get governments to act. This implies that *side payments* in another sector will almost always be necessary for forward linkages to occur if an overall balance of benefits is to be maintained.[8] By this interpretation, agriculture 'succeeded' because some governments (France, Netherlands, Italy) and some groups in each country (especially the efficient and modernizing farmers) expected its reorganization to bring about a redistribution of benefits to their advantage. In order to get the other governments and other interests to agree to this, it was necessary to open wide the bargaining process so as to provide concessions in other areas to 'deficit' countries. Unlike agricultural policies, national transport policies on the other hand were not widely regarded by their constituencies to have failed. There were apparently few actors who perceived that they would be better off with a common transport policy.

The nature of the redistribution 'solution' can vary and this variation will be an important determinant of potential success. Redistribution need not take the form of what game theorists call a 'zero-sum' solution, i.e. a situation where there is just so much of a resource to be divided and where whatever one player gains the rest automatically lose. The solution may instead range from large gains for some with only minor losses for others, to large gains for some combined with minor gains for the others. It is to be expected that the chances of a successful forward linkage will be greatest when the redistribution can be of this nature. This kind of solution will be possible when the resource to be divided is not constant, but is expanding. And this can happen either because economic conditions are very good (i.e. redistributing to the benefit of farmers doesn't hurt much when GNP is increasing by a larger increment); or because the act of integration itself adds to the resources available (as might be the case with the increased diplomatic influence of a united Europe).

Furthermore, the redistribution may involve primarily the outside world and not governments and groups within the Community. If the costs can be thus exported without resulting in a retaliation that might cost one Community country more than the others, we would expect forward linkages to be easier to attain.

All of the above points are by way of recognizing that integration involves changes in old and established ways, and that experience has shown that there are a host of built-in resistances in each country to such changes – attitudes, structures, vested interests. Only if there is no significant group or political actor in opposition to a proposed integrative move is it likely that it will

8. The problem for governments here will always be one of 'pricing', i.e. determining how to weigh concessions in one sector against gains in another.

be accepted without the promise of some kind of redistribution. It is possible, and functionalists are fond of so arguing, that a forward linkage might be forced upon the governments by some kind of major economic crisis like a depression. This would perhaps be a way of preventing a common calamity more than a way of achieving a redistributive solution. It is difficult to evaluate this argument since there have so far been no cases of such a situation in the Community. Some economists argue that such a crisis would lead to *ad hoc* solutions or to implicit coordination of policy, rather than to 'conscious coordination' or real joint policy-making involving Community institutions and procedures.

Governments do not need to be told, for instance, that excessive inflation in an open economy quickly leads to difficulties for themselves and their trading partners. They can see for themselves the rapidly deteriorating balance of payments, and pressures immediately arise for corrective actions. A 'hidden hand' toward policy coordination is directed by the market mechanism. . . . What is certain is that political integration will occur only as a result of a positive political decision to bring it about, not as a result of economic pressure alone (Krause, 1968, p. 24).

Of course, the functionalists might argue that *ad hoc* instrumental solutions like these are likely to be the opening wedge for a subsequent forward linkage. We are, however, inclined to hypothesize that it will result only when out of the crisis it is possible to devise a redistributive situation that will open up new positive incentives for significant actors. Without this what is more likely to occur is stopgap solutions and not the kind of commitment to policy-making that is the essence of forward linkages.

The other major point to arise out of our comparison of agriculture and transport was the apparent extent to which forward linkages are dependent upon particular leadership skills. One of our major conclusions was that, although transport may have had less inherent potential than agriculture for forward linkages, the Commission failed almost totally to take advantage of what potential there was. If we are correct in suggesting that in order to maximize chances for forward linkage, somebody must perceive real chances for a redistribution of benefits, that the redistribution should involve solutions other than the zero-sum kind, and that side payments in other sectors are probably necessary, then it follows that the Commission should do everything in its power to tailor its proposals and to plan its strategy with these considerations in mind. To be able to do this requires a high order of courage, independence and political skill. But not to do so greatly reduces the likelihood that any dependable growth pattern will be initiated. National leadership could conceivably accomplish these things only if it were to come from one of the larger powers (France, Germany or Italy) which could convincingly claim to be disinterested in the envisaged redistributive solution. This is not likely to occur very often.

One vitally important way in which redistributions can be facilitated and the bargaining process lubricated in general, is for specific integrative moves to be effectively symbolized in terms of the broader goals and purposes of European integration (e.g. avoiding future wars, achieving the welfare state, increasing Europe's influence in the world). This may cause a particular group to accept an unfavorable redistributive solution, because it sees itself contributing thereby to the greater goal of creating a united Europe. This would be a kind of symbolic side payment. There is evidence to indicate that this was indeed one of the reasons why German farmers became reconciled to the common agricultural policy.[9] Symbolic rewards would also help to activate the interest and attention of political actors and publics who are not directly affected by the particular case, but whose support may be necessary to keep the bargaining process moving.

9. Based on interviews carried out in 1964 by one of the authors with German agricultural interest group leaders. A public opinion poll carried out in 1962 also tends to support this interpretation. Fifty-seven per cent of the German farmers polled were in favor of a common agricultural policy and only 22 per cent were opposed, even though fully 49 per cent thought that German agriculture would suffer as a result (Gallup International, 1963, p. 121).

References

GALLUP INTERNATIONAL (1963), 'Public opinion and the European community', *J. Common Market Studies*, vol. 1, no. 2.

JENSEN, F. B., and WALTER, I. (1965), *The Common Market*, Lippincott.

KRAUSE, L. B. (1968), *European Economic Integration and the United States*, Brookings Institution.

LINDBERG, L. (1966), 'Decision-making and integration in the European community', in *International Political Communities*, Anchor.

POLITICAL and ECONOMIC PLANNING (1963), *Transport in the Common Market*, Broadsheet, no. 473.

SCHEINMAN, L. (1966), 'Some preliminary notes on bureaucratic relationships in the EEC', *International Organization*, vol. 20, no. 4, pp. 750–73.

SHANKS, M., and LAMBERT, J. (1962), *The Common Market Today and Tomorrow*, Praeger.

14 Helen Wallace

The Impact of the European Communities on National
Policy-Making

H. Wallace, 'The impact of the European Communities on national
policy-making', *Government and Opposition*, 1971, pp. 520–38.

The now fairly extensive literature on the European Communities, much of which sets out to analyse 'the European decision-
making process', has tended to concentrate on how this process
looks from the perspective of the Community itself and of its
institutions. National governments and actors in the six political
systems have been discussed primarily in so far as they are participants in the Community system. However, if we are to reach an
understanding of the impact of the Communities on national processes, then some attention must be given to how the Communities are viewed from the national capitals, to the extent to which
Community business impinges on the governmental systems in the
member states and to the importance given to European matters
among the competing issues which vie for prominence in national
politics. Any analysis of the politics of European integration
which looks from the Communities outwards makes the assumption that European issues are the only ones that count; but if
those same issues are examined from a national perspective, we
need to ask whether they represent simply one bundle of issues
among many, or whether they have come to add a new dimension
to the full range of governmental business and political debate.
In other words, has the advent of the European Communities
changed the political configuration of the six national systems,
and, if so, marginally or fundamentally?[1]

Clearly a broad approach is required into which can be in-

1. Studies of the European Communities since their establishment, both
European and American, have been overwhelmingly Community-oriented.
Some studies have, however, been made of the relationship between the
Community and national levels, notably in Institut d'Études Européennes
(1967) and Gerbert and Pépy (1969).

Two German projects on the relationship between national governments
(particularly the German government) and the E E C are now reported to be
under way, one under the auspices of the Deutsche Gesellschaft für Aus-
wärtige Politik, the other directed by Professor Karl Kaiser at Saarbrücken.

corporated a range of relevant questions, an approach which covers the domestic policy-making process.[2] The advantage of this is that it embraces both the procedures used for formulating policy and the involvement, whether actual or potential, of political actors in the process as they affect the decisions reached. Proponents of European integration might argue that to ask those questions about national policy-making familiar from more conventional studies of domestic politics would risk a failure to appreciate the revolutionary nature of the supranational experiment. But if the 'founding fathers' were correct in their assumption that the logic of the European Communities is to transform the politics of Western Europe, then what we should expect to find are unconventional answers to conventional questions.

The more striking aspects of the impact of the Communities on national policy-making will be illustrated by reference to three major areas:

1. The European Communities as an issue-area[3] in national politics.
2. National actors concerned with the European issue-area.
3. The implications of the growing arena of Community activity for national policy-making.

The European communities as an issue-area in national politics

The governments of the Six, like all governments, are faced with a mass of demands and recurrent problems competing for attention and for solutions. Where does Europe figure in this competition? Is it accorded similar treatment to other issues? How has the treatment accorded to European issues at the national level affected the attitudes of the six governments to the progress of integration and specifically to the development of the institutional structure of the Communities?

The weight of the evidence so far available suggests that the Communities have not penetrated dramatically into the national political scene, but have rather been confined predominantly within the executive (particularly within some departments) and within the sphere of certain national elites.

Some argue that this relates to the nature of the Community process: that, for example, 'it would not be an exaggeration to

2. The phrase is used here as defined by Lindblom (1968). For discussions of the distinction between the foreign policy and domestic policy processes see Rosenau (1967) and Wallace (1971).
3. The concept of 'issue-area' is taken originally from Dahl (1961).

characterize the entire Community as essentially bureaucratic and technocratic' (Lindberg and Scheingold, 1970, p. 79). Why should this be so? In part it is a consequence of the predominant role played by Ministries of Foreign Affairs in coordinating national positions on community policies and in setting the parameters of overall national policies. Despite the economic and social policy orientation of the Treaties, their adoption resulted from specific foreign policy actions by the six governments and their implementation has continued to be regarded at the national level as primarily a pursuit of a foreign policy objective. To some extent the consequence has been an erosion of the traditional distinction between foreign policy and domestic policy, a factor of which British diplomats have been particularly aware in considering the potential British governmental response to membership of the Communities. 'The most important lesson for the United Kingdom', a member of the Foreign and Commonwealth Office recently observed, 'is the prospect of the amalgamation of the two areas of foreign policy and domestic policy which, in the past, it has been possible to keep more or less separate'.

In the administrations of the Six, foreign affairs officials meet regularly with their colleagues from domestic ministries to discuss and to coordinate community matters.[4] In the West German administration there has been a shift from the Chancellery to the Foreign Office as the coordinating department – although strictly speaking the Foreign Office shares responsibility with the Ministry of Economic Affairs. The bulk of coordination is handled by the weekly meetings of experts, chaired by a Foreign Office official, which agrees point by point the instructions to the Permanent Delegation; if agreement is not reached at this level, the point of contention is sent to the fortnightly meeting of State Secretaries (from the Chancellery, Foreign Office, Ministries of Economic Affairs, Agriculture and Finance, with representatives of other functional ministries as occasion requires) or very occasionally to a meeting of ministers. The prominence of the Foreign Office has resulted partly from the growing respectability for West Germany of an active foreign policy.

4. Detailed accounts of the national coordinating machineries are to be found in Gerbert and Pépy (1969) in the series of articles on 'la préparation nationale de la décision communautaire' (pp. 165–255) by Theodor Holtz (Germany), Marie-Paule Mahieu (Belgium), Pierre Gerbert (France), Marco M. Olivetti (Italy), Guy de Muyser (Luxemburg) and Robert de Bruin (Netherlands). My information on Germany is supplemented by talks with various officials during a recent visit to Bonn.

In Belgium coordination is organized at the administrative level by the inter-ministerial Economic Committee and at the political level by the Ministerial Committee for Economic and Social Coordination, with the Ministry of Foreign Affairs often playing the role of arbiter. In principle instructions to the Permanent Delegation are centralized through the Ministry of Foreign Affairs, but in practice the formal machinery does not function smoothly, leaving much of the regular coordination to the Permanent Representative himself, this being possible because of the government's situation in Brussels.

In France coordination on major issues operates partly through the 'Inter-ministerial Committee for questions of European economic cooperation,' which dates from 1948 and has its own secretariat, and partly through the 'Technical Inter-ministerial Committee for questions relating to the application of the EEC and ECSC treaties', which has come increasingly under the competence of the Prime Minister. But the role of the Quai d'Orsay remains central in defining policy options, particularly through its 'General Direction for economic and financial matters', and in controlling the Permanent Delegation. In Italy the role of the Ministry of Foreign Affairs is even more central, as it is specifically charged with the coordination of all matters concerned with the Rome and Paris Treaties. At the administrative level there exists a Committee of Directors-General from the major ministries convened by the Foreign Affairs Ministry and at the political level there is the 'Committee of Ministers for international action on economic policy', usually chaired by the Minister of Foreign Affairs. In addition the Foreign Affairs Ministry organizes groups of experts for specific problems, an activity which is particularly significant as the distance between Rome and Brussels impedes direct contact between national experts and the Communities.

In Luxemburg too the Ministry of Foreign Affairs has the central responsibility for coordination and has tended to provide the full staff of the Permanent Delegation. The Luxemburg case is rather special in view of their reliance on the Belgian administration for much that concerns the Communities. In the Netherlands the decentralized system of administration has meant that coordination has not been clearly secured, particularly as there is uncertainty as to the demarcation of competences between the Ministries of Foreign Affairs and Economic Affairs. Weekly coordination is through an official committee convened by the

Ministry of Foreign Affairs; questions not resolved at this level go to the Commission of Coordination which precedes the Community Council meetings. The uncertain demarcation of responsibilities between ministries has also meant that the Dutch cabinet has become increasingly involved in the process of coordination, primarily through its European Committee.

So the evidence suggests that the similarities in national patterns are striking, although some governments have found more stringent mechanisms for coordination than others. The similarities are not, however, necessarily a reflection of similar political situations: for example, the Dutch and Italian patterns reflect in different ways the responses of the national administrations to their coalition governments. The aspect which is the most striking is the effort made by ministries of foreign affairs to reserve for themselves the position of gatekeeper between the national and community systems, a position reinforced by the development of substantial functional expertise on economic policies. Moreover, the tradition of the foreign-policy process has considerably influenced the handling of Community issues in the degree to which debate has been concentrated within the executive, partly because the foreign-policy area tends not to be concerned with legislation and hence to avoid regular involvement with parliament or with pressure groups. Thus in a sense the erosion of the rigid distinction between domestic and foreign policy appears in this context to have made Community policy-making more like foreign policy-making than like domestic policy-making. This has been facilitated by the legislative process of the Communities, by which regulations take direct force at the national level. In part this concentration within the executive may account for the attention given by pressure groups to activity at a Community level.

The response of domestic ministries has not been to broaden the area of debate on particular issues, but rather to try to preserve their own autonomy by seizing upon issues within their competence as technical'.[5] Thus issues are 'de-politicized' and handed to 'neutral experts' for advice. Ministries of foreign affairs have seen their function as to sort out issues into 'political' and 'technical'. Such a division rests on an arbitrary decision of definition; often politically sensitive and far-reaching points may

5. This phenomenon is widespread. See Mahieu in Gerbert and Pépy (1969, p. 191) on Belgium, de Bruin (p. 239) on the Netherlands, Holtz (p. 177) on Germany.

be concealed by a complicated 'technical' proposal. For example, the decision of the Council of Ministers of January 1970 to stabilize freight market conditions on the Rhine and Moselle rivers (by authorizing the payment of subsidies to barge owners who temporarily withdraw capacity from these waterways) has wider implications for German–Swiss relations at a high level.[6]

The pattern is one which minimizes participation. This is reinforced by the time table of decision-making. The welter of material to be reviewed is extensive and the need constantly to pass on instructions to the permanent delegations in Brussels leaves little time for thorough consultation at the national level. Failure to reach a decision on a coordinated national basis means either that the view of a particular government is absent from the matter in hand in Brussels or that the permanent representative is left to assume the attitude of his government. At this point the efficiency of the coordinating machinery is crucial. Another factor to be taken into account is the need for confidentiality in preparing bargaining positions for Council meetings.

Perhaps the most surprising aspect of the process is that it continues to work. Commentators have remarked that a crucial factor has been the personnel involved, that over the years more or less the same group of key officials has been concerned with Community matters both in the permanent delegations and in the ministries in the national capitals (Noel in Institut d'Etudes Européennes, 1967, p. 12; Gerbert in Gerbert and Pépy, p. 199). Their familiarity with the issues involved, with the breadth of views to be taken into account and with each other, has made it possible for the wheels to be kept in motion. The members of these key groups are as concerned with selling a European line to their own government or ministry as with representing that government or ministry, whether through the Committee of Permanent Representatives or through the national coordinating machinery. The experience of those British civil servants concerned with the applications for membership over some ten years has been strikingly similar. But this elite-oriented approach has reinforced the pattern of trying not to extend the policy debate beyond those who 'really understand' the problems.

To set this adequately in the context of the national political

6. I am indebted for this example and the point which it illustrates to a discussion with a member of the German Foreign Office. For the decision itself see *European Community*, London, February 1970, p. 4. The same official estimated that 95 per cent of Community issues were settled at the level of 'technical experts'.

scene requires more evidence than is available on the reaction of other political groupings not included in the charmed circle, on aspects such as intra-party discussions of affected policy areas or the accommodation of the consultative machinery of functional ministries to the problem. The exception in terms of studies so far published is agricultural policy.[7] Agriculture is moreover the significant exception to the pattern of an executive-dominated and non-participatory process described above. Yet it is the most highly integrated sector of community policy and has been portrayed as the model likely to be adopted as other sectors are integrated. However, a number of factors lead me to doubt that this will be the case. The relationship between government and agriculture is of a different order from that which obtains in other sectors of the domestic economy. In all European states agriculture receives considerable subsidies, and agricultural policy bears the mark of social as much as of economic considerations. The political power of agriculture is more effectively organized and more immediately brought to bear upon governments than that of most other sectors. The sensitivity of the agricultural market to daily fluctuations means that certain kinds of decisions have to be reached quickly and regularly through the management committees, and that the effects of those decisions are immediately evident to and readily identifiable by the farmers.

The evidence of public opinion surveys suggests a widespread agreement with the broad objectives of the Community.[8] Statements made by officials in ministries assume the principle of a commitment to European integration as an agreed political end. However, it does not follow from this support and commitment at a broad and generalized level that a parallel willingness exists on the part of national or sectional interests to subordinate their own interests on specific issues to a higher community interest. Furthermore the mode of resolving conflict adopted by the

7. Giancarlo Olmi, 'Le rôle respectif des institutions communautaires et nationales dans la mise en oeuvre de la politique agricole commune', in Instituts d'Etudes Européennes (1967, pp. 115f), Hélène Delorme, 'L'adoption du prix unique des céréales', and J. R. Verges, 'L'élaboration du système de financement de la politique agricole commune', both in Gerbert and Pépy (1969). Note too the extent to which evidence from the agricultural sector is relied upon in more general works.

8. See for example Lindberg and Scheingold (1970, pp. 45f); but note Table 3·5 on p. 75 which shows the consistent discrepancy between the percentages showing support for a united Europe and those listing European problems as among the most important.

national authorities affects directly both the policy outcome at the Community level and the evolution of the institutions of the Communities.

This can be illustrated by the gradual shift of emphasis from the Commission to the Council and the Committee of Permanent Representatives (CPR). Much of the analysis devoted to this has concentrated on a number of contradictions in the role of the Commission (Coombes, 1970; Noel and Etienne in Gerbert and Pépy, 1969, pp. 33–55).[9] These contradictions, it is argued, are founded in the dual administrative and political functions expected of the Commission and in the ambiguity of the relationship between the Commission and the Council. The shift of emphasis has also been seen as stemming in part from the failure to move from unanimous to majoritarian voting. Evidence cited has included the increasing attention given by pressure groups to the CPR (although access is not easy), the establishment of *Comités de Concertation* (groups of high officials, convened by the CPR, often at the request of the Council, to investigate particular problems) and the tendency for Commission proposals to be channelled by the Council into the national administrative hierarchies. These factors are seen as undermining the policy-formulation role of the Commission.

However, it has also to be borne in mind that this shift stems not only from the development of the Commission but also from the volition of the national governments. The Council of Ministers is still primarily a meeting of the representatives of the six governments. In this it presents a close parallel with other intergovernmental organizations. The practice has been such as not to encourage the strengthening of the Commission, because, unless the Council and the CPR keep community policy-making within their control, the national machinery will cease to be able to keep pace. It might even be argued that for the role of the Commission as the formulator of policy to predominate would require almost the by-passing of coordinated national postures, with consultations with experts in various fields not depending so heavily on their selection by national governments.

The models of Community decision-making based on the early years of the EEC (Sidjanski, 1967) described the detailed formulation of policy proposals as concentrated in the Commission.

9. Detailed information on more recent developments is drawn from papers presented in Manchester by Étienne on 9 February 1971, and by Nord on 10 November 1970.

The procedure consisted of a compilation of dossiers through working groups of experts, studies by professional organizations, questionnaires to ministries and 'information meetings with national experts *in their personal capacities*'. These dossiers then formed the basis of consultation with professional organizations, the European Parliament and governmental experts called in by the Commission. Only then were the final versions of the proposals handed to the Council and CPR for a decision on acceptance or amendment.

More recently the trend has been for proposals to be presented to the Council in a more general form and for these then to be transmitted by ministers to the national administrators for thorough examination at various levels.[10] Papers are prepared individually by the six governments and collated in the CPR. The detailed work of the Commission continues, but can be disputed more vigorously by the national representatives on the basis of their own substantive study. This trend is reinforced by developing efforts of the national coordinating machinery to keep a check on the experts involved in consultation with the Commission. Furthermore it has been a characteristic of national governments not to accommodate themselves to a process which would diminish their ability to press authoritatively a national attitude on any proposal, even though political tactics may on occasion lead a national attitude to be expressed in terms of a 'community solution'. The outcome of this maintenance of executive control at the national level has been to insulate the European issue-area from national politics and to lead to the pursuit of minimalist strategies (Camps, 1967, ch. 7, p. 196; Lindberg and Scheingold, 1970, p. 287).

National actors and the European issue-area

In the early days of the Communities commentators frequently remarked upon participation in Community decision-making as provoking 'a restructuring of activities and aspirations' for political actors, by which were understood 'high policy-makers and civil servants' (Lindberg, 1963, p. 286). The trend towards a Community spirit was anticipated as likely to intensify and to embrace a growing number of individuals and groups. The major

10. This trend was corroborated by Étienne and Nord in the papers cited above. More detail on the control of national governments over the participation of national experts can be found in the articles by Gerbert (p. 204) and Olivetti (p. 212) in Gerbert and Pépy (1969).

potential obstacles to this evolution were seen as the pursuit of Gaullist policies, direct pressures to reduce the role of the Commission, or the enlargement and possible dilution of the Communities.

In practice, the minimalist strategies of the national governments and the routinization of the process of policy-making have tended to act as a barrier to this type of socialization in a more subtle manner. On the one hand the existence of the Communities has enhanced the role of some national administrators who have gained a new dimension of activity and responsibility. But, on the other hand, the national machineries have not involved large numbers of national political actors in the Community process.

At a specifically Community level the national actors most involved are the members of the Council and of the permanent delegations. For the ministers the burden of attendance at Council meetings is large and increasing. It is especially heavy for ministers of foreign affairs in view of their commitments to other international organizations and their programmes of bilateral visits.[11] This burden must to a degree diminish the attention that these ministers can give to their other administrative and political duties and must lead to some uncomfortable compromises in terms of preliminary discussion and briefing. One German official complained of the difficulty of briefing ministers adequately for Council meetings. For the permanent delegations the burden of work is equally strenuous. Their task is complicated by their dual role, which consists of the representation of national positions in Brussels and the explanation of decisions agreed in Brussels to the national administrations. The two functions require that members of the delegations keep abreast with the minutiae of both national and community developments. Indeed, the demanding nature of the role is said to make some national civil servants reluctant to serve in the Brussels delegations.[12] On the other hand a period as permanent representative certainly does not impede a civil servant's career, and may perhaps even further it.[13]

11. In 1967 there were thirty-seven Council meetings covering sixty-eight days, distributed as forty-eight days for ministers of agriculture, twenty-eight for ministers of foreign affairs, sixteen for ministers of economic affairs, with a smaller number for other ministers. These figures include the presence of more than one minister per country at some meetings.

12. This point was made in interviews with Dutch and German civil servants.

13. Several former Permanent Representatives have moved on to high positions either in the Communities or in their national administrations.

At the highest national level the actors involved are the ministers of the relevant departments (primarily foreign affairs, economic affairs, finance, agriculture and other departments such as labour or transport as required), their top officials and members of the relevant directorates within ministries. In practice, as was described above, Community matters seem on the whole to be settled at the technical level and only to receive the attention of the higher echelons of ministries if they are either contentious or of great political significance. It is sometime argued that this results from the consensual nature of the problems under discussion.[14] It is, however, equally plausible to argue that this technicalization has tended to submerge disagreement, and that this is facilitated by the compartmentalization of European issues within ministries. Interministerial conflicts of opinion do exist (see the articles by Holtz p. 177, Gerbert p. 203, de Bruin, p. 254, in Gerbert and Pépy, 1969); also Newhouse (1967, p. 96), although conflicts over matters concerning the Communities reflect in part a more general competition among central departments to assert their authority in the national administration. This competition has tended to provoke more comment from journalists than from political scientists, perhaps because of the difficulty of finding hard data. John Newhouse, in his discussion of the 1965–6 crisis and particularly the Bonn meeting between de Gaulle and Erhard in June 1965, writes: 'The endless infighting between responsible ministries had for the moment been stilled in order to present a unified front.' The 'unified front' soon collapsed and added to the series of problems which lay behind the Luxemburg crisis. The 'in-fighting' can in part be attributed to the fragile balance of the German administration at that time, but it also relates to a more constant facet of policy-making in an area where decisions are not easily confined within individual ministries.

The role of the ministries of finance would be of particular interest to students of British politics familiar with the intricacies of Treasury control, and would certainly merit further study. Prior to the recent advances in plans for economic and monetary

Noel, in his article in Instituts d'Etudes Européennes (1967, p. 12), cites amongst others the examples of de Carbonnel (France) and Cattani (Italy), who each became secretary-general in their respective Ministries of Foreign Affairs.

14. This argument appears regularly in discussions of the Communities. See, for example, Lindberg and Scheingold (1970, p. 41), on the 'permissive consensus'.

union, ministries of finance were peripherally and intermittently involved with Community matters. Other ministries have none the less had to take their views into account through their participation in the coordinating bodies, and from time to time ministries of finance have tried to exert a more positive role. (Mahieu, p. 185, and Gerbert p. 198, in Gerbert and Pépy, 1969). In West Germany there has been a sensitive relationship between the Ministries of Economic Affairs and of Finance. This has been accentuated by Professor Schiller, who has to some extent used the development of Community policy to reinforce his own views on German economic policy, as for example over revaluation and the floating of the German mark. This tension, which culminated recently in the merger of the two ministries, can only have been exacerbated by the added dimension of the European Communities. It will be revealing to see the impact of further progress towards monetary union on attitudes within the finance ministries.

The prominence of ministries of foreign affairs, particularly in their transmission of instructions to the permanent delegations, has included efforts to control the channels of communication between domestic ministries and Brussels. In practice this control has more easily been exerted over written communication, and has failed to control direct communication by telephone between functional ministries and their seconded members in the delegations. Traditionally, bilateral contacts between functional ministries in different national capitals have been handled by ministries of foreign affairs, but in practice direct contacts have increased (Mathieu, p. 185). On occasion direct contacts have deliberately been made between German and French officials to find ways round impasses in Brussels.

The diplomatic content of the work done by functional ministries has increased. This is due to the involvement of officials in negotiation over Community matters and to the increasing foreign affairs dimension of many areas of domestic policy, including for example international transport problems or the growing international mobility of labour, neither of which areas is confined to Community level discussion. Functional ministries are involved, too, as the agencies for the implementation of community policy. For example, those substantial sections in the ministries of agriculture which deal with food markets and prices are now primarily concerned with the implementation of the common agricultural policy.

The executive orientation of the handling of Community matters has militated against the representation of a wider section of national attitudes. In terms of the structures of the Communities this was intended to be counter-balanced by the European Parliament. Discussions of this institution have been overshadowed by the continuing debate over the powers of the Parliament and over direct elections. Given the lack of progress on both questions, some attention is due to the involvement of the six national parliaments in the process and to the activities of members of the European Parliament within their national parliaments. Michael Niblock has usefully illuminated these points in his study (1971).[15]

It has been a feature of the European Parliament, which distinguishes it from the assemblies of parliamentarians attached to other European international organizations, not to encourage its members to promote the discussion of European issues in their national parliaments. There have been two major reasons for this: the first has been the concern of Europeans to establish the identity of the European Parliament as the representative organ of the Communities; the second has been a desire not to isolate European affairs as a discrete area. Despite its weak powers the Parliament's activities are time-consuming in terms both of full sessions, which cover some thirty-five sitting days per year, and of committee sessions. Thus its conscientious members find it increasingly difficult to play an active part in their national parliaments, often endangering their domestic political careers. The list system by which members are elected to the Dutch Second Chamber has made it easier for Dutch members of the European Parliament than for their colleagues, in that they need to spend less time on extra-parliamentary activities. It should also be noted that frequently the members selected by the national parliaments to serve in Strasbourg have represented the pro-European wings of their parties, a factor which has to be taken into account in assessing their contribution at both levels.

The direct impact of the Communities on the national parliaments has been relatively limited. The accountability of governments is restricted by their ability to explain Council decisions as required by particular circumstances and by their inability to renounce those decisions. The evidence suggests that national parliamentarians are more concerned with general postures than

15. The author elaborates in this study on many of the points summarized below.

with detailed examination of policy. The agricultural sector has been more thoroughly probed than other sectors for the reasons outlined above. The absence of detailed examination of most aspects of Community policy results from the lack of adequate information available to MPs, from their inability to influence their governments at the most crucial stages of policy formulation and from the highly technical nature of many of the issues. Those parliaments which have a well-developed committee system, notably West Germany and the Netherlands, are somewhat better placed. But the low level of parliamentary control over European issues as much reflects a general problem of parliamentary control as it denotes a limited interest in the Communities.

The role of national interest groups has been discussed in the literature, principally in relation to the development of community-level groups. Sidjanski, in particular, has emphasized this (1967; paper delivered at Manchester, 27 October 1970), partly to substantiate the arguments that elites and groups are highly adaptable to changing political situations, and partly to suggest their crucial role in building up support for further integration. A European strategy, he argues, is generally pursued where the groups can agree on a common position and it is only in the absence of agreement that national strategies are pursued. However, frequently agreement *á Six* can only be reached at a minimal level, leaving the national groups to press their particular views on their own governments. The German Trade Union Organization, for example, admits to concentrating its pressure on the Bonn government, because it feels that neither consultation with the Commission nor participation in the Economic and Social Committee is adequate.[16] On the other hand, the involvement of national groups with each other through groupings in Brussels does affect their attitudes and perspectives. The most striking example of this was the conversion of the German industrialists to the idea that economic planning was not a threat, as a result of its discussion in the *Union des Industries de la Communauté Européenne*. This in part accounts for the change of position by the German government, which facilitated the development of the medium-term economic programme.[17] Yet

16. The information on the Deutscher Gewerkschaftsbund is drawn from a recent visit to their headquarters. For a description of the general attitudes of national interest groups see Feld (1966).

17. For a detailed account of the German government's changing views see Denton (1967).

the predominant trend is for national groups to press their governments for a defence of their interests, and if necessary for a national antidote to an unfavourable Community policy.

This survey of national actors suggested that involvement is limited and is oriented to the development of coherent national positions, although the competitive relationship between ministries points to the difficulties of maintaining such cohesion. Fuller information on the implementation of Community directives in national legislation might illuminate these difficulties further.[18] But to date the process of policy-formulation at the national level has tended to protect the political establishment, which has thus so far avoided the consequences of allowing European issues to be caught up in the normal process of domestic politics.

The implications of the growing arena of community activity for national policy-making

Two major sets of implications are of interest: the effect of existing community policies on the policy options available to governments, and the possible effect of the expansion of Community activity to include sectors which may erode more drastically the distinction between national and community policies.

Community policies have been restricted so far either to sectors like agriculture and tariff policy, which are relatively well insulated from other sectors, or to fairly limited aspects of other sectors. Spillover from sector to sector has not occurred and even progress on policies like the free movement of labour and capital has had a lesser impact than many anticipated. The existence of such Community policies does close certain options for national governments, as, for example, the customs union has excluded tariff adjustments from the range of available policy instruments. Domestic economic planning has not yet been deeply affected. The French experience suggests that the work of the *Commisariat du Plan* has changed little (Gerbert in Gerbert and Pépy, 1969, p. 199; Hayward, paper delivered at Manchester, 2 March 1971). There are several reasons for this, partly that French planning is less far-reaching than its public relations activities suggest, partly that the agricultural sector was never properly integrated, and partly that international agreements, which for their purposes include community agreements, have not

18. Directives have not been much studied, but see the series in *Cahiers du Droit Européen*, covering in 1969 the Netherlands and in 1970 France.

been regarded as a component of the planning procedure, but rather as defining the parameters of action.

Evidence collated on the impact of Community policies on industrial management (Feld, 1970) suggests that the elimination of some of the obstacles to trans-national management has not had a great liberating effect. Few businessmen yet think in European terms; industrialists have not seen the European Communities as imposing a logic which makes it no longer reasonable to think in national terms. This is compounded by the persistence of many financial, legal and technical obstacles which make it easier to continue to use traditional patterns.

Perhaps the area of greatest impact has been the foreign-policy area.[19] The development of a common commercial policy and the association with developing countries in Africa and the Mediterranean basin have considerably altered the range of instruments available to foreign policy-makers and the scope of their activities. However, overall the effect so far of Community activity on national policy-making has been at most restrictive: it has narrowed the parameters of action, but its positive effect on the way policy alternatives are posed has been small.

Areas of potential community agreement imply a more profound effect on domestic policy-making. The implementation of the value added tax and its imposition at a common rate may influence national fiscal policies extensively; the adoption of a statute for a European Company might alter the configuration of European industry (Stephenson, 1970; European Communities Information Office, 1968; Thompson, 1969). More importantly, steps towards economic and monetary union, as envisaged in the Werner Plan, even if haltingly taken, are likely to affect national economic management substantially.[20] But it should be remembered that the experience to date has been that it is easier to reach agreement on something which it is simple to align in a technical sense, even though it may not go to the root of the problem in hand. Thus the principle of aligning exchange rates within the Community, even of establishing a common currency, may be agreed, but the far-reaching issues of economic management allied with it are more complex and more contentious: particular problems include the relationship between balance of payments

19. This point was developed by S. Henig in a paper given at Manchester on 24 November 1970.

20. The points which follow derive from the Werner Report (published as a supplement to Bulletin 11 of the European Communities, 1970), and from a paper given at Manchester by Peter Oppenheimer on 9 March 1971.

equilibrium and the level of employment, and the existence of regional imbalances. The nature of these problems calls into question the very ability of the Community institutions to fulfil a central function of economic management.

A similar range of problems arises in the technological sector.[21] The recognition of the strength of American business in Europe does not automatically lead to an acceptance of the solutions required, solutions which rest upon European purchasing policies, European companies and European programmes. All of these presuppose hard decisions as to which country will benefit in which sector, and which companies will receive which contracts. Such hard decisions are not made easier by the importance of the industries involved in terms of national prestige, national employment and high earning capacity.

The first areas chosen for Community policies were among those thought in the 1950s to be central, but which have, in practice, left national policy-making relatively immune. Potential and scheduled community policies are of a different order. The form in which they emerge and the methods of implementation will be interesting for their effect on policy-making at the national level. The argument so far suggests that the six governments generally pursue a minimalist strategy, but it is an open question as to whether this trend will continue.

Conclusions

From this we may draw a number of tentative conclusions. First, the lack of academic attention to the impact of the Communities on national politics has resulted in a failure to relate the stagnation of the Communities in the late 1960s and the changing emphasis in the Brussels institutions to the process of national policy-making on European issues. The executive orientation of this process, especially the predominance of Ministries of Foreign Affairs, has influenced both the minimalist strategies pursued in Brussels and the minimizing of participation at the national level. As far as can be judged, each of the six governments has been affected in a broadly similar way, although more detailed investigation would probably unearth interesting differences related to the variations in national political style.

Secondly, although the attitudes of administrators and public opinion surveys substantiate a broad acceptance of European

21. I am indebted to the paper given by Roger Williams at Manchester on 8 December 1970 for the arguments presented here.

integration, the stuff of policy-making has been relatively compartmentalized in the national processes. European issues have, in practice, tended to be regarded as one bundle of issues rather than as a new dimension pervading the political spectrum.

Thirdly, despite the intensity of activity generated by the European Communities, their impact on the national level seems to be different in degree rather than in kind from that of other international organizations. For political integration of the character envisaged by the founders of the Communities to be achieved, changes at the national level are as important as the development of the Community institutions themselves. So far such changes have not been extensive.

These reflections all add up to a view which does not see economic integration gradually and painlessly moving towards political integration. This derives from an assessment of the behaviour of national governments as impeding such an evolution. Indeed for this to occur far more positive and deliberate actions on the part of governments would be necessary. Their negative attitudes have not prevented political leaders from embracing apparently progressive positions on the development of the Communities – the Werner Plan is an outstanding example. The contradiction lies in the gap between the adoption of broad proposals and their translation into practice in a heavily mutilated version.

References

CAMPS, M. (1967), *European Unification in the Sixties*, Oxford University Press.

COOMBES, D. (1970), *Politics and Bureaucracy in the European Community*, Allen & Unwin.

DAHL, R. A. (1961), *Who Governs?*, Yale University Press.

DENTON, G. (1967), *Planning in the EEC*, PEP.

EUROPEAN COMMUNITIES INFORMATION OFFICE (1968), *Tax Harmonization in the European Community*, Community Topic no. 29.

FELD, W. (1966), 'National economic interest groups and policy formation in the EEC', *Polit. Sci. Q.*, September.

FELD, W. (1970), 'Political aspects of transnational collaboration in the Common Market', *International Organization*, vol. 24, no. 2, pp. 209–38, [Reading 19].

GERBERT, P., and PÉPY, D. (1969), *La Décision dans les Communautés Européennes*, Université Libre de Bruxelles.

INSTITUT D'ETUDES EUROPÉENNES (1967), *Institutions Communautaires et Institutions Nationales dans le Développement des Communautés*, Université Libre de Bruxelles.

LINDBLOM, C. E. (1968), *The Policy-Making Process*, Prentice-Hall.

LINDBERG, L. N. (1963), *The Political Dynamics of European Economic Integration*, Stanford University Press.

LINDBERG, L. N., and SCHEINGOLD, S. A. (1970), *Europe's Would-Be Polity*, Prentice-Hall.

NEWHOUSE, J. (1967), *Collision in Brussels*, Norton.

NIBLOCK, M. (1971), *The EEC: National Parliaments and Community Decision-Making*, PEP.

ROSENAU, J. N. (1967), 'Foreign policy as an issue area', in J. N. Rosenau (ed.), *Domestic Sources of Foreign Policy*, Free Press.

SIDJANSKI, D. (1967), 'The European pressure groups', *Government and Opposition*, vol. 2, no. 3, p. 400. [Reading 18]

STEPHENSON, P. (1970), 'Problems and political implications for the UK of introducing the EEC value added tax', *J. Common Market Studies*, June.

THOMPSON, D. (1969), *The Proposal for a European Company*, PEP.

WALLACE, W. (1971), *Foreign Policy and the Political Process*, Macmillan

15 L. J. Brinkhorst

European Law as a Legal Reality

L. J. Brinkhorst, 'European law as a legal reality', in M. Gaudet (ed.),
European Law and Institutions, Edinburgh University Press, 1968, pp. 7–25.

As a result of their training and of their ways of thinking, lawyers
belong to a traditional profession. They have a strong inclination
to explain new experiences in the light of their old ones – and to
fit them into their own familiar categories of law, even though
those categories are not appropriate and do not lend themselves
to this new purpose. So it is understandable that this general
tendency has had its application to the 'nascent law', nowadays
called 'European Law'. European law acts like a mirror to whoever cares to look into it. One recognizes those features with which
one is most familiar. The discipline to which the spectator belongs
often determines the observed image. This appears, for instance,
from the discussion which has been raging for many years about
the legal structure of the European Communities.[1]

It is significant that those who see European law mainly as a
law of nations, belong mainly to this latter branch of the law,
whereas those who work in the field of national law – constitutional and administrative law, social-economic law – usually put
the emphasis on the analogy with the internal structure of a
federal state as it is known in constitutional law. In its most extreme form, this discussion strongly resembles a *dialogue de
sourds* in which the others' arguments are not heard. It contri-
butes little to a clear insight into the legal phenomena concerned.
For each of these groups, the remark holds good 'that the positive-
ness of their persuasion is often greater than the persuasive-
ness of their position' (Polak, 1951, p. 6). The methods of deduction and analogy used by the disputants only reflect part of the
reality of law. The inductive method, which I wish to follow here,
shows more clearly the nature of European law.

I shall concentrate on four aspects: (1) the way in which this

1. Literature on this question exists in abundance. Recent reviews can be
found in Hay (1966); Ophüls (1965); Von Simson (1964); Waelbroeck
(1964); Wagner (1965).

law is formed; (2) its contents; (3) its legal effects; (4) its interpretation. However, before I continue, the term *European law* demands some explanation. Used as a geographical description it includes the legal expression of all forms of cooperation between European states such as the Council of Europe, Benelux, Western European Union and the North Atlantic Treaty Organization, as well as the law of the European Communities. However, more and more is there a tendency to use this expression particularly in connection with the last-named organizations. The aim of several periodicals of this name is the study of European law, especially in connection with the European Communities.[2] There is no objection to this, but it should not lead to any exclusivity. For scientific exposition the notion 'European law' only has significance in so far as it concerns the description of special legal phenomena. These exist undoubtedly in the European Communities, but also in the European Convention for the Protection of Human Rights, of which the Human Rights Commission declared that the *aim* was the creation of 'a common public order', a European public order, and not merely the creation of mutual obligations between states.[3] In this sense, there is a strong analogy with the pronouncement of the Court of Justice of the European Communities in the case of *van Gend en Loos* 'that the Community constitutes a new legal order in international law'.[4]

The formation of law

In recent years, most of the discussion about the character of the European Communities has been in connection with the decision-making process within these organizations. It is on this point that the procedures of the Communities vary strongly from the way in which policy is made in the more classical forms of intergovernmental organizations. In the latter the policy to be followed is exclusively decided by the representatives of the member states who are under instruction from their governments and can only take binding decisions by unanimity. There are exceptions, but

2. *Cahiers de Droit Européen, Rivista de Diritto Europea, Revue Trimestrielle de Droit Européen, Europa Recht.* The Netherlands Social-Economic Legislation has since 1967 as its sub-title: *Review for European, Netherlands and Belgian Social-Economic Law.*

3. Decision Commission of 11 January 1961, in the case Austria *v.* Italy (*Pfunders*), *Yearbook of the European Convention on Human Rights* (1961), p. 138.

4. Case 26/62, Rec. IX, p. 23.

these are little more than minor exceptions to a general principle, embellishments which do not destroy the main architectural structure.

Two sets of provisions of the EEC Treaty, to which Treaty I will now limit myself, depart, in particular, from the above principle: (1) there are those which relate to the right of initiative which lies with the Commission of the European Communities, and (2) the related rules that the Council of Ministers can decide by a qualified majority. In the institutional set-up both aspects – and it is useful to emphasize this – are indissolubly interwoven and are what Pescatore called 'la clé du succès' (1965, p. 55). Although the most important economic-political decisions lie with the Council, in most cases the Council can only take these decisions on a proposal of the Commission.

In this way continuous cooperation is created between the European Commission, which, as an independent institution, has the task of giving *shape* to the general interest of the Community, and the Council, in which the representatives of the six member states give emphasis to their national interests. Because of the introduction of the rule of qualified majority voting in the Council the position of the Commission is greatly strengthened, and the authority of its proposals is increased. Thus the Commission is not merely the mediator between divergent national interests, as it is or may be whenever the Council has to decide by unanimity but, in Hallstein's (1965) term, it is also an arbitrator which, on the condition that it is supported by a majority, can help to promote a decision of the Council which takes into account, in a reasonable way, both the interest of the Community and the interests of the minority. The right of initiative is greatly strengthened by the existence of the rule[5] that only by unanimity can the Council amend a proposal of the Commission.

In this system, as laid down in the EEC Treaty, two points are of importance. On the one hand, the conditions are created for quick and efficient decisions, in which the opinion of the Commission has a strong weight and an advantage over the ideas of others. On the other hand, this procedure gives a guarantee against a haphazard overruling of the minority by the majority. For the misuse of the majority principle is prevented by the requirement that a majority decision must conform to the Commission's proposal which, by definition, serves the interests of the Community as a whole. Only where there

5. Article 149, para. 1, EEC Treaty.

exists a consensus in the Council which derogates from the Commission's proposal does this consensus prevail. In this situation there is no need for special protection of the minority. In theory at least, this system seems to offer every guarantee for a balanced development.

What is the state of the application of this principle in practice? Interesting studies by Haas (1958; 1967); Lindberg (1963, 1965); and Hoffmann (1966), representatives of the political sciences, have shown us the reality behind the legal constructions and the dangers of too much confidence in the 'constitutional documents and formal structural arrangements of international agencies'. For 'their actual operation can only be understood with reference to the world of politics' (Claude, 1964, p. 7). The intrusion of states into the process of decision-making can be seen in numerous ways and on numerous levels; this disturbs the carefully balanced equilibrium between the European Commission and the Council of Ministers. It cannot yet be foreseen whether the prophecy of the former president of the High Authority, René Mayer, will come true: that one can administer the French only *une dose de supranationalité par génération*: nor whether others will more readily accept such doses. It is a fact, however, that the doses laid down in the Treaties of Paris and Rome of 1951 and 1957 have proved to be insufficient to prevent the procedures, which are followed at present, sliding further and further to the level on which decisions are reached in strictly intergovernmental organizations. This could already be seen in the *décisions négociées* of the High Authority in which little is left of the concept of its independent role as described in the Dutch Government's Explanatory Memorandum on the ratification of the ECSC Treaty:

Therefore the decisions of the High Authority should not have the character of the common denominator of the national interests or be the result of a compromise between those interests, but they should give the objective opinion of this institution as to what, in a given situation, should be done in the interest of the Community as a whole (Annex, Hardelingen Tweede Karner II, Session 1950–51, no. 2228, p. 10).

Instead of an increasing independence of the supranational authorities we see an increasing entanglement in a network of national civil-servant groups, committees and working parties. The fear, expressed eight years ago by Samkalden, becomes true 'that the compromise between the national viewpoints overshadows the viewpoint of the Community' (1960, p. 16). In an escalation of nationalism – in Samuel Johnson's words, 'the last refuge of a scoundrel' – it is more and more the states who are the real authorities. Many symptoms bear this out. The Committee of Permanent Representatives, modestly called the preparatory body of the Council's activities and the executive body of the Council's instructions,[6] has developed into a central turn-table of the decision-making process. The right of initiative of the Commission is undermined when the Council invites this body (and not the Commission) to prepare drafts for decisions, as happened in the field of the common transport policy. The Council's decision[7] in this matter – originating from a communication of the Commission and a memorandum of one of the member States – cannot be seen otherwise than as a barely veiled violation of the Treaty. Deringer[8] was right when in his excellent parlimentary report of 1962 he already warned against an evolution in which the Council would be the scene of a battle for national interests. In the Council of Ministers, in the structure of which the tensions between Community spirit and the defence of national interests are already felt most strongly, more and more priority is given to national interests. The horse-trading in agricultural products with package deals and marathon sessions is the vivid proof of this evolution. Quite apart from the physical strain for those personally involved, the consequences have not failed to make themselves felt. The application of the rule laid down in the first paragraph of Article 149 EEC, mentioned before, that the Council may only by unanimous vote deviate from a proposal put before it by the Commission – the crux of the institutional set-up[9] – is in jeopardy. Houben was right when he saw as its general purpose the idea that the Council should not be able to change too light-heartedly the Community view as formulated by the Commission (1964, p. 109). In practice, this rule is completely robbed of its *ratio* and of its value when the proposals put before the Council are mere starting points for negotiations, instead of being the finishing line of a legislative process, departure from which should only take place in cases of obvious necessity (Samkalden, 1962, p. 689).

6. Art. 4, Fusion treaty of 8 April, 1965, S. & J ed. no. 157, p. 501.
7. 67/790/EEC, J.O. 1967, no. 322/4. See about what happened before Rutten (1968).
8. Documents de Séance, European Parliament 1962–3, doc. 74, p. 34.
9. M. *v.* T. *EEC*-Treaty, Annex to Reports II, Session 1956–7, no. 4725, p. 35.

This has also meant that a situation has gradually emerged in which neither the national nor the European parliamentary responsibility for Community decisions gets its due. Here the fundamental weakness becomes very real, a weakness which was always a potential one, namely that the political status of the European Parliament (which was given consultative powers only, in the process of decision-making) is completely dependent on the European Commission. Although the European Parliament can, in theory, dismiss the Commission by accepting a motion of censure, in practice this right has no more value than a fig-leaf to cover its nakedness.

As, gradually, the Commission has turned more and more towards the Council as the body responsible in final analysis for the decisions of the Community and in which to reach a compromise acceptable to all, so the political authority of the European Parliament has gone further into decline. An inquiry into the effect of parliamentary recommendations has recently confirmed that the influence of the European Parliament on the process of legislation is negligible. Only where there is not primarily a conflict between national interests, but merely one between views on society and on economic interests, does it make a real contribution (Kapteyn, 1968, pp. 110–19). This was clearly the case with regulation no. 17 – the basic decision in the field of economic competition. During its preparation two schools of thought, on cartels in particular, confronted one another. There were those who wanted an antecedent control on the question of whether a particular set of facts in the field of competition would be in line with the rules, and there were those who wanted the judges to have a supervision *a posteriori*, or *ex post facto* control. Examples like these, however, are rare.

The Council has made a very circumspect use of the possibility of strengthening the position of the Commission by means of the delegation to it of regulatory powers, especially in cases in which such delegation would have given discretionary powers to the Commission. In such cases, the Council kept the execution in its own hands, often with a different procedure from the one foreseen in the Treaty. In cases where powers were delegated, the Council insisted on the inclusion of committees of civl servants, a procedure which has meant a further limitation of the independence of the Commission (Haas, 1967). It must be stated, however, that, e.g. the so-called Management Committees ('*beheerscomités*'; *comités de gestion*) in the field of agricultural

policy were not such a menace to the Commission as had been
expected when they were first set up (Bertram, 1967–8).[10] The story
is getting monotonous. A further illustration is what happened
in the field of external relations, especially in the field of Treaty-
making power. Although articles 228 and 238 give a central place
to the autonomy of the Community by providing that Association
agreements should be concluded by the Council as a Community-
institution, the practice grew up of the so-called mixed agreements, which only take effect after ratification by the national
parliaments (Testa, 1966). This is an expression of the fact that
the real power does not lie with the Community as such, but has
been kept in the hands of the states.

Finally, as the most striking expression of these tendencies,
mention must be made of the so-called Luxemburg Agreement,
which, in January 1966, put a formal end to the crisis which had
paralysed the Communities since July 1965. The statement of
the difference of opinion between the member states on the question of the cases in which majority-voting should be decisive,
cannot be classified in terms of law, although this has been tried.[11]
The title or description of an 'agreement to disagree' can hardly
be called a classification. The French reservation that unanimity
is necessary when very important interests are at stake, hangs as a
black cloud over the Community. This reservation is born of the
same way of thinking as was the 'honour and vital interest' clause
of article 9 of the Hague Convention on the peaceful settlement
of conflicts of sixty years ago and is typical of that era: the
refusal by the state to be bound by legal institutions. So far there
is nothing new under the sun. As a political decision, the Luxembourg Agreement means that it has become even more unlikely
that the Council will be willing to take majority-decisions of any
importance. Thus, the activating influence of the majority-rule
on the attitude of the states is threatened and might well get lost.
This opens the way for an evolution in which unwritten constitutional law can make infractions upon the letter of the Treaties
(Kaiser, 1966, p. 24). Seen in this way, the compromise means
disintegration. Therefore, Lindberg's conclusion that the decision-

10. See, however, on recent developments, with respect to the Committees on the origin of goods, on customs value, and the permanent
veterinary committee, *Second General Report of the European Commission*
(1969), S S 639–72.

11. See Mosler, 'National- und Gemeinschaftsinteressen im Verfahren
des E W G-Ministerrats', Zaö R V Bd.26, 1–31, who stated that the agreement is legally binding for the states.

making process in the Community has become a

'system in permanent crisis' is right. Gone is the 'sense of "engagement", of being in the same boat, of being "condemned to succeed", of being committed to solve mutual problems by give-and-take in an institutionalized setting in which failures are excluded and sensitivity is shown to each other's needs and preoccupations' (1966).

The contents of the law

It may be true that many procedures for law-making do not at the moment function, or function only in a defective way, as a result of which the structure of the Communities has lost a large part of its stability; nevertheless the Treaties contain more than a system of cooperation totally dependent on the whims of a political use of power. With the establishment of the three Communities a 'new legal order' has come into being. This term has obtained a specific meaning. To quote once again the Court of Justice:

Namely that the member states – by creating a community of unlimited duration, having its own institutions, . . ., with real powers[12] . . . have limited their sovereignty, albeit in a limited field, and therefore have created a system of law applicable both to their citizens and to themselves.[13]

It can be said of most international organizations that, as they occupy themselves more with technical or administrative problems which do not endanger their independence, there is a greater willingness on the part of the constituent states to grant legislative or executive powers to those organizations (Falk, 1967, p. 191). None the less, of all specialized organizations of the United Nations, the World Health Organization (WHO) and the International Civil Air-Transport Organization (ICAO) alone have more than advisory and coordinating powers (Friedmann, 1964, pp. 278–9). In a regional organization such as the Council of Europe, with its very general aim 'of promoting a greater unity between its members, in order to safeguard and thus to realize the ideals and principles, which are their common heritage, and to promote their economic and social progress' (article 1a) the lack of means for direct intervention in the systems of law of the member states is striking. Somewhat simplified, this phenomenon could be typified thus: in most international organizations, universal as well as regional, the extent of the powers which have

12. The official Dutch text says, wrongly, 'practical'.
13. *Costa* v. *ENEL*, case 6/64, Rec. x, p. 1159.

been entrusted to that organization is inversely commensurate with the breadth of the field of action in which they can operate. Rightly therefore, Tammes concludes that in the means of action of international organizations real legislation only plays a very minor role (1958).

In the European Communities the picture is a very different one. They are distinguished by the nature and the scope of interests which the states have entrusted to them. By reason of its content, European law must be built out of those branches of national law in which the most fundamental social and economic interests of the member states have been incorporated. In future these interests can only be promoted in common. It is not important whether one sees this as a quantitative or as a qualitative difference from other organizations provided one remains conscious of the consequences. It is no longer a problem of a mere adaptation of the national legal rules to incidental international obligations (Riphagen, 1960, p. 16), such as the acceptance of the clause of the most favoured nation of the GATT, or the fixing of minimum standards in social legislation as a result of participation in the conventions of the ILO or of the acceptance of the European Social Charter (Koopmans, 1966, p. 192). Certainly, in the Communities we also meet elements like these in the rule of equal pay for equal work for men and women (article 119 EEC), or in the shape of the general prohibition of discrimination on the grounds of nationality (Article 7 EEC); but both principles are also serving a wider perspective, i.e. the establishment and the functioning of the common market.

Furthermore, however, the substantive law included in the Treaties is subject to independent European regulations and is thus taken away from the national systems of law. In the Treaty establishing the European Coal and Steel Community this is particularly clear in the rules on investments, production, prices, and competition. As to the EEC one thinks in the first place of the European marketing rules which have, for a large number of agricultural products, taken the place of national systems of legislation, and which contain uniform rules for the whole of the Community. Target prices and intervention prices, levies and repayments – the bases of the agricultural policy – are fixed by the institutions of the Community. Thus the role of the national authorities is, to a large extent, reduced to a role of technical execution. There already is a European set of rules on cartels which – albeit by fits and starts – has come into effect and which now, as far as inter-state commerce within the Community is concerned, has pushed the application of national law into the background and according to some has even excluded it (Van den Heuvel, 1966-7).[14]

Again, in the field of European transport the Council of Ministers was given important powers of regulation. Although progress has been slow so far, there is a start towards the enactment of a regulation to put an end to discriminations concerning freight charges and conditions of transport, and recently it was agreed that new measures will be taken before 1 July.[15] Finally, in the field of turnover taxes, it was decided, in 1967, to introduce a uniform system, i.e. the TVA system, although not yet to accept uniform rates.[16]

In many cases the national legislator and administrator are closely involved in the execution of Community law. They have retained a freedom of action to a greater or lesser degree, but they may not exceed the limits set by the Community institutions.[17] The examples make it clear that certain powers are no longer in the hands of the states. The states no longer possess the instruments to look after the matters involved in a completely independent way. It is increasingly more difficult for them – and from time to time even impossible – to refuse their cooperation in the taking of specific decisions. In this way, the increasing economic integration brings along with it interpenetration in the field of law even without the moment having been reached (which is decisive for the existence of a federal system) at which the member states can no longer free themselves from the whole. In this process of interpenetration, however, their freedom of choice between cooperation and non-cooperation in decisions has largely been restricted. In fact as long as they are not willing to put an end to their membership, they are condemned to cooperation as a consequence of the legal framework which they have created (Von Simson, 1964, pp. 94-8). We cannot speak anymore

14. See too the judgement of the Court of Justice in Case 14/68, a preliminary ruling at the request of the Kammergericht Berlin, 13 February 1969 AWD. (1969), 144.

15. These measures have now been taken, see J.O. (1968), no. L/175/1.

16. Council Directives 67/227/EEC and 67/228/EEC of 11 April 1967, resp. J.O. 1301/67 and 1303/67.

17. e.g. Execution of Community law by the Netherlands public authorities, Reports by Brinkhorst, Koopmans, Peiffer, Phaf and van Poelje, *Vereniging voor Administratief Recht* (1968), no. 60. See also Constantinides-Megret (1967, p. 131).

of the 'un-tied and un-tieable sovereign state' (Van Vollenhoven, 1918, p. 71).

The legal effects

It is here that we must look at a further aspect of European law. The force of this law is that the regulations do not only affect the states, but, over their heads, the regulations also directly affect all the participants in the economic process. It is the latter who are the 'infrastructure' of the process of integration. Thus the circle of subjects of law has been made much wider: citizens are in immediate contact with European law. In the jurisdiction of the Court of Justice much emphasis is laid upon this function of the individual citizen. The Court declared that the citizens cannot obtain rights only by positive assignment in the Treaty, but also 'as a repercussion of the clear obligations which the Treaty imposes upon individuals, the member states and the common institutions alike'.[18] As a sequel to this reflex, various stand-still obligations of the states have been given direct application. This has even been held to be the effect of a provision which next to a prohibition – no discrimination between taxes on indigenous and on imported goods – also contained an obligation to act, i.e. to abolish existing provisions which are contrary to this rule (article 95 EEC).

Because of these decisions the national judge, in upholding the law, has an important responsibility. He is called upon to fulfil a function in the system of law of the Communities, by which the integration of Community law into national law finds its expression. In a striking phrase Scelle characterized this as 'dédoublement fonctionnel' (1955, p. 324). This decision has not remained without consequences: after the judgement mentioned above German enterprises lodged 200,000 complaints with administrative institutions and in no less than 15,000 cases there was an appeal before the Finanzgerichte[19] against the levy of compensatory turnover tax. In seven cases the Finanzgerichte asked the Court of Justice for a preliminary decision on the interpretation of the Treaty provision (articles 95 and 97 EEC).[20] This illustrates the increasing degree to which national jurisdic-

18. Case 26/62, note 5, p. 23.
19. First general report on the activities of the European Communities (1968), p. 500, note 2.
20. See cases 7/67, 13/67, 20/67, 25/67, 27/67, 28/67, 31/67, 34/67, reported XIV Rec. 211. See also 6 C.M.L.Rev. 1968–9, pp. 132–8.

tions are involved in the application of Community law. As of 31 December 1967, the Commission knew of 187 published judgements on European law, apart from the fifty cases in which preliminary decisions were requested on the interpretation or the validity of Community rules.[21] Judges from each of the member states have followed this procedure in various fields of Community law, which aims at guaranteeing a uniform interpretation of Community law. Among the courts making such requests were some of the highest jurisdictions, such as the Belgian Council of State, the *Bundessozialgericht*, and *Cour Supérieure de Justice* of Luxembourg, the *Bundesfinanzhof*, the French *Cour de Cassation*, and in the Netherlands the Tariff Commission, the *Centrale Raad van Beroep* and the *College van Beroep voor het Bedrijfsleven*. They all turned to the Court of Justice when confronted with problems of interpretation. So far, only the Italian judges and the French *Conseil d'Etat* have failed to do so,[22] although there, also, many possibilities of so doing have presented themselves.[23] In this respect the *Conseil d'Etat* often bases itself on the French theory of the '*Acte clair*'. According to this ancient theory, requests to give a ruling are only necessary in cases of reasonable doubt on the interpretation of legislative rules (Gaudet, 1966, pp. 215–19). Whether the *Conseil d'Etat* always applied the theory with the necessary care is a question of reasonable doubt. If, however, one looks at the whole field of the application of European law by national courts, the picture is encouraging. They have become aware of the fact that European law has added a new dimension to national law.

This does not mean, however, that all problems have been solved. Because European law interferes directly in the relations between citizens since, as to its content, it covers the same areas as national law and is applied to the same subjects of law, yet is based upon sources of law of its own, a clash between this law and divergent national law is sometimes unavoidable. The question then is which of the two has priority. Thus, one finds oneself on the slippery slope of the relations between international and national law, for which there are as yet no uniform traffic rules.

21. See general report (1968), Table 24 and Table 23A.

22. e.g. *Shell-Berre*, 19 June 1964 A.J. (1964), p. 438 and *Synd. nat. des imp. fr. en prod. laitiers et avic. et Decker*, R.D.P. (1967), p. 781 (judgement of 27 January 1967). *Synd. gén. de fabricants de semoules*. C.E. March 1, 1968, D. (J.) 285.

23. See written question Westerterp, Session Eur. Parl. 1967–8, no. 100 (1967), J.O. no. 270/2.

In the Netherlands this question is of merely theoretical interest because the Constitution clearly puts rules of international origin above divergent national rules.[24] But elsewhere, where this happy situation does not exist, a fierce discussion has been raging for a very long time on the consequences of a possible conflict. The traditional dualistic doctrine according to which international law and national law move, so to speak, on two separate traffic lanes, communication between which is only possible by means of national feeder lanes, is clearly insufficient for organizing the traffic between Community law and national law. In fact, this way of looking at the problem leads to the consequence that direct application of Community law in each of the member states, as stipulated *expressis verbis* by article 189 EEC, is only ensured in so far as the constitutional law of each individual state allows for it. If the contents of Community law could vary from country to country, there would be a strong tension indeed between the 'Sein' and the 'Sollen'.

There are, however, encouraging signs that in those countries where this theoretical dualism prevails, the special character of the European Community structure is also starting to be acknowledged. Thus, in Italy, the *Corte Costituzionale*, in its decision of 27 December 1965,[25] already moved some way from the viewpoint it earlier expressed;[26] namely, that in Italy Community law only ranks with ordinary legislation which may therefore be repealed by later ordinary legislation. Under the influence of the Court of Justice[27] the Corte arrived at the view that, side by side with national law, Community law gives shape to an independent system of law, and that, therefore, its validity does not exclusively depend on the Italian Constitution. It is true that thus the priority has not yet been accepted in all respects, but opinions are clearly changing. Again, in Germany, a change of direction is clearly visible. After the *Bundesverfassungsgericht* had already declared inadmissible[28] a 1963 request by the *Finanzgericht* of Rheinland-Pfalz to declare the EEC Treaty contrary to the Constitution, this same *Bundesverfassungsgericht* declared itself unqualified to

24. See Van Panhuys (1964) and the recent discussions between Meuwissen and Lauwaars in *Ars Aequi* (1966) p. 303 and (1967) pp. 271–6, resp. (1967) pp. 150–52.

25. *Foro ital.* (1966), no. 1, col. 8.

26. Judgement of 7 March 1964, *Foro ital.* (1964), no. 14, col. 465. Abridged version *C.M.L.R.* (1964–5), pp. 201–22.

27. *Costa* v. *ENEL*, case 6/64, Rec. x, pp. 1158–60.

28. Decision of 5 July 1967, *NJW.* (1967), 1707. 5 *C.M.L.R.* 481.

express a view[29] on the alleged invalidity of certain EEC regulations, and it based this standpoint on the special character of the European law. 'The institutions of the EEC', according to the *Bundesverfassungsgericht*, 'are exercising sovereign rights of which the member states have divested themselves in favour of the Community set up by them. . . . Thus a new and autonomous authority which is not dependent on the authority in the various member states has been created. . . . The rules of law enacted by the institutions of the Community (in the execution of their powers under the Treaty) form a special legal order whose rules are neither international law nor national law of the member states.' Are not these refreshing sounds coming from the country of Triepel, the patriarch of dualism? The importance of this evolution is, furthermore, that now the door is being opened to the direct infiltration of law of other international origins, which answers to the same conditions. In any case it is certain that these judgements shed a new light on the whole problem of the relationship between international and national law.

The interpretation of law

In this new structure of law – as is already apparent in many ways from what has been said so far – the Court of Justice, as an independent body, plays an essential part. Its decisions have given a strong impetus to the construction of a complete system of law in which totally new phenomena and problems make themselves felt. This is the last aspect of European law I shall discuss. The Court of Justice is called in to 'ensure the observance of law and justice in the interpretation and application' of the Treaties (article 164 EEC). To its jurisdiction states, institutions and citizens alike are subjected, and its judgements are binding in each country of the Community ('Elle participe ainsi *du dedans* a l'œuvre créatrice de la communauté dont elle fait partie.') (La Grange, 1958). By its existence the decisions of the institutions get a life of their own and these decisions can be tested in their own right. It is especially because of the existence of the Court of Justice that the cohesion of European law is guaranteed. Its methods of interpretation are based on a clear conception of the politics of law. This conception is characterized by what, in

29. Decision of 18 October 1967, *A.W.D.* (1967), 477. 5 *C.M.L.R.* 483. Only the question whether and in what measure Community law can be compared with the fundamental civic rights contained in the German constitution was left open. See on this latter point the further decision of the *Bundesfinanzhof* of 11 July 1968, *AWD.* (1968), 354.

another context, Koopmans[30] called 'embedding into a framework'. The Court always places the basic Treaties and decisions against the background of the fundamental targets of the Communities as a 'living constitution'. In this way a framework for reference is gradually taking shape into which the individual rules are fitted. In this context the establishment of the common market is always the goal, i.e. the disappearance of the frontiers between member states, and a common attitude and activity versus the outside world. First and foremost this applies to the obligations concerning the customs union. In fact, the Court declared that

it appears from the clear, specific and unreserved formulation of articles 9 and 12, from the logical context of the rules and from the Treaty as such, that the prohibition of new tariffs, together with the principle of the free flow of goods, is one of the most important rules and that therefore each potential exception, which by the way must have a strict interpretation, should be clearly foreseen.[31]

The rules on economic competition of the EEC Treaty are seen by the Court of Justice in the same perspective. Interstate agreements restricting competition are especially forbidden as they are barriers for the mutual flow of goods and prevent economic interpenetration.[32]

This 'embedding into a framework' or this teleological approach is very clearly visible in the rules concerning the social security of migrant workers. For the interpretation of the term 'worker or somebody in a similar position' in regulation no. 3 it was regarded as decisive that this regulation was in execution of article 51 EEC, that this article formed part of the chapter of the Treaty of Rome on 'Workers' which, in its turn, belonged to the part of the Treaty concerning the foundations of the Community. Therefore, it had to be given a uniform 'common meaning'.[33] It was thus agreed, notwithstanding the fact that the history of regulation no. 3 made it clear that the only intention was to create rules for dealing with the conflict of law. It might then have been natural to take the phrase in question in the sense in which it was used in national legislation. By choosing, despite this, to

30. Contractueel Stippelwerk, oration Leyden (1965), p. 14.

31. *EEC-Commission* v. *U.E.B.L.*, Joint cases 2 and 3/62, Rec. VIII, p. 827.

32. *Grundig-Consten* v. *EEC-Commission*, Joint cases 56 and 58/64, Rec. XII, p. 429 et seq.

33. *Unger* v. *Bestuur Bedrijfsver.* Detailhandel en Ambachten, case 75/63, Rec. X, pp. 349 et seq. esp. pp. 362–3.

put the emphasis on the contents of Community rules, the Court of Justice ensured an application of article 51 EEC of the greatest uniformity and efficiency. These same principles also played an important role in the judgements on the famous system of the scrap-iron equalization system in the ECSC. Under this system enterprises had to pay a levy on scrap they bought. To reach a uniform application of the system the Court however, for the purposes of Community law, interpreted the phrase 'scrap-iron purchased' as meaning iron actually delivered, notwithstanding the fact that in the common law of various member states purchase does not comprise delivery. Had the Court of Justice regarded the word 'buying' or 'purchasing' as referring to the national law of the enterprises using scrap-iron, the inevitable consequence would have been an uneven working of the equalization system.[34]

The Court of Justice reasoned in the same way in the question whether it would be permitted to reserve the property in scrap which was the subject matter of future deals. Such a reservation could have been important in connection with a possible exemption from the equalization-levy on scrap-iron. Here, again, there was no analysis of whether such a reservation was permissible under national common law, but the judgement was given exclusively from the viewpoint of the aims and objects of the equalization mechanism:[35] acceptance for one country might lead to unequal treatment of the scrap consumers in other states.

These examples show that the Court of Justice strongly emphasizes the completeness and independence of European law in relation to national law. On the other hand, the Court of Justice calls widely on the systems of law of the member states in cases where the Treaties themselves do not provide any or an inadequate basis for the evolution of rules of law for the Communities as such. Since this has already been emphasized it is enough to make only a brief mention of it. As the Advocate-General La Grange rightly said in one of his *conclusions*, the object is not 'merely to reach a solution by means of some kind of mathematical average between the various national solutions, but to choose from the legal systems of each of the member states those solutions that seem the best ones in view of the aims of the Treaty'.[36] In fact,

34. *Forges de Clabecq* v. *High Authority*, case 14/63 Rec. ix, pp. 749–50.
35. *S.A. Métallurgique d'Espérance Longdoz* v. *H.A.*, case 3/65 Rec. xi/ii, pp. 1340–1.
36. *Kon. Ned. Hoogovens* v. *H.A.*, case 14/61 Rec. viii/3, p. 539.

there is no other way, except by comparison, that one can establish basic principles of the responsibility of the Community for non-contractual liability, which (second para. Article 215 EEC) must be 'in accordance with the general principles common to the laws of member states'. In this framework comparative law, both in the fields of public law and of private law, acquires a new meaning (Coing, 1966). The point is no longer merely to get a better comprehension of our own law through the study of comparable foreign systems. In European law comparison of law is conditional for the creation of new law, a twentieth-century 'ius commune'.

I must now conclude. What I have said so far has made it clear that European law cannot be understood through simple analogies with international law or national law. The reality of European law is more complicated than that and is based upon four pillars: the formation of law, the contents of law, the effects of law and its interpretation.

It is in the creation of European law that the penetration of the elements of international law is the strongest; here it is more difficult than in the other fields to say where the borderline lies between law and power. But we also saw that European law cuts itself free from its international origins as soon as it is in operation; in this way it gets a life and quality of its own. New roads have been taken and thus it got a character different from, but for the moment inspired by, both international and national law. The latter it fertilizes because it stimulates fresh thought about old and familiar ideas. That there are differences from international law in general does not mean that connections with international law have been broken. In this respect emphasis must be laid upon the warning given by Van Panhuys that regional law must not be twisted into bastions, or, in the words of Charlier, into 'citadelles d'exclusivisme' (1961, p. 164). This danger does not exist when European law is seen, in the first place, as an advance guard of modern international organizations. Thus, European law opens up perspectives for wider cooperation. This is important at a time when there is a growing consciousness of the fact that existing frameworks of society and organizations within it do not match up to the necessities of our time.

In European law the central point is the endeavour to find a legal order of a wider scope than that imposed by national frontiers. The fascinating fact is that European law is in full construction. The foundations are there, but the building is not yet finished. There still are many imperfections: there are no windows yet, for some seams old mortar has been used which may not bind strongly enough to hold the stones in place, and various hinges are not yet well enough fixed to carry the weight of the doors. But the stonework is there. To finish the building one needs the courage to analyse the validity or essential strength of the existing structures, the perseverance to get over set-backs, and the conviction that only continued efforts will be able to achieve a real legal order.

References

BERTRAM (1967–8) 'Decision-making in the EEC: the management committee procedure', *CMLR*, vol. 5, pp. 246–65.

CHARLIER (1961), 'Regional or general international law? A misleading dilemma', *Netherlands International Law Rev.*

CLAUDE, (1964), *Swords into Plowshares*, Random House.

COING (1966), 'Gemeines Recht and Gemeinschaftsrecht in Europa', *Festschrift für Hallstein*, pp. 116–27.

CONSTANTINIDES-MEGRET (1967), *Le droit de la CEE et l'ordre juridique des états membres.*

FALK (1967), 'New approaches to the study of international law', *AJIL*, p. 491.

FRIEDMANN, W. (1964), *The Changing Structure of International Law*, Columbia University Press.

GAUDET (1966), 'La Cooperation judicaire, instrument d'edification de l'ordre juridique commentaire', *Festschrift fur Hallstein.*

HAAS, E. B. (1958), *The Uniting of Europe*, Stanford University Press.

HAAS, E. B. (1967) 'The uniting of Europe and the uniting of Latin America' *J. Common Market Studies*, pp. 315–43.

HALLSTEIN (1965) 'The Commission: A new factor in international life', *ICL*, pp. 727–41.

HAY (1966), *Federalism and Supranational Organization*, University of Illinois Press.

HOFFMANN, (1966), 'The fate of the nation-state', *Daedalus*, pp. 862–915.

HOUBEN (1964), *Les Conseils de Ministres des Communautés Européennes.*

KAISER (1966), 'Das Europarecht in der Krise der Gemeinschaften', *Europarecht*, p. 24.

KAPTEYN, (1968) Institutionele beïrvloeding van de besluitvormende organen: Europees Parlement en Economisch en Sociaal Comite', *Besluitvorming in de Europese Gemeenschappen: theorie er praktijk.*

KOOPMANS (1966), 'De bovennationale norm in het arbeidsrecht', *Hedendaags Arbeidrecht*, Opstellen Levenbach.

LA GRANGE (1958), 'L'Ordre juridique de la CECA vu à travers la jurisprudence de la Cour de Justice', *R.D.P.* p. 849.

LINDBERG L. N. (1963), *The Political Dynamics of European Economic Integration*, Stanford University Press.

LINDBERG L. N. (1965) 'Decision making and integration in the European Economic Community', *International Organization*, pp. 56–80.

MAAS, (1967), 'Delegatie van bevoegdheid in de Europese Gemeenschappen', *SEW*.

OPHÜLS (1965), 'Staatshoheit und Gemeinschaftshoheit: Wandlungen des Souveränitätsbegriffs', *Recht im Wandel*, pp. 519–91.

PESCATORE, (1965), 'La fusion des institutions et des pouvoirs', *La Fusion des Communautés Européennes*.

POLAK, C. H. F. (1951), 'Ordening en Rechtsstaat', speech at Leyden.

RIPHAGEN (1960), 'De relaties tussen volkenrecht en nationaal recht in de regeling van het economisch verkeer' speech at Rotterdam.

RUTTEN, (1968), 'Het samenspel tussen Commissie en Raad', *Besluitvorming in de Europese Gemeenschappen: theorie en praktijk*.

SAMKALDEN (1960), 'Structuur en Bestuurskracht van Internationale Organisaties', speech at Leyden.

SAMKALDEN (1962), 'Gemeenschapsrecht en parlemenataire stelsel', *Sociaal Economische, Wetgeving*.

SCELLE (1955), 'Le phenomène juridique du dédoublement fonctionnel', *Rechsfragen der intenationalen Organisation, Festschrift fur Hans Wehberg*.

TAMMES (1958), 'Decisions of international organs as a source of law', *Rec. Cours*, vol. 2, p. 344.

TESTA, (1966), 'L'intervention des états membres dans la procédure de conclusion des accords d'association de la CEE', *Cahiers de Droit Européen*, pp. 492–513.

VAN DEN HEUVEL (1966–7), 'Some unsolved problems in community law concerning restrictive trade practices', *CMLR*, vol. 4, pp. 180–88.

VAN VOLLENHOVEN (1918), *De drie treden van het volkenrecht*.

VAN PANHUYS (1964), 'The Netherlands Constitution: a decade of experience', *AJIL*, pp. 88–108.

VON SIMSON (1964), 'Der politische Wille als Gegenstand der europäischen Gemeinschaftsverträge', *Festschrift für Otto Riese*, pp. 83–98.

WAELBROECK, (1964), 'Contribution à l'étude de la nature juridique des Communautés Européennes', *Mélanges Henri Rolin*, pp. 506–16.

WAGNER (1965), *Grundbegriffe des Beschlussrechts der europäischen Gemeinschaften, Kölner Schriften zum Europarecht*.

Part Four
Sources of Support for European Integration

Integration is not merely a question of agreement between national governments, but also involves changes in the attitudes and behaviour of the various groups in society which hitherto have looked to the national political process for satisfaction of their demands and resolution of their disputes. As yet there is little evidence of a major shift of loyalties and expectations from the national to the Community level, although Ronald Inglehart finds that the attitudes of the post-war generation are more favourable towards European integration than those of earlier generations. Arnold Rose has investigated the treatment of migrant workers in West Europe, and concludes that few nationals of these countries think of themselves as really interchangeable with their immigrants.

While popular attitudes have in general remained national in orientation, it was hoped by many advocates of European integration that national groups would combine across frontiers to seek joint advancement of their interests. Dusan Sidjanski argues that although the establishment of the European Community has encouraged the formation of such transnational interest groups, particularly in the field of agriculture, they only play a marginal role in supporting integration, and the main focus of activity remains at the national level. Werner Feld's analysis of transnational business ventures in the Community indicates that this type of collaboration is increasing, and with it the pressure for harmonization of company taxation and regulation. Once such harmonization has been achieved, the pressure for further integration will disappear, and the main concern of these transnational business enterprises will be to safeguard the level of integration already attained.

16 Ronald Inglehart

Public Opinion and Regional Integration

R. Inglehart, 'Public opinion and regional integration', in L. N. Lindberg
and S. A. Scheingold (eds.), *Regional Integration: Theory and Research*,
Harvard University Press.

Public preferences and national decision-making

For the time being, at least, survey data is relevant to the study
of regional integration chiefly in so far as it gives an indication of
the influence of the public (and various elite groups) on the
decisions of the respective national governments – and vice versa.
As integration progresses in given regions our focus may change,
and we may become primarily interested in the degree to which
given groups direct support or demands toward supranational
institutions. But for the present the basic question seems to be:

To what extent do public preferences constitute an effective influence on
a given set of national decision-makers, encouraging them to make
decisions which increase (or diminish) regional integration?

In attempting to answer this basic question we are led to examine
the nature of elite-mass linkages and to attempt to specify the
conditions under which public opinion is likely to play a relatively
important, or relatively insignificant, role. In regard to our basic
question one might even ask, 'Does the public have *any* influence
on foreign-policy decisions?' It seems to us that the answer is 'yes'
although the degree of influence can vary widely. To the extent
that a given polity permits free elections, referenda and demonstrations in the streets, the public can exert pressure on their
decision-makers. It seems reasonably evident, for example, that
the American public had a significant influence on the 1968 decision to halt the bombing in the Democratic Republic of
Vietnam (North Vietnam) and on President Lyndon Johnson's
decision not to seek reelection. Similarly, one of the burning
questions in British politics recently was whether public opinion
would cause Prime Minister Harold Wilson to reverse his stand
in favor of entry into the European Economic Community
(EEC). The sudden decision to hold general elections in the
spring of 1970 diminished the immediacy of this pressure, but by

no means excludes it as a factor bearing on the negotiations. Even in an extreme situation, such as that of the Czechoslovak Socialist Republic today, occupied by foreign troops, it would appear that the Czech public is able to effect at least a slight modification in the behavior of their decision-makers through such techniques as work slowdowns. The vital question, then, is the empirical one, 'How much influence – and under what conditions?' This question is by no means easy to answer.

For one thing, the direction of causality is not usually clear. If it is true that public preferences can generally exert at least some degree of pressure on national decision-makers, it seems equally evident that opinion leaders can often influence public opinion. Thus, the Labour Party's reversal of position regarding entry into the Common Market seems to have led a number of members of the Labour electorate to modify their views (at least temporarily): Prior to this decision Labour supporters were less favorable to entry than was the Conservative electorate; afterward, they were relatively *more* favorable. Conversely, Charles de Gaulle's opposition to supranational European integration during his last several years in power may have led his electorate to migrate from a position of one of the groups most favorable to European integration to a rank, in 1968, of least favorable. The change was only relative (a majority of Gaullists were still favorable) and was probably the result of his losing the support of a certain number of pro-European voters as well as a reflection of his personal influence. Nevertheless, one suspects that the phenomenon was at least partially a case of influence from the top down. We see the relationship between public preferences and political decision-makers, then, in terms of a feedback model.[1] But the relative importance of the societal input is conditioned by at least three main factors:

1. The structure of the national decision-making institutions: Are they pluralistic or monolithic? To the extent that there is institutionalized competition between alternative groups of decision-makers they are likely to bid against each other for societal support. In the Union of Soviet Socialist Republics, for example, during succession struggles various members of a collective leadership have frequently tried to mobilize support from lower levels of the party hierarchy or from the broader public in order

1. See Easton (1967) for a discussion of some basic concepts underlying our analysis.

to strengthen their position; with the consolidation of power in the hands of a given leader, fewer concessions seem to be made to the preferences of societal groups and a harder line may be taken behind a single policy.

The norms and perceptions of elite decision-makers are also important. A closed, hierarchical decision structure seems likely to be reinforced by norms which play down the importance and legitimacy of independent inputs from the public: mass demonstrations of support may be encouraged, but this represents manipulation of the public more than influence by the public. To the extent that the leaders of such a system are guided by an explicit or implicit political ideology, deference to public preferences is of secondary importance since the leaders already *know* what is best for the public. Their appraisal of the public interest may be correct; in any case, it is formed more in reference to the ideologues' internalized values and perceptions than on the basis of an investigation of the distribution of preferences in the society. Public opinion polling techniques are likely to be viewed as of little value.

The same tendency seems to apply to political systems having institutionalized competition, provided the elite groups can maintain cohesion on a given issue: as long as no genuine alternative is offered to the public, its influence can be minor. Thus, in the face of overwhelming public support for a return to capital punishment British political party leaders maintained a more or less solid front in rejecting it recently; similarly, as long as all three leading parties remain committed to entry into the Common Market, none of them risks paying a political price for their stand. The situation would be quite different if one of them broke the cartel.

2. *The distribution of political skills within the society.* In virtually all modern societies there exists a stratum of individuals who play a largely passive role in the national decision-making process. One indication of the existence of this group is the presence, in public opinion survey results, of respondents who consistently give no opinion about national issues and who seem likely to be non-voters. The relative size of this stratum apparently varies considerably from one society to another; within Western Europe, for example, it tends to be larger among samples of the Italian public than among the French public and smaller still among the British public. Within given nations it may vary from region to region: The 'no-opinion' stratum seems to be larger in southern

Italy and the islands than in the rest of Italy. In regard to given issues this stratum could be seen as consisting of those individuals who lack interest in, and knowledge about, the given topic. One might distinguish between the uninformed public and the informed public – or the 'attentive public', to use James Rosenau's term (1961). This could be a short-term distinction, the parameters of which might be changed substantially by an information campaign. But this stratum may also reflect a long-term difference: an absence of basic political skills which enable an individual to participate effectively in the politics of an extensive polity. Perhaps the most basic of these skills is literacy – but it is also a matter of a whole group of formative experiences which provide the habits and knowledge needed to cope with the bureaucratic organizations which make most of the national-level decisions in modern societies. Karl Deutsch's distinction between the 'politically relevant' (1961; 1966) and 'politically irrelevant' segments of society is useful to describe the long-term situation. In settings where most of the public remains 'parochial' (Lerner, 1958) in its skills and orientation public opinion data is of little significance to the study of regional integration (although surveys of elite attitudes may be useful). It would seem that decision-making in regard to regional integration in East Africa, for example, remains the province of a very restricted elite (Nye, 1970). In Western Europe, by comparison, public opinion seems to have a greater potential influence.

3. The degree to which the given decision relates to deep-seated values among the public or evokes only relatively superficial feelings. Here again, we must attempt to distinguish between a feedback relationship based on short-term and long-term effects. There is substantial evidence that certain aspects of an individual's political orientations tend to be formed relatively early in life and to persist thereafter with a relatively low probability of change. Specific age cohorts whose basic orientations are formed under conditions differing from those shaping the socialization of other cohorts may therefore retain a distinctive outlook over a period of years. The formation of political party identification seems to fit this pattern: levels of support for a given party may fluctuate, but there is an underlying tendency for given individuals to prefer a given party consistently over time. Angus Campbell, Philip Converse, Warren Miller and Donald Stokes, for example, have pointed to the existence of certain age cohorts which have tended to show a relatively high proportion of vote for the Democratic

Party over time; they explain this in terms of formative experiences associated with the New Deal (Campbell *et al.*, 1960). David Butler and Donald Stokes find evidence of a somewhat similar phenomenon among the British Labour Party electorate which they attribute to the lasting effect of formative experiences associated with the Second World War (1969, ch. 5).

An individual's sense of national identity also seems to have a tendency to be formed early and to persist through later life. Jean Piaget found that Swiss children had generally formed a sense of nationality by the age of twelve (Piaget and Weil, 1951; cf. Jahoda, 1963). Applying this line of reasoning to the study of regional integration, it has been argued that changes in the conditions governing the socialization of different European age cohorts would lead us to expect differences in the degree of support for European integration: the older cohorts, who received their basic socialization in the nationalistic atmosphere prevailing in most Western European countries up through the first World War, would retain a relatively nationalistic basic attitude which would tend to work against the acceptance of supranational integration. The cohorts who received their basic socialization in the period after the Second World War – an atmosphere in which traditional nationalism had recently been discredited and European community institutions existed and were widely regarded as beneficial – would lack these underlying reservations and would more readily support proposals for European integration. Preliminary evidence seemed to support this interpretation (Inglehart, 1967). To the extent that a sense of national (or supranational) identity does represent an early instilled and relatively deep-seated orientation it is resistant to short-term manipulation; it is an input into the political decision-making process which the decision-makers can modify only marginally and gradually – largely through the socialization of new cohorts. We would expect a substantial time lag between changes in the conditions governing socialization of a given age cohort and the impact of these changes, through recruitment into political relevance (and, eventually, into decision-making roles) of the individuals.

Let us sum up these hypotheses about the impact of mass and elite preferences on political decision-making. To do so we will make use of two diagrams. The first illustrates the short-term relationship between society and decision-makers and consists of a familiar input–output diagram supplemented by a decision funnel or pyramid to emphasize the different roles played by different groups in the society (see Figure 1). The decision-makers themselves play the central role, but outside this limited circle there are a variety of groups having various degrees of influence: Far out on the periphery we find individuals who may be unaware, or only vaguely aware, of the decision being made and who have little or no influence on it;[2] close to the decision-making center we find individuals playing elite roles, possessing information, skills and contacts which enable them to exert a relatively strong influence on the decision-makers themselves. The results of public opinion surveys then provide a potential means of analysing the importance of societal pressures favorable or unfavorable to integrative decisions – but the data cannot be interpreted in an undifferentiated way. The preferences of certain individuals are likely to have much greater weight than the preferences of others. Moreover, the impact of public preferences can be blocked at various levels: thus (in Figure 1) we indicate the inputs to the decision-making process by a line which is broken at the frontier between the mobilized and the unmobilized public; at the level of influential elites;[3] and at the level of the national decision-makers. 'Blockage' occurs when a set of values prevailing among the public is not transmitted into political decisions. The most common case, perhaps, is one in which a given issue is of low salience at a given time – and hence potentially relevant values are not perceived by decision-makers. Such cases are trivial to the extent that a deep-seated value is not relevant and the prevailing preference may be easily changed. Blockage at the elite and decision-making levels can more readily occur to the extent that the decision-making structure tends to be monolithic rather than pluralistic. In a totalitarian system a tightly disciplined decision hierarchy acts on behalf of a set of values already internalized at the top, inhibiting the communication of information about non-compatible values at lower levels. Figure 2 (p. 332)

2. An individual may be located on the periphery for a variety of reasons: In a short-term sense he may be there in regard to a given decision simply because he is not interested or informed on the topic. In a long-term sense he may be there because he has not attained cognitive mobilization, is below the age of political relevance, or belongs to a category which is coercively excluded from participating in the decision-making process.

3. For our purposes defined as individuals who normally transmit the preferences of the unorganized public to the actual decision-makers and as such occupy positions of above-average influence–especially elected representatives and governmental officials but also leaders of labor, business, agricultural, scientific, military and other groups.

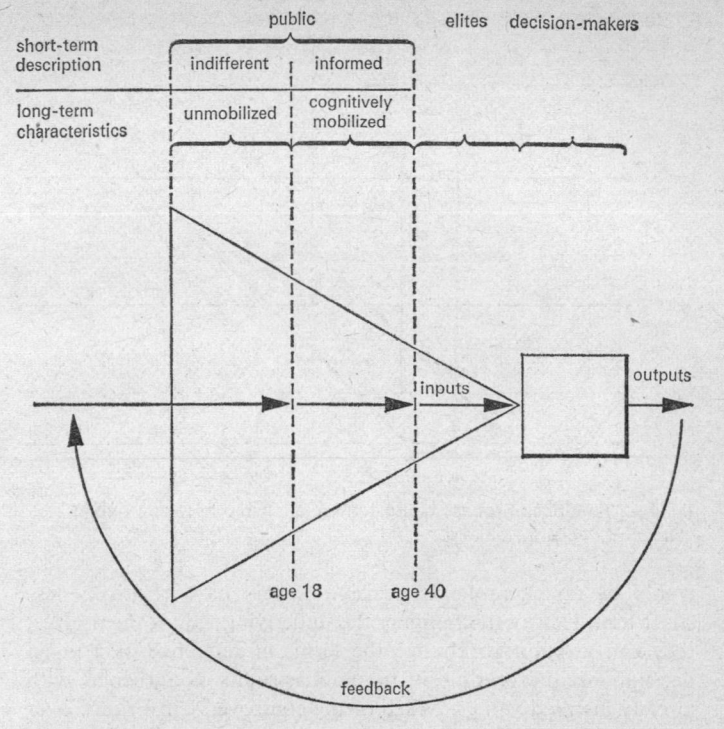

Figure 1 Feedback process: short-term relationship between public, elites and decision-makers.

illustrates the long-term relationship between society and decision-makers, emphasizing the time lag between formation of basic skills and values and their role as political input – and the implicit possibility of intergenerational differentiation linked with the tendency toward persistence which presumably characterizes these aspects of an individual's character.

The first type of feedback relationship is likely to apply to the more or less rational assessment of immediate advantages or disadvantages resulting from political outputs – what Stanley Hoffmann has called 'low politics'. Probably the most important example would be economic conditions. Political decisions on this level can produce relatively rapid changes in public support.

The second type of feedback relationship describes the less rational level of 'high politics'; the legitimacy of a given regime

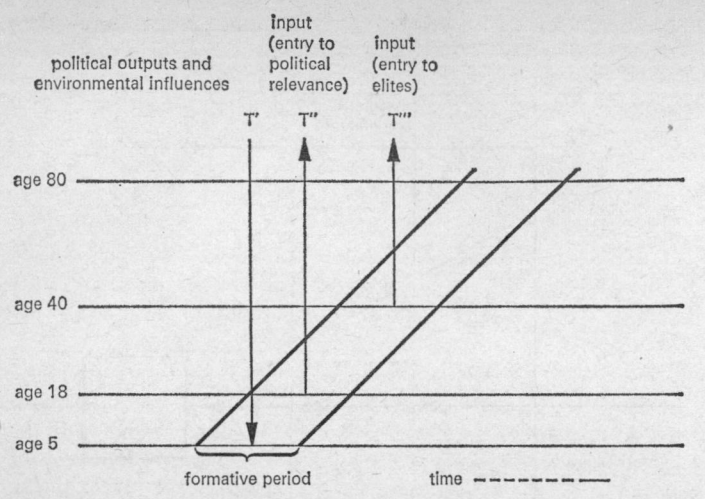

political outputs and
environmental influences

Input
(entry to
political
relevance)

Input
(entry to
elites)

T'   T''   T'''

age 80

age 40

age 18

age 5

formative period   time — — — — — — —

Figure 2 Feedback process: long-term relationship between public,
elites and decision-makers.

would be an example. If decision-makers have relatively less
short-term leeway in changing the underlying values themselves,
they can attempt to change the terms of reference of a given
decision – reinterpreting it to emphasize its congruence with
already instilled values. Much of the controversy in France over
the European defence community, for example, was based on
whether the individual saw it primarily as a means to defend *la
patrie* – or as the rearming of an ancient enemy.

It will be noted that our analysis tends to associate stable
preferences with early instilled ones. Strictly speaking, this is not
necessarily the case. Some individuals may well form deep and
lasting political orientations relatively late in life. Nevertheless it
seems that by the time they have reached adulthood, most
politically relevant citizens have already formed a basic set of
value priorities; later learning will take place in reference to these
values, and it is probably more difficult to unlearn an existing set
of orientations than to learn a new outlook from the start. We
have suggested elsewhere that a certain degree of 'structural
commitment' impedes changes in an individual's outlook once
basic socialization has taken place (see Inglehart, 1967; cf.
Abramson and Inglehart, 1970; Merelman, 1966). An analogy
might be seen in the relative ease with which young people learn

foreign languages; it is relatively rare (although not impossible) that an adult learns to speak a new language with perfect fluency and without a foreign accent.

Finally, we must distinguish between salience and stability of opinion. The two may tend to go together but they are certainly not identical. Under given conditions a previously unimportant issue may become the object of heated public feelings. Our hypothesis is that, except to the extent that such feelings reflect relatively early instilled attitudes, they probably cannot be regarded as an independent input to the political process as much as the reflection of current political outputs and environmental influences.

Public opinion survey responses at any given time represent a mixture of these two types of feedback, and it is difficult to separate the two elements. But in so far as we are dealing with the former, public opinion is probably more largely a reflection of elite decisions than an influence on them. To the extent that a decision evokes deep-seated values decision-makers must deal with something they cannot change quickly; they may have to accept certain limits to their policies or pay the political costs of public disaffection (which, of course, vary from system to system).

We have suggested a set of conditions under which societal opinion is likely to be an important factor relating to regional integration. Our ideas are drawn from impressionistic evidence; they remain to be validated empirically. They suggest a research strategy: ideally, we should measure the preferences of elite and mass samples, representing each of the structural levels of the decision process; furthermore, we must attempt to distinguish between deeply internalized values and relatively superficial preferences. We would need to make such measurements at a series of points in time in order to analyse the relationship between societal preferences and integrative (or disintegrative) decisional outputs.[4] The latter could, perhaps, best be measured by an expert-rating system similar to that suggested by Leon Lindberg and Stuart Scheingold (1970). An extensive series of these measurements would be necessary in order to enable us to control for the effect of environmental variables – changes in economic conditions, trade flows, external threats, etc. Public

4. Another interesting (and related) line of investigation lies in the analysis of monochronic correlations between public opinion and the perceptions, preferences, and behavior of elite representatives. This approach clarifies only part of the process – the elite-mass linkage – but has the advantage of immediate feasibility. For an example see Miller and Stokes (1966).

opinion may be an important influence on the decision process, but it is almost certainly only one of several major factors.

Clearly, this would necessitate a costly research effort continuing over many years. It seems, however, that any definitive conclusions about the role of public/elite preferences in foreign-policy decisions would have to be based on a data base of this kind. Properly done, such an analysis could enable us to begin to move toward making predictive statements about the probable outcome of integrative processes.

While we still have a long way to go, a fair amount of time-series data on the topic of European integration does already exist. What is needed is a more continuous effort with greater attention to achieving comparability in the data gathered and a clearer knowledge of the degree to which given survey items tap relatively basic attitudes.

In the meantime, we can only draw some tentative conclusions about the impact of societal preferences on regional integration based on fragmentary evidence. It may be worthwhile to do so by way of indicating progress to date and some problems still to be solved. Our observations will be limited to integration in Western Europe – the only region for which a substantial data base exists.

European opinion and decision structures: a permissive consensus?

For many years what might be called a 'permissive consensus'[5] seems to have existed among the Western European publics regarding European integration. There was a favorable prevailing attitude toward the subject, but it was generally of low salience as a political issue – leaving national decision-makers free to take steps favorable to integration if they wished but also leaving them a wide liberty of choice. It seems, for example, that the Schuman Plan was launched by a small elite working in almost conspiratorial fashion and able to maneuver swiftly and effectively in part *because* of the lack of public involvement. This margin may be growing narrower as time goes by.

Since the early 1950s majorities of the public in the Federal Republic of Germany (West Germany), France, Italy and the United Kingdom, have supported the general idea of uniting Western Europe. In response to a question concerning 'efforts to unify Western Europe', support dropped below the 50 per cent level only twice during the 1952–62 decade: in France in 1955 (the year after the defeat of the European defence community, and in

5. The term is from Lindberg and Scheingold.

the United Kingdom in 1962 (the year of public controversy over the Conservative Party's decision to try to enter Europe). Apart from these special cases a majority of the French public has consistently supported the general idea of 'unification', with only about 12 per cent in declared opposition (a sizable group giving no opinion). The favorable majority in West Germany has generally been above 70 per cent (dropping to a low of 69 per cent in 1955); in Italy it has been at least 55 per cent (the low point, again, being 1955); and in the United Kingdom it has remained at least 58 per cent, with the exception noted.[6] Despite these fluctuations the relative positions of the various national publics nearly always have been rather consistent, the Germans (with the Dutch, when data is available) nearly always ranking as most pro-European. In all four countries a low point was reached in the aftermath of the defeat of the projected European defence community. The decline associated with this crisis was especially marked in France – the country in which the European defence community debate had been sharpest. Somewhat similarly, the British public registered a sharply depressed level of support for European unification during the 1962 debate over British entry into the Common Market. After a subsequent recovery of British support, this phenomenon seems to be repeating itself at present when another possible leap into the unknown looms before the British public. Since de Gaulle's first veto of British entry into the Common Market, levels of public support for European integration in all four countries have been below their peak level of the 1950s – if we use this very general question as our indicator.

This item concerning 'efforts toward unifying Western Europe' has the advantage of having been used in an exceptionally long time series. It has the disadvantage, however, of having what might be called a 'floating referent': it does not ask whether an individual is for or against a specific measure (such as a European army) but tends to refer to whatever topics are currently salient in the public eye. Consequently it probably does not reflect more

6. This data is from United States Information Agency (USIA) surveys of 1952 through 1962, reported in Merritt and Puchala (1968, pp. 283–5). This book contains a rich collection of additional background data on the subject. The above remarks are also based on supplementary data from a 1962 survey (using the same item) sponsored by the European Communities Information Service and similar data from the 1964 USIA surveys, tabulated by myself. For additional evidence concerning the development of public support for European political integration over the past ten years see Rabier (1966; 1967); and Bissery (1968).

specific developments going on in public opinion. Among the most important of these developments seems to be a convergence of opinion within the European community in support of measures which would have been considered unfeasible a decade or so ago and the development of a European public within which nationality is a variable of secondary importance (ranking behind such variables as formal education, age, social class and sex as a predictor of attitude).[7] This emerging European consensus seems to support supranational political integration – it apparently is ready for a 'United States of Europe'. The homogenization of opinion seems to have been achieved by a process in which the slow pace may have disappointed German expectations but gave the French a chance to catch up. In 1955 a two-thirds majority of the German public already favored building a 'United States of Europe'. This figure rose to a peak of 81 per cent by 1961 in the early days of the Common Market. By 1967 it had declined to 78 per cent, fell to 73 per cent in 1968, and was only slightly above its 1955 level (with 69 per cent in favor) in early 1970.[8] Available data for France is only very roughly comparable, but it appears that as of 1957 only 35 per cent of the French public were in favor of a 'federation of Western Europe'. This figure rose gradually to 38 per cent (1962), 42 per cent (1964) and 55 per cent (1966). Approximately the same percentage (57 per cent) was favorable to a 'United States of Europe' in 1968 – a level which rose to 67 per cent in 1970.[9]

For a dozen years the publics of the six European community countries have lived under common institutions having limited but real powers. They have shared a certain set of experiences and they seem to be taking on a common perspective. But while this

7. A tree analysis of predictors of pro-European attitudes based on survey data from Britain, France, Germany and Italy gathered in 1963 and in 1968 bears this out while suggesting the growing importance of a cleavage between the publics of the United Kingdom and the European community (see Inglehart, 1970a).

8. The 1955–67 figures are from *Deutschland und die Europäischen Gemeinschaft*, Table 10; 1967 figures are from *Die Einstellung der deutschen Jugend zur Vereinigung Europas* (Allensbach: Institüt für Demoskopie, 1967); 1968 figures are from a cross-national pilot survey undertaken by Leon Lindberg, Stuart Scheingold, and myself; 1970 figures are from a cross-national survey sponsored by the European Communities Information Service.

9. Data for 1957 is calculated from tables in Merritt and Puchala (1968); 1962–6 data appears in Rabier (1966, p. 24); 1968 and 1970 figures are from the respective sources cited in the preceding footnote.

development has been going on, there is evidence of a growing differentiation across community borders: specifically, between the publics of the Six and the British. Although in the 1950s and early 1960s the British public appeared to be about as pro-European as the French, there was an extraordinary reversal of opinion at the time of the second veto of British admission in late 1967, followed by a downward trend continuing to the present. Thus, in early 1970 a survey of the adult publics of the United Kingdom and the five largest members of the Six obtained the following responses to a series of proposals for European integration (Table 1): perhaps the most striking aspect of Table 1 is the contrast between the Europeanism of the British and the European community publics. Equally important, however, is the high level of support among the publics of Europe for certain proposals which imply far-reaching supranational political integration. These are not simply 'motherhood and virtue'-type items with which one must inevitably agree: it is possible for a reasonable man to reject them (and heavy majorities of the British do). The breadth of the majority which supports them within the community, then, is all the more impressive – as is the relative homogeneity of the European consensus.

As we move farther up the decision pyramid, we find results which are consistent with the public preferences indicated above. In a group of elite interviews conducted in 1964 Karl Deutsch found that among a sample of French elites 83 per cent were at least conditionally in favor of further limitations on national sovereignty, as compared with 13 per cent who were opposed. Among a sample of German elites the respective figures were 91 per cent in favor and 4 per cent against (1967b; cf. Deutsch, 1967a).[10]

As is true at the mass level, the French – and especially the German elites – find support for European integration compatible with support for integration with another region:

When asked to choose between policies of strengthening mainly European institutions, such as EEC, and strengthening NATO, 40 per cent of the 124 articulate French respondents prefer EEC, whereas only 4 per cent favor NATO. . . . [Among the German respondents] a 72 per cent majority refuses to choose and insists on supporting both –

10. Deutsch's samples consisted of leaders in the fields of business, politics, administration, journalism and academic life – men who, while not the actual decision-makers themselves, were reputedly influential in the national political system.

Table 1 **Levels of support for five European integration proposals**
(Percentage responses by country, February 1970)

	For	Undecided	Against	N
1. 'United States of Europe'				
Germany	69	22	9	(1731)
Netherlands	64	19	17	(1482)
France	67	22	11	(2130)
Belgium	60	30	10	(1155)
Italy	60	33	7	(1941)
United Kingdom	30	22	48	(2147)
2. British entry into Common Market				
Germany	69	24	7	
Netherlands	79	13	8	
France	66	23	11	
Belgium	63	29	8	
Italy	51	40	9	
United Kingdom	19	18	63	
3. Election of European Parliament				
Germany	66	25	9	
Netherlands	59	20	21	
France	59	26	15	
Belgium	56	34	11	
Italy	55	39	6	
United Kingdom	25	20	55	
4. Supranational European government with common defence, foreign and economic policies				
Germany	57	24	19	
Netherlands	50	18	32	
France	49	23	28	
Belgium	51	30	19	
Italy	51	39	11	
United Kingdom	22	18	60	
5. Would vote for president of 'United States of Europe' from a country other than respondent's own				
Germany	69	19	12	
Netherlands	63	19	18	
France	61	17	22	
Belgium	52	24	24	
Italy	45	36	19	
United Kingdom	39	20	41	

Source: Survey sponsored by European Communities Information Service, with collaboration of the author.

a middle way favored also by a French plurality of 49 per cent (Deutsch *et al.*, 1967b).[11]

A series of elite interviews carried out in 1956, 1959, 1961 and 1965 in France, Germany, and the United Kingdom yield similar results. In reporting their findings Daniel Lerner and Morton Gorden place heavy emphasis on the emergence of a pragmatic consensus among West European elites – overriding time-honored cleavages between left and right and between nationalities. The consensus was especially strong regarding European *economic* integration:

By 1965, two thirds of all panels even believed that European integration had passed the 'point of no return'. At worst, they believed that delays might occur. But essentially, time was on the side of European integration (Lerner and Gorden, 1969, ch. 5).[12]

At the elite level the evidence seems to demonstrate the existence of a consensus favorable to at least a limited measure of further integration – even in France (and even among Gaullist elites). But when we examine the political outputs of recent years, we find another story.

Major attempts to broaden and strengthen the European community have met with failure over the last several years[13] – and the European esprit has suffered severely. Negotiations for British admission have twice ended in a unilateral veto; a far-reaching set of proposals to strengthen the role of the Commission of the European Communities was stalemated in early 1966 after a demoralizing six-month boycott of the European community by the French government.

Despite the prevailing consensus in favor of broadening and strengthening the community why has policy-making not followed the path indicated by these underlying pressures? To answer this question we must move to another level of analysis – that of personality. In this case we must examine the personality of General de Gaulle. It appears that in regard to certain issues prevailing pressures within the French (and hence the European) decision structure were, for a limited time, successfully blocked at the very top level – by a strategically located individual.

11. Deutsch reports that only 7 per cent of the French and 3 per cent of the German elites indicated that they did not wish to strengthen *either* European or NATO institutions (p. 122).

12. These elite samples are drawn from approximately the same groups as those interviewed by Deutsch, and others.

13. We should not, however, ignore indications of a gradual expansion of the scope of European decisionmaking activities (see Lindberg and Scheingold, 1970).

It seems almost too simple to explain major historical events in terms of the influence of one man: surely there are 'deeper' causes – causes to be found, for example, in the socio-economic structure of the society. As a general rule this view is probably correct; only in rare cases do individual actors have a major influence on shaping events. Fred Greenstein has summarized the circumstances under which this can happen (1967). According to him, it depends on:

1. Location of the actor in a given environment. A limiting case would be that of a dictator in a totalitarian system; here there is a tendency for political machinery to become 'a conduit of the dictatorial personality' (Tucker, 1963). While certainly more limited in his powers than a totalitarian dictator, de Gaulle had the advantages of a seven-year term, plenary emergency powers, and a reserved domain in foreign affairs – reinforced by a widespread belief that he was indispensable to France. In the realm of foreign policy de Gaulle alone was in effective control of France.

2. The degree to which action admits of restructuring – in this case, *can* an individual in effective control of French policy contrive to block European political integration? As long as the European decision system is based on international unanimity, open to unilateral vetoes, the answer is yes.

3. Personal strengths (or weaknesses) of the actor. De Gaulle's strengths – his skill as a politician and as an actor in the theatrical sense – were exceptional. 'Strength of character' is another important aspect: his insensitivity to personal popularity constituted a great strength from this viewpoint. To an extraordinary degree de Gaulle was a man who acted on the base of internalized values rather than in response to external stimuli.[14]

Thus, survey data by itself can predict political outcomes only to a limited extent; both mass and elite preferences can be overruled by a tiny minority or even a single individual within given decision structures.

But, to the extent that the analysis of survey data delineates the existence and character of given political generations it may even aid us in interpreting such apparently unpredictable factors as a de Gaulle. De Gaulle tended to act on the basis of deeply internalized values. In 1940 this trait redounded to his great honor,

14. This corresponds approximately to Karl Deutsch's definition of 'will': the closure of a communications network against new messages (see Deutsch, 1963).

and in a great many respects his unique role after 1958 was highly positive. In certain of his decisions relating to European integration he may have represented an extreme case of delayed feedback into the political system – imposing a perspective which lagged behind current realities of French and European society. For in 1963, as in 1940, he acted in a way which was faithful to his early formation – that of a member of the French bourgeosie, trained as a military officer, who came to maturity in the intensely nationalistic period preceding the First World War. It is not surprising, then, that de Gaulle was strongly committed to a balance-of-power view of the world, one which reacted chiefly according to concepts of domination/subordination, rather than perceiving the possibility that integration could represent cooperation among equals.

As a result of his exceptional situation de Gaulle was able – for a limited number of years – to make foreign policy decisions almost without reference to the prevailing trends in French mass and elite opinion. This applied to a number of issues apart from those of European integration. Deutsch found, for example, that 'the idea of a *national nuclear deterrent* is unpopular among the elites of France, where it is official government policy' (1967a). Similarly, his withdrawal from NATO, his gestures in support of *Québec libre*, his anti-Israeli posture during the Six-Day War of June 1967 were apparently received with a mixture of chagrin and astonishment by the bulk of the French people.

Lerner and Gorden provide some quantitative evidence on this score: they selected approximately twenty questions each from their 1961 and 1965 surveys of elite opinion in France, Germany and the United Kingdom. Questions were selected for which a clear government policy had been enunciated (and agreed upon by a panel of judges). They then examined the degree of congruence between official policy and elite opinion as reflected in their surveys (see Table 2).

Table 2 **Elite-government-policy congruence**

| | United Kingdom | | France | | Germany | |
| | 1961 | 1965 | 1961 | 1965 | 1961 | 1965 |
	$n = 19$	$n = 19$	$n = 21$	$n = 21$	$n = 23$	$n = 18$
Degree of congruence as percentage	79	89	61	48	83	82

Source: Lerner and Gorden (1970, appendix 4); adapted from a working paper by John Child, Jr. The number of issues rated is shown for each year and country.

The results show a consistently high level of congruence between elite preferences and government policy in both Germany and the United Kingdom – and, by contrast, a low and declining level of congruence in France. Indeed, by 1965 congruence existed between the French government and the French elite sample on less than half of the items rated!

We hypothesized that the role of public opinion tends to be minor when the political institutions of a given country do not present genuine alternatives. In a special sense this situation describes France under de Gaulle. To be sure, the institutions of competitive political parties and other independent organizations existed. But France had known a long series of political crises, leading up to the revolt which toppled the Fourth Republic in 1958, followed by a series of abortive revolts continuing until the achievement of Algerian independence in 1962. Despite divergences between himself and prevailing societal preferences on the European issue and other questions during the mid-1960s, de Gaulle was widely regarded as indispensable – the one man who could provide something valued even more highly: domestic political and economic stability. He was thus, to a certain degree, insulated from the pressures of public opinion on lesser issues. Nevertheless, it would be inaccurate to conclude that the European issue could not impose certain political costs; the December 1965 French presidential election seems to indicate the contrary. This election was held during de Gaulle's boycott of the European Communities, and the European question became the central issue, with both of the general's leading opponents taking pro-European stands. A specifically European candidate, Jean Lecanuet, was launched by the Center, competing directly for the votes of socio-economic groups which in the recent past had supported de Gaulle. Lecanuet – almost unknown previously – succeeded in winning a considerable segment of these votes in the first round. French farmers seem to have reacted particularly sharply to the charge that de Gaulle was anti-European and to the fact that he was boycotting the Common Market, but the bulk of the Lecanuet vote seems to have been from the middle class.

To be sure, de Gaulle polled 45 per cent of the vote on the first round against Lecanuet's 16 per cent. But this left de Gaulle with a level of support far below what he had won in previous referenda and forced him into the humiliation of a run-off election. His claim to speak for all of France was made less plausible. Upon his elimination from the race, Lecanuet announced, 'The question of Europe will be the determining factor in the choice I and my friends of the Democratic Center will make on 19 December' (the date of the run off election). On the basis of this issue he threw his support to de Gaulle's opponent, François Mitterrand, and a good half of his voters followed him. These voters – who moved across the chasm which normally prevents partisans of the French Center (or Right) from voting for a candidate who has Communist support – may well have been largely motivated by the European issue. While a minority of the electorate, they nevertheless constituted a significant bloc. Furthermore, the campaign may have contributed to a polarization according to age-group which has to become increasingly important: the vote in 1965 was age-related to an unprecedented degree. A survey made by l'Institut français d'opinion publique (IFOP) shortly before the election found that in the twenty-one–thirty-four-year-old age-group, among those voters who had made up their minds, only 35 per cent had decided in favor of de Gaulle, while 21 per cent chose Lecanuet. If the franchise had been limited to this age-group, de Gaulle might have lost the election in the second round.

It would seem, then, that de Gaulle paid a certain price for his boycott of Europe: it did not cost him his job, but it did tend to undermine his prestige. His relative immunity, however, was due to an exceptional position which an eventual successor would be unlikely to maintain.

On the basis of an analysis of the elite and mass opinion data cited above (and an examination of transaction flow data) we concluded in 1967 that de Gaulle's successor would probably need to conciliate the Center; this *tendance* appeared to be the most strongly pro-European of the French political families, at both elite and mass levels. Consequently, we conjectured that:

De Gaulle is likely to remain in power through 1972 at the latest. From that point on . . . the various underlying pressures which have been discussed here should again begin to be reflected in elite-level political activity. Other things being equal, we would expect that:
1. The United Kingdom will be admitted to the European Community.
2. The movement toward supranational organization of Europe will be resumed.
3. French anti-American and anti-Canadian politics will diminish (Inglehart, 1968).

Certainly, we failed to foresee the substantial shift in British public opinion which began later that year – and which may yet prevent British entry into the European community. But in its application to French politics our analysis appears to have been accurate. Let us examine the series of events leading up to what some observers have called the European *relance* at the Hague in December 1969.

The revolt of May–June 1968 had a critical impact on the French national decision structure. The strength of de Gaulle's position, we have argued, was based on a widespread feeling that he was the only man who could provide political and economic stability for France. The events of May demonstrated that not even he could provide it – and that an alternative existed. By comparison with de Gaulle (who sometimes seemed to be losing his grip) the premier, Georges Pompidou, performed very coolly during the crisis, emerging with a prestige within the government which rivaled de Gaulle's own and a popularity (as reflected in public opinion polls) which was even higher than de Gaulle's. From the general's viewpoint the solution was clear: Pompidou had to go. He was dismissed shortly after the Gaullist legislative electoral victory which he had largely engineered. Nevertheless, a certain alternative now existed. And it seems likely that the April 1969 referendum, on which de Gaulle gratuitously staked his presidency, was held, in part, because he hoped to reestablish his position as the paramount national leader independent of Pompidou. The referendum was voted down for a variety of reasons. Among the most important, it seems, was the fact that Pompidou now was waiting in the wings, a discreet but distinctly available candidate for the succession, and the fact that once again a not widely known centrist (this time Alain Poher) came forward to campaign against the referendum, introducing the European issue as one of his major themes. It appears that it was the erosion of support from the centrist constituency which brought about de Gaulle's defeat in the referendum, leading to his immediate resignation (Lancelot, 1969).

In the presidential campaign which followed Pompidou made great efforts to appear at least as European as his leading rival, Poher. One of his first steps was to conciliate the Independent Republican leader, Valéry Giscard d'Estaing (who had worked against the referendum): converted, Giscard campaigned with posters of himself plastered all over France bearing the words: 'Liberal and European, I support the candidacy of G. Pompidou'. After a face-to-face radio interview in which he gave the right answers to the European question Pompidou won over another leading European, Jacques Duhamel; in doing so, he succeeded in splitting the centrist electorate with which both Poher and Duhamel were linked. In the first round Pompidou got 44 per cent of the vote to Poher's 23 per cent (the rest was split among four candidates of a seriously divided Left). Pompidou won the run off by a comfortable margin due (in part) to the fact that the Communists abstained massively. His new government included leading Europeans in several key positions (including the ministries of agriculture, economy and finance, and foreign affairs).

There are indications that the current regime is relatively sensitive to public opinion, including, specifically, the results of public opinion polls (which predicted the defeat of the 1969 referendum). It may be significant, for example, that shortly before the Hague conference (December 1969) French survey results showing high levels of support for supranational integration were commented on in prominent articles in *Le Monde*, *L'Express*, and *Paris Match*; in all three cases the findings were interpreted in a context which took for granted that President Pompidou would not only be aware of them but would be influenced by them in his actions at the Hague.

Pompidou's role there was far from simple: he had to avoid the risk of an open break with the orthodox Gaullist faction in his own party, preserving the appearance of continuity with the general's foreign policy (to which he gave lip service) while accepting major revisions. At that conference and in subsequent negotiations the leaders of the Six agreed to form a European economic and monetary union; to reopen negotiations on British entry by mid-1970; and to provide the European institutions with their own financial resources, independent of contributions from the national governments. These resources, for the immediate future, are very modest in size, but the principle involved represents one of the essential first steps toward the creation of an autonomous supranational government and reverses an important aspect of the stand taken by de Gaulle in his 1965–6 boycott. Moreover, in requiring approval of the budget at Strasbourg the agreements give a measure of real power to the European Parliament. Europe has a very long way to go, but it is possible that it has begun moving again. And it seems that within the community the public consensus in favor of European integration is becoming increasingly capable of influencing that movement.

Cognitive mobilization: the changing balance of political skills

Some evidence has been presented that public opinion is becoming increasingly important in relation to decisions concerning European integration. We pointed to various fragments of evidence which suggest the presence of an increasingly favorable distribution of values as well as recent structural changes which tend to produce a greater openness to societal inputs in France. But there are other reasons to believe that, as a long-term trend, the role of public opinion is becoming increasingly significant in Western Europe. One of these reasons relates to the changing distribution of political skills in these countries. To explain this we will briefly trace a certain broad historical development.

In the small traditional polity, based on word-of-mouth messages and face-to-face loyalties, political communication was accessible to all, as far as possession of the relevant skills was concerned. Hence, an equalitarian decision process is frequently found within the tribe or peasant village, based on a consensus reached by all mature males (and, sometimes, all mature females). Such a process is rarely or never found in the more complex and extensive traditional monarchies or bureaucratic empire. With the development of an extensive political community fundamental changes necessarily take place in the making and executing of political decisions: it becomes a question of making decisions involving millions, rather than hundreds or thousands, of people and of coordinating the activities of a geographically scattered population rather than a group assembled in one place. New techniques of communication and control must be developed, and, increasingly, an elite must be differentiated which possesses specialized skills. Personal loyalties no longer suffice; a system of legitimacy must be developed which is based on impersonal roles to at least some extent. Word-of-mouth communications no longer suffice; records must be kept based on abstract symbols. Perhaps the most significant of the new skills is literacy; but others are also important: skills in bookkeeping, the ability to conceptualize authority relations at a distance and over long periods of time. To sum up these skills in one general concept we might view them as the ability to manipulate political abstractions. We will refer to the process by which these skills become increasingly widely distributed as 'cognitive mobilization'.

In a subsistence economy it is very unlikely that the entire population will have sufficient leisure time to develop these skills. They tend to become the monopoly of a differentiated minority:

royal officials, a priestly caste, mandarins, etc. The differentiation of such an elite, in a sense, is a great leap forward in political development. It permits the formation of extensive polities, maintaining order over large areas, based on the resources of relatively large numbers of people. But the resulting shift in the relative distribution of political skill implies, almost inevitably, a diminution of popular control and participation. During this phase the politics of the political community tend to move out of the ken of the common man and become the sphere of a relatively skilled and cosmopolitan elite. By comparison the great bulk of the population of traditional monarchies or bureaucratic empires is parochial.[15] Likely to have a low level of awareness and comprehension of national-level politics, the majority finds it difficult to project themselves into the role of a distant political authority. As a consequence they tend to be politically inert.

With increasing economic and technological development resources become available which make it possible to begin to readjust the balance of political skills between elite and mass. It is probably not by sheer coincidence that, in the political development of European nations, expansion of the electorate tended to be linked with expansion of public education: a literate citizenry could keep in touch with national-level politics via the printed mass media.

Although they attained widespread literacy decades ago, the great majority of the publics of Western European countries still have no more than a primary education. By contrast, the bulk of government officials at a policy-making level have university educations; a citizen with a primary-school education is scarcely on an even footing. The bureaucrat operates at a level of abstraction which is scarcely comprehensible to the average citizen; it is unlikely that the latter will be able to articulate his grievance effectively – quite possibly he will not even be able to figure out which official he ought to contact.

The massive expansion of higher education in recent years has tended to equalize this balance of political skills at least among the younger cohorts. Increased student activism may represent, in part, the type of input described in Figure 2: the attainment of political relevance by cohorts which possess relatively high levels of political skills and, in some respects, different basic value priorities from those of older cohorts.

15. Our use of the terms 'parochial' and 'cosmopolitan' is based on Daniel Lerner's classic work (1958).

On the whole, increasing cognitive mobilization seems to favor European integration. It is perfectly conceivable that it could be associated with rising feelings of nationalism; indeed, this pattern seems to have characterized an earlier stage of the process in nineteenth-century Europe. Cognitive mobilization increases an individual's capacity to receive and process messages relating to remote political objects: The effect of exposure to such messages depends, in large part, on the *content* of the messages. In the Western European environment since the Second World War the content of communications relating to European integration seems to have been predominantly favorable. Hence, we would expect individuals with high skill levels to take a relatively favorable position. There are additional reasons why we might expect this. Increasing familiarity with European-level politics may make them seem less remote, more familiar. For the less sophisticated public the Brussels institution may remain dimly understood, perhaps somewhat threatening.

Survey evidence bears out this expectation. If we take formal education as an indicator of cognitive mobilization, we find a consistent tendency for the more educated to give a higher level of support to proposals for European integration. In part this is because the more educated are notably more likely to have an opinion on the subject. But even controlling for this effect we find a general tendency for the more educated to be relatively pro-European (see Table 3). It might be argued that the linkage

Table 3 **Percentage 'for' supranational European government, by education among those giving an opinion** (France and Germany, 1968)

Educational level	France	Germany
Primary school only	52 (500)	50 (946)
Beyond primary school	71 (598)	69 (471)

between education and Europeanness is spurious – that it simply reflects an association between higher education and higher social class, higher income level or distinctive political party preferences. In fact the correlation between education and Europeanness tends to be stronger than the correlation between Europeanness and these other variables; it may be more plausible to view part of the linkage between higher income and Europeanism as resulting from the effect of education rather than the other way around (Inglehart, 1970a).

Again, our evidence is not conclusive. But there are indications of a long-term trend toward an increasingly active role for public opinion in Western Europe, and there is reason to believe that this more active public is relatively favorable to European integration.

Internalized values: a delayed feedback into the political system

In a previous article we hypothesized that certain basic political orientations tend to become crystallized during an individual's preadult years and are relatively unlikely to change greatly during the remainder of the individual's life (Inglehart, 1967).[16] It follows from this hypothesis that when substantially different conditions govern the political formation of two or more respective age cohorts these differences should be reflected in the attitudes of the age-groups in later life. One's sense of national identity, we argued, is one of these basic orientations. If this is true, then those Western European age cohorts which were formed in the intensely nationalistic period preceding the First World War, for example, should show a relatively nationalistic response pattern even today, by contrast with the cohorts formed after the Second World War – in an atmosphere in which traditional nationalism had recently been discredited and influenced by the existence of supranational European institutions and by the absence of violent hostilities between Western European nations.

On the basis of these assumptions we predicted (and found) age-group differences in the indicated direction in response to a series of proposals for European integration which presumably tapped a basic nationalism/internationalism dimension. We would, furthermore, except the magnitude of these age-group differences to vary according to the recent historical experience of the given country. Among the four which we analysed, age-group differences were largest in Germany which had undergone cataclysmic changes from the chauvinism of the Kaiserzeit to the anti-nationalistic reaction following the defeat of Adolf Hitler.

16. This article was based on secondary analysis of cross-national public opinion surveys carried out in 1962 (sponsored by the European Communities Information Service) and in 1963 (sponsored by the Reader's Digest Association). For descriptions of this data and a presentation of some findings see, respectively, *Journal of Common Market Studies*, November 1963 (vol. 2, no. 4), and *Products and Peoples* (Reader's Digest Association, 1963).

Age-group differences were smallest in the Netherlands, already characterized by a relatively internationalistic outlook in the pre-1918 period, with France and the United Kingdom falling between these two extremes.

Table 4 **Percentage 'for' four proposals for supranational integration, by country and age-group: 1970**

Age-group	Germany	Nether-lands	France	Belgium	Italy	United Kingdom
For 'United States of Europe'						
21–34	75	69	71	67	66	33
35–49	75	61	66	67	63	30
50–64	64	65	71	61	57	30
65+	57	60	60	42	42	24
Age spread:	+18	+9	+11	+25	+24	+9
For British entry into Common Market						
21–34	75	80	69	60	58	23
35–49	73	78	64	71	54	20
50–64	65	80	65	59	49	17
65+	59	73	66	57	36	14
Age spread:	+16	+7	+3	+3	+22	+9
For European Parliament						
21–34	73	64	64	54	60	30
35–49	70	57	56	61	60	25
50–64	62	61	63	57	51	23
65+	55	54	50	43	38	19
Age spread:	+18	+10	+14	+11	+22	+11
For supranational European government, responsible for foreign affairs, defence and economy						
21–34	66	54	53	52	57	28
35–49	60	49	51	60	53	22
50–64	53	51	51	51	49	21
65+	42	45	40	37	33	14
Age spread:	+24	+9	+13	+15	+24	+14
Would vote for president of a 'United States of Europe' from another country						
21–34	81	73	73	58	59	54
35–49	71	67	63	60	45	42
50–64	61	57	59	51	40	34
65+	54	47	46	33	25	20
Age spread:	+27	+26	+26	+25	+34	+34

In Table 4 we replicate the previous age-group comparison, using data gathered in 1970 (see Table 4).[17] The expected age-group differences appear and in the predicted direction (younger cohorts showing a rather consistent tendency to give higher levels of support for supranational European integration). Moreover, the *relative* magnitude of the age-group differences again conform to our expectations: among the four countries examined previously the differences are greatest in Germany and smallest in the Netherlands, with France and the United Kingdom again falling into intermediate positions. An Italian sample has been added to our analysis this time, and it proves to have the largest age-group differences of all. In part this reflects unusually high non-response rates among the older Italian cohorts (which we would interpret as indicating relatively low levels of cognitive mobilization). However, we cannot uniformly discount non-response as simple absence of opinion: there is reason to believe that among certain individuals it reflects reticent opposition, an intermediate position between outright opposition and outright support.[18]

17. The items asked were:
1. 'Are you in favour of, or against, Britain joining the Common Market?'
2. 'Assuming (in these next four questions) that Britain *did* join, would you be for or against the evolution of the Common Market towards the political formation of a United States of Europe?'
3. 'Would you be in favour of, or against, the election of a European parliament by direct universal suffrage; that is, a parliament elected by all the voters in the member countries?'
4. 'Would you be willing to accept, over and above the British Government, a European Government responsible for a common policy in foreign affairs, defence and the economy?'
5. 'If a President of a United States of Europe were being elected by popular vote, would you be willing to vote for a candidate *not* of your own country, if his personality and programme corresponded more closely to your ideas than those of the candidates from your own country?'
18. Evidence exists that those who take a minority position in regard to prevailing norms are relatively likely to give 'no response' to relevant survey items. Thus, for example, support for the French Communist party is consistently and substantially underrepresented in surveys as compared with its actual vote in elections. For a theoretical treatment see McCroskey (1967–8). In previous research we found that the older cohorts who give a relatively high non-response rate on European integration proposals seem relatively likely to shift from support to neutrality or from neutrality into opposition in the face of events which weaken overall support (and hence, the strength of the majoritarian norm). This finding seems consistent with our interpretation, according to which these older cohorts have under-lying orientations less supportive of European integration: In a relative sense they tend to be 'fair-weather friends' (see Inglehart, 1967).

We would view the Italian historical experience as parallel to that of Germany in several respects: the older Italian cohorts (like the Germans) were formed in what might be called a period of nascent nationalism after a relatively recent struggle for unification. Basic socialization of the younger cohorts, on the other hand, took place in an atmosphere influenced (as in Germany) by the fact that an aggressively nationalistic regime had been discredited by defeat in the Second World War. The relative magnitude of the Belgian age-group differences presents few problems, but the internal pattern shows certain anomalies: For one, the youngest age-group shows no sign of being more European than the next oldest, if anything, it seems less so. Has the recent renewal of intensity of Belgium's traditional linguistic conflicts tended to shift the focus of political identification toward a narrower, rather than a broader, community? For the time being we will sidestep this question.[19]

Our cross-sectional analysis has possible cross-temporal implications. We interpret the findings as indicating a process of gradual political change: if our hypothesis is correct concerning the relative stability of these attitudes, then as new age cohorts are recruited into the electorate (and eventually into the decision-making elite) one would expect to find increasing support for European integration. This interpretation, however, raises important methodological questions:

1. Are the differences due to life-cycle changes rather than inter-generational change?
2. Are the given age-groups really comparable?
3. Are the differences stable?

We will deal briefly with each of these problems. In regard to the first the cross-national pattern of age-group differences gives us some reassurance that the differences are not simply inherent in the process of aging: they tend to correspond to the historical

19. Similarly, the importance of this internal conflict may have reduced the pressure on the oldest age-group (the presumed 'fair-weather friends' of internationalism) to conform to post-Second World War internationalist norms – which might account for the surprisingly large gap between them and the next younger age-group. Our data, which has just become available, permits certain more detailed analyses which might shed light on this question (as well as the non-response problem); we have not yet undertaken these analyses. Nevertheless, we felt it would be interesting to present at least the broad outlines of the most recent cross-national survey on the subject.

experience of the given nations in a reasonably orderly way.[20] And a recent analysis of American survey data seems to support the hypothesis that such age-cohort differences can persist over long periods of time. In an analysis of twenty national sample surveys, carried out at five-year intervals over the period 1946–66, Cutler examined the deviations among attitudes within both age-cohort and life-stage groups. Analysing the results of polynomial regressions on foreign-policy attitudes of each of the respective groups, Cutler concludes that both the aging process and the generational interpretation explain part of the observed differences in public opinion; the generational cohorts, however, provide a relatively stronger explanation than do life-cycle groups: Foreign policy has relatively higher salience for the younger American cohorts and given cohorts have maintained their relative position over a period of decades (1968).

The question remains: 'Are the age-groups in our European data really comparable?' In theory a representative national sample should contain a number of respondents in their early twenties proportionate to their distribution in the total population and approximately similar to the rest of the sample in social background factors other than age. In fact, this youngest adult group is very often undersampled: it is less likely to be found at home. To cope with this problem we adopted a technique which permits us to examine the problem of intergenerational change in a different fashion. We asked the adults sampled in our 1968 pilot study whether they had any children in certain specified age categories (fifteen–sixteen and nineteen–twenty).[21] In case of affirmative response we recorded names and addresses of those children – who were interviewed the following year in a survey carried out by the European Communities Information Service. In this way we obtained responses to three items concerning European integration from parent–child pairs.[22] While this tech-

20. Nor are youth necessarily more internationalistic: in the mid-1950s the youngest adult cohort gave only moderately favorable responses, at least in France; only in the 1960s – when the post-Second World War cohorts began to reach maturity – did the youngest age-group begin to show the highest level of Europeanness (see Bissery, 1968, pp. 43–5).

21. Cross-sectional analysis of these three national samples also revealed age-group differences in the predicted direction (see Inglehart, 1969).

22. Text of questions:

1. 'If a United States of Europe were being established, would you be for or against having Britain become a part of it?'

2. 'Would you be for or against having the British army become part of one unified European army?'

nique has the disadvantage of being relatively costly in relation to the number of responses obtained, it has certain advantages: The two age-groups being compared are from *precisely* the same households – exerting automatic controls for ethnicity, region, religion and family background. The results of this direct inter-generational comparison are presented in Table 5.

Table 5 **Parent–child comparisons as percentage: 1968–9 surveys**

	Germany		France		United Kingdom	
	Parents	Youth	Parents	Youth	Parents	Youth
'United States of Europe'						
For	71	92	65	83	31	76
Neutral	21	5	26	15	22	10
Against	8	3	9	2	48	15
European army						
For	54	72	47	57	32	47
Neutral	26	16	35	25	18	11
Against	20	11	18	18	50	42
European government						
For	37	50	46	48	21	45
Neutral	31	20	31	17	12	7
Against	31	30	24	35	67	48

Note: Respective numbers of parent–child pairs are: 80, 98, 166.

A rather striking set of intergenerational differences appears: in every case the youth give a higher level of positive response than their parents – sometimes by 30 per centage points or more. Indeed, the differences here are greater than those which would be expected on the basis of a cross-sectional analysis of the adult survey. It is possible that our cross-sectional analysis tends to *under*estimate the degree of intergenerational change. This would be the case if, for example, there were a systematic tendency to undersample a more mobile, and more European oriented, type of youth.

The question of the stability of the age-group differences found in our European data cannot be resolved conclusively: to do so would require a longitudinal study lasting several decades. Never-theless, the presumption that they are indicative of long-term factors gains a certain amount of support from the fact that the

3. 'Do you think that the government of a United States of Europe should have the right to overrule the government of Great Britain on some important matters?'

predicted differences have been found in cross-sectional analyses of a substantial number of national samples carried out over the past several years as well as in the comparison of parent–child pairs just cited.

The interpretation of these findings depends on the extent to which a given item tends to tap short-term reactions (of the type depicted in Figure 1) or basic early instilled orientations (the long-term feedback depicted in Figure 2). Our problem is complicated by the fact that the former pattern is likely to be superimposed on the latter. To the extent that a given item referring to European integration does tap a basic sense of national-supranational identity we would expect overall response levels to that item to change only gradually over time, largely as a result of the recruitment of new cohorts into a given population.

Most of the European-integration items for which we have time-series data seem to conform to this latter criteria reasonably well although support levels *do* fluctuate, apparently in response to important national and international events. The decline in support for a series of European integration items from 1962 to 1963 is an example (Merritt and Puchala, 1968), the key event presumably being the first veto of British admission (see Table 6). But a notable exception exists to this rule of limited fluctuation; it

Table 6 **Mean percentage 'for' four key measures, 1962 and 1963, by country**

	1962	1963	Change
The Netherlands	78·5	73·0	−5·5
West Germany	68·2	61·8	−6·4
Belgium	67·0	60·0	−7·0
Italy	62·0	60·8	−1·2
France	58·8	54·4	−4·4
(United Kingdom)		(56·5)	

Note: These proposals concerned abolition of tariffs, free movement of workers and businesses, a common foreign policy, and use of national taxes to aid poorer countries of Europe.

concerns the attitudes of the British public toward entry into the Common Market. In this case the recent shift is so sudden, and its magnitude so extreme, as to make it dubious that this item taps a basic sense of national identity – one might even ask whether such an orientation exists. We cannot exclude the possibility that it does not.

We can, however, point to similar phenomena in the realm of electoral behavior where sharp swings are known to take place and yet where the bulk of the evidence points to the persistence of a long-term sense of political party identification among significant numbers of people. In the two most recent American presidential elections, for example, there was a shift from the landslide victory of the Democratic Party in 1964 (when it won 61 per cent of the votes cast) to that party's defeat in 1968 (when it polled 42 per cent of the vote). Yet during that period the percentage of those reporting that they considered themselves Democrats, or closer to the Democrats, changed only slightly – indeed, these figures had changed very little since 1952.[23] The changes in vote seem largely due to public shifts on given issues and especially in assessment of the various candidates.

Does a measure of political party identification have any value if it does not necessarily correspond to the way a person votes in a given election? It is widely conceded that it does:

1. Despite a certain amount of slippage it is a good indicator of how an individual will actually vote (much of the shift seems to come from those who have a weak or non-existent sense of partisan identification).

2. The measure is of value in analysing long-term trends.

There is evidence that a sense of political party identification is often instilled in one's family of orientation and tends to persist through adult life (Campbell, 1960; Converse and Dupeux, 1966). We would think that a sense of national identity is likely to be at least equally early instilled and long lasting. Our problem is to find items which effectively tap this underlying orientation. We would expect such items to show

1. Relative stability over time.

2. In the contemporary Western European setting these items would be expected to show relatively great age-group differences, the old being more nationalistic.

Early in this article we hypothesized that short-term attitudinal shifts are relatively likely to be influenced by conscious, rational considerations; the type of feedback shown in Figure 1 is likely to be shaped by an assessment of immediate economic consequences, for example. Long-term feedback (illustrated in Figure 2) is more

23. See marginals from Survey Research Center surveys, 1952–68.

likely to reflect prerational considerations – one's reaction to symbols of national prestige or sovereignty, for example.

At any given time the two types of effects may be superimposed on each other, but it would seem that the British public today reacts to the question of Common Market membership largely in terms of what it will do to the cost of living. In a survey carried out in late 1969, 67 per cent of the British public expressed the fear that if Britain joins the community, prices will go up (by comparison, only 11 per cent gave this response in 1961).[24] Fears of loss of political identity were mentioned by only 10 per cent (about the same level as in 1961) (*Gallup Political Index*, December 1969, no. 116).

We appear to have a problem of measurement: If the item about Common Market entry does not tap one's basic sense of national identity, do any items exist which do? Perhaps the answer is 'yes': In the survey just cited the same British respondents were asked about 'closer political relations with Europe'; 55 per cent said that they would be a 'good thing' (*Gallup*)[25] – a figure close to the long-term level of support for other European integration proposals.

In our more recent survey we find something similar: while the British public opposed entry into the Common Market by a 3:1 margin, the same respondents – despite the possible effect of response set[26] – divide almost evenly on the question about a foreign president of Europe. Could it be that the latter item is a relatively accurate indicator of a long-term sense of national identity? To the extent that the size of age-group differences (shown in Table 4) reflects the persistence of long-term orientations this latter item appears to tap the relevant dimensions more effectively. The age-group difference associated with it is greater than those found with the other items; among the British public it is nearly four times as great as those associated with the item concerning entry into the Common Market (a difference of 34 percentage points as compared with a difference of 9 points). This does not seem to be accidental; the age-group differences produced by this item are consistently the largest among any of the five items within all six national samples. The item itself seems

24. If this is the case, further analysis should show two relatively distinct dimensions appearing in British responses, corresponding to these two sets of orientations.

25. Only 13 per cent said it would be bad.

26. The latter item was asked only a minute or two after the one concerning entry into the Common Market.

to tap something which older cohorts find harder to accept than younger ones. We suggest that, prior to 1967, items concerning British entry into the Common Market did tend to be answered by the British (as they still are by the European community publics) in terms of an underlying nationalism/internationalism. Levels of support for this and other European integration proposals were roughly comparable, and responses to the various items tended to have relatively strong positive correlations. An analysis of data gathered in 1964–5 among youth in France, Germany, the Netherlands and the United Kingdom indicated that for respondents from the three European community countries a relatively well-defined structure of attitudes toward European integration existed. Among the British respondents attitudes favoring European integration were more loosely structured and less distinct from a general internationalism; however, responses to an item concerning British entry into the Common Market was at the heart of this general cluster (Inglehart, 1970b). At that time attitudes toward British entry served as a fairly good predictor of this group's attitudes toward other aspects of European integration.

Since 1967 levels of support for British entry have begun to diverge from the levels of support for other European integration items, and it is possible that the former question now tends to tap a different dimension from the nationalist/internationalist orientation. The shock of a second failure, in late 1967, brought about a profound negative reaction in British public opinion (see Table 7). By December 1967 a strong plurality was already

Table 7 **Trends in British public opinion regarding entry into European community as percentage**

	February 1965	February 1966	February 1967	December 1967	June 1968	November 1969	February 1970
For	59	59	59	38	36	36	19
Don't know/ No answer	22	22	21	12	21	19	18
Against	19	19	20	50	43	45	63

opposed to entry: having twice proposed marriage and twice been refused, they tended to dissociate themselves from Europe, perhaps as a matter of ego defence. This prepared the ground for widespread acceptance of negative economic arguments which became widely disseminated thereafter and gave a reassuring rationale for not wanting to go in: the woman who had jilted you wasn't so lovely after all. Thus, the frame of reference for the EEC-entry item may have shifted after 1967 from a basic nationalism/internationalism to a skeptical assessment of immediate economic effects.[27]

Ironically, then, the British public is now predominantly unfavorable to joining Europe at the very time when entry has at last become possible. And it seems that this public now reacts to entry into the Common Market on the basis of a negative evaluation of its immediate economic consequences; they react relatively favorably to the idea of political integration – which may tap an underlying nationalism/internationalism dimension to a greater degree. Current opposition to Common Market membership, then, may be relatively responsive to short-term factors; it my decline as rapidly as it rose.

Life would be much simpler if a given item always tapped the same underlying orientation. Unfortunately, this may be an unrealistic expectation. There is no guarantee that the question about British entry to the Common Market ever did tap a deeply instilled orientation of the British public. The relatively close correlation found earlier between responses to this item and a variety of Europeanism and internationalism items suggests that up to 1967 perhaps it did; the subsequent instability of response levels, as well as the apparent bifurcation between responses involving economic, as compared with political integration, indicates that after 1967 it did not.

This item, then, may give a poor basis for comparison of the basic nationalism or Europeanism of the British, as compared with the European, publics: the two are probably closer together than it would indicate. Nevertheless, the situation appears very serious from the perspective of European integration. There are indications of convergence toward a European consensus supporting supranational integration among the public of the community. At the same time the British public seems to be moving in the opposite direction. If British entry does not take place in the immediate future (despite public preferences) it may become an increasingly remote possibility at any future time.

27. The economic arguments are less than persuasive: in October 1969, 81 per cent of a sample of ninety-two British financiers and bankers – a group presumably well informed on the probable long-term economic effects – were favorable to British entry (see *Grand Bretagne et Marché commun*, Paris: Agence économique et financière, March 1970).

Conclusions

We have argued that the role of public opinion in regional integration must be examined in the light of three types of conditioning factors: institutional structure, the distribution of skills and the internalization of values among the public. We have discussed some available evidence about how these three factors have influenced the relationship between public opinion and European integration. Recent changes in the French national decision structure seem to have led to a somewhat greater openness to societal preferences ('*ouverture en continuite*', as Pompidou has put it). The increasingly wide distribution of politically relevant skills also appears likely to enhance the role of public opinion in Western Europe. Finally – apart from the possible exception concerning British attitudes toward entering the EEC – there are indications that public attitudes toward European integration tend to reflect long-term orientations. Taken together, these findings suggest that public preferences are likely to constitute an increasingly effective long-term influence on political decision-makers, an influence which (in the community, at least) is basically favorable to supranational integration.

References

ABRAMSON, P., and INGLEHART, R. (1970), 'The development of systematic support in four western democracies', *Comparative Political Studies*, vol. 2, no. 4.

BISSERY, J. (1968), *L'opinion des français sur le Marché Commun et l'unification européenne*, L'Institut français d'opinion publique.

BUTLER, D., and STOKES, D. (1969), *Political Change in Britain: Forces Shaping Electoral Choice*, Macmillan.

CAMPBELL, A. *et al.* (1960), *The American Voter*, Wiley, ch. 7.

CONVERSE, P., and DUPEUX, G. (1966), 'Politicization of the electorate in the US and France', in A. Campbell *et al.*, *Elections and the Political Order*, Wiley.

CUTLER, N. E. (1968), *The Alternative Effects of Generations and Aging upon Political Behaviour*, Oak Ridge National Laboratory.

DEUTSCH, K. W. (1961), 'Social mobilization and political development', *Amer. Polit Sci. Rev.*, vol. 55, no. 2, pp. 497–502.

DEUTSCH, K. W. (1963), *The Nerves of Government*, Free Press.

DEUTSCH, K. W. (1966), *Nationalism and Social Communication*, MIT Press.

DEUTSCH, K. W. (1967a), *Arms Control and the Atlantic Alliance: Europe Faces Coming Policy Decisions*, Wiley.

DEUTSCH, K. W. *et al.* (1967b), *France, Germany and the Western Alliance: A Study of Elite Attitudes on European Integration and World Politics*, Scribner.

EASTON, D. (1967), *A Systems Analysis of Political Life*, Wiley.

GREENSTEIN, F. I. (1967), 'The impact of personality on politics: an attempt to clear away underbrush', *Amer. Polit. Sci. Rev.*, vol. 61, no. 3, pp. 629–41.

INGLEHART, R. (1967), 'An end to European integration?', *Amer. Polit. Sci. Rev.*, vol. 61, no. 1, pp. 91–105.

INGLEHART, R. (1968), 'Trends and non-trends in the Western Alliance: a review', *J. Conflict Resolution*, vol. 12, no. 1, p. 128.

INGLEHART, R. (1969), 'Regional integration, political development and public opinion', Conference on Regional Integration, Madison, Wisconsin.

INGLEHART, R. (1970a), 'Cognitive mobilization and European identity', *Comparative Politics*, vol. 3, no. 1, pp. 47–72.

INGLEHART, R. (1970b), 'The new Europeans: inward or outward looking?' *International Organization*, vol. 24, no. 1, pp. 129–39.

JAHODA, G. (1963), 'The development of children's ideas about country and nationality', *Brit. J. Educ. Psychol.*, vol. 33, nos. 1 and 2, pp. 47–60, 143–53.

LANCELOT, A. (1969), 'Comment ont voté les français le 27 avril et les ler et 15 juin 1969', *Projet*, no. 39, pp. 926–47.

LERNER, D. (1958), *The Passing of Traditional Society: Modernizing the Middle East*, Free Press.

LERNER, D., and GORDEN, M. (1969), *Euratlantica: Changing Perspectives of the European Elites*, MIT Press.

LINDBERG, L., and SCHEINGOLD, S. (1970), *Europe's Would-Be Polity*, Prentice-Hall.

MCCROSKEY, J. (1967–8), 'The significance of the neutral point on semantic differential scales', *Public Opinion Q.*, vol. 31, no. 4, pp. 642–5.

MERELMAN, R. (1966), 'Learning and legitimacy', Amer. Polit. Sci. Rev., vol. 60, no. 3, pp. 548–61.

MERRIT, R. L., and PUCHALA, D. J. (1968), *Western European Perspectives on International Affairs: Public Opinion Studies and Evaluation*, Praeger.

MILLER, W., and STOKES, D. (1966), 'Constituency influences in Congress', in A. Campbell *et al.*, *Elections and the Political Order*, Wiley.

NYE, J. (1970), 'Comparing common markets; a revised neo-functional model', *International Organization*. vol. 24, no. 4, pp. 796–835.

PIAGET, J., and WEIL, A. M. (1951), 'The development in children of the idea of the homeland and relations with other countries', *International Soc. Sci. Bull.*, vol. 3, no. 3, pp. 561–78.

RABIER, J. R. (1966), *L'opinion publique et l'Europe*, Institute of Sociology, Brussels.

RABIER, J. R. (1967), *Deutschland und die Europaischen Gemeinschaft*, Institut für Demoskopie, Allensbach.

ROSENAU, J. N. (1961), *Public Opinion and Foreign Policy: An Operational Formulation*, Random House.

TUCKER, R. C. (1963), *The Soviet Political Mind*, Praeger.

17 Arnold Rose

The Integration of People

A. Rose, 'The integration of people', from R. H. Beck *et al.*,
The Changing Structure of Europe, University of Minnesota Press, 1970,
pp. 192–220.

The movement during the post-Second World War era toward a
more politically integrated Europe has been largely created by
highly placed policy-makers. Some were idealists, who believed
that economic development and political stability could only be
achieved in larger than national units. Others were opportunists,
seeking more power for their relatively important nations or
responding to American pressures to develop greater European
strength. Probably both the idealists and the opportunists were
reacting to the threat of Russian expansionism and sought safety
by joining forces. These and other factors at first worked on a high
level of leadership and made little impact on the broad masses of
the Western European population. The economic benefits of reduced trade barriers and of the lesser efforts at economic collaboration were soon felt by the European 'man in the street', and
he generally came to approve of such international arrangements
as the European Economic Community and the European Free
Trade Association (Rabier, 1965, 1966; Gallup International Poll,
1962, 1966; Reader's Digest Poll, 1963; Annuaire Européen,
1962; International Research Associates, 1966; MIJARC, 1966;
Le Monde, 1967). But in no sense could the development toward
various international organizations in Europe be considered a
mass movement with broad popular support.

Public opinion is developing on various aspects of European
integration as a result of direct experience with them and publicity
concerning them. The average European, as noted, has had direct
experience with the economic aspects of integration agreements
and has come to approve many of them. These economic aspects
of integration involve an increasing transfer of goods and services
across international borders. But the political and sociological
aspects of integration – thus far less developed than the economic
aspects – involve some kind of transferability of people themselves across international borders; indeed, full political and
sociological integration entails one national group's regarding

itself as interchangeable with another national group for such purposes as elections, granting powers over themselves, social participation in friendship, and so on. People need direct, personal contacts with others if they are to accept them as their 'own kind', suitable for living with in a common political and social community. It is not that all such direct contacts lead to acceptance – other conditions must exist for this to happen; but direct contacts are a necessary requirement.

Some of this transfer or interchanging of peoples is now going on in Europe, and experience with it today can provide some clues to the probable reaction its more extensive and expanded forms will evoke tomorrow. The author suggests that the integration of people is just as important for the creation of 'Europe' as the agreements of statesmen, that the agreements of statesmen will be able to go only so far without the further integration of people (although it must also be recognized that certain agreements of statesmen can facilitate the integration of people), and that the achievements to date in the creation of 'Europe' will be reversed and nullified if there should be a large-scale rejection of the integration of people. The agreements among European nations so far have been more or less opportune for all the signatory powers; they have not yet had to face the test of making sacrifices for the benefit of their 'brother' Europeans. Only the integration of a 'European people' will get them over that hump. Without that basic integration, the promising international agreements of today will be as weak in the face of crisis as was the socialist ideology in 1914 in the face of war. All the talk about 'class solidarity across national lines' did nothing to inhibit the First World War, nor did the cross-national cousinly relationships among the aristocratic elite. In the face of challenge, the people of Europe did not think of themselves as the 'people of Europe'; they thought of themselves as Frenchmen, Germans, Britons and so on. Yet history shows that new nations *can* be born: the United States was born (Lipset, 1963) out of these same Britons, Germans, Frenchmen; Germany was born out of Prussians, Bavarians, Hessians, etc.; and Italy was born out of Piedmontese, Tuscans, Calabrians, etc.[1] The question before us is whether Europe, in this sense, is being born today.

1. Some Italians raise the question whether the Italian people have yet, by and large, accepted Italian nationality, or whether provincial and local loyalties are stronger. It is an interesting question, but no attempt will be made to answer it here (see the *Economist*, vol. 222, no. 6447, 18 March 1967, pp. 26–8).

What is meant here by 'the integration of people'? It means their acceptance of each other as members of a common nation, their having a sense of belonging to the same 'community'. It does not mean complete abandonment of self-identification as Greek or Swede or Frenchman, but it does mean a general tendency – for many purposes – to place self-identification as European *above* being Greek or Swedish or French. It does not mean the elimination of the old national cultures and institutions, but it does mean allowing a new cross-national culture and set of institutions to be built parallel to the old. Americans are not less loyal to their family or church or ethnic background for being loyal to the United States, and some are also loyal to their separate states. Germany, France, Belgium, Norway, Spain, and the other nations will have to take on the psychological character of states in the American sense, or of ethnic groups, before there can be an integrated Europe. It is not necessary to go so far as to say that there must be the creation of a 'United States of Europe', a new state, before there can be integration, but there must be a much stronger sense of mutual acceptance and of common Europeanness than Europe has ever had before, and probably some sort of political confederation.

Various other terms have been used which bear a close relationship to 'integration'. Eisenstadt (1954) speaks of the 'absorption' of Jewish immigrants of various national and cultural backgrounds into Israel; Zubrzycki (1966, pp. 165-75) speaks of the 'accommodation' of Polish refugees into Britain after the Second World War; and American sociologists for several generations have spoken of the 'assimilation' of at least the white-skinned immigrants into the United States. This chapter will not get into a discussion of whether the 'melting pot', 'cultural pluralism' or 'conformity to the dominant national culture' is the best relationship for nationality groups occupying the same territory to have toward each other, or even whether migration across national lines should be temporary or permanent. If there is to be an integration of people in Europe, economic factors will largely decide how temporary or how permanent a migration is to be, and sociological and psychological factors operating through individuals and families will decide whether there is to be 'melting pot' or 'cultural pluralism' or adherence to one dominant culture. Policies of government or private organizations can affect the outcome by modifying the influence of economic, sociological, or psychological forces. It is not intended here to suggest either the value premises for giving direction to such policies or the techniques by which one or the other set of goals can most effectively be reached.

Not only have European countries been politically and economically divided, but there are considerable differences of culture and 'national character' among them. The medieval synthesis, provided by the Catholic Church and the Holy Roman Empire in much of Europe, has long since disappeared, and national differences have provided the outstanding facts about Europe during the past several centuries. Along with efforts at political and economic integration after the Second World War, efforts have been started toward social integration – cultural and educational exchanges, international meetings for all sorts of purposes, modification of school curriculums to orient children toward Europe and the world as well as toward their individual nations, the encouragement of tourism, businessmen's collaboration on common enterprises, special efforts to aid in the adjustment and assimilation of cross-national migrants, etc. Some of these were not entirely novel, and had antecedents going well back before the First World War, but the considerable extent to which they were planned and effectuated was a distinctive characteristic of the post-Second World War era. If Europe is to have internal peace, if it is to act even in small ways as a unified whole, it must integrate its culture and people to some extent – at least so it is felt by those who think in terms of 'Europe'. It is the purpose of this chapter to examine the most extensive of these efforts – the encouragement of migration of peoples across national lines – and to test certain hypotheses concerning its success or lack of success. That is, the chapter is limited to a consideration of the contribution which cross-national migration is or is not making to the integration of Europe.

Recent cross-national migration

In the discussion to follow, 'migration' refers to situations in which individuals move across international boundaries and take employment, sometimes permanently but at least for a 'season' (usually nine months). Thus excluded are tourism, study abroad, international meetings, diplomatic missions, daily frontier-crossing for work, and other situations in which there is usually no motive for the person who crosses the border to think of himself as a part of the country to which he travels. Most migrants in the sense used here expect to return to their home countries, but practically all of them also intellectually entertain the possibility that they will remain permanently in the country to which they move.

Cross-national migrations are not new in Europe, although their directions are somewhat so.[2] In the years before the First World War not only was there the tremendous emigration from southern Europe overseas to the Americas, but numerous north Italians moved across the frontier to Switzerland and France; neighboring Spaniards, Belgians and Swiss and more distant Poles also migrated to France; Austrians, Poles,[3] Serbians, Belgians and Dutch went to Germany; Germans, Dutch, Italians and Poles moved to Belgium. The early migration to France and Germany was mainly into agriculture; that to Belgium was mainly into mining. While many of the worker immigrants were seasonal rather than permanent, their numbers were substantial. In 1910 foreigners constituted some 15 per cent of Switzerland's population, only slightly less than the 17 per cent attained in 1964, and in 1907 the proportion of foreign workers in Germany's labor force was higher than that in 1965. The proportion of foreigners in France did not reach a peak until 1931, but then it was significantly higher than today. France was the leading country of immigration during the interwar years of 1919–31, with most of its economic immigrants coming from Poland and Italy, and refugees coming from White Russia and Armenia (in Turkey). With the partial exception of France, Europe in this period was much less permissive about cross-national migration than it had been before the First World War. Part of this was due to poor economic conditions, but part was due to growing nationalism and xenophobia.[4] The post-Second World War years

2. An excellent history of cross-national migrations is contained in Taft and Robbins (1955). For the specific period of the Second World War; see Schechtman (1946). Also see Borrie (1959).

3. Germany allowed Poles to come as seasonal laborers and as miners. Poland, along with Italy, was a leading emigrant country in the pre-Second World War era. Zubrzycki (1966, p. 27) states that there were 1,485,600 'permanent' emigrants between 1919 and 1938, of which 348,200 returned – leaving a permanent net emigration of 1,137,400. Many of these were dependents rather than workers only. The classic study by Thomas and Znaniecki (1919), examines the causes within Poland for the extensive emigration largely in terms of the breakdown of primary group controls.

4. For example, France returned some 117,000 Poles to their home country during the depression years 1931–5; see Zubrzycki (1956, p. 28). During the occupation years 1940–45, the Pétain government deported many foreigners, some of whom were sent to the slave-labor camps of Germany;

saw a resumption of the liberal policy, and there was an increase of immigration – mainly of refugees at first. For France this included a liberalization of the law on naturalization, which caused the number of Frenchmen of foreign birth to rise sharply. By 1962, there were 1,266,680 naturalized persons and 1,815,740 foreigners – respectively 2·72 per cent and 3·9 per cent of the French population (La Documentation Française, 1964).

The first decade after the end of the Second World War saw the relocation of many refugees in Europe (Taft and Robbins, 1955; Vernant, 1953; Murphy *et al.*, 1955; Holborn, 1956; Joint Statistical Project on European Migration, 1958). French, Belgian, Dutch and other Allied nationals who had been forced into the German 'work camps' during the war now returned home, while Germans who lived in Prussia, the Sudetenland, and other eastern territories were now expelled into a narrower Germany. There was little in the way of strictly economic migration within Europe, since most of the Continent was still recovering economically from the war, although economic motives for migration were undoubtedly mixed with political and ideological ones. The chief direction of economic migration, and much of the refugee relocation also, was overseas. During the decade 1945–55, 'The chief countries of emigration have been Germany, Austria, Italy, Greece and the Netherlands; the chief countries of reception, the United States, Australia, Canada, Argentina and Brazil' (Taft and Robbins, 1955).[5] Table 1 shows that Europe was not the major destination of most of the European displaced persons or other migrants in the decade following the Second World War. Some eight million Europeans moved across international lines between 1946 and 1954, but only three of the ten countries leading in their reception were European and these were at or near the bottom of the list. The leading European country of immigration in that period was the United Kingdom, which recovered economically from the war more rapidly at first than the other war-involved nations of Europe.

see Taft and Robbins (1955, p. 188). Probably under the influence of Hitlerism, some xenophobia developed in France during the 1930s and 1940s; see Domenach (1966), and Doublet (1965).

5. For a general discussion of post-Second World War international migration besides Taft and Robbins (1955) see Thomas (1959), Bouscaren (1963) and Thomas (1954).

Table 1 **Leading countries of immigration, 1946 to 1954**

Country	Number of immigrants
United States	1,700,000
Canada	1,100,000
Australia	900,000
Israel	790,000
Argentina	760,000
Venezuela	500,000
United Kingdom	440,000
Brazil	410,000
France	390,000
Belgium	290,000

Source: Borrie (1959, p. 17).

The chief sources of cross-national migration in Europe after 1955 were from within Europe itself, as shown by Table 2. West Germany drew from all labor-exporting countries of southern Europe, with the number from Greece, Spain, Turkey and Yugoslavia growing each year. France, as noted, kept up a stream from Italy, but its immigration from Spain and Portugal[6] became even larger. France also had a major repatriation of its colonials, especially from Algeria, in the years 1962–3 (Rognaut and Schultz, 1964; Toujas-Pineda, 1965). Switzerland kept its primary reliance for immigrant workers on Italy – although now they were from southern rather than northern Italy – but increasing numbers came from Spain. In 1963, Switzerland adopted a policy of forcing its employers to cut down on their number of foreign workers, and in the succeeding years it became an exporter, rather than an importer, of foreign (non-Swiss) labor. Immediately after the Second World War, Sweden was the beneficiary of immigrants – both skilled and unskilled – from the Baltic countries (now absorbed politically into the Soviet Union). Its continuing labor shortage led to an agreement among the Scandinavian nations for free movement of labor, and Sweden came to rely most heavily on Finland for [unskilled labor, although significant numbers of workers came also from Italy, Greece, Yugoslavia and Turkey. The Benelux countries drew on labor

6. 'L'Immigration Portugaise', *Population*, vol. 21, no. 3 May–June 1966, pp. 575–6; 'L'Immigration Portugaise', *Hommes et Migrations*, no. 105, 1966, p. 203.

from all of southern Europe, as well as a small stream from Asia and Africa. The United Kingdom kept its traditional reliance on Ireland for unskilled labor but otherwise obtained very few workers from Europe; the United Kingdom also for a while relied heavily for labor on the colored Commonwealth countries of India, Pakistan, and the West Indies. For over a century after 1841, Ireland's emigration was larger than its natural increase so that the country reduced its total population from 6,529,000 in 1841 to 2,818,300 in 1961; even after 1961 emigration absorbed most of Ireland's natural increase (Jackson, 1967, p. 1). Table 3 highlights emigration and immigration trends in the nations of Europe.

Although the official statistics (including those in Table 3) are inadequate and somewhat inaccurate, they permit us to draw the following conclusions:

1. While before the Second World War, France and Switzerland were the main immigrant countries of Europe, the Federal Republic of Germany had by 1960 surpassed them in the number of immigrants; these countries, then, are the ones to which the largest *number* of migrants go. The United Kingdom had a period of heavy immigration between 1960 and 1962.

2. In terms of *percentages* of foreigners in the active working force, Switzerland (with 32·3 per cent) and Luxembourg (with 21·7 per cent) are by far the highest ranking countries. Intermediate positions are held in Belgium, France, the United Kingdom, West Germany and Sweden – in that order. Western European countries with low percentages of foreigners in their active working force are the Netherlands (with 1·6 per cent), Austria (with 1·2 per cent, mostly seasonal workers), Norway (with 1 per cent) and Denmark (with 0·5 per cent). Among the latter, only the Netherlands since 1960 has been receiving a steady, if small, flow of immigrants, and it will be considered a 'country of immigration' for the purposes of this study, even though a significant small proportion of its own nationals emigrate overseas.

3. Spain has now surpassed Italy as the leading European 'country of emigration' in terms of absolute *numbers*.

4. In terms of *proportions* of their total population emigrating, Ireland, Portugal, Greece and Spain are leading in that order, with Yugoslavia and Turkey coming up. Italy has greatly reduced its net emigration, and Spain has begun a relative decline.

Table 2 Origin of foreign labour force in immigrant countries (in thousands)

Country of emigration	Belgium in 1964	France in 1962	Germany (FR) in 1965	Luxembourg in 1964	Netherlands in 1965	Sweden in 1966	Switzerland in 1965	United Kingdom[a] 1960	United Kingdom[a] 1966
Greece	6·0	4·4	181·7	b	2·2	5·5	7·3	3·4	3·4
Italy	64·9	305·0	335·8	15·0	7·8	5·8	454·7	68·1	24·6
Portugal	0·7	30·1	10·5	0·5	0·9	0·4	b	2·3	3·9
Spain	12·9	312·0	180·6	2·5	16·0	3·2	77·3	17·1	26·6
Turkey	5·3	7·5	121·1	b	5·8	1·3	4·8	0·8	1·3
Yugoslavia	1·2	10·1	64·1	b	1·1	11·9	5·3	8·9	1·4
EEC countries (except Italy)	45·2	68·4	116·9	13·5	29·0	18·7[c]	150·3[d]	e	e
Special countries	25·0[f]	219·3[g]	59·6[h]		5·2[i]	105·6[j]	39·8[b]	k	k
Stateless or uncertain	1·2	10·9	12·4	1·0	2·9	5·4[l]	12·3[m]	4·4	b
Other European countries	5·4	117·6	34·0	0·5	4·4	17·0	58·4	239·5	57·4
Non-European countries (except special countries)	5·3	73·4	47·8	0·5	4·4	0·5	b	66·6	45·9
Total[n]	172·9	1,065·2	1,164·4	33·5	79·6	175·4	810·2	405·9	164·5

Source: For Belgium and France, estimated by OECD from census figures. For Germany and the Netherlands, semiannual tally of work permits. For Luxembourg, estimated on the basis of work permits issued and placements registered, but does not include frontier or detached workers. For Sweden, aliens registered as being gainfully employed. For Switzerland and the United Kingdom, census figures; for Switzerland figures do not include workers not under federal control. Since a variety of definitions, categories, and dates are used in calculating the labor force in various countries, the figures in the table are not strictly comparable.

[a] Figures reported are only for those registered with the police; since 1961 aliens have not been required to register after four years' residence in the United Kingdom. For this reason, the figures as of 31 December 1960, are also offered.

[b] Very small number; included in appropriate other category.

[c] Germans and Dutch only.

[d] Germans and French only.

[e] Included in other European countries; 1960 figures include Polish and Hungarian refugees.

[f] Mostly from Belgium's former colonies.

[g] Estimate of 200,000 Algerians and 19,300 Moroccans.

[h] From Austria.

[i] Mostly from the Netherlands' former colonies.

[j] Including 72,811 Finns, 19,379 Danes, 13,377 Norwegians.

[k] Estimate of 500,000–600,000 immigrants from other parts of the Commonwealth plus 350,000 from the Irish Free State in 1963, but these are considered citizens, not foreigners, and so are not included in the figures.

[l] Including 1937 Balts and 3466 Hungarians.　　　[m] Hungarians only.

[n] Because of rounding, columns do not add precisely to totals.

Table 3 Trends of immigration (+) and emigration (−) in European countries, 1950 to 1965
(net migration in thousands, with statistical adjustments)

Country	Annual average 1950–54	1955–9	1960	1961	1962	1963	1964	1965
Countries of immigration								
Belgium	+3·2	+10·6	+7·0	−1·0ᵃ	+19·0	+34·0	+49·0	+31·0
France	+27·8	+156·0	+140·0	+180·0	+860·0	+250·0	+195·0	+141·0
Germany (F.R.)	+221·4	+297·2	+336·0	+419·0	+283·0	+224·0	+302·0	+344·0
Luxembourg	+0·9	+0·6	+0·6	+2·4	+2·8	+1·6	+3·1	+3·0
Netherlands	−20·6	−3·2	−13·0	+6·0	+17·0	−8·0	+14·0	+19·0
Sweden	+9·2	+9·8	+11·0	+14·0	+11·0	+12·0	+23·0	+33·0
Switzerland	+22·8	+32·0	+76·0	+101·0	+88·0	+57·0	+48·0	−1·0
United Kingdomᵇ	−33·6	−3·2	+39·0	+198·0	+97·0	+43·0	+7·0	+10·0
Countries of emigration								
Greece	−13·8	−25·0	−26·0	−19·0	−49·0	−56·0	−44·0	−43·0
Ireland	−34·8	−44·4	−41·0	−30·0	−16·0	−17·0	−24·0	−24·0
Italy	−100·8	−127·4	−192·0	−177·0	−137·0	−56·0	−81·0	−85·0
Portugal	−64·2	−68·0	−68·0	−32·0	−55·0	−47·0	−55·0	−53·0
Spain	−51·8	−104·0	−138·0	−133·0	−119·0	−126·0	−158·0	−135·0
Turkeyᶜ				−1·5	−11·2	−30·3	−66·2	−52·1
Yugoslavia					−34·0	−34·0	−56·0	−80·0

Source: For all countries except Turkey and Yugoslavia, 1950–59 figures from I.L.O Automation Programme, *International Differences Affecting Labour Mobility* (Geneva: I.L.O., 1965), pp. 12–14, and from O.E.C.D, *Manpower Statistics 1950–62* (Paris, 1963); 1960–64 figures from O.E.C.D, *Manpower Statistics 1954–1964* (Paris, 1965), corrected by unpublished O.E.C.D statistics; 1965 figures from unpublished O.E.C.D statistics. For Turkey, Turkish Employment Service. For Yugoslavia, 1965 figure from *Migration Today*, no. 5 (December 1965), p. 62; earlier figures from *Ekonomska Politika*, 15 October 1966, p. 1320.

[a] Not including correction from census.

[b] Figures for the United Kingdom do not include migrants from Ireland and, before 1962, do not include migrants from Commonwealth countries. Thus the data indicate a net emigration for Britain during the 1950s when in fact it was experiencing very heavy immigration from India, Pakistan and the West Indies.

[c] Net immigration figures for Turkey are not available; reported here are the 161,300 persons aided by the Turkish Employment Service from 1961 through 1965. However, few Turkish emigrants had returned permanently by 1965, and for these five years only some 20,000 Turks emigrated without using the facilities of the Turkish Employment Service. Hence, the Turkish figures are roughly comparable to the O.E.C.D figures given for the other countries.

The study of adjustment to migration

There has been a vast amount of literature, published and unpublished, on the subject of adjustment to cross-national migration, and a significant amount of this has been summarized in a separate volume by the author of this chapter (Rose, 1969).[7] That volume's original contribution to the study of cross-national migration rests on the use of a combination of approaches, not all of which have been utilized together even in the many superb monographic studies previously published.

1. This study is comprehensive and systematic, although it does not go into depth on all the many facets of the complicated problem.

2. This study is comparative, not for the purpose of making invidious distinctions among nations, but because comparison is the only satisfactory technique for making data on cross-national relations meaningful and measurable. It has not been possible to get every item of relevant information for every country studied, so there are a significant number of gaps, but nearly every fact is presented in a comparative context.

3. This study is couched in a framework of theory; that is, it is not purely descriptive, although description takes up the majority of its pages.

4. This study uses a great variety of data, including published and unpublished statistics, public opinion polls, direct and indirect case observations, historical and contemporary description from library materials, legal documents, interviews with specialists, and even some documents produced by the migrants themselves.

The economic factors of differential wages and differential opportunities for job mobility, twelve policies or programs which countries of immigration have adopted or practised toward the migrants, public opinion toward immigration and immigrants, and six other non-policy factors facilitating the integration of foreign workers – all have been described and measured in the author's full-length work, in so far as data are available for measuring them, for each of the eight countries of immigration. Similarly, eight conditions prevailing in each of the seven European countries of emigration that facilitate or retard the adjustment to migration are described and measured there. And finally,

7. The material in the balance of this chapter is adapted from this volume.

five indexes of acceptance and adjustment are presented to give some idea of what is happening to the migrants themselves. Perhaps needless to say, systematic data on these subjects are incomplete and not always comparable among countries, but the author sought to make the best use of what was available to him.

In this chapter an attempt is made to give the high points of the longer analysis.

International agreements for the benefit of cross-national migrants

Several deliberate institutional arrangements, agreed to by various combinations of nations, to protect and otherwise benefit cross-national migrants will be the subject of this section. While not nearly as far-reaching in their implications as the NATO agreement on defence or the EEC agreement on trade, they are on the same order, relating to the institutional integration of Europe rather than to the integration of people which forms the central interest of this chapter. For lack of space, only the main facts will be presented here.

Two groups of nations, by multilateral treaties, have established completely free internal labor mobility, with no more required of the migrant than an identity card issued by his country of citizenship. These are the four Scandinavian countries plus Finland (in an agreement signed in 1954, called the Nordic Labor Zone Agreement, later called the Scandinavian Common Market for Labor) and the three Benelux countries (in an agreement signed in 1956). The United Kingdom once had a similar arrangement with Commonwealth nations throughout the world, but its unilateral statute of 1962 restricting immigration from all but a few remaining colonies ended that. However, the statute seems to be applied systematically only to the colored nations; migrants from the Irish Republic (and presumably from Australia, Canada and New Zealand if they had ever wished to migrate) continue to enter freely into the United Kingdom, despite the law. In 1965, this law was strengthened so that now only a few hundred per year from the Commonwealth colored nations can migrate to the United Kingdom for work and permanent residence.

The EEC has had a three-stage plan for free labor mobility. Articles 48 and 49 of the 1957 Treaty of Rome specified that full freedom of labor mobility was to be achieved by the end of 1969.[8] The treaty looked forward to 'the abolition of any discrimination

8. The treaty provisions and subsequent adaptations are summarized in Weil (1965, pp. 259–65).

based on nationality between workers of the member states as regards employment, remuneration, and other working conditions', and stated that the individual rights which it includes shall be subject to limitations only where justified by reasons of public order, public safety and public health. The first stage was inaugurated by EEC Council regulation 15 issued 16 August 1961, which included five main provisions: labor permits are to be given automatically to member-state nationals in the case of occupations in which there is a labor shortage; the domestic labor administration can restrict job opportunities to its own nationals for only three weeks, after which it must make the openings available to other member-state nationals regardless of pre-existing restrictive members or quotas; foreign workers for whom an employer has called by name will in certain cases be granted a permit without reference to the domestic labor market; member-state nationals are to be given preference in filling jobs over other foreign workers; member-state nationals are granted the right to renew their labor permits for the same occupation after one year of regular employment, for any other occupation for which they are qualified after three years, and for any kind of paid work after four years of regular employment.

The second stage, inaugurated by regulation 38 issued 25 March 1964, restricted the priorities accorded to the domestic labor market to certain labor-surplus occupations and regions only, extended the rights and privileges of member state migrant workers, gave them the right to vote in factory elections after three years of employment by the same firm, gave them the right to bring in dependent forebears and descendants – in addition to spouse and children under age – if the worker could offer them satisfactory accommodation, and facilitated clearing offers of and applications for employment within the community. There remained a 'safeguard clause' which enabled member states to reintroduce priority for national workers in certain occupations and areas where there is local unemployment. By November 1966, all the member states had renounced this opportunity except France (EEC press release no. 2549, 8 November 1966, p. 6).

The third stage, scheduled for inauguration in 1968, is to be devoted to the abolition of the last obstacles standing in the way of free movement, so that workers of all member states will be assured of access to paid employment in each member state on the terms that apply to nationals of that state. They will have equal right of worker representation in the firm's organizations, will be able to bring in their families without proving that they have adequate housing, will be granted equal tax arrangements and social benefits. However, if unemployment occurs, member states are to discourage migration. On 7 April 1967, the EEC Commission proposed the institution of a community-wide identity card for all workers to replace the existing work permits given to foreign workers. This card – if adopted by the member states represented in the EEC Council – would eliminate all documentary distinctions among workers, nationals or foreign, if they are citizens of any of the Six (*Le Monde*, 8 April 1967; EEC press release, 13 April 1967). Italians have been the main workers affected by all these provisions because, among the Six, they have been the most frequent migrants and because they are least likely – due to the geographic position of Italy – to be frontier workers with privileges obtained through earlier bi-national agreements. In the first six years, 1961 through 1966, during which EEC regulations on freedom of movement within the Six were operative, an average of 270,600 first work permits a year were issued to workers of the member states moving from one community country to another (EEC press release, 13 April 1967). Of these, 80 per cent were Italians. If the community-wide identity card should be adopted, all nationals of the Six would be benefited, and a portion of Europe would move a significant distance toward international integration.

The Organization for Economic Cooperation and Development – when it was still the Organization for European Economic Cooperation – on 30 October 1955, and 20 December 1955, made recommendations to its member states (twenty-one in number after 1960) to liberalize the international movement of workers. The OECD does not have the power to require the adoption of its recommendations, and its member states have adopted the recommendations only in part and gradually over a period of years. The OECD Council does, however, have the instrumentality of an annual report prepared by its staff to note the progress of each member state in accord with its recommendations, which are from time to time expanded on authorization of its Manpower Liberalization Group. The most important recommendation of the OECD, which is adhered to by most European countries, is that work permits must be issued as soon as it is established that no suitable workers are available on the home market, and that this determination should take place within a month. The OECD also has a labor exchange information system through which each country provides to all other member countries information about its labor market and working conditions, and this information can then be made available to workers.

The OECD recommendations have perhaps been useful in indicating possibilities to member states, but they are too general to cover all the special circumstances involved in the migration from one specific country to another. For that reason, various pairs of immigrant and emigrant countries among the OECD member states have agreed to bilateral treaties. Each of these treaties has somewhat different stipulations but touches on the same general points as all the others. They all provide a mechanism for getting migrants directly into a job in the country of immigration, for wages equal to those of national workers, for some vocational and language training, for transfer of earnings back to the home country, and for specification of the migrant's rights (e.g. to change jobs, to gain social security benefits, to get vacations).

National statutes restricting freedom of cross-national migration will not be dealt with here. Suffice it to say that Switzerland and the United Kingdom among the countries of immigration and Portugal and Spain among the countries of emigration had, in 1967, especially strong restrictions. Nor will the complex social security legislation governing foreign nationals be considered in this chapter.

The agreements among the Scandinavian countries and among the Benelux countries providing for the free flow of workers within these regions gave the workers from the other signatory countries all the rights and privileges of an economic and social nature which nationals of the countries of immigration have. These immigrants might just as well be in their native countries as far as their economic and social rights are concerned, except of course they do not have the right to vote in political elections (they can vote in firm or union elections) or hold political office. Language similarities often prevailing within each regional group make meaningful the provision for 'equal access' to work information and training offered in the language of the immigrant country – which is seldom true for foreigners from outside the region who have different native languages.

The Common Market is working in the same direction as the regional pacts, and in these matters of social policy the Common Market has made consistent progress. This is because the Treaty of Rome gave a number of specific authorizations to the EEC

Commission, and probably because the treaty requirements fit into trends within the nations making up the Common Market. Even during the years 1963–6, when it looked as if political and economic developments in the Common Market might be checked or reversed and when occasionally there was some pessimism about the future of the Common Market, steady progress was being made in extending and equalizing the social policies of the member states in regard to workers from other member states. Of course, it should be recalled that there was only one major country of emigration – Italy – in the Common Market, and Italy's rate of emigration was declining. Other cross-national migrants within the Six were largely frontier or seasonal workers who created few difficulties for the countries to which they migrated. Still, the application of the social security programs of member states for the benefit of workers from other member states covered about two million people and involved expenditures of about $80 million in 1964 (Sandri, 1966, p. 3). By July 1966, the EEC Commission had sent two recommendations to member states: one on social services for community nationals working in another community country and the other on housing for these workers and their families (although there is little evidence that the member states have acted on these recommendations). By the end of December 1965, the European Social Fund – set up by the Treaty of Rome, and one of the few examples of independent administrative activities of the EEC on a supranational basis – had allocated $31·7 million for the retraining and resettlement of 454,000 workers (275,000 of whom were Italians) (Sandri, 1966, p. 4).[9] Plans are being formulated by the Commission for more independent and developmental use of the Social Fund, for a European-wide industrial health and safety system (including protection of young people and working

9. However, Sandri, a vice-president of the EEC Commission, states that the Social Fund has not had the impact expected and also has run into political opposition from the Council because of its supranational character. Vocational training is handled on a national basis, with the Social Fund paying 50 per cent of the cost retroactively (the remaining 50 per cent is often divided according to an agreement between the country of emigration and the country of immigration). The Social Fund may also be used to pay for resettlement of workers whose firms have been adversely affected by modification of trade barriers and other development programs within the EEC. Most resettlement is within the country affected, not cross-national, and the country requesting Social Fund allocations for resettlement must pay half of the costs.

women), and for harmonization of certain social security provisions but no action has yet been taken on these.

The EEC has made considerable progress in encouraging the improvement of working and living conditions, usually where the Treaty of Rome specified that certain things were to happen. The treaty set the end of 1964 as the date at which there should be equal pay for men and women, although some loopholes remain; the aforementioned steps toward free movement of workers and the training of workers have taken place; social security for migrant workers has been established under existing national laws. The EEC Commission lacks both legal powers and funds to go much further, however, and future developments will depend on authorization and funds that may be granted by member states acting through the Council (Sandri, 1966, p. 7). Thus far, the member states have agreed to almost nothing beyond what was specified in the Treaty of Rome, even in regard to such matters as standardizing statistics collection and terminology. In sum, considerable progress in the social field – particularly in matters affecting migrating workers – has been achieved, mainly because of far-reaching commitments of the member states when they signed the Treaty of Rome, but this progress cannot be continued beyond 1969 unless the member states make further commitments. The major exception may be the Social Fund, since there is some flexibility in its use and it can set rules for granting aid, if one or more of the member states do not actively oppose extended uses for it. The exchanges of information, through conferences and Commission studies, are also likely to have a continuing influence on member states, even though no powers are inherent in them.[10] The best example of achievement through exchange of

10. Exchanges of information have also been sponsored by ILO, through several conventions and resolutions, and by UNESCO, through its conference at Havana in 1956 (reported in Borrie, 1954). The Office of Social Affairs of the European Office of the United Nations, in cooperation with Swiss authorities, convened an expert group at Mont-Pélerin in Switzerland in 1962 and a more extensive seminar at Madrid in 1964. The OECD held international conferences at Gröningen in 1960 (see Krier, 1961); at Paris in 1961 (see Barbichon, 1962); at Wiesbaden in 1963 (see *Adaptation of Rural and Foreign Workers to Industry, Final Report, International Joint Seminar, Wiesbaden, 10–13 December 1963*, OECD, 1965); and at Athens in 1966 (see *Emigrant Workers Returning to Their Home Countries, Final Report, International Management Seminar, Athens, 18–21 October 1966*, OECD, 1966). The studies, conversations, reports, and periodicals of the International Catholic Migration Commission (see its periodical *Migration News*, and its Migration Informative Series no. 4, *Catholic Migration Activities*),

information has been some movement toward an alignment of national social security programs. Some alignment may also have come about as a result of the opening up of the economies of the Six to each other – a kind of 'rub off' effect. It is hard to know whether the trend toward equalization of wages, hours of work, paid holidays, and other conditions of work actually has been influenced by a Common Market program (other than those developments which benefit the economies generally); equalization here might simply be due to the overcoming of economic backwardness in the relatively backward countries of the EEC.

There are many matters on which coordination among the Six in regard to migrant labor could yet take place, although to accomplish some of these would require more political authority than now exists in the community.[11] There is almost no co-ordination among the Six of manpower recruiting policies in non-EEC countries, and each country of immigration is in competition with every other one. Vocational guidance and training to meet the special needs of migrants is yet in its infancy except for notable spot achievements by the Germans and a retraining program in Italy under the European Social Fund. Since 1963, migrants from one EEC country to another can use the educational facilities of the country of immigration on the same terms as its own nationals. Reduction of differentials in social security, social assistance, and other welfare programs has a way to go. There is scope for much more imagination in the use of the Social Fund. Whether these things will or will not develop depends on the general political direction of the EEC, a matter which is considered elsewhere in this book.

The European Coal and Steel Community also created a Social Fund when it was established by the same six nations in 1952.[12] Its objective was to provide aids for workers whose employment

the World Council of Churches (see its periodical *Migration Today*), and the Intergovernmental Committee for European Migration (see its periodical *International Migration*, and Ladame, 1958) have also had a considerable intellectual impact on those private persons and public authorities who provide various services to migrant workers. For information about these organizations, also see OECD Division of Social Affairs, 'Etude de Politiques et Mésures d'Ordre Pratique: Organisations Internationales', MS/S/2657/13 (Paris, 23 October 1964).

11. The point of view of this paragraph has also been guided by Sandri (1966, p. 10).

12. Information for this paragraph is taken from Schnitzer (1966, pp. 70–73). Also see *Social Policy in the ECSC, Community Topics* no. 20, European Community Information Service, 1966.

was reduced or suspended as a result of the elimination of all barriers to the free flow of trade in coal or steel. Specifically, it offered assistance for occupational retraining, allowances for re-settlement in the same country or any of the five other countries, and compensatory payments for workers whose employment was temporarily or wholly terminated as a result of closure or conversion of their enterprise to other production. Over 10 per cent of the coal mines received some form of assistance from the inauguration of the program in 1954 up through 1964. But few used the aid for financing relocation – partly because the coal miners were reluctant to leave their home region and partly because the economic boom in their home countries allowed them to find other employment nearby. Two thirds of the miners benefited were in West Germany (the nation with the most rapid economic expansion during 1954–64) and only 3·5 per cent were in Italy (the only nation of emigration among the Six). The reason for this, of course, is that Germany has many more mines than Italy, but the differential benefit to these two countries shows that not all the Social Fund activities are equalizing.

The extensive cross-national migration of labor in post-Second World War Europe necessitated international agreements regarding social security.[13] A convention held among the Scandinavian countries in 1955 resulted in a unified program. One of the first actions of the Common Market – taken in 1958 and put into force from 1 January 1959 – was to coordinate national systems among the Six, replacing the eighty bilateral agreements (and several multilateral agreements) they had worked out between 1946 and 1958. Beginning in 1965, the Council of Europe, with the help of the International Labour Organization and the EEC, began to work on a European Social Security Convention, but by 1967 it was far from adoption.

The EEC agreement was based on three principles:

1. Equality of entitlement to social security – including family allowances, health care, old-age and unemployment benefits, and compensation in case of employment injury or occupational disease – for all nationals of the Six under the laws prevailing in the country of residence, except that family members domiciled in countries other than that of the insured worker receive medical and family allowance benefits at the level prevailing in their country of domicile (usually their country of birth).

13. This paragraph is based on Ribas (1965, pp. 10–13).

2. Aggregation of periods of insurance and employment in more than one country, both for entitlement to benefit and for calculation of its amount.

3. Payment of most benefits in any community country.

The third principle – which went beyond most of the earlier binational agreements – was a step toward the 'harmonization' of social security systems among the Six, toward which the EEC has made some other advances. The implementation of the detailed regulations based on these principles presents many problems of interpretation, and a committee – composed of the directors of the six social security bodies with representatives of the EEC and the ECSC – meets monthly to settle these questions. Sometimes the committee calls in representatives of workers', employers' and farmers' organizations. Special regulations for seasonal workers and frontier commuters were adopted in 1963, and came into force on 1 February 1964. Special regulations are also being developed for seamen and for self-employed persons. The second major interest of the EEC in social security – that of 'harmonization' or 'leveling upwards' the diverse systems among the Six – generated an enormous amount of study, discussion, and differences of opinion, but by July 1963, an agreement was reached on general guidelines and a short-term program which goes only part way toward harmonization. The latter, in revised form, is now being implemented, but full harmonization had not been achieved by 1967.

There is another multilateral agreement – that of the Council of Europe – which supports free movement of workers, subject only to restrictions based on cogent economic and social reasons, and the right of migrant workers to protection and assistance for themselves and their families in the territory of any other contracting nation. This agreement, called the European Social Charter, includes these two points that affect migrants in a much larger framework of the rights of citizens to get various social benefits from their states without discrimination on grounds of color, race, sex, religion, political opinion, national extraction or social origin. Most European countries signed the charter after it was drawn up in 1961, but it did not come into force until 26 February 1965, when the required five nations had ratified it. By 1 January 1966, it was ratified – and therefore presumably in operation – in the United Kingdom, Norway, Sweden, Ireland, Germany (FR) and Denmark. These countries 'have undertaken to accept a number of broad aims of social policy, to observe a large proportion of the detailed provisions of the charter and to notify [*sic*] those they cannot immediately undertake to implement' (British Information Services, 1966, p. 11). The difficulty with the Social Charter is that it leaves a number of loopholes and is not detailed: it is almost an expression of high ideals rather than a concrete agreement. However, it is an important step in that it indicates that the three major countries of immigration which are ratifying powers – the United Kingdom, Sweden and Germany – have the intention of granting to all foreign workers the same kind of rights and privileges which the EEC nations grant to each other's nationals.

Another significant development of the same type – worked out jointly by the Council of Europe and the ILO – is the European Social Security Code, which was opened for signature on 16 April 1965. It sets out a series of standards (higher than those in the 1949 ILO convention) which member countries should apply to their national health schemes and social security provisions. It also provides for equal treatment of migrants and nationals.

The ILO has a convention ratified by France, West Germany, Italy, the Netherlands and Norway as of 1 June 1964, recommending that signatory states facilitate the departure, journey, and reception of migrant workers by providing information, accommodation, food and clothing on arrival, vocational training and other access to schools, recreation and welfare facilities, equal employment conditions (Erixon, 1965, pp. 18–19). This recommendation is also unenforceable, but it indicates the intention of the ratifying immigrant countries of France, Germany and the Netherlands to do what they can to aid immigrant workers. Northern Italy is in the process of becoming an immigrant territory – especially for Greek and Spanish workers – so Italy's signature to the ILO convention is also important.

Conclusions about the acceptance of cross-national migrants

During the period from 1955 through 1966, at least eight million Europeans voluntarily left their homes to take up residence and work in some other country of Europe, most of these migrating from some southern country to some northern or central country. A couple of million among these have returned to their homelands, and another significant minority (perhaps a million) have become citizens of the country to which they had migrated (nearly all naturalizations of those migrating after 1955 have been in France, the United Kingdom, Sweden and the Netherlands); at the end of the period there remained at least five million Europeans living and working as foreigners in European countries, plus their dependents. The economic recession in the winter and spring of 1966–7 sharply reduced the rate of migration, which might be presumed to have an upswing with the end of the recession. But for reasons too complex to consider here, the rate of migration will never return to what it was in the early 1960s. Some 4 per cent of the people of Europe outside the Soviet bloc had voluntarily changed countries, and both economic and social-psychological factors were operating to reduce the rate of migration.

This movement has profound implications aside from the economic ones which largely stimulated it. (Since the economic impacts of the migration are not central to the problem here, they will not be considered further in this chapter.[14]) To mention some minor effects first, it should be noted that those who had special dissatisfactions in their native countries used migration to avoid these dissatisfactions, and presumably successfully so in the majority of instances. Among the dissatisfactions thus eliminated have been political repression, uncongenial dominant ideologies, obnoxious marital ties where divorce was legally impossible, repressive social customs (such as those restricting the freedom of women). The more libertarian and democratic countries of northern and central Europe provided sanctuaries from such kinds of political and sociological restrictions at the same time that they posed new social–psychological problems for the migrants.

The whole category of problems of adjustment to migration is the second set of effects that should be pointed out. The disruption of traditional patterns of behavior and accommodation to new ones – symbolized in such sociological concepts as culture shock, cultural conflict and alienation – was probably experienced in one form or another by each of the migrants. Some of this was painful and damaging, especially to the tiny minority who manifested psychiatric symptoms, but in many cases it was just as constructive (in providing release from social constraints) as it was destructive. All change – including tourism – is disruptive; the question is what are the long-run and countervailing conse-

14. See Rose (1969), for a discussion of the important economic impacts of the migration.

quences of the disruption. Considering that most of the migrants were moving from a rural to an urban culture at the same time as they were crossing national (and cultural) lines, the disruption was considerable. But probably in only a small minority of cases did the long-run negative effects outweigh the long-run positive effects.

Table 4 summarizes the large amount of information gathered on the policies, programs and practices of countries of immigration toward immigrants as indexes of 'acceptance' and of facilitation of adjustment. Not included in the table is the very important policy toward admission of foreign workers, since this is a function of the economic needs of a country, of the proportion of foreign workers already present, and of the concern for 'balance' of religious categories, linguistic groups, political parties, etc., rather than an index of 'acceptance' and facilitation of adjustment of immigrants already admitted. (The only way it could be justified as the latter is in a psychological sense: If a country is open to further immigration, it probably gives the present immigrants a feeling that they are wanted.) Here it will suffice to indicate that France seems to be the country of immigration most open to new immigration, while Switzerland and the Netherlands are the countries most closed to further immigration. The table does, however, provide ratings on the policy toward admission of the foreign worker's wife and children, since this is clearly an index of 'acceptance' and of facilitation of the adjustment of immigrant workers.

Twelve policies are evaluated for each country in terms of a three-point scale. For seven of the policies – openness to immigration of foreign workers' families, avoidance of segregation, social security provisions, language training, special educational programs for immigrant wives and children, availability of housing for families, and openness to naturalization – there seemed to be enough information available about different policies and enough differences to use all three points in differentiating countries. For the other five policies – vocational training, orientation to work, orientation to country, availability of housing for single workers, free-time programs – there seemed to be smaller differences between countries or merely enough information available about different policies to justify using only two of the three possible points. In the table, number 1 is used to characterize a relatively favorable policy toward immigrants, number 3 to characterize a relatively unfavorable policy toward

Table 4 Policies of countries of immigration favorable or unfavorable to immigrants[a]

Policy	Belgium	France	Germany (F.R.)	Luxembourg	Netherlands	Sweden	Switzerland	United Kingdom
Vocational training programs	2	1	1	2	2	1	2	2
Language training programs for adults	1	1	1	1	1	1	1	1
Orientation to work	3	2	3	3	3	2	3	2
Orientation to country	2	1	1	2	2	1	2	1
Social assistance programs	2	1	1	2	2	1	3	2
Educational programs for immigrant wives and children	2	1	2	2	3	2	3	1
Housing for single workers	2	1	1	1	2	2	2	2
Housing for families	1	2	2	1	2	2	3	2
Free-time programs	1	1	1	2	2	1	2	2
Openness to immigration of workers' families	1	1	2	1	3	1	3	1
Discouragement of segregation of immigrants	1	2	3	3	2	2	2	1
Openness to naturalization	2	1	1	1	1	1	3	1
Total	20	15	19	21	25	17	29	18

[a] The number 1 is used to characterize the most favorable policies toward immigrants, 3 the least favorable.

immigrants. Thus, the lower the total score, the more favorable is the country's policy toward immigrants.

The weaknesses in such a table are obvious:

1. The policies chosen and the number of points used in evaluating each policy are arbitrary, although arguments could be made in their support.

2. For many of the policies there was not sufficient information, and in all cases published and unpublished reports and arbitrarily chosen informants had to be relied on rather than direct observation and measurement. As mentioned, where information was sparse, only two points were used, rather than three, to differentiate countries.

3. The judgements are inevitably partly subjective, possibly even biased, although they do not conform to what the author anticipated when he began the study. The judgement of the degree of segregation encouraged by the country's policies is especially subjective. Because of these weaknesses the table is offered only tentatively, and it should be considered open to criticism and revision.

The advantages of having such a table are that

1. It permits a summary view of the many pages of description of policies that have been included in the author's full-length monograph cited earlier.

2. It permits a correlation – made elsewhere in this report – of policy with certain indexes of adjustment or integration of immigrants.

Of course, the table also permits an invidious distinction to be made between countries. If the ratings are incorrect, an unfair slur has been cast on certain countries; if they are correct, an evaluation is being made of what is going on in Europe today. Many of those who have written reports on which the author has partly relied as source material are officials of international agencies and their position prevents them from making any invidious distinctions publicly. This limitation should not apply to an independent scholar. The evaluation, crude as it is, may be said to indicate the importance which the receiving country puts on facilitating adjustment of foreigners.

There were many more indexes of acceptance and adjustment that the author hoped to obtain when he began his study, such as the proportion speaking the language of the country of immigration, the proportion joining unions or other occupational associations, the proportion with close friends among nationals; but the data were not available. The relatively few indexes of dependent variables on which data were obtained are summarized in Table 5. Again, the low scores in the table indicate the greatest degree of acceptance and adjustment. While the data are not so adequate, nor the method so precise, as to permit incontrovertible conclusions, these are the findings: Sweden, the Netherlands and the United Kingdom have the most adjusted immigrants; Switzerland has the least adjusted while those in Germany and Luxembourg are only a little better adjusted; immigrants in France and Belgium are in the middle ranges of adjustment.

Some of the specific findings of this study are here tentatively presented in summary form.[15]

1. Economic factors are the main ones in motivating individual workers to migrate, but policy factors seem to be most important in facilitating or retarding their acceptance in the country of immigration and their adjustment to that country. (This does *not* refer to policies excluding immigrants or reducing their number after they are in the country. It refers only to policies and practices toward foreigners already permitted to work in the country.)

2. There are gaps in each immigrant country's organized activities to aid in the acceptance and adjustment of its immigrants. A country may have an excellent program in several respects, but have little activity in other respects.

3. Nevertheless, it is possible to discern different central tendencies among countries in the intensiveness and extensiveness of their programs. France and Sweden lead in the variety and completeness of their organized efforts. At the other end, Switzerland does the least.

4. The multilateral international agreements – especially those of the EEC, the Council of Europe, the ILO and the Scandinavian Common Market for Labor – have done a great deal to upgrade the programs and activities of their ratifying countries. While the benefits are specifically for the nationals of the member states, they tend to 'spill over' and be applied to other migrants.

5. Italy and Spain are the only emigrant countries to have significant programs to aid in the adjustment of their nationals

15. Further discussion and supporting data are found in Rose (1969).

Table 5 Indexes of acceptance and adjustment in countries of immigration[a]

Index	Belgium	France	Germany (F.R.)	Luxembourg	Netherlands	Sweden	Switzerland	United Kingdom
Turnover of immigrants	1	1	1	1	1	1	3	2
Percentage of cross-national marriages	1	2	2	2	1	1	2	
Ratio of naturalized foreigners to foreign labor force	3	2	3	2	1	1	3	2
Crime rate	3	2	2	2	1	1	1	1
Lag between repatriation peak and migration peak	1	2	3	3	3	—	3	1
Total	9	9	11	11	7	5-7	12	7-9

[a] Number 1 indicates the greatest degree of acceptance and adjustment, 3 the least.

going abroad, although Greece has also recently set up missions in several cities of Germany.

6. Private employers, trade unions, local governments, churches and voluntary associations are significantly aiding the reception, training and adjustment of foreigners.

7. While progress has been made in the past decade, the inadequacies of the programs to aid cross-national migrants make an adjustment – in the light of their initial handicaps of cultural limitations, rural background, low educational level, poor vocational preparation – suggest that, by and large, the life of the cross-national migrant is not a pleasant one. The inadequacies of housing and the exclusion of the family of the worker are probably the most unpleasant features. A large number of immigrant workers are being exploited economically without compensatory social advantages – or mistakenly think they are exploited because of insufficient orientation. Despite the progress, and despite the efforts of several countries and many groups throughout western and northern Europe, policies, programs and practices toward migrant workers cannot be considered as generally favorable forces toward the future integration of Europe.

8. Sweden offers its workers the highest wages, for any given occupation, of any country in Europe, with Germany coming second. In occupational level, the immigrants to the United Kingdom rate the highest, mainly because that country no longer accepts many immigrants who are not skilled. Opportunities for upward occupational mobility are best for the immigrants into France and Sweden.

9. Public opinion polls indicate there is a good deal of dissatisfaction with the free migration policies now prevailing in most countries of northern and central Europe, as well as significant antagonism toward the migrants.

10. On the non-policy factors facilitating the integration of immigrants, France stands in the best position. These factors are ideology favoring integration of immigrants, flexibility of social structure, Catholic religion, Romance language, closeness to country of emigration, and attractiveness of climate.

11. In so far as the culture and social structure of the countries of emigration facilitate the adjustment of their emigrants, Italians have the greatest likelihood of adjustment and Turks the least, among the seven European peoples studied.

12. The indexes used here, which are inadequate, suggest that the best adjustment has been made by immigrants to Sweden, the Netherlands and the United Kingdom.

To turn now to a test of the main hypotheses of this chapter, the relevant facts have been assembled in Table 6. These hypotheses are that integration and adjustment of foreigners into a host society is a function of

1. The openness of the host society.

2. The degree of attachment of the immigrants to their society of origin (that is, the inverse of this should be correlated with measures of integration into the host society).

3. The similarity of the cultures, respectively, of the country of emigration and the country of immigration. As throughout this study, no attempt will be made to weight the diverse variables measured; instead a weight of 1 is arbitrarily assigned to each. In other words, they are all treated alike.[16] The dependent variables – that is, the measures of acceptance, integration, and adjustment – are important ones, but they may not be enough to cover what happens to the immigrants as they are intended to do. There may also be defects in the reliability of the data themselves, although they came from official government sources. Nevertheless, the summary index of dependent variables (item 6 in Table 6) was related to each of the summary indexes of independent variables (items 1–4).

The one significant correlation that appears is that between the summary index of dependent variables and the summary index of openness of a country's policies, practices and programs in regard to immigrants (item 1). Using the rank-order coefficient of correlation for all eight immigrant countries, the author found a rho measure of 0·47, which means that there is a moderate relationship. This is a positive finding for the first hypothesis. One country is an obvious deviant in the relationship – the Netherlands. Its deviancy lies in the fact that immigrants make a good adjustment in the Netherlands, even though the country's policies, programs and practices are not very open to them.[17] This seems

16. If there are a large number of variables, as is partly true in this study, there is mathematical support for using the arbitrary weight of 1 (see Guttman in Horst, 1941, pp. 251–364).

17. France is also somewhat of an exception – but to a smaller extent and of an opposite nature. France's immigrants do not have the highest integration and adjustment even though it is the most open country in terms of its policies, programs and practices. The reason would again appear to lie in public opinion – which in France is not always hospitable toward immigrants.

easy to explain: the Netherlands is the poorest example of our immigrant countries – in fact, it is only marginally an immigrant country, having almost as many emigrants as immigrants. The Netherlands can afford to do very little for the immigrant, but Dutch public opinion is pro-immigrant, compared to that found in most other countries, and in this *informally* favorable atmosphere, immigrants make a relatively good adjustment. The author made no attempt to relate public opinion statistically to the dependent variables index, since the measuring instruments were noncomparable. If the Netherlands is left outside the correlation, rho jumps to 0·73, which is a fairly high correlation for complex data such as these. The author thus considers the first hypothesis confirmed – that integration and adjustment of immigrants is related to the openness of programs, policies and practices of immigrant countries. The Dutch case indicates that if comparable measures of the openness of public opinion had been available, the indexes would be even more closely related.

But the other hypotheses do not hold up under correlation of the indexes. The findings give no reason to believe that the degree of attachment of the immigrants to their society of origin inhibits good integration or adjustment to the immigrant country (rho = 0). And they give no reason to believe that similarity of cultures in the country of immigration and the country of emigration makes for better integration and adjustment of the immigrants (rho = ·10). These hypotheses have *not* been disproved but there has been a failure to prove them. If the true relationships should be zero, as the crude indexes here suggest they are, this is indeed a most valuable finding, even if it does go against current sociological thinking: It would mean that the cultural and political background of the migrants – by country, not as individuals – has little or nothing to do with the kind of adjustment they make to the immigrant society, and that, in a significant sense, all cross-national migrant groups – on the average for their country – start off on the same foot when they migrate. The data here have shown that what is important for integration and adjustment is the openness of the *immigrant* country – certainly in its overt policies, programs, and practices and probably in its informal attitudes as well.

An important qualification needs to be made to these generalizations. The data being dealt with are macroscopic – that is, information applying to all national groups. No information is presented here on individual cases or on variations among indi-

Table 6 Summary indexes for independent and dependent variables related to acceptance and adjustment of immigrants[a]

Variable	Belgium	France	Germany (F.R.)	Luxembourg	Netherlands	Sweden	Switzer- land	United Kingdom
1. Openness of policies of immigrant country[b]	5	1	4	6	7	2	8	3
2. Economic factors of immigrant country	2	2	1	1	3	1	2	1
3. Attachment to culture of emigrant country, according to distribution from various countries of emigration	2	2	3	2	1	1	1	3
4. Differences between countries of emigration and countries of immigration[b]	2	1	4	2	4	3	4	4
5. Summary of rankings for independent variables[b]	11	6	12	11	15	7	15	11
6. Summary of rankings for dependent variables	4	4	5	5	2	1	6	3
7. Summary of rankings for independent and dependent variables	15	10	17	16	17	8	21	14

a The lower the number, the greater the degree of acceptance and adjustment.

b The indexes are rank orders based on the total sums of [...]

viduals. It could still be true that *some* individual migrants are very much affected by their ties to their national and local backgrounds. It could still be true that a small number of immigrants find the different climate, language or religion of the country of immigration to be such an obstacle that they cannot make an adjustment. And it could even be true that some immigrants make an excellent adjustment even when the immigrant country is least open and most hostile (within the range examined in this study). It is thus important to emphasize that the data here are *grouped*, macroscopic, that the correlations are of the type which have taken on the technical misnomer of 'ecological',[18] and that the findings do not apply to all individuals.

The indexes which made up a measure of the openness of a country to immigrants as indicated by its formal policies, programs and practices were summarized earlier in this report. There France, Sweden and the United Kingdom, in that order, were found to be on the top, and the Netherlands and Switzerland to be on the bottom. In other portions of this report several other measures affecting or indicating the integration or adjustment of immigrants were presented. Drawing them all together makes for a theoretically meaningless index, but one which may have practical utility. Such a summary of summaries, presented in item 7 of Table 6, might be called an 'index of favorable conditions' affecting immigrants. It shows where, among the eight countries of immigration studied, the immigrants are best off and where they are worst off. Sweden was ahead of France on this final measure, and the Netherlands and West Germany are, after Switzerland, the worst countries for the immigrant. These measures are all relative to each other: certainly no country is really very bad for immigrants; if it were, immigrants would soon cease to go or stay there. And certainly no country offers perfection for immigrants, although Sweden and France make a conscious national effort to do as well as they can.[19]

18. They should be known as 'grouped-data' correlations. 'Ecological' refers to a theoretical viewpoint which interprets social facts in terms of location and distance. It is true that ecology works with grouped data, but not all grouped data are ecological. There is nothing 'ecological' about the present study, for instance. Ecology was a branch of sociology and geography for thirty years before the misnomer 'ecological correlation' arose in the late 1940s.

19. Public opinion polls suggest that the Swedes cooperate more than the French with their government, big employers and big trade unions in a conscious national effort to be pro-immigrant.

This 'index of favorable conditions' for the countries of immigration harks back to one of the basic themes with which this chapter opened: To what extent are the people of Europe today changing their conception of themselves to think of themselves as Europeans and not merely as Frenchmen, Germans, Swedes, etc.? It was assumed at the outset that if this is not to be regarded as merely a verbal change, with no substance, it must take the form of European peoples accepting nationalities other than their own *as their own*. This applies to the total population of Europe, of course, but this chapter has concentrated on cross-national migrants and their hosts. In a very important sense, the migrants and their hosts are the best persons to test the question of acceptance: Their mutual presence is real, not academic or something to fill in on a questionnaire; it is of some duration, not for a few days of superficial tourism or convention going; the relationships occur under conditions of everyday living, not of the best behavior with which diplomats or experts confront each other at conferences. Cross-national migration provides an almost experimental situation for judging whether European peoples are accepting each other.

In this study the hosts have been examined to a greater extent than the migrants themselves, simply because there are more relevant data on them, and also the hosts provide a more critical test of the acceptance of others because they have more power and freedom than the migrants, who in a sense *must* accept the hosts. In speaking of the acceptance by the host peoples, the author does not refer to any hypothetical willingness to accept all foreigners under any and all conditions. Every nation has limits on its expansibility, and every nation must set limits on the rate of immigration, for economic reasons if no other. The purpose of this study was to find out whether the host people, who have invited the immigrants either to take the least desirable jobs in their countries or to fill in occupational gaps which their own nationals cannot fill, treat these migrants as they treat their fellow-nationals. This is what is meant by 'acceptance' among the host people. All the host countries' policies, programs and practices for which objective information could be obtained were examined, along with public opinion polls and indexes of the adjustability of the migrants. The author's conclusion is that there are gaps and faults in every country, but that France and Sweden have made significant formal efforts to accept the immigrants. 'Formal' efforts are emphasized because the public opinion poll data show a considerable rejection even in those countries, and in France the efforts seem to be conditioned on the immigrants' becoming 'francisized'.[20] The United Kingdom, Belgium and Luxembourg follow behind the two leaders, with the British making an obvious effort to face up to their short-comings, through studies, much public discussion, and legislation. Germany's policy apparently has been to be very formally correct in regard to the immigrants, to treat them well materially, but in no sense to accept them as equivalent peoples. The German policy is expressed in the term used to designate the migrants – 'guest workers'. The Netherlands represents almost a contrast-conception to France and Germany: It does little to help the immigrants formally, but its attitudes are more open than those in most countries and the immigrants generally find it easy to adjust to the Netherlands despite the lack of formal aids. Only Switzerland has chosen the conscious path of rejection to the point of overt and explicit chauvinism. To repeat, this is not because of Switzer-land's restrictions on immigration, but because of the treatment which it metes out to the immigrants it has accepted into the country. While the 'rejection' is clearest in Switzerland, it exists to some extent among all the immigration countries, and few nationals of these countries think of themselves as really inter-changeable with their immigrants.

On the migrants there is less information. The naturalization and intermarriage rates presented offer important clues to the extent to which the migrants accept their hosts as interchangeable with people of their native nationalities, defined here as 'accept-ance'. But clearly 'acceptance' means something beyond assimi-lation, and both naturalization and intermarriage refer to acceptance only so far as it also means assimilation. Even if an immigrant returns to his home country and takes a spouse from among his native people, he can still accept his former hosts as 'my own kind of people', as interchangeable with his own nationality for social and political purposes. It has not been possible to measure this kind of opinion, except very crudely by scattered references to such things as participation in cross-national voluntary associations. Very few emigrants leave their home countries with the intention of never coming back except

20. In the mid-1960s the Swedes were having a great debate about whether they should encourage the immigrants to be like Swedes or let them be like anyone they wanted to be. The very existence of such a debate indicates a degree of openness in Swedish society that no other European country had achieved at that time.

maybe for a visit. But the fact that only a minority have returned is a crude index that the majority have accepted their host country as their adopted country, whether the law and those who apply it allow them to be naturalized or not. Except for those who return with bitterness or with psychological problems to their home countries, the migrants seem to show a great deal of tolerance, if not outright acceptance toward their hosts.

This study lacks a real contrast or comparison, which probably could be best provided today by Canada, Australia and some countries of Latin America. To make this comparison would take a separate study. But the author would guess that mutual acceptance is greater among migrants and their hosts in these countries than in Europe.

A few comparisons can be made with the migrants who came from Europe to the United States in the century and a half before the quota-restriction laws of the 1920s cut them off. The times were so different that the comparison is hardly appropriate: It was an era of *laissez-faire* for government, so the programs and practices toward immigrants were largely those of private organizations, which did much to aid the foreigners but not nearly as much as is done today by governments. It was a migration of much longer distance, and – although no information is available about whether the migrants initially dreamed of returning to their homelands – they found it much more difficult to return, even for a holiday. Other profound differences could be specified.

Mutual acceptance was dominant in the immigration to America in the pre-1921 period. There were those Americans who insisted that the immigrants adapt to an 'American' cultural norm, those who looked forward to a more cosmopolitan 'melting pot', and those who favored an equalitarian cultural pluralism. But – even at the height of the agitation for putting restrictions on further immigration, and even at the fever pitch of racist hatred – there was almost no one who insisted that the migrants return to their homelands after a period of labor in the United States. Different conceptions prevailed about how the European immigrant was to become an American, but there was no doubt that he could become an American and that he should have full legal and political rights as an American. There was a norm of acceptance that made integration – despite many personal hardships attending the process – ultimately inevitable.

From the migrants themselves there are no comparative systematic data, but the historical studies of Marcus Hansen,

Oscar Handlin and others suggest that the immigrants to America also quickly thought of themselves as permanent Americans, not that many adopted assimilation as their personal goal, for many retained a sentimental and cultural loyalty to the 'old country'. But there was a transfer of political loyalty, which has yet to be measured among the intra-European migrants of today. Some of the American immigrants returned to their homelands, especially the Italians, but there is no evidence that this involved repudiation of the United States: some returnees were trapped by European wars and new American immigration restriction laws into staying in the homelands when they originally had intended to go back to the United States after a holiday or a settlement of family affairs. The European immigration to the United States was a successful, integrative migration, if the evidence of history can be trusted. The study here raises a question whether there has been as much mutual acceptance among European migrants and their hosts in Europe today.

References

ANNUAIRE EUROPÉEN (1962), *L'opinion publique et l'Europe*, vol. 10, p. 46.
BARBICHON, G. (1962), *Adaptation and Training of Rural Workers for Industrial Work*, OECD.
BORRIE, W. D. (1959), *The Cultural Integration of Immigrants*, UNESCO.
BOUSCAREN, A. T. (1963), *International Migrations since 1945*, Praeger.
BRITISH INFORMATION SERVICES (1966), *The Council of Europe*, Central Office of Information.
DOMENACH, J. M. (1966), *Esprit*, vol. 34, no. 4, p. 529.
DOUBLET, J. (1965), 'Les Mouvements migratoires en Europe', *Revue Internationale des Sciences Sociales*, vol. 17, no. 2, pp. 304–17.
EISENSTADT, S. N. (1954), *The Absorption of Immigrants*, Routledge & Kegan Paul.
ERIXON, I. (1965), 'Adaptation and training of rural manpower moving from population surplus area to industrial regions and countries', OECD.
GALLUP INTERNATIONAL POLL (1962), *L'Opinion publique et L'Europe des Six*, Institut Français d'Opinion Publique.
GALLUP INTERNATIONAL POLL (1966), 'Big majority keen on joining Europe', *Daily Telegraph*, 12 December, p. 18.
HOLBORN, L. W. (1956), *The International Refugee Organisation: Its History and Work, 1946–52*, Oxford University Press.
HORST, P. (1941), *The Prediction of Personal Adjustment*, Social Science Research Council.
INTERNATIONAL RESEARCH ASSOCIATES (1966), *L'Image de L'Europe unie dans l'opinion publique*, Brussels.
JACKSON, J. (1967), 'Experience with emigrants returning to the home country: Ireland', *Emigrant Workers Returning to their Home Countries: Final Report*, OECD.

JOINT STATISTICAL PROJECT ON EUROPEAN MIGRATION (1958), *A Decade of Post-Second World War European Migration*, CIME, ILO, OEEC and UN.

KRIER, H. (1961), *Rural Manpower and Industrial Development: Adaptation and Training*, OECD.

LADAME, P. (1958), *Le role des migrations dans le monde libre*, Droz.

LA DOCUMENTATION FRANÇAISE (1964), *Les Travailleurs Etrangers en France: Notes et Etudes Documentaires*, no. 3057, 23 January, p. 15.

LE MONDE (1967), 'Les français et l'entrée de la Grande Bretagne dans le Marché Commun', 24 January, p. 3.

LIPSET, S. M. (1963), *The First New Nation*, Basic Books.

MIJARC (1966), *8000 jeures Rivaux nons disent . . .*, 'Louvain'.

MURPHY, H. B. M. *et al.* (1955) *Flight and Resettlement*, UNESCO.

RABIER, J. R. (1965), *L'information de européens et de l'intégration de l'Europe*, Institute of Sociology, Brussels.

RABIER, J. R. (1966), *L'opinion publique et l'Europe*, Institute of Sociology, Brussels.

READER'S DIGEST POLL (1963) *Products and People*, Readers Digest.

RIBAS, J. J. (1965), *Social Security in the European Community*, European Community Information Service.

ROGNAUT, J. L. and SCHULTZ, J. (1964) 'Les rapatriés d'Afrique du Nord dans L'Hérault 1954–64', *Société Languedocienne de Géographie*, Bulletin Trimestrial, vol. 35, pp. 283–417.

ROSE, A. M. (1969), *Migrants in Europe: Problems of Acceptance and Adjustment*, University of Minnesota Press.

SANDRI, L. L. (1966), *Social Policy in the Common Market, 1958–65*, European Community Information Service.

SCHECHTMAN, J. B. (1946), *European Population Transfers, 1939–45*, Oxford University Press.

SCHNITZER, M. (1966), *Programs for Relocating Workers used by Governments of Selected Countries*, US Congress Joint Economic Committee.

TAFT, D. R. and ROBBINS, R. (1955), *International Migrations: The Immigrant in the Modern World*, Ronald Press.

THOMAS, B. (1954), *Migration and Economic Growth*, Cambridge University Press.

THOMAS, B. (1959), 'International migration', in P. M. Hanser and O. D. Dancan (eds.), *The Study of Population: An Inventory and Appraisal*, Chicago University Press.

THOMAS, W. I. and ZNANIECKI, F. (1919), *The Polish Peasant in Europe and America*, Badger Press.

TOUJAS-PINEDA, C. (1965), 'Les rapatriés d'Algérie dans la région Midi-Pyrenees', *Revue Geographique des Pyrenees et du Sud-Ouest*, vol. 36, pp. 321–72.

VERNANT, J. (1953), *The Refugee in the Post-War World*, Yale University Press.

WEIL, G. L. (1965), *A Handbook on the European Economic Community*, Praeger.

ZUBRZYCKI, J. (1956), *Polish Immigrants in Britain*, Martinus Nijhoff.

18 Dusan Sidjanski

Pressure Groups and the European Economic Community

D. Sidjanski, 'Pressure groups and the European Economic Community',
Government and Opposition, vol. 2, no. 3, 1967, pp. 397–416.
Translated from French.

The development of the power of the European Economic Community has given rise to a reaction from those interests which are
most directly affected. In order to make sure both that they are
informed and that their interests are represented and defended,
the various groups concerned have been led to create for themselves new structures at the level of EEC. A parallel relation has
thus emerged between the official powers of EEC and the private
powers affected by it. These groups, formed on the European
level, naturally have neither the solidity not the effectiveness of
professional representation on the national level. Moreover, since
such groups are themselves a part of the process of evolution of
the political structure, they adapt themselves readily to new
political circumstances. But if these European professional organs
are not comparable to the national groupings, they cannot be
seen as similar to the international associations. They are more
numerous – 350 to 400 gravitate towards the European Community. Their action is both more intense and more concrete than
that of the international associations, and corresponds to questions with which the community is concerned.

On the whole, the birth of new groups, as well as the strengthening of the weak links which existed before, was, and is, caused
by the emergence of a new centre of decision at the continental
level. In turn, this centre of decision needs to win over and to
consolidate support.

The four phases of formation

Roughly speaking, the emergence of the socio-economic groups
within the regional European framework has passed through four
phases:

The first wave appeared when the Marshall Plan and OEEC
were launched. Ninety new organizations were set up to establish
relations between the interests and OEEC (today OEDC); sixty

of them were formed between 1948 and 1957. But they were mostly groupings with a very loose structure, mirroring in this sense the loose powers with which OEEC and later OEDC were invested. The main purpose of these organs was to ensure that information was transmitted in two directions – from the organization to the members of the groups and from the groups to the organization. These can best be described as potential pressure groups.

The second wave appeared during the setting up of ECSC itself, from 1953 onwards. It was limited, but more intense, as was ECSC itself. About ten new organs, grouping together the main interests saw the light of day: in 1953 the federation of the iron and steel workers of the European Communities (FEDEREL), the liaison committee of the European metallurgical industries, the committe for study of the coal producers (CEPCEO), the club of the steel producers, as well as two European specialized offices of the confederation of free trade unions and of the confederation of Christian trade unions were set up. These groups were not content simply to inform and be informed, but tried to intervene in the decision-making process of ECCA.

The third wave arose with the entry into action of the European Economic Community in 1958. It was vaster and had more profound effects. From then on, the creation of multiple professional organizations began in earnest. Following the example of EEC itself, these organizations were concerned with the main sectors of economic and social activity. Some, such as the union of the industries of EEC (UNICE), COPA (committee of professional, agricultural organizations of EEC) and the trade unions' secretariat of the Six came into being the moment the institutions of EEC were formed; others, such as the committee of consumers and interprofessional or specialized organs (COMITEXTIL) were set up at the same time as and according as the regulatory powers of EEC began to take effect and to influence various interests. Sometimes the formation of these organs was spontaneous. Sometimes it was prompted by an invitation or even by some pressure from the Commission, as in the case of the consumers' organizations. Whatever their origin their action in the field of simultaneous information and consolidation between the members and exertion of influence corresponded to real needs. The form of these groups and the intensity of their action varies from case to case, the best structured organs often being those whose interests are most directly affected or threatened. In short, whatever the original motivation of these professional groups, they all have, in various degrees, the object of bringing pressure to bear on the authorities of the European Community. For it is true to say that the European Community does not have all-embracing political powers. It can only use a still imperfect political procedure, taking decisions in the last resort. Moreover, these procedures, contrary to what happens in national politics, apply only to certain specific economic and technical matters.

The fourth wave which again was a weaker one, coincided with the emergence of the European Free Trade Association (EFTA) of which fifteen professional organizations are members. However, the national groups have not felt any urgent need to be reconstituted in this intergovernmental organization because, as in OEDC, they can use the classic, intermediary channel of their own governments. This channel of influence suffices them because the decisions of the new centre of decision-making – the Council – are taken with the participation of national representatives.

Of course, the formation of the European Economic Community has created a new situation. The powers of the Community no longer belong exclusively to an intergovernmental institution. They are the result of an organic and often obligatory collaboration between the Council and the Commission. To the extent that the Commission fulfills an autonomous function, either by taking its own decisions or by working out proposals for the benefit of the Council, it becomes a centre of special interest for the groups. The tandem, Council–Commission, is the central mechanism of EEC and this centre of decision naturally attracts the groups. Certainly, the groups do not completely ignore other bodies such as the Economic and Social Committee. But in so far as it carries no effective weight in the decisions of the Council and of the Commission, the groups treat it rather as a future than as a present channel of intervention. Their relation with the European Parliament is even more ambiguous since, for the time being, it is only an indirect conveyor for resolutions which produce no results.

Plan of decisions

Figure 1 shows the way in which decisions are reached in EEC and illustrates the role of various institutions in the elaboration of community acts. It outlines the longest path for the production of the basic rules or directives. The line thus drawn can be reduced, cut or altered. It is only a model for reference. For instance, if the basic regulations for agriculture have followed a longer route, the complementary rules for their implementation have been established by many short cuts. As these policies had already been decided upon, there was no need for the same long series of preliminary consultations.

But the figure must be altered in the opposite direction in cases in which the Council alone takes decisions. This does not often happen. But when it does, it is usually on important matters (the transition from the first to the second stage, the solution of the 1965 crisis). Then the whole Commission phase is practically suppressed.

The more the Council works alone, the more it tends to monopolize the attention of the groups. Their action is closely related to our figure, though not identical with that of the inter-governmental organizations. In fact, as the professional structures at the community level in EEC start to function, the national groups can bring pressure to bear either directly or through them on their governments by working on public opinion. It will be observed that the Court of Justice, an important institution in EEC, is missing from the figure. Yet its role in annulling or adjusting, or on the other hand in confirming the decisions of the Council and of the Commission is well known. But the Court remains, whatever its influence on Community decisions may be, the one institution of control which is the most impervious to pressure. This explains its absence from a figure which is designed to illustrate pressure groups and influences.

Birth of the professional structures

The acts of the institutions of EEC differ from their counterparts in the other organizations in that not only are they binding and compulsory but they also have direct results. That is to say, they bring pressure to bear directly on groups and individuals without passing through the apparatuses of the respective states. A direct relationship is thus established between the Community organs and groups or individuals. No wonder that in these circumstances the groups should have tried to set up a defensive mechanism against the power of EEC. Over and above the protection and the resources with which they are already supplied they strive to counterbalance this power by endowing themselves with permanent structures on the scale of EEC. Organized action of the groups is correlated to collective action by states and by the

first phase of the Commission

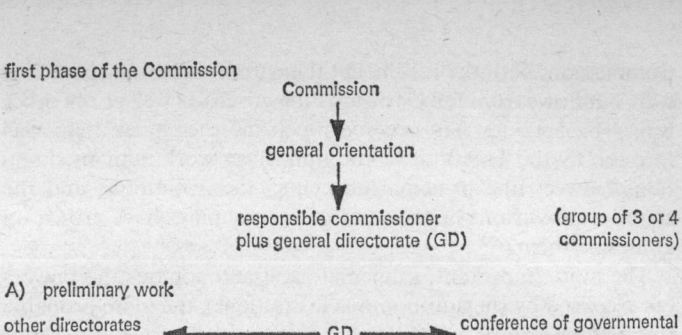

Commission

↓

general orientation

↓

responsible commissioner   (group of 3 or 4
plus general directorate (GD)   commissioners)

A) preliminary work

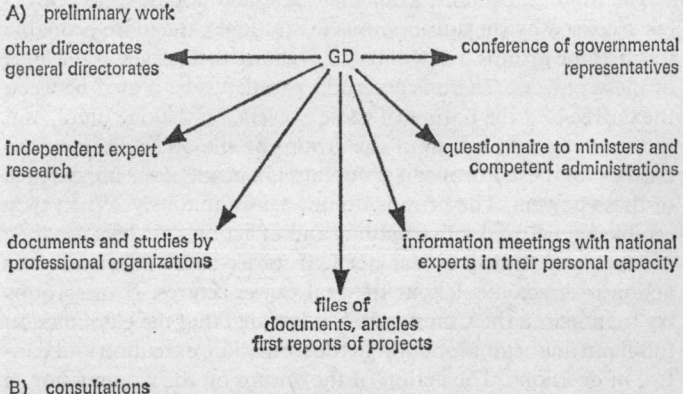

other directorates ◄——— GD ———► conference of governmental
general directorates   representatives

independent expert   questionnaire to ministers and
research   competent administrations

documents and studies by   information meetings with national
professional organizations   experts in their personal capacity

files of
documents, articles
first reports of projects

B) consultations

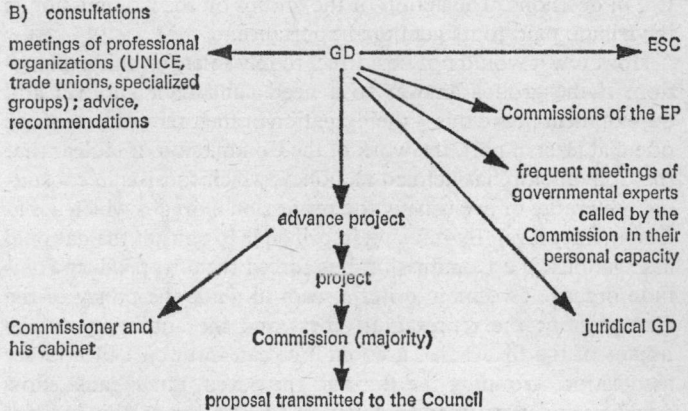

meetings of professional ◄——— GD ———► ESC
organizations (UNICE,
trade unions, specialized
groups); advice,   Commissions of the EP
recommendations

                                                          frequent meetings of
                                                          governmental experts
                                                          called by the
advance project   Commission in their
                                                          personal capacity

↓

project

↓

Commissioner and   Commission (majority)   juridical GD
his cabinet

↓

proposal transmitted to the Council

Sources : Treaty, basic statutes, proposals and initiatives of the
Commission, initiatives of the Council, government or private
organizations

Figure 3 European Economic Community : Diagram illustrating how basic
decisions are made

Commission, with the result that the current is no longer all one way, but flows from EEC towards the groups as well as the other way. The network has become much more complex than was foreseen by the Treaty of Rome; influences work in many directions between the principal elements – the institutions and the states – and various groups and many groupings have grown up alongside them.

The more important, immediate and autonomous the powers (as exercised by the autonomous institutions), the more probable it is that the groups will will try to organize themselves at the level of these powers. There is a certain parallel to be drawn between the degree and the nature of these powers, on the one hand, and the structure and action of the groups on the other. Besides, the creation of these European groupings is a proof of the importance of these powers. The groups do not act gratuitously. When they establish a network of structures and of action, it is because they are trying to satisfy a real need. In order to be effective, their action is directed solely at the real power-centres. If the groups try to influence the Commission, it is a sign that the Commission fulfills an important function in the formation, execution and control of decisions. The action of the groups on the Commission is the tribute paid to its genuine importance.

However, it would not be correct to rely solely on this explanation. If the groups answer to a need – and their survival and development prove this – their creation or their reinforcement are often, at least in part, the work of the Commission. It is clear that the Commission has defined its policy, which consists in consulting preferably or exclusively the professional organs which act at Community level. By refusing in principle to consult the national associations, the Commission has forced them to produce common organs. Two main criteria seem to guide the policy of the Commission: the representativeness and the autonomy of the organs of the Six. Thus, a committee can form part of a larger association, grouping the Six and the Seven, but it must show a sufficient degree of independence. In addition to this indirect pressure, the Commission has been sometimes the driving force: the consumer's committee is the result of the initiative of M. Mansholt who also played a part in the establishment and strengthening of the structures which group the activities connected with agriculture.

The motives behind this active policy of the Commission are many, of which the most important are:

1. The Commission prefers to avoid intervention in the interests of professional bodies; problems should be discussed by the groups themselves within their common organs, which should then present the institutions of EEC with agreed positions or take note of disagreement among their members.

2. The Commission also needs these organs not only to obtain technical information, but in order to use them as a network of information on the problems of the Community.

3. In this way a sphere of support for its activity is formed around the Commission. During the recent crisis in the Economic Community, most of the groups adopted positions favourable to the Commission and rose in defence of the Community when it was seriously threatened.

4. Lastly, and by way of exception, the Commission can sometimes try to influence governments by using the national groups which are members of the European organs.

Up to a point, the preparation by the Commission and the adoption by the Council of the list of exceptions for the 'Kennedy round' provide a notable example of this procedure.

When speaking of the activity of the pressure groups, one thinks not only of a unilateral pressure, but also of the influence which institutions exert on the groups, or through them, on the national centres of power. It would be difficult, however, to say which of these two counter-influences is stronger. The action of the groups is conditioned by circumstances, by the relative importance of the respective group and by its position with regard to other groups.

Structure of the groups

According to various estimates, there are 350 groupings at the Community level, of which two thirds possess statutes and formal organs. As on the national level, the groups correspond to three great categories: employers, agriculture and labour. The employers, for example, have a central organ for industry (UNICE), one for trade (COCCEE), one for banking (BFEEC); about one hundred organs in branches, sections or subsections in industry and about sixty commercial organs (agricultural activities). If, for instance, one were to look in greater detail at the organization of the industrial groups one would find three main structures: the central organizations (UNICE), the intermediary or inter-professional organs (COMITEXTIL for textiles or ISCI for the chemical industries) and the specialized organs (plastics, detergents, pharmaceutics or wool and cotton, etc). The two latter types of organs do not take part directly in UNICE, with which they keep in touch. At the level of economic policy, of planning and general problems (for example, anti-trust legislation) UNICE is responsible to the whole industry. This distinction on the structural and functional plane determines to some extent the action of the groups. The division of work is established, in particular along the dividing line between general, intermediary and specialized functions. In exercising these functions, UNICE is called on to try to coordinate the positions and the claims of other organs. This is an arduous task in an environment in which the responsibilities and the links are still ill-defined. In practice, the various organs maintain contacts, collaborate and give each other mutual support, in spite of the lack of organic links.

Other factors also influence the behaviour and activity of the groups. The predominance of vertical interests over horizontal (as for instance the permanent conference of the chambers of commerce of EEC countries) is one. Another is the multiplicity of specialized organs in the representation of a particular sector of economic activity. In this case, while the former take a stand on general questions, the latter restrict themselves to defending their particular interests. But the limitations on the range of their activity do not reduce its amount. Indeed, these organs tend to express their opinion on general questions quite as much as on matters which directly concern them. But one may well consider if the action of these specialized groups does not gain in effectiveness when it is confined to their area of interest.

From the point of view of this article, it is not irrelevant to ask whether the organs which undertake an action belong in their own right to the Six, or if they are only a subgroup, for action at ECC, of a wider association. For, even if the subgroup has sufficient functional or organic autonomy, it will probably have a tendency to consider the interests of the whole association, while at the same time stressing those of the Six. How far such a group can reconcile these two objectives depends very much on the structure and the links between the subgroups as well as on conditions in the relevant branch of the industry. To take an example, there is the case of ORGALIME (the organization of liaison of the European metal industry) and of the European confederation of the timber industry. At first glance, these two associations seem to have characteristics of a large structure with two subgroups, one at EEC and the other at EFTA. In reality, they differ considerably. The timber confederation has two commissions, one for the Six and one for the Seven. But, in fact, the commission for EFTA is inactive, whereas the executive commission for the Common Market fulfils many functions and its structure develops in response to the growing demands (constitution of subcommissions). Thus a discrepancy arises between the two commissions, which is not without effect upon their activities. On the other hand, ORGALIME, and its two EEC and EFTA committees carry on their activities in a way which is at the same time more continuous, more balanced and better oriented towards the objectives common to the thirteen countries concerned and their twenty-seven associate members. What probably happens is that each committee takes more account of the interests of the other, even when it is acting primarily in its own interests.

Typology of channels and of influence

If one admits the close relation between the groups and the centres of decision, one is justified in distinguishing between the main and the secondary channels in the Community. The first are found at the level of the Commission, of the Council and of the governments; the second at the level of the Economic and Social Committee and of the European Parliament. One can also divide methods of action into informal and official – the latter taking on forms which are more or less institutionalized.

Direct and indirect action. At the European level more than at the national, the central organizations, unions or associations resort to general action and often try to intervene through declarations. On the national plane, organizations representing interest groups often take effective and decisive action. Thus, when the trade unions of the workers or of the farmers want to influence public opinion, they use a wide range of methods, from warnings to mass meetings, even strikes. But on the European plane, these methods are unknown. UNICE, COPA and the unions organize congresses, meetings (the assembly of COPA at Strasburg and the trade-union meeting in Dortmund, for example) and publish declarations.

Indirect influence is often intended to support the direct pressures which are brought to bear on the institutions of EEC. UNICE, COPA and the trade unions took a stand – as did many other organs – during the most recent EEC crisis. They tried to bring their weight to bear directly on the governments, since the Commission was not involved. In these conditions, direct pressure could only be exercised on the governments on a national scale. As the French government was the cause of the crisis, most of these interventions were addressed to it. For the same reason the French groupings were called upon to play a more active role. Thus, the French farmers acted on two levels: as the driving-force within COPA, which only endorsed the text which they had composed – a supporting action which was intended to mobilize European public opinion. On the other hand, on the internal level, the French farmers acted as a pressure group by using direct channels, making representations to the governments, or taking part in the presidential campaign. Because of the particular form the crisis took (opposition of one government to the Commission and to the other governments) we can observe the difference between direct and indirect action on the two levels, national and European.

Channels at the level of the Commission. In principle, the Commission has not adopted the procedures of the UN or of the Council of Europe whereby consultative status is granted to international or European associations. But the Commission does accept some of the groups as spokesmen and acknowledges them as correspondents. The Commission is guided in this pragmatic choice by the criterion of representativeness and autonomy of the respective professional groups. Yet there are many cases in which it maintains only informal contacts with organs which seem to fulfil both conditions.

Informal channels

We have drawn a distinction between informal and official channels. The first include every kind of contact which the professional groups establish and maintain with the Commission: meetings, private discussions, etc. However discreet and difficult to follow they may be, they are none the less effective. Besides, the content as well as the range of these relations depend on the ultimate influence of the groups. The content of the relations varies from simple exchanges of news, data and technical information to the tendering of advice and guidance. Although these contacts are private, they can take the form of genuine consultations. Their nature is not fundamentally different from those which develop at the national level.

Informal relations can be established between the different types of groups (groups of national interests, business groups, groups of European interests) and the branches of the Commission. Nevertheless, one fundamental difference persists, according to the groups concerned: for the professional European groupings, and in particular for those which are regarded as the spokesmen for their sector, this is an additional channel which supplements the official one.

This supplementary quality does not diminish its importance which, as national experience has shown, is far from negligible. On the contrary, when a European group is not consulted officially by the Commission, the informal channel remains the only avenue available. This lends prominence to the channel which becomes privileged, as in the case of business concerns. Informal channels can also be particularly important for those groups which do not dispose of a complete set of channels at official level. Thus, for example, the Permanent Conference of the Chambers of Commerce has no official channels: the Commission does not consult it and it has no representative in the Economic and Social Committee, in which it has the status of observer; its general-secretary no longer takes part in the press conferences called by EEC. In these conditions, informal channels become a precious instrument. The secretary-general of the Permanent Conference, with offices in Brussels, undertakes personal contact with the officials of the Commission. Fairly intensive technical activity is also undertaken.

A similar kind of monopoly is found at the level of the national organizations and the business groups, but with the difference that they can both use official channels as well, by means of the European professional groups of which they are members. The employers or the French farmers can try to influence the attitude of UNICE or of COPA and thus ensure that their wishes are taken account of by the Commission. The Commission in principle does not maintain official contacts with the national groups. But some of them take part in the work of the Economic and Social Committee and of the various consultative agricultural committees.

Official contacts for the groups of business interests are more often undertaken by intermediaries. Indeed, they must pass both through the national professional organs and through a European one to reach the Commission. Here the distance becomes greater, but sometimes it is made up for by the weight of influence of these gigantic concerns. It is clear, for instance, that this distance is reduced to a minimum for the European organization of the motor-car industry. In addition, the sheer weight of these concerns allows them to develop effectively all available informal channels.

Although the European organs often act through official channels, they do not neglect the informal ones. Regular contacts are established at every level. Thus the presidents of the central federations represented in UNICE hold regular meetings with the Commissioners. On the permanent staff level, relations are closer and almost daily; the secretary-general of UNICE and the permanent delegates are in constant touch with the high officials of the Commission; the same holds good for contacts at the level of experts and cadres. Contacts are often easier between compatriots. They are also smoothed by professional or personal affinities, and the fact of belonging to the same social circle or political party can be a positive factor.

Official channels

These may take institutionalized or non-institutionalized forms. Among the non-institutionalized channels one can count various types of 'hearings' and information meetings. During the Kennedy negotiations, genuine hearings took place, organized by the Commission. During the drawing up of the list of exceptions, the interested groups were consulted and they collaborated in apportioning the exceptions. These information sessions have dealt with the problems of EEC, its commercial policy, the associate status of Greece, etc.

The most interesting aspect of this non-institutionalized collaboration is the contribution of the groupings to the drawing up of proposals or other acts by the Commission. They intervene on several planes: in the phase of study, the Commission allows them to contribute by asking them for technical information; in turn the Commission supplies the groups with its documentation and keeps them informed of its various plans. At this stage, the action of the groups is neutral or objective; experience has shown that this is by no means the most negligible method of influence used by professional groups. At the more advanced stage, the Commission goes on to hold consultations with the European organs and the national experts, in a personal capacity. Without dismissing the effective role of the groups, it is generally admitted that the national experts carry most weight during the process of elaboration – a point which it is necessary to remember, in order not to overestimate the influence of the groups. This influence which is difficult to assess exactly, is exercised by their participation in various working-parties called by the Commission, by their individual attitudes, by their advice and studies as well as through direct and informal contacts. These interventions occur at the level of professional experts in the working-parties as well as at the highest levels, as for instance when the president of UNICE addresses the president of the Commission directly.

These various activities mostly arise over projects of the Commission itself. The intervention usually follows on the activities of the Commission, but sometimes it precedes them. Group initiatives have lately become more frequent. To take only one example, the federation of bankers of EEC has formulated several proposals: the elimination of discrimination arising out of legislation or regulations, the suppression of all taxes on cheques and commercial drafts with EEC. COMITEXTIL and many other groups continuously put forward their own proposals and suggestions to the Commission. In this way, they take an active part in the development of the Community, by urging and helping the Commission to undertake and to fulfil a multitude of tasks.

Institutionalized channels can be classified under two headings: those channels giving access to participation in the preparation of general policy decisions; and those giving access to participation in administrative functions. In the first case, the Economic and Social Committee provides a channel, if only on a consultative basis, for the various categories of interests which are represented on it. Whereas the mechanism of informal consultation is reserved essentially for the European organization, it is the national groups who sit in the Economic and Social Committee, although this is not tantamount to formal representation. The European organizations are brought into the committee as coordinating bodies. UNICE, for instance, coordinates the representation of the employers, or COPA that of the farmers; the secretariats of the European trade unions fulfil the same function with regard to the trade unionists who are members of the Committee. Thus, the central organs which, as previously mentioned, participate in the preparation of the Commission's proposals, are also present at a later stage of the process, namely at the moment when the complex negotiations between the Commissions and the members of the Council are embarked on. As for participation in the administration, the Consultative Committee for Social Welfare and the consultative committees of various agricultural sectors provide the best examples. Their practices do not differ much from those of similar committees in the administrations of various governments. Here again, whereas national groups are called to sit in the European organizations, groups such as COPA assume the function of coordination according to categories of members. In this way, the groups intervene both at the level of execution and of administration.

By and large, these are the main channels at the level of the Commission. Their effectiveness certainly varies, but none of them appears to be neglected by the European groups, which tend to penetrate all the mechanisms at all levels. One of the rapporteurs of the union of craftsmen of EEC(UAEEC) recommended in 1963 that each national federation of craftsmen should try to obtain a seat in the consultative committees. This *will* to be present does not necessarily reflect the actual effectiveness of the organs in question. But the existence of such a desire indicates that the strategy of the groups is aimed at placing their spokesmen in all the channels which bring them or could one day bring them nearer to the power-centres of the Communities.

Other channels. It is generally admitted that it is very difficult for the European groups to influence the Council as such. The groups often submit their studies and documents to the Council but find it somewhat inaccessible. Direct intervention is an exception, as for instance the dispatch of telegrams by COPA, during the agricultural 'marathon' (a term which describes a specific procedure during discussion of some general issues, on which a decision must be taken in order to avoid complete deadlock in the machine; hence day and night meetings are held over long periods). Indirect access can be obtained by using the institutionalized channel of the Economic and Social Committee which is consulted by the Council. As a rule, however, the national groups press in the classic manner through their own governments: direct contacts with the Council and with the permanent representatives take place very rarely. One may assume that some national groups try occasionally by private contacts to influence the position, if it is not too rigid, of their permanent representative in Brussels.[1] Sometimes the European

1. It seems that the German and Dutch representatives are more open to this dialogue with some groups than are the other representatives.

organs, when there is complete agreement between their members (which seldom happens), can attempt to influence the Council through these members and their national governments.

Among the *secondary channels*, we have already noted the role of the Social and Economic Committee. The role of the European Parliament is scarcely more important. Having no real grip on the power of the Community, the European Parliament is rarely lobbied by the groups. At most its documentation on the Communities can interest them. In addition, since it has only a consultative function and its powers of political control remain on paper, it offers, in contrast to the Economic and Social Committee, merely an indirect channel.

The activity of the groups

Figure 2 shows the activity of the groups at the national and community level. It certainly does not cover all the possible situations. In the case of ISCI (the international secretariat of the chemical industry of EEC) and of UNICE, the diagram can be said to be accurate. But if one replaces the ISCI, for instance, by COMITEXTIL the situation is changed because COMITEXTIL is a group which does not willingly act through UNICE and prefers to approach the Commission directly. In spite, however, of such discrepancies and inadequacies, the figure can be of help in summarizing the complex character of the activity of the groups and the combination of typical pressure group action on the one hand, and action on the European scale, on the other.

Taking as a point of departure the particular interest of a national federation, one can think of several possibilities. Thus, at the community level, this interest may coincide with the interests of the other federations which are members of the European organ: in the present example this would be ISCI. In such a case, action will take place on the plane of EEC, and of the Commission in particular, with ISCI acting as spokesman through the available channels. If the action concerns a purely professional question, three possibilities are theoretically open: the action of ISCI might suit the policy of UNICE, in which case UNICE would support it; or it might be a matter of indifference to UNICE, which would then remain neutral; but ISCI could also be opposed to the policy of UNICE, thus giving rise to a conflict between two European organizations. Finally, if the action of ISCI were to involve more general interests, the same patterns would be reproduced, but with the

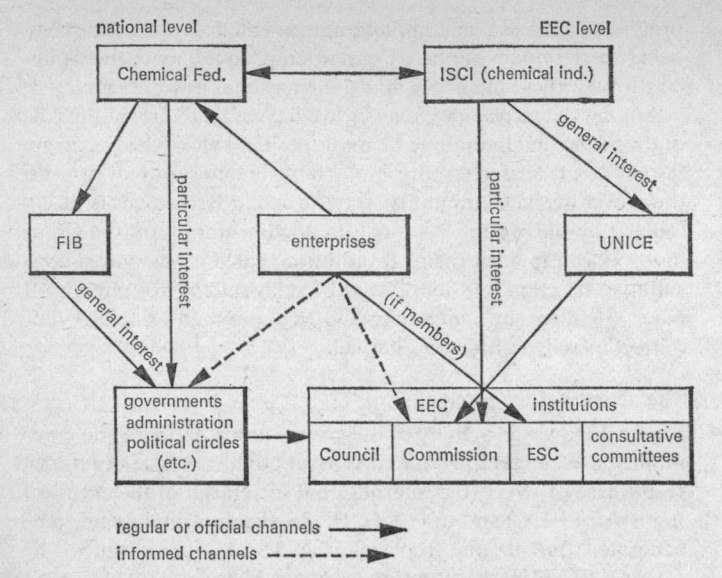

national level   EEC level

regular or official channels ⟶
informed channels ⟶

Figure 2 Diagram of action (Groups of socio-economic interests in the EEC)

difference, this time, that the agreement or the conflict would be upon matters which are within the jurisdiction of UNICE. The coincidence of the particular interest and of the wider point of view of UNICE leads, as happened in the struggle against anti-trust legislation, to common action. What about the other central organs? On the whole, at the national level, a central federation or central organization can face three situations. In the first, the interests of a national group coincide with the interests of other federations which are members of the European grouping. In this case, the action of a national group, through the channel of its own government, goes in the same direction as that of the European group and provides it with additional support. For example, in the case of the most recent crisis in EEC, the pressure of the French farmers on their government was extended to the community level through COPA, which acted as inter-mediary. The second situation arises when the interests of the national group run contrary to those of the European group. In such a case the national group may make common action im-possible and bring pressure to bear on its own government. This occurred with the German farmers' opposition to a uniform price. Alternatively, the national group may align itself with others on a general question, but oppose through its own government the application of a particular measure. This occurred, for instance, when the French National Council of Employers, although supporting EEC, later opposed the expected application of the customs union. A third situation occurs when the interests of the national organ do not conflict with the European interests. In these circumstances, the national groups are free to act through the traditional channels. The above are only a few examples of possible contingencies. In reality, the main variations, the complex network of organs (central, intermediary, specialized, both European and national, plus business groups) provide an infinite variety of combinations.

One last remark about this figure, in connection with its one-way appearance. In fact, the influences are not all one-way, running from a group towards the Commission. The Commission frequently tries to influence the groups and to win their support. For its technical and specialized work, it often requires the recommendations of professional organs (the work of COMITEXTIL, of specialized groups), their advice and suggestions. This need explains the process of consultation. In cases of difficulty or of crisis, the supporting action of the groups is of considerable value, as their reaction to the 1965 crisis showed. On other occasions, the Commission can rouse or stimulate the action of the groups. Indeed it may well be that during the 'marathons', the Commission asked the groups for their help in furthering its proposals or achieving successful compromises. The drawing up of the list of exceptions for the 'Kennedy round' is one example which is often quoted: during its hearings and negotiations with the groups, the Commission succeeded in drafting a list of exceptions, and the groups undertook to bring the necessary pressure to bear on their own governments. Thus a precarious compromise was in the end confirmed by the Council. In these cases, the groups did not bring pressure to bear on the Commission, but acted in favour of it. Thus, they have not always been the originators, but sometimes the objects of influence.

Conclusion

In principle, for a group to be able to act, it must have a clear view of the desired goal and it must be able to count on the support of its members. This double will is expressed in many organizations by the requirement of unanimous agreement of their members, an agreement which reflects the configuration of forces enabling the member groupings to act. Indeed, the European organization generally takes a confederal form, which provides the best guarantee for the protection of the particular interests of its members. And yet this confederal form acts as a brake on the efficient functioning of a European group: COPA, for instance, was paralysed during the discussions of the question of the uniform price for lack of unanimity. This is why the groups have adopted in practice and often in their statutes, the rule allowing the expression of minority opinion, together with that of the majority. Thus the functioning of the group is assured, without a brutal suppression of differences of opinion. More and more frequently the groups present an agreed opinion. In exceptional cases, this unity of action can be assured by reference to the qualified minority. The statute of COCCEE, for instance, incorporates this principle for its own organ of decision, basing itself upon article 148 of the Treaty of Rome.

The central groupings concentrate more often on action of a general character, and leave more specialized activity to sectional or subsectional groupings. UNICE acts as the authorized spokesman for the industries of the Six on all problems of general interest, or on those problems which touch upon questions relating to the common policy of the central organizations which are members of it. In so doing, UNICE does not try to cover all industrial activities, but retains for itself questions of common policy or of general interest. The specialized federations are all free to organize themselves and to act in their own field.

Specialized action is within the competence of technical organizations. In COMITEXTIL the general activities of the textile industry coexist with the particular interests of the sectors. Cotton, for instance, does not necessarily take up the same position as wool. Each of these sectors can make its own approach to the Brussels authorities. At the level of common textile interests, the organization of the entire branch intervenes. It is clear that in reality, both at the level of the central organization and of the intermediary or specialized ones, many combinations and much friction and opposition can arise. Without venturing on generalizations, one may say that the predominance of specialized organizations bears witness to the effectiveness of limited technical action. General action is difficult to define, and general agreement is often the result of compromise. To the extent that action directed to general questions is vague and fluid, it has less chance of exerting real influence. A proposal to regulate beer or jam suggested by European organizations has a better chance of being adopted by the authorities of EEC than a general trade or anti-trust policy proposed by a central organization. In the actual state of European integration, influence is exerted more effectively in the domain of technical matters than on general questions.

Finally one may raise the question of the relationship between the groups and the political parties, and their respective activity. The political parties have established only weak and ineffectual links, except for the socialist parties of the Six. This prolonged absence of the parties from the European political stage may lead to a lack of balance favouring the interest groups, with serious consequences for the future of European democracy. This situation is easily explained in the light of the parallel between the powers of the Community and the groupings at the same level: to the extent that the European Parliament lacks real power, the parties do not feel the need of widescale common action at the Community level and are content with a token presence in the Community. Indeed, their action is geared mainly to their national policies.

At the same time, some professional groupings, organized at the European level, occasionally give the impression, in their general declarations, of wishing to promote a political idea. This is why the European trade unions, as well as other groupings, periodically demand that the power of the European Parliament should be enlarged. But the situation is still far from clear. Both functions and powers are more intertwined and more fluid than on the national plane, where the action of pressure groups and of political parties occurs within a framework both global and better defined.

Within the Community, the structures of powers and of groups are in process of transformation. Moreover, the position is even more complex because a new scale is superimposed upon the national and local levels. But this new scale has not yet acquired the powers and the articulation of a national community. Indeed, in spite of a certain shift the principal and original power remains in the national units and groups. And the European groups attempt to maintain a minimum of coordination and common action between them. It appears that both in matters of policy reserved to the states, and in economic and social matters, the division of functions and activities in the European Community is still fluid and obscure.

Tendencies such as have been described here can develop in a variety of ways. However, to the extent to which developments continue in practice in the direction outlined here and to the extent to which the powers of the Community are enlarged, especially through the strengthening of the European Parliament or through the creation of an effective Senate, the division of functions between the future political formations and the pressure groups will tend to become more precise. For the moment, the groups, but above all the parties, tend to play only a marginal role in supporting integration. Active power is concentrated in the member states and in the central Council–Commission tandem of the European Communities.

19 Werner Feld

Political Aspects of Transnational Business Collaboration in the Common Market

W. Feld, 'Political aspects of transnational business collaboration in the Common Market', *International Organization*, vol. 24, no. 2, 1970, pp. 209–38.

Transnational business collaboration is a phenomenon that can be observed in many parts of the world. It may assume special significance when it is carried out on an extensive scale within an international region where an economic integration scheme is being implemented, as is the case in the European Economic Community (EEC). And indeed, a rising trend of transnational business collaboration within the EEC has become manifest during the last decade. Focusing on certain political aspects of this collaboration, this article will

1. Examine the principal objectives pursued by collaborating enterprises that require for their attainment action by the national authorities of the EEC member countries or by the community institutions.

2. Make a preliminary assessment of the effect that transnational business collaboration within the Common Market might have on political integration.

The empirical data presented in this study stems from fifty in-depth, open-ended interviews and conversations with executives of firms engaged in transnational ventures and with officials of interest groups, political parties, national administrations and the EEC. Data is also drawn from secondary sources and a variety of statistical compilations.

The nature and pattern of transnational collaboration in the Common Market

As understood in this study, transnational business collaboration refers to long-term collaborative endeavors across national borders by two or more economic entities located in different countries of the EEC. It goes beyond a mere export and import trade relationship under which orders are placed with different suppliers according to the most favorable terms available. Rather, it aims at partnership in a broad sense – ideally with a well-defined common interest – and suggests a border-crossing interlacement of efforts on the part of the entities involved in the collaboration. This interlacement must not be understood merely in terms of technical contributions to the cooperative efforts by the collaborating entities and their staffs. There is also an emotive side to such efforts which produces in the staff members concerned with collaboration a distinct feeling of being involved in a 'united or cooperative' endeavor (Friedmann and Kalmanoff, 1961, pp. 5–6). This is an important dimension of transnational business collaboration because it points to the social and human relations created by the collaboration schemes in addition to economic and administrative transactional flows.

A major motivation for the rising trend of transitional business collaboration in the ECC has been the prospect of a unified regional market offering new opportunities for increased sales and permitting cost reductions through the use of economies of scale and more efficient allocation of resources. A reinforcing factor has been the Treaty Establishing the European Economic Community (Rome Treaty) which provided a measure of assurance for a definite direction in economic development and thereby constituted a risk-reducing element in the calculations of firms considering border-crossing collaboration. Another important motivation has been and continues to be in many instances the desire to combat what is perceived occasionally as the 'economic colonization of Europe by foreign capital' (Marchal, 1968, p. 31). The main targets, of course, are the large United States companies whose European subsidiaries have been able to capture over the years an increasing share of the market in the EEC, especially in the so-called 'growth' industries. Finally, an essentially ideological motivation becomes at times apparent, namely, the assurance of the continued progress of integration, and through it the ensured future of Europe.[1]

1. These motivations emerged from the interviews with executives of firms engaged in transnational collaboration ventures and are confirmed largely by a study undertaken in 1968 by the Comité européen pour le progrès économique et social (CEPES) entitled *Grenzüberschreitende Unternehmungskooperation in der EWG* (Stuttgart: Forkel Verlag, 1968, pp. 29, 149–57). In this study 1448 cases of transnational business collaboration in Western Europe have been analysed. The cases were culled from European newspapers and professional journals dating back over several years. The information received from these sources was supplemented by a number of interviews with business executives. In 1136 cases the main activity is within

The particular objectives of the collaboration ventures vary. The closest kind of collaboration involves the joint rationalization of production either by assigning the manufacture of whole products or the production of parts of a particular item to the various plants of the partners or to a jointly owned subsidiary. The advantages of this kind of collaboration are not only opportunities for optimum production runs but also shared development costs and risks. The most frequent objective sought, however, is the establishment of joint marketing arrangements permitting the partner located in one country to use the sales and service facilities of the partner in the other country and perhaps employing joint facilities in the remaining EEC countries. Through these arrangements the potential for EEC market penetration of the collaboration partners is enhanced. A third objective of collaboration quite frequently pursued is the creation of joint research operations. In view of the extremely high cost of research in the aeronautical, electronic and chemical industries the benefits of joint research may be considerable, and the results are likely to contribute to narrowing the technological gap between Europe and America. Other objectives of the collaboration partners may be the arrangement of joint purchasing agreements and the improvement of their credit positions in order to finance the expansion of plants or long-term delivery contracts.[2] In some cases collaboration agreements have included several of the listed objectives; in other cases the exchange or acquisition of licences or other activities have become part of the agreements.[3]

The forms of transnational collaboration endeavors differ greatly. The tie between the collaborating units may be an agreement which leaves their corporate structures untouched and excludes any investment schemes between the partners. A more intense collaboration is likely to be established when the agreement includes the financial participation of one of the partners in the enterprise of the other. Finally, in a number of cases new corporate structures have been created, either in the form of a hold-

the Common Market, but transnational relations exist also with enterprises in non-EEC countries. 706 cases are concerned exclusively with intra-Common Market ventures. Thirty case studies are published in detail (see also Marchal, 1968, pp. 44–8).

2. For additional details see the CEPES study, pp. 33–52.

3. At times licence exchanges or acquisitions are forerunners to production collaboration ventures.

ing company, a jointly owned subsidiary, or two corporations – as in the case of Agfa-Gevaerts.[4]

Do wholly owned subsidiaries established in one EEC country by a parent company in another EEC country fall under the term of transnational collaboration? In such cases it may be inappropriate to speak of 'partnership' in a technical sense since a hierarchical relationship exists between the parent company and its subsidiary. Nevertheless, since it is the border-crossing flow of various transactions between the two entities (including those of a social and human nature) which has particular relevance for our study, the inclusion of wholly owned subsidiaries under the term of transnational collaboration seems warranted.

In view of the limited scope of our study it is immaterial whether enterprises engaged in transnational collaboration or parent companies of subsidiaries situated in other EEC countries are owned or controlled by firms whose main headquarters are located outside the Common Market. The salient point is that the collaboration takes place between entities located in different Common Market countries. This also furnishes us the clue as to how to relate multinational corporations to transnational collaboration in the EEC. Many of these corporations such as Philips, Nestlé, IBM, and others have been operating in the member states prior to the establishment of the Common Market. As defined by Raymond Vernon, they are 'a cluster of corporations of diverse nationality joined together by ties of common ownership and responsive to a common management strategy' (1968, p. 114). They operate therefore in the different countries basically as national companies. This fact is often politically very significant, for example, in the case of defence orders which national governments usually prefer to bestow on national enterprises. Of course, in terms of top-level management the multinational corporations act in a transnational manner. Moreover,

4. In this venture the most prominent producers of photographic equipment in Germany and Belgium, Agfa Aktien Gesellschaft and Photo Produits Gevaerts, established in each country in 1964 two new corporations, the Agfa-Gevaerts Aktien Gesellschaft in Germany and the Gevaerts-Agfa Naanloze Venootschap in Belgium, each of which has the same capitalization and is owned equally by the founding companies. Both of the new corporations have the same management and substantially the same board of directors and have taken over all activities of the old companies. A similar arrangement has been used in 1969 for the collaboration between the Dutch airplane manufacturer, Fokker, and the German producer of planes, Vereinigte Flugtechnische Werke. The two firms together employ 20,000 workers (see Communauté européenne, June 1969, no. 131, p. 19).

they can also engage operationally in border-crossing activities; an illustration would be the rationalization of production by using the best-suited manufacturing facilities in different EEC countries for a particular product. Opel, the General Motors German affiliate, has started this process by having the body of one of its models built and assembled in France while its mechanical parts come from Opel's West German factory. Philips is also beginning to do this in the production of radio sets, closing production lines in one EEC country and using longer production runs in another.[5]

The growth and scope of transnational business collaboration in the Common Market can be appreciated best by the introduction of selected statistical data. We must stress, however, that the statistical information currently available is less than satisfactory because it does not uniformly cover the full range of the collaboration endeavors and does not contain data on the size of many of the entities involved, on their sales records, capitalization and employees. Only when rather large enterprises are participants in transnational ventures – and quite a few of Europe's large corporations are – can the latter information be found periodically with relative ease.[6] Nevertheless, the statistics available are at least suggestive, and the data presented in Table 1, which covers collaboration ventures involving financial participations and the establishment of subsidiaries, indicates a definite upward trend of border-crossing endeavors, with 1968 being a banner year. The full implementation of the customs union on 1 July of that year may well have been the reason for the remarkable increase in collaboration ventures since many enterprises may have seen this as the signpost that the movement toward full economic integration had passed the point of no return. We should note, however, that over the years there have also been failures of collaboration ventures, and some wholly owned subsidiaries may have been abandoned. Since failures are rarely publicized widely, it is difficult to estimate their number. The failures were often caused by socio-psychological factors which created dissatisfaction and friction between the managements of collaborating enterprises.[7] Although these difficulties have moti-

6. *Fortune*'s annual listing since 1963 of the top 200 industrial companies outside the United States.

5. This process is a politically sensitive undertaking and requires careful balancing of activities in the countries involved.

7. These obstacles were inability to overcome the language barrier,

vated some firms to opt for national collaborations, it is evident that others have not been discouraged from engaging in new transnational endeavors.

Table 1 **Transnational collaborative ventures in the EEC**

	1959	1960	1961	1962	1963	1964	1965	1966	1967	1968
Financial participations and wholly owned and jointly owned subsidiaries Total = 1425	24	30	71	68	93	121	151	138	164	565

Adapted from Saclé (1968, p. 116); Weber (1968, p. 262; 1969, p. 392).

It is also interesting to observe the national distribution of newly established marketing and production subsidiaries as well as financial participations within the EEC during 1967 and 1968. This distribution can be seen in Tables 2 and 3. For comparison purposes we have also included British and American transnational activities in the Common Market.

The distribution of marketing subsidiaries during both years suggests a strong West German interest in the French market and a strong French interest in the German and Belgian markets. The Italians show a predilection for the French market during both years, but the Dutch shift from a major interest in the French and Belgian markets in 1967 to a predominant concern with the German market in 1968.

A somewhat different picture is revealed by the distribution of wholly and jointly owned production subsidiaries and financial participations. The German enterprises show a strong interest toward the French industrial complex, whereas the French industry is mainly drawn toward Belgium, Luxembourg and Italy; Italy, in turn, is interested only to a limited extent in expanding its industrial orbit and for this prefers France and the Belgium–Luxembourg area. The Dutch seek some industrial penetration in all EEC countries except Italy, where its interest is minimal.

In view of the United Kingdom's application for full ECC membership it is noteworthy that the figure for British marketing subsidiaries in the Common Market compares favorably with

differing conceptions of doing business, differing expectations of the monetary results of joint ventures, and fears of take-over on the part of smaller firms engaged in transnational collaboration with a larger company.

Table 2 Total of marketing subsidiaries[a] established during 1967 and 1968 within the EEC

Receiving country	Originating country															
	Germany		France		Italy		Netherlands		Belgium/Luxembourg		Total		Great Britain		United States	
	1967	1968	1967	1968	1967	1968	1967	1968	1967	1968	1967	1968	1967	1968	1967	1968
Germany		16	43	3	6	4	48	5	13	28	110	2	23	26	60		
France	10	47			6	30	8	13	4	2	28	92	7	18	30	47
Italy	14	20	3	11			3	5	1	2	21	38	4	14	15	32
Netherlands	4	23	2	4	0	7			1	3	7	37	8	13	10	21
Belgium/Luxembourg	6	20	5	31	2	5	7	30			20	86	6	16	22	46
Total	34	110	26	89	11	48	22	96	11	20	104	363	27	84	103	206

[a] Includes service organizations for 1968.
Tables 2 and 3 are adapted from Weber (1968, p. 264) and Weber (1969, p. 393 and p. 394) respectively.

Table 3 Total of production subsidiaries and financial participations[a] established during 1967 and 1968 within the EEC

Receiving country	Originating country Germany		France		Italy		Netherlands		Belgium/Luxembourg		Total		Great Britain		United States	
	1967	1968	1967	1968	1967	1968	1967	1968	1967	1968	1967	1968	1967	1968	1967	1968
Germany			1	4	0	0	3	12	1	4	5	20	10	14	29	53
France	11	40			2	12	3	8	5	9	21	69	6	30	34	54
Italy	2	5	5	14			1	0	0	4	8	23	3	18	25	31
Netherlands	3	11	2	3	0	0			0	6	5	20	3	20	19	39
Belgium/Luxembourg	2	20	7	24	2	8	10	18			21	70	7	39	34	39
Total	18	76	15	45	4	20	17	38	6	23	60	202	29	121	141	216

[a] Includes holding companies in 1968.

those of the Federal Republic of Germany (West Germany), France and the Netherlands and is substantially higher than those of Italy and the Belgium–Luxembourg complex. For production subsidiaries and financial participations British enterprises show considerably higher initiatives in the EEC than any of the member states. The 1968 figure for these British initiatives is the same as the combined total for France and West Germany and six times as high as that of Italy.[8]

The percentage increase in the establishment of United States subsidiaries in the Common Market and of financial participations by American firms in EEC enterprises between 1967 and 1968 has been substantially smaller (173 per cent) than that of EEC-based and British companies (344 and 366 per cent, respectively). In 1968, for the first time, the United States figure (422) fell below the number of intra-ECC ventures (565).[9] We must remember, however, that these figures merely record the number of joint ventures without saying anything about their size and scope.

The statistical information regarding the distribution of transnational ventures by type is also fragmentary. Data is available for intra-EEC wholly and jointly owned subsidiaries as well as for financial participations during the 1959–66 period. Of the total of 696 transnational ventures recorded during these years (Table 1) 277 are wholly owned subsidiaries (39·8 per cent), 244 are jointly owned subsidiaries (35·1 per cent), and 175 are financial participations (25·1 per cent) (Saclé, 1968, p. 116). Another source of data adds collaboration agreements without financial participation and 'failures' to the breakdown but excludes wholly owned subsidiaries. The source is the *Comité*

8. In 1967 the preferred EEC countries for British marketing subsidiaries were the Netherlands, France and Belgium–Luxembourg, respectively; for production units and financial participations they were Germany, Belgium–Luxembourg and France. In 1968 the preferred EEC countries for the former category were Germany, France and Belgium–Luxembourg and for the latter category Belgium–Luxembourg, France and the Netherlands.

9. In 1967 and 1968 the preferred EEC countries for all United States-established subsidiaries and financial participations were France, Germany and Belgium–Luxembourg although the order of rank has shifted slightly from category to category and year to year. It is noteworthy that plant and equipment expenditures by Common Market affiliates of American corporations dropped from $1437 million in 1967 to $1194 million in 1968 but increased again to $1584 million in 1968 (estimate) (see the Department of Commerce *Survey of Current Business*, September 1969, vol. 49, no. 9, p. 20.

européen pour le progrès économique et social (CEPES) study of transnational business collaboration conducted in 1968 and the data stems from 1136 existing (not necessarily new) cases in which the main activity was centred within the Common Market although some of the partners were also located outside the ECC.[10] The figures presented in Table 4 show that 44·2 per cent of the border-crossing ventures were collaborations without financial

Table 4 **Distribution of transnational collaboration ventures by type**

Country of main activity	Collaboration without financial participation	Collaboration with financial participation	Jointly owned sub-sidiaries	Failures	Total
Germany	150	40	135	12	337
France	152	40	125	1	318
Italy	106	9	59	2	176
Netherlands	48	20	88	1	157
Belgium/ Luxembourg	46	26	75	1	148
Total	502	135	482	17	1136

Adapted from the CEPES study, pp. 208–13.

participation, 11·9 per cent included such participation, 42·4 per cent were jointly owned subsidiaries, and 1·5 per cent were failures. While the above figures are merely suggestive and cannot be correlated satisfactorily, they indicate that inclusion of wholly owned subsidiaries in the CEPES study statistics would result in a substantial reduction of the percentages of the other categories (Weber, 1969, pp. 396–7).

The industrial branches most deeply involved in transnational collaboration ventures are the machinery and automobile industries, the chemical industry, and the electric and electronic manufacturers. This is not surprising since, as we have already noted, the research expenditures in the latter industries are extremely high whereas in the machinery and automobile industries the

10. See footnote 1. The number of failures reported is apt to be too low since failures are rarely publicized widely. Cf. pp. 51–4 of the study.

division of labor and the concentration on certain products are likely to reduce production costs. Of course, enterprises in other economic sectors, including especially the food processing and textile industries, have also engaged in transnational joint ventures. It seems, however, that the more technologically advanced industries with high research and development costs engage in transnational ventures to a larger extent than those which are less efficient and more labor-intensive (CEPES study, p. 206; Weber, 1969, pp. 394–5).

Despite the weakness of the statistical data it does reveal that a substantial and increasing number of enterprises in two or more EEC countries are engaged in border-crossing collaboration although the emerging network of transnational interlacement is not entirely symmetrical in terms of national participation. The effects of this growing interlacement are likely to go beyond the direct benefits sought by the collaborating enterprises and have an EEC-wide impact. In fact, the increasing use of the economies of scale where feasible, the technological improvements due to expanded research made possible by cost sharing, the enhancement of competitiveness in the enlarged market as the result of greater marketing efficiency and reduced production costs, and the more efficient utilization of resources can be seen as some of the indicators that economic integration is proceeding successfully (Balassa, 1961, pp. 10–14, 21–5, 102–4, 118–34, 163–7).[11] While 'measures designed to abolish discrimination between economic units belonging to different national states' (Balassa, 1961, p. 1) are essential for the process of economic integration, the national economies must 'grow together' (Pinder, 1969, p. 3) in order to ensure the optimal operation of the total economy of the region and its positive contribution to welfare (Balassa, 1961, pp. 11–14, Tinbergen, 1965, pp. 57–62). However, as Bela Balassa points out, to achieve total economic integration also requires unification of national, fiscal, economic, monetary and other policies. Similarly, to secure optimal conditions for transnational business ventures in the Common Market necessitates that obstacles stemming from divergent fiscal and other laws as well as from disparities in the national policies of the member states be eliminated. Since demands to that effect, although motivated by economic self-interest, require for their satisfaction in most cases action by national authorities or ECC institutions, they seek an

11. Another indicator would be an increase in economic growth. See also the interesting article by Lecourt 1968.

'authoritative allocation of values' and thereby become essentially political objectives.

Political aspects and implications

As stated in the beginning of this article our interest is centered on the political objectives of enterprises engaged in transnational business collaboration and on the effect that this kind of collaboration might have on the process of political integration. Our working hypothesis is constructed as follows: the spreading net of transnational business collaboration is likely to generate increasing pressures for the pursuit of political objectives aimed at the elimination of government-related obstacles to the optimal functioning of the collaboration ventures such as divergent national laws, regulations and policies. The more successful is the attainment of these objectives, the higher will be the extent of legal and policy harmonization in the community. Since effecting this harmonization carries with it the implicit, if not explicit, obligation of the EEC member governments not to make any further unilateral changes in the areas involved, the autonomy of the member states in a decision-making will tend to be restricted in proportion to the extent harmonization has been carried out. At the same time, the powers of the EEC institutions, especially those of the Commission of the European Communities, are apt to be enhanced, as future changes probably will only be made jointly by the community authorities and the member governments, with the former perhaps also being assigned new supervisory powers in the functional areas where harmonization has taken place. The consequence of this chain of events would be a likely rise in the level of political integration. High integration is conceived as a condition in which decisions on all or most important functions are made in the community system rather than by individual states. Other conditions of a high level of integration would be strong tendencies to assign additional functions to the ECC institutions (as well as full acceptance of the institutions and practices of the system) and acknowledgement of their legitimacy by political actors in the member states (Lindberg, 1967).

In the analysis that follows we will first identify the principal objectives of enterprises planning or engaged in transnational collaboration and examine briefly the techniques employed as well as the present status of goal attainment. This will be followed by an appraisal of forces and factors both favoring and impeding the successful attainment of these objectives. Finally, we will draw tentative conclusions as to the effect of transnational collaboration of political integration.

The political objectives

In view of the multilevel interaction between EEC institutions, national authorities and interest groups in evolving decisions and policies affecting Common Market activities demands of enterprises engaged in transnational ventures may be addressed directly to or channeled indirectly through interest groups or political parties to the national administrations as well as tō the EEC institutions. If addressed directly to or channeled through the former, interest groups, parties, and national bureaucracies perform the function of 'gatekeepers'. As such they control the flow of pertinent demands which as a consequence may be moved forward, killed, delayed or modified. Similar functions may also be carried out by European level interest group federations such as ' *Union des industries de la Communauté européenne*' (UNICE), the subdivisions of the EEC Commission, the Committee of Permanent Representatives and its working groups, and others. The Council of Ministers has the final decision-making authority, but when this body issues directives to the EEC member governments,[12] their execution depends on the bureaucracies of the national administrations which then are placed in a position to exercise for the second time their gatekeeping power. This power includes the decisional latitude as to the form and means for the implementation of the directive, the authority to interpret its meaning through which both the thrust and the details of the implementation can be influenced, and simply procrastination in carrying out the directive.

The particular demands actuated by transnational business collaboration and the specific objectives pursued vary depending on whether they are to be obtained prior to or after the conclusion of the collaboration agreements. We will begin our examination of these objectives and their attainment status by focusing on the precollaboration period.

The precollaboration period

In order to conclude collaboration agreements some kind of authorization of the national governments in whose territories the

12. When the Council of Ministers promulgates a 'regulation', it 'shall be binding in its entirety and take direct effect in each member state' (article 189, EEC treaty).

firms involved are located may be required when financial participations of one prospective partner in the enterprise of the other are to be made. In Belgium, Germany and Luxembourg the criterion of control seems to be more general; France, Italy and the Netherlands are more specific in distinguishing between the more welcome and the less desirable foreign investments. But even in the countries where the authorization is mainly a formality or is only required for special cases, the national governments tend to oppose informally substantial investments that are regarded as contrary to the 'national interest' (Balekjian, 1967, pp. 46–60). The requirement of authorization seems to contravene the aim of the EEC treaty which, in articles 67–73, insists on the progressive abolition of restrictions on capital movements within the Common Market except in the event of temporary balance-of-payment and other difficulties. Specifically, this clause seeks the elimination of any discriminatory treatment of persons or firms based on nationality or place of residence or on the place in which capital funds are to be invested.[13] However, most of the member governments are apprehensive about large outflows of capital since such outflows may hurt their social and economic policies. Moreover, they prefer these funds to be invested in their own countries in order to assure maximum employment. The concern of the governments is especially pronounced when investments in prominent national firms by companies of other EEC countries might signify a shift of control. The persistence of the national perspective, the burden of the protectionist past, and the uncertainty about the future of Europe reinforce the attitudes of the member governments which have a decided predilection for national solutions for collaborations between enterprises.[14]

The foregoing should not be construed to mean that consent for financial participations in border-crossing ventures is generally

13. The Commission has recently charged that a French law of January 1969 requiring prior authorization by the French finance ministry for *all* investments in France by foreign companies, including those from EEC countries, violates the EEC treaty. It has taken action to bring this violation before the Court of the European Communities (*Journal of Commerce*, 17 October 1969).

14. See the interesting comments by Drancourt and LePage (1968). In a survey of Dutch firms engaged in one way or another in border-crossing ventures France and Italy were singled out for the politico-psychological difficulties encountered (cf. de Jong and Alkema, 1968). These difficulties as well as the socio-psychological difficulties referred to in footnote 7 have encouraged national collaborations, thereby playing into the hands of the member governments.

refused; in fact, in most cases, permission seems to have been eventually granted.[15] It suggests, however, some reluctance on the part of the member governments toward this kind of activity and the desire to exercise control over it. For this reason in all cases requiring governmental consent its procurement has highest priority, and political influence and pressure must at times be exerted to achieve this objective without which the collaboration venture cannot be started.

One of the best illustrations of the problems encountered in obtaining governmental consent has been the conclusion of the collaboration agreement between Fiat and Citroën in October 1968. The agreement envisages joint programs of research, production, sales, purchases and investment; its legal structure includes a holding company in which Fiat has a substantial minority interest. We should note the extent and complexity of this arrangement. Fiat, the largest automobile manufacturer in Europe in terms of cars produced and an economic concern engaged in other far-reaching industrial endeavors in Italy, already controlled truck and tractor manufacturing plants (Unic and Someca) in France. Citroën, on the other hand, has control of 99 per cent of the stock of Berliet, the foremost manufacturer of heavy trucks in France; in turn, 56 per cent of Citroën is owned by Michelin, the prominent French tire manufacturer.

In Italy the leftist unions and parties opposed the collaboration agreement on the grounds that the massive outflow of capital resulting from it would harm future Italian employment and economic development prospects, especially in the south (*International Herald Tribune*, 9 October 1968; *Le Monde*, 10 October, 1968). Nevertheless, the Italian government gave its full approval to the agreement with only little persuasion on the part of Fiat.

To obtain the French government's consent was a much more difficult undertaking. The final decision was that of President Charles de Gaulle whose government announced on 10 October that it objected to the financial arrangements of the agreement on the grounds that they could unfavorably affect the independence of an important French industrial company (*International Herald Tribune*, 5, 6, 7, 8, 13, 14 October 1968). Renault and Peugeot, France's other two major automobile producers, may have had

15. No data is available for the number of refusals. In important cases as reported in the following pages the press uncovers them; in other cases the prospective partners may prefer to keep their unsuccessful efforts for collaboration hidden from any publicity.

a hand in the rejection because they feared stiffer competition as the result of the Fiat–Citroën collaboration. Some of the French unions, especially the powerful, Communist-oriented General Confederation of Labor, also strongly opposed the Fiat–Citroën agreement and expressed fear of grave repercussions on the employment of French labor (*Le Monde*, 11, 12 October 1968).

Condemnations of the French government's decision were voiced all over Western Europe, including France. The Italian government, in particular, deplored the French decision and considered it another veto in Common Market affairs (*International Herald Tribune*, 12, 13 October 1968; *Le Monde*, 12 October 1968). In France the powerful Patronat expressed support for the agreement through the issuance of a statement by its president denouncing the interference of the government in projects of collaboration between private firms.

In the meantime the chief executives of Fiat, Citroën and Michelin negotiated a revision of their agreement and engaged in a coordinated effort to persuade the top-level officials of the French government to change their attitudes. These efforts were aided by the relatively easy access which, according to press reports (*Le Monde*, 5, 13, 14, 27, 28 October 1968) and the interviews, Pierre Bercot, director-general of Citroën, and François Michelin had to Prime Minister Maurice Couve de Murville and other ministers, if not also to General de Gaulle. Mr. Umberto Agnelli (brother of the board chairman of Fiat, Giovanni Agnelli) who at that time was president of Fiat-France, the twenty-sixth largest company in France, also had many useful acquaintances in high French government circles.

On 25 October the French government reversed its initial decision after Fiat had agreed to a reduction of the planned financial participation in the joint enterprise. This reduction of Fiat's financial interest apparently dispelled French governmental fears of a threat to the ownership or the control of France's second largest auto manufacturers (*International Herald Tribune*, 29 October 1968).[16] However, the widely voiced criticism and various pressures exerted in France itself most probably played an equally

16. In response to the apprehension expressed by French labor unions mentioned earlier that Citroën would cut its work force or that an Italian-controlled company would give priority to the employment of Italian labor a communiqué issued by Citroën and Fiat pointed out that the collaboration of the two firms should permit an increase of their competitive position which was the sole guarantee of the stability of employment and future growth (*Le Monde*, 27–28 October 1968).

important role in persuading the French government to tolerate a Fiat presence in Citroën.

An example of unsuccessful political pressures exerted for the procurement of governmental approval for a transnational business venture has been the attempt by the Compagnie française des pétroles (CFP) to obtain a 30 per cent participation in the Gelsenkirchener Bergwerks-Aktien Gesellschaft (GBAG). This was to be done through the acquisition of a large bloc of shares held by the Dresdner Bank of West Germany which the bank was willing to sell. The GBAG is principally a coal mining concern which also owns petroleum resources in Libya, possesses substantial refinery installations, and participates in the control of a widespread marketing organization for gasoline and oil products. The French government supported the CFP in its endeavor and hoped for the approval by the West German government, particularly after it had consented to a collaboration venture between the powerful German chemical firm, Farbwerke Höchst, and the very important pharmaceutical French company, Roussel-Uclaf, which involved a significant financial participation of Höchst in the French firm. However, despite the fact that Charles de Gaulle and French Minister of Economics François-Xavier Ortoli lobbied strongly during their semiannual meeting with German government leaders in September 1968 for Franco–German collaboration in the petroleum business as proposed by the CFP and despite continued high-level pressure on the part of the French the West German government refused to approve it. Its professed reason was to first bring order into the fragmented petroleum market by pooling the interests of the German oil companies, with GBAG as the nucleus for a viable German petroleum industry. After a national solution for this strategically important industry had been achieved, collaboration with EEC partners could be considered. Despite these understandable reasons this is a clear case where nationalistic considerations of a member government have won out.[17]

To overcome, or at least reduce substantially, the obstacle of governmental consent for financial participations in border-crossing ventures would require the full implementation of articles 67–72 of the EEC treaty, coupled perhaps with an appropriate harmonization of economic and monetary policies of the member governments. But so far very little progress has been made in the

17. See *Le Monde de l'Economie*, 11 February 1969, for an interesting and detailed account of the CFP-GBAG affair.

full liberalization of capital movements within the Common Market and proposals by the Commission dating back to 1964 have not received approval by the Council of Ministers (*Report of the Commission Regarding the Activities of the Communities 1968*, Brussels–Luxembourg, February 1969, paragraphs 144 and 145). One proposal for a directive setting into motion the progressive abolition of restrictions on capital movements is now in the process of being submitted to the Council and companion proposals are also being prepared (*Agence Europe Bulletin*, 27 March 1969). Their fate, however, is far from certain, considering the attitudes of most member governments related earlier.[18]

We should note that the vice-chairman of the French Patronat specifically demanded in the summer of 1969 that the free movement of capital become a reality in the Common Market and that a liberal policy on foreign investments be introduced (*Agence Europe Bulletin*, 19 June 1969). On the other hand, there is little evidence that companies contemplating transnational ventures have undertaken systematic initiatives through any channels to generally seek the elimination of the consent for financial participations required by national governments.[19] They seem to accept this requirement as a fact of political life although as members of their national confederations of industry such as the Patronat they undoubtedly share the sentiments expressed by that organization.

Chief collaboration objectives

Once a transnational collaboration agreement has been successfully concluded, the main political goal of the firms engaged in border-crossing ventures becomes the creation of optimal conditions for the efficient functioning of these ventures. For this purpose, the following major objectives can be identified:

1. The complete elimination of border customs check points within the Common Market.

18. It is noteworthy that the German anti-trust agency (Kartellamt) recently pronounced itself in favor of controlling all mergers and the German government may well share this view. It based its position on the assumption that optimum production conditions may often be found in medium-sized enterprises and that the superiority of large firms in research and development is not confirmed (*Agence Europe Bulletin*, 4 and 18 June 1969).

19. Perhaps one indication is the declaration of the president of the powerful Société générale de banque (Belgium), a firm strongly engaged in transnational activities, urging the integration of the capital markets of the Six (*Agence Europe Bulletin*, 22 April 1969).

2. The harmonization of fiscal laws.

3. The harmonization of national laws setting technical standards for industrial products.

4. The creation of a European patent law.

5. The elaboration of a 'European company' statute either through Community regulation or the promulgation of identical national laws.

6. The liberal application of the EEC anti-trust laws.[20]

These objectives are also supported by many firms not engaged in transnational ventures. However, they are especially significant for collaborating firms because of the very direct effect that their attainment would have on the economic results of the collaboration.

It is difficult to determine in detail the methods used by European companies for the presentation of their demands and the lobbying efforts undertaken in support of them. European business executives prefer to conceal such activities as much as possible and like to claim that they are interested only in economic matters and not in politics.[21] Nevertheless, companies engaged in border-crossing collaboration have a special opportunity in the pursuit of their objectives inasmuch as they can coordinate their demands addressed directly to or channeled indirectly through the national and EEC authorities. The benefits of such coordination can be all the more significant when collaboration ventures include firms in more than two EEC countries or when firms such as Höchst Farbwerke and others are participating in several of these ventures. While the extent of such

20. These major objectives are suggested by the CEPES study and survey cited in footnote 1 and are in general confirmed by the interviews and conversations of the author and by de Jong and Alkema (1968). Collaborating firms are naturally also interested in promoting the coordination of the economic and monetary policies of the member governments since such coordination would have beneficial effects on their collaboration ventures. However, this interest has not evolved into use of their specific major objectives. We should note that the Commission has submitted proposals for such coordination to the Council of Ministers (*Agence Europe Bulletin*, 13 February 1969). While member governments agree in principle, they also manifest various reservations and cite difficulties flowing mainly from their desire to retain their full autonomy over these policy areas.

21. For a general discussion of tactics used by large companies in Europe and their capacity to influence governmental and community decisions see Meynaud and Sidjanski (1967, pp. 129–204); and Feld (1966).

coordination cannot be fully ascertained, the interviews conducted with executives of collaborating firms suggest that it is practised on a fairly large scale although with varying degrees of intensity. Since enterprises in France, Germany and the Netherlands have been in the forefront of initiating and operating transnational collaboration ventures, they have also been particularly active in elaborating coordinated demands. Companies collaborating in production and marketing schemes are especially interested in the coordination of demands since they are prime beneficiaries of favorable responses. But joint research ventures may also benefit, particularly from advances toward uniform patent protection.

From the interviews the impression was gained that mainly large companies are involved in the coordination of demands. When wholly or jointly owned subsidiaries located in EEC countries other than the company headquarters are small, it is usually considered best to leave them out of the coordination scheme as under these conditions the politcal benefits have proven to be minimal.

We should note that when presenting coordinated demands, aggressiveness in content and form is generally avoided. Rather, the demands are couched in more or less academic language, and a climate of restraint and objectivity is regarded as beneficial for their discussion. In other words, no obvious and strong political pressures are used in the pursuit of these demands. For the successful presentation of coordinated demands the business executives interviewed considered the national level most important and the highest political level as most rewarding (witness the Citroën–Fiat affair).

When national interest groups are tied in with the pursuit of the above objectives there is consensus among the business executives interviewed that coordinated demands receive much more effective backing by specialized groups, for example, associations of chemical firms, than by the more general organizations such as the French Patronat or the Federation of Netherlands Industry. The fact that the membership of these two organizations is highly diffuse makes it difficult, if not impossible, to generate concentrated support for demands favoring only particular industries.

On the European level the specialized confederations, numbering more than 300, are also considered more potent to press coordinated demands of collaborating firms than UNICE although we should note that the effectiveness of these confederations varies widely.[22] The main task of these confederations is to ensure that these demands become official proposals or positions of the Commission. For example, the European Federation of Mechanical and Metal working Industries recently approached the Commission in order to urge liberal interpretation of the community anti-trust laws for collaborating ventures even if they constitute a certain restriction of free competition (*Agence Europe Bulletin*, 1 February 1969).

In a few cases collaborating firms have established their own liaison bureaux in Brussels and some large corporations like Fiat or Shell maintain either their exclusive offices or permanent representatives in that city. Their basic functions are more or less the same as those performed by the confederations, but they are able to provide more individual treatment for the demands of their principals, thereby enhancing in some instances the potential for success.

Political parties appear to be employed only to a very small extent for the channeling of coordinated demands. However, a few companies insist on 'full orchestration' of the lobbying efforts, and it may be assumed that these efforts include parties in EEC countries where they have a measure of effectiveness in influencing the governmental decision-making process.

The interviews with executives of firms engaged in transnational collaboration reveal that fiscal harmonization is considered a prime objective[23] and that a great deal of energy is spent seeking this objective. This is not surprising because the disparities in fiscal tax structures and rates have a multiplicity of damaging effects on the functioning of border-crossing ventures. They are in part responsible for the continued existence of customs check points along the national borders despite the elimination of internal tariffs because certain taxes such as value added taxes and others have to be levied on goods entering a member state, and value added taxes may have to be reimbursed for goods leaving a country where such a tax exists.

In the last few years harmonization has been enhanced through the introduction of similarly constructed value added taxes in all member states except Italy. However, because the application of this tax tends to accentuate inflationary pressures that already

22. Some of the confederations seem to provide mainly a center for entertainment for visitors from the national groups with little serious work being accomplished.

23. See also de Jong and Alkema (1968, p. 156) whose survey of Dutch companies involved in transnational activities tends to agree with this view.

exist, Belgium has postponed application until 1 January 1971, and Italy has delayed introduction and application until 1972 (*Agence Europe Bulletin*, 1, 17 October 1969).[24] We should note, moreover, that the tax rates in the member countries are not uniform. Therefore, if the costly delays in the movement of goods across the borders are to be eventually eliminated, these rates must be made uniform. Moreover, since the value added taxes are consumer taxes, a clearinghouse mechanism must be developed through which member governments can remit tax funds levied on goods shipped to another EEC state to the government of that state. The Commission is now in the process of studying procedures and elaborating proposals for the progressive unification of value added tax rates and the necessary mechanism to permit the elimination of border delays for the adjustment of these taxes (*Agence Europe Bulletin*, 21 April 1969). Obviously, this will be a long, drawn-out project whose success is anything but certain at this time.

Differing national tax structures and tax rates on a variety of industrial products also impose burdens on border-crossing collaboration from a different angle. For example, the tax rates applied by France and Germany on the weight per axle of trucks vary greatly. This affects unfavorably the rationalization potential of joint production and marketing arrangements between Maschinenwerke Augsburg Nürnberg (MAN) and Saviem, prominent truck manufacturers in Germany and France. These arrangements aim at the production of heavy trucks by MAN and of lighter trucks by Saviem as well as at a division of labor in the manufacturing of parts. Both MAN and Saviem have lobbied in their respective countries for the equalization of the pertinent national tax systems regarding utility vehicles, an objective which has received strong support by the Commission and by the European Parliament (*Agence Europe Bulletin*, 7 May 1969). However, at least so far, a pertinent directive proposed by the Commission has not been adopted by the Council.

Other impediments of a fiscal nature for transnational ventures include the differing national taxes and tax rates applicable to mergers, financial participations, and dissolutions of enterprises and the double imposition of taxes on company headquarters and subsidiaries located in different EEC countries. The Commission has submitted to the Council of Ministers proposals for two

24. The Netherlands had to impose temporary price controls after the value added tax became effective.

directives which would establish a uniform tax structure and eliminate existing discriminations against transnational ventures. So far no action has been taken by the council since the national governments have expressed a variety of reservations (*Agence Europe Bulletin*, 16 January, 27 May 1969).[25]

Equally serious obstacles for transnational ventures emerge from divergent national laws setting technical standards for industrial products. Returning to the MAN-Saviem collaboration, it is obvious that different French and German standards for brakes, lights, body size, etc., can be frustrating and harmful to the full rationalization of production and marketing. The two companies have elaborated and presented coordinated demands for the elimination of these disparities to the pertinent French and West German ministries. In addition, the Franco–German Committee for Industrial Cooperation has been tied in with the efforts of the two firms. In the meantime the Commission has worked up a general program for eliminating the disparities of national laws with respect to industrial products which has been accepted by the Council of Ministers and which is to be implemented through council directives by the end of 1970 (*Agence Europe Bulletin*, 26 March 1969).[26] Clearly, without uniform technical standards (including health regulations) there can be no elimination of border control points and consequently no true Common Market with full freedom of movement of goods.[27]

25. See also Agence Europe Document no. 519, 'European Commission guidelines on the tax system applicable to shares and interest in debentures', and Mailander (1968) For a comprehensive discussion of this problem see the reports by Kauffman and Hutchings, (1968). We should note that the last kind of disparity in fiscal laws may at times constitute also an incentive for transnational ventures in order to take advantage of a particular low tax rate in one of the member states. Collaborations in the banking field involving movements of capital and the establishment of holding companies come to mind. But most collaborations are concerned with movements of goods across borders in one way or another and therefore full fiscal harmonization remains a preferred objective.

26. As far as standards for pharmaceutical products are concerned, the Council had already adopted a harmonization directive in 1965, but this directive has not been implemented by some of the member governments (*Agence europe bulletin*, 18 April 1969).

27. Some progress has been made in the spring of 1969 in the harmonization of national customs regulations after many efforts dating back to 1962 had failed. The EEC Council of Ministers adopted a number of directives for the member governments which constitute, when translated into national legislation, at least the beginning of a 'European' customs code (see *Le Monde*, 4 March 1969).

The creation of a European patent law has made progress, partially as the result of energetic demands made by Agfa–Gevaert and supported by a number of pharmaceutical and chemical companies in the EEC. Although patents are not covered by the EEC treaty, the Council of Ministers, acting in the capacity of the representatives of the Six, agreed in March 1969 to initiate negotiations aiming at two multilateral conventions through which inventors in the EEC and other Western European countries would receive uniform patent protection and which would eventually create a truly 'European' patent (*Agence Europe Bulletin*, 3, 5 March 1969).[28]

Less promising than the developments in the patent field are the prospects for elaborating a common statute for a 'European company'. Although transnational collaboration agreements have been successfully concluded without the existence of such a law (in fact, most collaborations do not aim at a merger) its absence suggests a climate of legal insecurity which in an indirect way is likely to act as a brake on the trend toward border-crossing joint ventures and thus hinder mergers where they are desired (Mailander, 1968; CEPES study, pp. 191–5).

One major source of difficulties in evolving common rules for a European company is the attitude of the labor unions. The German Federation of Labor and most German political parties will support a European company law only if it does not reduce the labor participation rights presently existing in Germany. The labor unions in the other five member states disagree with the Germans on these demands to varying degrees.[29] Until the labor unions can find a compromise solution that is also acceptable to the employers and the national governments, no progress can be expected on the question of the European company. But even if the problem of labor participation were solved, another hurdle, the very complex registration system of shares in Italy which is strongly defended by the Italian government as a means of tax control, would have to be overcome before success could come within sight.

In the application of the anti-trust provisions of the community

28. For details of the planned conventions see *Agence Europe Bulletin*, 12 February 1969. For a discussion of a related problem, the harmonization of trademark laws, see Wertheimer (1967).

29. See *Le Monde*, 6 and 7 December 1968, *Der Spiegel*, 28 October 1968 (22nd Year, no. 44), pp. 46–70, and Vetter (1968). The Italian labor unions oppose the labor participation provisions because they consider 'sitting on both sides of the fence' would reduce their bargaining power.

treaties the Commission has a means to promote and strengthen the integrationist tendencies produced by transnational collaboration agreements. In fact, the attitude of the Commission is basically liberal and sympathetic to these agreements because it recognizes their value for the process of integration and the need for sufficiently large units that can compete effectively with the American business giants. However, the views of the commissioners are not uniform in this respect, and in the opinion of several of the business executives interviewed the overall tenor of the decisions handed down by the Commission is ambiguous. In an official declaration issued in July 1968 the Commission welcomed specifically the collaboration between small and medium-sized enterprises inasmuch as it would contribute to an increase of their capabilities and competitive positions in an enlarged market. With respect to the collaboration of large enterprises, however, the backing of the Commission was more qualified (*Journal officiel des Communautés européennes*, No. C75, 29 July 1968; see also the *Report of the Commission Regarding the Activities of the Communities 1968*, paragraphs 22–33). Clearly, the Commission opposes all collaboration agreements which contain restrictions on the economic interchange between the member countries.[30]

The effects on political integration

We had hypothesized earlier that the effect of transnational business collaboration in the Common Market on the process of political integration would depend on the degree of achievement of the major political objectives set by firms engaged in such collaboration, in particular those aiming at fiscal and legal harmonization. We also assumed that the closer this collaboration was, the more pressures for goal attainment it would generate. We will now examine the factors and forces which tend to favor goal attainment and those which impede it. It is fair to assume that the larger the circle of persons in the member countries having a stake in the achievement of the objectives of the col-

30. For an analysis of pertinent Commission decisions see Waelbroeck (1968). Cf. also Meynaud and Sidjanski (1967, pp. 58–69). An additional problem for transnational collaboration stems from the double application of community and national anti-trust provisions where the latter exist. For example, Germany pursues the 'doctrine of two barriers' and sometimes the German anti-trust provisions tend to be more restrictive than the application of the community provisions. German firms engaged in transnational collaboration would like to see the community anti-trust law be predominant.

laborating firms and the more the politically powerful among them are committed to European values and to the procedures and norms of conduct of the community system, the better are the prospects for goal attainment. But equally important, if not more so, are likely to be the responses of other influential political actors in the community to the demands of transnational ventures.

Evidently, the more enterprises that are engaged in transnational collaboration, the greater is the circle of potential beneficiaries if the objectives delineated in the preceding section are attained. But these enterprises, whose number is relatively small when compared with the total number of business enterprises existing in the EEC countries, are not the only ones which would benefit. Thousands of other companies in the member countries which have accepted the Common Market rather than their national markets as the proper framework for their marketing activities would also be beneficiaries. In other words, the collaborating enterprises would have acted as something of a special shock force for the benefit of much of the EEC business community, and the resulting allocation of values would be perceived as important by an appreciable number of persons in the community.

One could also be tempted to argue that the circle of potential beneficiaries would be greatly enlarged if savings in the cost of production and marketing resulting from the elimination of border check points and the harmonization of fiscal and other laws were passed on to the consumers in the form of lower prices. However, whether these cost savings would lead to price reduction is not certain. Some doubt for such a development arises from the insistence of the collaborating firms on a liberal application of the community anti-trust provisions. Moreover, certain European studies made recently on industrial concentration where cost savings may be expected suggest that no correlation exists between increased industrial concentration and the formation of prices. On the other hand, these studies disclose a positive correlation between the degree of industrial concentration and the payment of higher wages (Phlips, 1969; de Jong, 1969, esp. Table 3). As a consequence one could expect a definite enlargement of the circle of beneficiaries by adding the employees of firms engaged in border-crossing collaborations.[31]

31. The number of employees of fifteen EEC-based enterprises engaged in transnational ventures of different types that are listed among the fifty largest corporations outside the United States totals a respectable 2,074,931 (*Fortune*, 15 August 1969, vol. 80, no. 3, p. 107). The total civilian labor force in the EEC is nearly seventy-four million.

But despite this rise in wages that is likely to be engendered by the expansion of transnational business collaboration the attitudes of the labor unions toward this collaboration have been less than favorable. We have already mentioned in the discussion of the Fiat–Citroën agreement their concern about the possible loss of jobs – transnational ventures may exploit labor cost differentials in the member states – and about the uncontrolled outflow of national capital resulting from these ventures. We have also pointed out their critical positions toward the project of a 'European company' statute. Some of the unions, especially those of the Left, also have ideological grounds for their opposition to transnational business ventures which in their opinion may result in capitalistic monopolies entirely devoid of any state control (de Pamphilis, 1968).

While these concerns and fears tend to lower the unions' support level for the objectives of transnational ventures, the latter have also stimulated the pursuit of certain union goals which indirectly might strengthen this support. In response to expanding transnational collaboration by business enterprises the unions have been spurred to turn their attention increasingly to trans-national bargaining in order to 'level up' labor's benefits. Although it is most likely difficult at present to bargain on a community-wide basis with respect to wages because the social legislation in the member states varies widely and therefore social benefits and charges differ from country to country, the unions have already begun to meet with employers in the Common Market to discuss the harmonization of working conditions and retraining programs across national boundaries.[32] Therefore, since improved operating conditions for transnational ventures may lead to higher wages and better working conditions, it may be in the unions' interest to support the political objectives of collaborating enterprises, at least on a selective basis. Moreover, the eventual harmonization of social legislation may also serve the long-range interests of labor and this may be achieved with greater ease when considered as a natural sequel to the harmonization measures sought by transnational business collaboration.

32. These topics were discussed, for example, during meetings held in 1967 and 1969 between Christian and Socialist unions and management staff members of Philips (*Agence Europe Bulletin*, 4 July 1969). In 1968 an agreement was concluded between the EEC Comité des organisations professionelles agricoles (COPA) and the Christian and Socialist union confederations which covers working hours and rest periods of agricultural workers (see *European Community*, June 1969, no. 124, p. 18).

While it was difficult to determine during the interviews the precise attitudes toward European unity held by executives of firms engaged in transnational ventures, a large majority, including French executives, seems to have a substantial commitment to the community system and to European unification although much skepticism was expressed about the latter's realization. Some of the chief executives clearly are acknowledged 'Europeans'. One example is Giovanni Agnelli, chairman of the board of Fiat, who not only has expressed himself on many occasions with great vigor for moving European unification forward but also has explicitly stated that the collaboration with Citroën was motivated strongly by this goal (*International Herald Tribune*, 17 January 1969). Another example is Karl Winnacker, president of Höchst, who is equally interested in the pursuit of this goal and who is surrounded by a remarkably Europe oriented top leadership group (*L'Express*, 9–15 December 1968).

Commitment to European values may also be triggered or deepened as the result of the continuous transactional flows between collaborating firms and the necessary interaction of their management and technical staffs. The coordination of the joint activities is usually carried out through a network of committees and working groups composed of an equal number of officials from the collaborating firms. Depending on the size of the firms and the range of the joint activities, fifty to two hundred officials may be involved in the coordinating operations. Meetings of the committees and working groups are held at least once a month, sometimes more often, and the meeting places generally alternate between the headquarters of the collaborating firms.[33] Although the interviews indicated that frictions and frustrations are not infrequent, especially because of diverging viewpoints on technical matters, the development of a feeling of belonging to a group with shared goals eases communications between the individuals involved and sometimes leads to close personal relationships. Because many members of this group perceive their activities as related to the framework of the Common Market, one can observe among them an increased identification with European values and ideologies, a process which may be seen as some kind of political socialization toward 'European' consciousness. To a great extent, the members of this group 'socialize

33. The committees of Agfa-Gevaert meet at a motel midway between the locations of their respective headquarters. Significantly, the name of the motel is Euromotel.

themselves' (Dawson and Prewitt, 1969, pp. 38–39; Almond and Verba, 1965, pp. 266–306).[34] However, a positive though subtle influence toward the adoption of 'European' values and norms may also be exerted by leaders of companies engaged in joint ventures who are outspoken in their support for European integration and who then take on the role of 'socializing agents'. This group, which is bound to grow in members as the number of transnational ventures expands, may develop into a special type of a Europe oriented business elite. Since many members of this group are relatively young, their positions of power are likely to be still on the rise and therefore their outlook and influence may in time lend increasing, potent support to the full attainment of the objectives pursued by border-crossing business ventures.

Summarizing our discussion of the last few pages, we find that a substantial number of potential beneficiaries in the member states have a stake in the attainment of the political objectives of transnational ventures and that this number is increasing. While many of the potential beneficiaries are conscious of this stake, others, especially the workers, may not be. The labor unions, although looking askance at border-crossing collaboration, may emerge as reluctant allies because of partly converging interests. Many members of the business elite involved in transnational ventures are committed to European values and to the community system procedures and norms of conduct. Some of them are politically powerful and their number is likely to expand. Nevertheless, despite this array of forces favoring the attainment of the objectives of collaborating firms and despite the support of the EEC institutions we have seen that progress has been slow and spotty, especially as far as fiscal and legal harmonization have been concerned. What seem to be the underlying reasons? Although firm data is scarce, certain suggestions come to mind.

We have already alluded several times to the nationalistic orientations of the member governments and their strong penchant for continued autonomy despite repeated broad declarations over the years by at least five of these governments that they strongly favor European unification. Specific examples were the attitude of the French government toward the Fiat–Citroën agreement and that of the German government toward the attempted

34. Individuals socializing themselves adopt, thereby, new values and beliefs of a political nature.

CFP participation in the GBAG. Another example involves the Italian government which in 1968 imposed a national solution for collaboration on the chemical industry when it permitted the state-controlled Ente nazional di idrocarburi (ENI) and Instituto per la riconstruzione industriale (IRI) conglomerates to take control of Italy's foremost chemical enterprise, the privately owned Montecatini–Edison group. This effectively prevented any possible transnational collaboration of Montecatini–Edison with chemical companies of other EEC countries, collaboration which could have been used for the infusion of needed new capital and for the improvement of Montecatini-Edison's lagging competitive position (*Le Monde*, 15 October 1968).[35]

These actions and other manifestations of national preference on the part of the EEC member governments stem in part from the attitudes of many civil servants in the national ministries who, as pointed out earlier, exercise far-reaching gatekeeping functions. Motivated, perhaps unconsciously, by the fear of reduced functions with a corresponding loss of their positions of power in a Europe where the important decisions would be made on a higher level than the national plane, they seem to be in no hurry to move the harmonizing and coordinating activities in the EEC forward. Being technical experts in the preparation of legislative and administrative proposals, they can find many reasons why the harmonization of specific laws and policies should be delayed. Moreover, the *status quo* is always easier to defend than are reasons for innovation (Loch, 1969; Kriedemann, 1969).[36] Even if some members of the national parliaments were really enthusiastic and were willing to push through legislation needed to aid transnational collaboration in the Common Market, they usually do not possess the necessary staff nor the expert knowledge to prepare the required legislative proposals. Thus, they are at the mercy of the national bureaucrats who, if they want to, can easily and subtly sabotage the wishes of the legislators. With respect to these problems Franz-Josef Strauss, the West German

35. Private shareholders of Montecatini-Edison continue to oppose the take-over but with only limited success (see *Frankfurter Allgemeine Zeitung*, 29 April 1969).

36. The attitude of national civil servants is highly complex and should be a fruitful field for further research. Officials in the EEC countries (except France and Italy) with whom the author had conversations stressed at first their support for European unification. But later in the conversations a variety of reservations and objections appeared, almost reversing their first views.

minister of finance and a man who should know, made the following significant comments:

Sometimes short-sighted ambition of nationalistically oriented bureaucracies as well as lack of decisiveness on the part of responsible politicians leads to an overgrowth of egocentric interests. We observe not without apprehension that after the dismantlement of the tariff walls new national paper walls are being erected surreptitiously through the issuance of drawn-out indeterminable regulations. The re-nationalization of ideas is followed by the re-nationalization of secret bureaucratic decisions. With the slogan of the sovereignty of the states and the pursuit of their own interests, it is quite easy to manipulate [the bureaucratic schemes] (1968).[37]

While the national bureaucracies may intentionally seek to delay or sabotage the harmonization of fiscal and other pertinent laws, the major political parties and most parliamentary deputies seem generally to lack the positive will to push ahead rapidly and energetically with this task despite the fact that most of the party programs emphasize varying degrees of support for European unification. In fact, the parliamentary party of the Christian Democratic Union/Christian Socialist Union specifically advocates the coordination of economic and fiscal policies and the harmonization of the appropriate laws (*Süddeutsche Zeitung*, 20 June 1969). But these expressions of support must be seen in the context of how they actually affect the outcome of concrete elections. Studies made on the role that the European questions actually played in elections (the Netherlands elections in 1967 and the West German elections in 1965) suggest that these questions aroused little interest and that their impact on voter motivation was minimal (De Vree, 1967; Jäger, 1965). A somewhat different situation existed during the French presidential elections in 1965 when the Common Market crisis provoked by President de Gaulle's boycott of community proceedings caused serious apprehension among the French farmers about the future of the common agricultural policy and thereby raised the level of interest in European questions. Nevertheless, it was the consensus of the persons interviewed by the author that in the election of a candidate to political office his support for political unification, or specifically for fiscal and legal harmonization, would have practically no influence on the outcome of his election. This should

37. It is noteworthy that in Germany young officials are beginning to be interested in being assigned to ministerial sections dealing with European questions. This may suggest a slow change of bureaucratic attitudes.

not be taken to signify that the majorities of the electorates in the EEC countries are 'anti-European', but simply that other issues are decisive.[38]

We must also point out that parliamentary deputies are only infrequently urged by firms engaged in transnational collaboration ventures to press their demands energetically, as these firms do not use party channels often for the promotion of demands. On the other hand, small businessmen who frequently regard transnational collaboration coupled with industrial concentration as a threat to their survival and for whom the national markets remain the proper framework for their activities request protection, sometimes vociferously, in parliamentary committees, professional organizations, and from the national governmental agencies (Gingembre, 1968). For these businessmen fiscal divergence and legal disharmony, especially as far as technical standards are concerned, constitute important protective devices against competition from other EEC countries. Since the claims of small businessmen are often permeated by nationalistic overtones, they are not easily disregarded by the political parties.

One may wonder why the business elites interested in obtaining optimal conditions for transnational ventures have not been able to mobilize sufficient support for the objectives among the national administrative and political elites to speed up goal attainment. In our discussion of the presentation of demands by collaborating firms we have mentioned that strong pressures and bluntness are avoided. We should add that these demands clearly fall into the category of what Ernst B. Haas calls 'pragmatic-interest polictics'. The interests pursued are pragmatic and generally not reinforced with deep ideological or philosophical commitment. Although many top-level executives in enterprises

38. It is noteworthy that the strong backing of European unity prominently displayed in the election program of French presidential candidate Alain Poher, announced six days before the first election run in 1969, did not gain him additional votes; in fact, his percentage of votes received during this election run was substantially lower than that indicated in the public opinion polls taken just prior to the announcement although no causality between the announcement and the poor election result can be assumed. (*Le Monde*, 28 May 1968, and *Le Soir*, 2 June 1969).

A number of new parties dedicated chiefly to European unification have sprung up during the last few years, but they have been able to attract only a tiny number of voters. For an account of two such creations, the Europa Partei and the Parti socialiste européen, see *Agence Europe Bulletin*, 19 May 1969. In the West German elections of September 1969 the Europa Partei received less than 0·5 per cent of the votes cast.

engaged in transnational collaboration are committed to European values and the community system, they are not prepared to man the ramparts for European political unity. Rather, they accept gradual, incremental progress and seek to obtain their goals through persistent but undramatic efforts. Thus the pursuit of their objectives can be slowed down or halted without too much difficulty. As Haas has pointed out, 'a political process that is built and projected from pragmatic interests . . . is bound to be a frail process susceptible to reversal' (1968, p. xxxiii).

On the other hand, the reluctance of the national bureaucracies to move ahead promptly with legal harmonization and policy co-ordination is not only related to the pursuit of their own vested interests but is buttressed often by a strong nationalistic ideology. The same may be said of the fears of small businessmen in the EEC to accept the Common Market as the proper framework for their business activities. This and the other factors discussed above seem to be largely responsible for the slow progress made so far by those who would like to see the political obstacles to the effective functioning of transnational business collaboration removed as quickly as possible. They suggest, at least for the time being, essentially negative responses to the demands of transnationally collaborating enterprises by important political actors whose cooperation is needed for full goal attainment.

Conclusions

From the foregoing analysis we can conclude that while the increasing rate of transnational business collaboration in the Common Market over the last ten years has produced a more intensive degree of economic integration, the effect on political integration as measured by a rise in the powers of the EEC institutions has been slight thus far, producing only small incremental advances. The main effect has been strongly motivated assistance, even leadership by collaborating firms for bringing about the initial steps toward fiscal and legal harmonization. If the harmonization process is permitted to move forward, the autonomy of the member governments is likely to be whittled down and larger incremental advances in political integration can be expected. We have already observed that legal harmonization and perhaps also policy coordination by the member governments carries with it at least the implicit obligation of no further unilateral changes; as a consequence, the powers of the EEC authorities would be gradually enhanced as the process of harmonization and coordination progresses. In addition, the development of a European patent law may result in the assignment of new functions and powers to the EEC institutions, either de facto or through multilateral conventions between the member states.

We should also recognize that certain by-products of transnational business collaboration may have favorable implications for the future progress of political integration. Increasing numbers of firms and persons have both a direct and indirect stake in the harmonization measures and other objectives of collaborating enterprises. As pertinent harmonization measures are instituted, many of them are likely to perceive the continuation of these measures as vested interests. They therefore constitute an increasingly powerful force which, if it could be fully mobilized, would probably resist attempts to lower the level of political integration by reinstituting the full autonomy of the member governments in the fiscal and other areas of concern. If such attempts were made, they might well develop into domestic political issues in the member states similar to those raised by the French farmers in 1965 following de Gaulle's boycott of the ECC institutions. As a consequence, the European question may assume greater significance in the outcome of forthcoming elections which, in turn, might create a greater interest in integration and the community system by elected political elites and elicit more genuine support for its institutions, procedures and norms.

Another by-product with potentially favorable implications for political integration is the gradual emergence of an expanding, relatively young, Europe oriented business elite as the result of the subtle political socialization process operative in the coordinating mechanisms of collaborating entities. While it is impossible to determine the precise effect of this elite on the progress of political integration, its members are likely to perceive having a vested interest in the maintenance of the integration level achieved. In addition, they may be in time influential, through cross communication with other elites, in soliciting support by the member governments for harmonization measures and for the community system in general. A concomitant contribution may be a rise in the legitimacy level of the community institutions and procedures.

Preliminary and very tentative figures indicate that the upward trend of transnational business collaboration has continued in

1969.[39] As the conditions for transnational business collaboration improve as the result of greater fiscal and other harmonization measures and the eventual disappearance of border control points, this trend is apt to receive additional impetus. In turn, the clamor for full implementation of these measures is likely to rise further. Eventually, however, a plateau of satisfactory conditions for transnational collaboration ventures may be reached. At that time the stimulus for political integration will cease to operate and the main concern will be the maintenance of the level of integration attained. Although the incentive for integration growth will have disappeared, certain effects, such as the increased legitimacy level of the EEC institutions and procedures and the greater commitment of business and perhaps other elites to European values, would probably persist and remain influential for possible further progress of political integration in the future. Moreover, the acquisition of vested interests in a certain level of integration would constitute a bulwark against regression or dismantlement of the community system and enhance its stability.

39. Important examples are the collaboration agreements between l'Union chimique belge, the Dutch chemical group Algemene kunstzijde unie (AKU), and the German Glanzstoff Aktien Gesellschaft; the Dutch steel maker Hoogovens and the German steel firm of Hösch; and Fokker Aircraft of the Netherlands and Vereinigte Flugtechnische Werke of Bremen, Germany (see *Le Monde*, 16–17 March 1969, *Agence Europe Bulletin*, 24 March 1969, *International Herald Tribune*, 13 May 1969, and *Süddeutsche Zeitung*, 17 July 1969). However, national collaborations and mergers also continue to show a very strong trend. Recent examples are the Volkswagen-Neckarsulmer Motorenwerke merger and the Rhone-Poulenc acquisitions (*International Herald Tribune*, 10 June 1969). For explanations of this phenomenon see de Jong 1968, especially p. 197, and Jürgensen and Berg (1968).

References

ALMOND, G. A. and VERBA, S. (1965), *Civic Culture: Political Attitudes and Democracy in Five Nations*, Little Brown.

BALEKJIAN, W. H. (1967), *Legal Aspects of Foreign Investment in the European Economic Community*, Manchester University Press.

BALASSA, B. (1961), *The Theory of Economic Integration*, Irwin.

DAWSON, R. E., and PREWITT, K. (1969), *Political Socialization: An Analytic Study*, Little Brown.

DE JONG, H. W. (1968) 'Specialisations, concentrations et Marché Commun', *Revue de l'économie du Centre-Est*, vol. 10, no. 46, pp. 192–213.

DE JONG, H. W. (1969), 'De concentratiebeweging in de Westeuropese Economie', *Economisch – Statistische Berichten*, 22, 29 January, 5, 12 February.

DE JONG, H. W. and ALKEMA, M. (1968) 'Communications', *Revue du Marché Commun* no. 109, pp. 143–55.

DE PAMPHILIS, N. (1968), 'Azione sindicale e concentrazioni industriali', *Conquiste del lavoro*, vol. 21, no. 47, p. 7.

DE VREE, J. K. (1967), 'Le thème européen dans les elections générales de 1967 au Pays-Bas', Europa Institute, University of Amsterdam.

DRANCOURT, M., and LE PAGE, H. (1968), 'Obstacles psychologiques (et politiques) au concentrations et fusions intercommunautaires', *Revue du Marché Commun*, no. 109, pp. 131–42.

FELD, W. (1966) 'National economic interest groups and policy formation in the EEC', *Polit. Sci. Q.* vol. 81, no. 3, pp. 392–41.

FRIEDMANN, W. G., and KALNAROFF, G. (eds.) (1961) *Joint International Business Ventures*, Columbia University Press.

GINGEMBRE, M. L. (1968) 'La création d'entreprises à l'échelle européene: l'avenir des petites et moyennes entreprises, Free University in Brussels, mineograph.

HAAS, E. B. (1968) *The Uniting of Europe*, Stanford University Press.

JÄGER, A. (1965) 'Das Thema "Europa" in Bundestags wahlkampf', University of Cologne.

JÜRGENSEN, H., and BERG, H. (1968) *Konzentration and Wettbewerb in Gemeinsamen Market – Das Beispel der Automobilindustrie*, Vanderhok and Ruprecht.

KAUFFMANN, J., and HUTCHINGS, G. (1968), *Revue du Marché Commun*, no. 109, pp. 749–74.

KREIDEMANN, H. (1969), 'Die Gemeinschaft ist in grössten Bedrängnis' *Europaische Gemeinschaft*, October, pp. 6–7.

LECOURT, R. (1968), 'Concentrations et fusions d'entreprises: facteurs d'intégration européenne', *Revue du Marché Commun*, no. 109, pp. 6–24.

LINDBERG, L. N. (1967), 'The European Community as a political system: notes toward the construction of a model', *J. Common Market Studies*, vol. 5, no. 4, pp. 344–87.

LOCH, T. M. (1969), 'Warten auf ein Wunder', *Europäische Gemeinschaft*, October, pp. 4–5.

MAILANDER, K. P. (1968), 'Mergers and acquisitions in the EEC: problems under corporate tax and anti-trust law', *New York University J. International Law and Politics*, vol. 1, no. 11, pp. 19–30.

MARCHAL, A. (1968), 'Necessité économique des fusions et concentrations intracommunautaires', *Revue du Marché commun*, no. 109.

MEYNAUD, J., and SIDJANSKI, D. (1967), *L'Europe des affaires: Role et structure des groupes*, Payot.

PHLIPS, L. (1969), 'Effets économiques de la concentration industrielle; essai d'analyse empirique', mimeograph.

PINDER, J. (1969) 'Comecon: An East European Common Market', paper presented at the Semaine de Bruges.

SACLE, R. (1968) 'Cooperations – concentrations et fusions d'enterprise dans la CEE', *Revue du Marché Commun*, no. 109.

STRAUSS, F. J. (1968), 'Phrasen schaffen kein Europa', *Europäische Gemeinschaft*, December.

TINBERGEN, J. (1965) *International Economic Integration*, Elsevier.

VERNON, R. (1968), 'Economic sovereignty at bay', *Foreign Affairs*, vol. 47, no. 1.

VETTER, H. O. (1968) 'Mitbestimmung ist Fortschritt', *Europäische Gemeinschaft*, September, pp. 5–7.

WAELBROECK, M. (1968), 'Cooperation agreements and competition policy in the EEC', *New York University J. International Law and Politics*, vol. 1, no. 1, pp. 5–18.

WEBER, A. P. (1968), 'Les monvements de concentration en Europe et la penetration industrielle et commerciale', *Direction*, no. 148.

WEBER, A. P. (1969), 'Concentrations en Europe', *Direction*, no. 160.

WERTHEIMER, H. W. (1967), 'The principle of territoriality in the trademark law of Common Market countries', *International and Comparative Law Q.*, vol. 16, no. 3, pp. 630–62.

Further Reading

The books and articles listed below supplement those referred to in the introduction and readings. The most recent and comprehensive bibliographies on the subject are:

C. A. Cosgrove, *A Readers' Guide to Britain and the European Communities*, Chatham House/PEP, 1970.

E. B. Haas, 'Regional integration: selected biography', *International Organization*, vol. 24, pp. 1003–20, 1970.

Part One
Why Europe? The Origins and Achievements of European Integration

R. Albrecht-Carrié, *The Unity of Europe: An Historical Survey*, Secker & Warburg, 1969.

H. Bliss (ed.), *The Political Development of the European Community*, Ginn, 1970.

H. Brugmans, *L'idée européenne 1918–1965*, de Tempel, 1965.

D. Calleo, *Europe's Future*, Hodder & Stoughton, 1965.

M. Camps, *Britain and the European Community 1955–1963*, Oxford University Press, 1964.

M. Camps, *European Unification in the Sixties*, Oxford University Press, 1967.

M. Crouzet, *The European Renaissance since 1945*, Thames & Hudson, 1970.

S. de la Mahotière, *Towards One Europe*, Penguin, 1970.

J.-F. Deniau, *The Common Market*, Barrie & Rockliffe, 1967.

W. Diebold, *The Schuman Plan: A Study in Economic Co-Operation 1950–1959*, Praeger, 1959.

N. Heathcote, 'The crisis of European supranationality', *J. Common Market Studies*, vol. 5, pp. 140–71, 1966.

R. Mayne, *The Recovery of Europe*, Weidenfeld & Nicolson, 1970.

R. Mayne (ed.), *Europe Tomorrow*, Fontana, 1972.

M. Palmer and J. Lambert, *European Unity: A Study of the European Organizations*, PEP, 1969.

S. Patijn (ed.), *Landmarks in European Unity*, Sijthoff, 1970.

R. L. Pfaltzgraff, *Britain faces Europe*, University of Pennsylvania Press, 1970.

W. Yondorf, 'Monnet and the Action Committee: the formative period of the European Communities', *International Organization*, vol. 19, pp. 885–912, 1965.

F. R. Willis, *France, Germany and the New Europe, 1945–1967*, Oxford University Press, 1968.

F. R. Willis, *Italy Chooses Europe*, Oxford University Press, 1971.

Part Two
European Integration: Theoretical Perspectives

M. Beloff, 'International integration and the modern state', *J. Common Market Studies*, vol. 2, pp. 52–62, 1963.

M. J. Brenner, *Technocratic Politics and the Functionalist Theory of European Integration*, Cornell University Press, 1969.

J. A. Caporaso, 'Theory and method in the study of international integration', *International Organization*, vol. 25, pp. 228–53, 1971.

J. Galtung, 'A structural theory of integration', *J. Peace Research*, vol. 5, pp. 375–95, 1968.

P. E. Jacob and J. V. Toscano (eds.), *The Integration of Political Communities*, Lippincott, 1964.

D. J. Puchala, 'Of blind men, elephants and international integration', *J. Common Market Studies*, vol. 10, pp. 267–85, 1972.

B. M. Russett, *International Regions and the International System*, Rand McNally, 1967.

P. C. Schmitter, 'A revised theory of regional integration', *International Organization*, vol. 24, pp. 836–68, 1970.

Part Three
The Dynamics of European Decision-Making

S. V. Anderson, *The Nordic Council: A Study of Scandinavian Regionalism*, University of Washington Press, 1967.

W. A. Axline, *European Community Law and Organizational Development*, Oceana, 1968.

D. T. Cattell, 'Multilateral co-operation and integration in East Europe', *Western Political Quarterly*, vol. 13, pp. 64–9, 1960.

P. Coffey and J. R. Presley, *European Monetary Integration*, Macmillan, 1971.

G. R. Denton (ed.), *Economic Integration in Europe*, Weidenfeld & Nicolson, 1969.

W. Feld, *The European Common Market and the World*, Prentice-Hall, 1967.

Geneva Graduate Institute of International Studies, *The European Free Trade Association and the Crisis of European Integration*, Humanities Press, 1968.

A. Green, *Political Integration by Jurisprudence*, Sijthoff, 1969.

W. Hallstein, *United Europe: Challenge and Opportunity*, Harvard University Press, 1962.

G. Ionescu (ed.), *The New Politics of European Integration*, Macmillan, 1972.

M. Kaser, *COMECON: Integration Problems of the Planned Economies*, Oxford University Press, 1965.

E.-S. Kirschen, *Financial Integration in Western Europe*, Columbia University Press, 1969.

U. W. Kitzinger, *The Politics and Economics of European Integration*, Praeger, 1963.

M. Lagrange, 'The European Court of Justice and national courts', *Common Market Law Review*, vol. 8, pp. 313–24, 1971.

J. Lukaszewski, 'Western integration and the people's democracies' *Foreign Affairs*, vol. 46, pp. 377–87, 1968.

M. Niblock, *The EEC: National Parliaments in Community Decision-Making*, Chatham House/PEP, 1971.

E. Noël, 'The Committee of Permanent Representatives', *J. Common Market Studies*, vol. 5, pp. 219–51, 1967.

R. L. Pfaltzgraff and J. L. Deghand, 'European technological collaboration: the experience of the European Launcher Development Organization', *J. Common Market Studies*, vol. 7, pp. 22–34, 1968.

J. Pinder (ed.), *The Economics of Europe*, Charles Knight, 1971.

S. Scheingold, *The Rule of Law in European Integration*, Yale University Press, 1965.

L. Scheinman, 'Euratom: nuclear integration in Europe', *International Conciliation*, no. 563, 1967.

D. Swann, *Economics of the Common Market*, Penguin, 1972.

D. G. Valentine, *The Court of Justice of the European Communities*, 2 vols. Stevens, 1965.

E. Wall, *Europe: Unification and Law*, Penguin, 1969.

Part Four
Sources of Support for European Integration

R. C. Beever, *European Unity and the Trade Union Movement*, Sijthoff, 1960.

J.-P. Dubois, 'The economic interest group at Community level, the institutional context and political integration', *Common Market Law Review*, vol. 8, pp. 168–83, 1971.

H. S. Feldstein, 'A study of transaction and political integration: transnational labour flow within the European Economic Community', *J. Common Market Studies*, vol. 6, pp. 24–55, 1967.

H. Günter (ed.), *Transnational Industrial Relations*, Macmillan, 1972.

S. Henig and J. Pinder (eds.), *European Political Parties*, PEP, 1969.

A. Sampson, *The New Europeans*, Hodder & Stoughton, 1968.

P. Sanders, 'The European company on its way', *Common Market Law Review*, vol. 8, pp. 29–43, 1971.

D. Sidjanski and J. Meynaud, *L'Europe des affaires: rôle et structure des groupes*, Payot, 1967.

D. Thompson, *The Proposal for a European Company*, Chatham House/PEP, 1969.

J. Vaizey, *Education* (*Studies in Contemporary Europe*), Macmillan, 1971.

R. Weissberg, 'Nationalism, integration and French and German elites', *International Organization*, vol. 23, pp. 337–47, 1969.

Acknowledgements

Permission to reproduce the following readings in this volume is acknowledged to the following sources:

1 Royal Institute of International Affairs
2 Johns Hopkins Press
4 *Die Zeit*
5 Doubleday Books Inc.
6 Prentice-Hall Inc.
7 Royal Institute of International Affairs
8 Weidenfeld & Nicholson
9 Princeton University Press
10 Basil Blackwell
11 George Allen & Unwin Ltd
12 Editions de L'Université de Bruxelles
13 Prentice-Hall Inc.
14 Macmillan Co.
15 Edinburgh University Press
16 Harvard University Press
17 University of Minnesota Press
18 *Government and Opposition*
19 World Peace Foundation

Author Index

Subject Index

Accra, 91
Action Committee for European
    Constituent Assembly, 64–5
Action Committee for the United
    States of Europe, 67
Adenauer, K., 51, 70
Administrative Committees of
    EEC, role in implementing
    common agricultural policy,
    259, 260–61
Africa, 57, 91, 300, 369
  East, 29, 328
  and study of regional integration,
    184, 188, 194
Agfa-Gevaert, 424, 444, 448
Agnelli, Giovanni, 436, 448
Agnelli, Umberto, 436
Agriculture, 73, 75, 78, 79, 102
  EEC common market in, 137–8,
    148, 241, 243, 247
  levies on, in EEC, 142, 249,
    251–2, 266, 277, 312
  marketing rules in EEC,
    312–13
  policies, 26, 70, 76, 80, 82, 84,
    136, 197
  pressure groups, in EEC, 407
  protection of, in EEC, 242–3
  relationship between national
    governments and EEC policy,
    291
  world market for, 242, 243,
    250
  see also Common Agricultural
    Policy (CAP)
Aid, economic, 53, 58, 59, 66
  military, 63, 66
  regional, 144
  US, 94, 105
  see also Marshall Aid
Algeria, 342, 368

Amalgamation
  amalgamated security
    communities, 15, 16, 110–14,
    115, 119, 121
  background conditions for,
    112–13
  conditions for disintegration,
    113–14
  and functionalism, 117
  opposition to, 120–21
Anarchism, 37
Anti-trust regulations, in EEC,
    444–5, 446
Argentina, immigration, 367
Arms and armaments, 99–100,
    106, 109, 111
  nuclear, 67, 341
  see also War
Asia, 91, 184, 369
Atlantic Council, 63
Atlantic Pact, 63, 64
Atlantic Union, 108
Australia, 45, 159, 375
  immigration, 367, 398
Austria, 43, 102
  and emigration, 367
  and migrant labour, 369

Balance of Payments, 125
  and common markets, 143–8
  and effects on free trade, 130
  and EEC common policies, 136
  and level of employment in
    EEC, 300–301
Balance-of-power politics, 341
Bangkok, 91
Behrendt, President, 86
Belgium, 14, 40n, 46, 77, 81, 102,
    171
  and business interests in EEC,
    426, 429, 434

Common Agricultural Policy of
EEC (CAP)
common organization of
national markets, 246–8, 253,
258, 263
example of cereals, 248–52
institutional regulations for
establishing, 245–6, 248,
253–5, 258
price policy, 255–6, 277
structural policy, 246, 277
success of, compared with
transport policy of EEC,
270–84
and transfer of power from
national governments to
community, 243–4, 245
see also Council of Ministers;
European Commission
Common markets, 65, 67, 69, 78,
90, 99, 101
and case for economic union,
127, 134, 142
Central American, 189
East African, 189
economic achievements of,
195–8
and effect on trade see EEC,
effects of customs unions on
trade
as end of negative integration,
126
EEC agricultural, 137–8
incentive for business, 422
and regional liberalization of
trade, 180
Commonwealth, British, 46, 369,
375
Communications, social, 15, 16,
18, 37, 110
international, 16–17
Communism, 48, 52, 57, 59, 62
in France, 60, 343, 345, 351
Community, sense of, 15–16, 19,
20
Gaullists' view of, 207, 212

political, 205
relationship with sovereignty
concepts, 205–10, 217
socio-psychological, 205, 206,
208, 209, 210, 214–15, 217,
219, 220–21
Compagnie française de pètroles
(CFP), 437, 450
Conflict resolution, 91, 92–6,
96–7, 111–12
integration as a means to, 117
Conservatism, 59, 66, 116
Conservative Party, Great Britain,
326, 335
Constitutions, British, 44
European, 65, 68, 83–6
United States, 45
Consultative Committee for
Social Welfare, EEC, 414
Consumer goods, 51, 102
consumer groups see
COMITEXTIL
COPA (committee of
professional agricultural
organizations of EEC), 402,
409–10, 411, 413, 414, 416,
418, 447n
Coudenhove-Kalergi, Count,
43–4
Council of Europe see Council of
Ministers of EEC
Council of Ministers of EEC, 59,
60, 64, 72, 75, 78–9, 84, 86, 94,
96, 98, 103, 107, 138, 147, 193,
226, 275–6, 305, 410, 438
and conventions, 100
cultural activities, 99
decisions on transport policy,
265, 290
legislative powers in relation to
member states, 311–12
and pressure groups, 404, 407,
409, 414–15, 433
proposals for transport policy,
265, 266
and refugees, 97, 106

Council of Ministers of EEC –
contd.
  regulations on labour mobility,
    376, 377, 380, 382, 383, 384, 389
  role in coordinating national
    policy making, 292–3, 294
  role in definition and
    implementation of CAP,
    245–6, 249, 251–2, 255, 257–63
  and role of EEC Commission,
    225, 226, 228, 238, 306–11,
    403, 404
  and the Saar, 97
Court of Justice, European, 98,
  141, 311, 314, 315, 316
  independence from pressure
    groups, 404
  and interpretation of
    Community Law, 317–20
  see also Law, and the EEC
Couve de Murville, Maurice, 435
Currency, 28, 60, 70, 80, 300
  convertibility, 99, 101
  currency union, a, *see* Monetary
    union
  devaluation, 130
  see also finance
Customs unions, 38, 69–73, 82,
  196–7
  competitiveness and
    complementarity, 151, 161–5,
    176–9
  dynamic effects, 130, 177–9, 180
  and economies of scale, 151, 176,
    177–8, 180
  effect on welfare, 151, 152
  empirical evidence for their
    effects on trade, 165–75, 179,
    181
  and EEC policies, 136
  ex ante and *ex post* approaches
    to, 165–6, 169, 173, 174
  nineteenth-century German, 116
  policy criteria for, 155–8, 179
  and role of European Court of
    Justice, 318

  size of, 159–61, 162, 179
  static effects of, 127–9
  theory of, and its limitations, 90,
    151, 152–4, 178, 180–81
  and theory of second best, 152,
    160, 165
  and trade creation and diversion
    see Trade
Cybernetics, 15
Czechoslovakia, 36, 326

Davignon Report, 77–80, 85, 86
Decision making, 14, 18, 21, 22,
  23, 26, 28, 97, 98, 201
  decentralization of, 42
  intergovernmental bodies and,
    106
  national, and public preferences,
    325, 329–34
  roles of Commission and
    Council of EEC in, 306–11,
    403–7
  and sense of national
    identification, 329
  structure of national institutions
    for, 326–7
  transfer of power for, from
    national to European
    institutions, 204, 208, 211
Defence policy, 25, 100, 109, 190
  in Europe, 63, 94, 104, 191, 193
  and security, 78
Democratic Party, United States,
  328–9, 356
Democracy, 11, 12, 55
  and Catholicism, 49–50
  Christian, 50
  in Eastern Europe, 52, 57
  and European government, 72,
    75, 82, 83, 85–6, 419
Denmark, 49, 159, 170, 369, 383
Depression, the, 45
Diplomacy, 93
  parliamentary, 94–5, 96–7, 99
  see also National policy making
Disease, prevention of, 21

Dollars, 40
Duhamel, Jaques, 345

Eastern Europe, 49, 52, 57, 58,
    140
    see also Comecon
ECCA, 402
Economic and Social Committee
    of Council of Europe, 73, 279,
    298
and pressure groups, 403, 409,
    411, 413, 414, 415
Economic integration, and
    economic union, 25–6, 74, 79,
    80, 84–6, 94, 95
benefits of, 181
case for, 142–8
definitions of union, 124–6, 127
and negative integration, 126–7,
    135–7
and positive integration, 126–7,
    135–7, 139–40
related to political integration,
    185–6, 188, 189, 192–3, 196–7,
    302, 362
'spread' and 'backwash' effects,
    197–8
Education, 79
and mass and elite politics, 347
and social integration, 365
and support for European
    integration, 348–9
Einaudi, Luigi, 43
Eisenhower, General D. D., 64
Elites, 12–14, 18, 20–21, 23, 24,
    26, 27–9, 103
and 'cognitive mobilization',
    346–7
and influence of public opinion
    on national decision making,
    325, 327, 330, 333
institutional, 215, 217
and launching of Schuman Plan,
    334
and opinion data, 109, 337, 339,
    341–2

and pluralism, 101
and roles in integration process,
    114–15, 117–19, 192, 193
trans-national, 97
Empire, idea of, 44, 45
Employment, 125
employers, 73, 407, 417
unemployment and retraining,
    144–5
Energy, EEC policy on, 138–9
    see also ECSC; Euratom
England, 16, 45, 52, 58–9, 108, 116
elite role in integration of
    Britain, 114
English–Irish Union of 1801, 116
and functional amalgamation,
    116–17
as strong economy, 132
    see also Great Britain
Ente nazional di idrocarburi
    (ENI), 450
Equilibrium analysis
and customs unions, 127–8, 165,
    166
and growth theory, 132
Erhard, Dr, 135, 147, 295
Ethnic problems, 42
Euratom, 23, 24, 26, 38, 95, 139,
    141
'Europe des Patries', 26
European Coal and Steel
    Community (ECSC), 9, 13,
    23–4, 26, 56, 61–2, 63, 65, 95,
    99, 101, 106, 138, 139, 151,
    383, 402
High Authority of, 24, 139,
    307–8
scrap-iron equalization system,
    319
Social Fund, 381–2
taxing powers, 141–2
Treaty, 261, 267, 307, 312
European Commission, 34, 69–73,
    74–5, 81, 85–6, 138, 211,
and 'Acceleration' decision of
    1960, 225, 228

Finanzgerichte, 314
German–Swiss relations, 290
industry, 137
integration of, 108, 115, 116, 363
labour unions, 444
and migrant labour, 366, 368, 369, 381, 382, 383–4, 389, 395, 397
military position, 95, 100
and national and Community law, 316–17
neo-liberals in, 147
rebuilding after the war, 60–63, 66
refugees, 367
tax rates on road transport, 442
Third Reich, 50
wages in, 391
Zollverein, 160, 161
Giscard d'Estaign, Valéry, 84, 344
Great Britain, 12, 27, 35, 39, 40, 44, 86, 95, 129
as amalgamated security community, 111
amalgamation of foreign and domestic policy, 287
application to join Common Market, 35, 38, 75, 130, 197, 220, 325–6, 335
British Empire, 45–6
and business in Common Market, 426–9
consensus in favour of European integration, 334–5, 337, 339
division of political skills in society, 327
economic growth, 130
effect of tariff reductions on trade, 173
and European Social Charter, 383, 384
and Federal Union Movement, 44–7
foreign trade, 168

gains from joining a wider market in Europe, 130–33
and immigration, 367, 375, 395, 397
integration of, 114, 115, 210
leadership of elite groups in mobilizing public opinion, 327
and migrant labour, 369, 378, 385, 389, 391, 392
payment crises and OEEC, 105, 106
Polish refugees, 364
political parties, 102
and post-war European policy, 58–9, 60, 61, 63
shifts in public opinion on European integration, 355–9
Greece, 101, 102, 103
emigrants, 367, 368, 369, 391
Treaty of Association with EEC, 140, 412
GNP
increases in, and free trade, 129–30, 152, 153, 156, 159, 165, 174–5, 176, 177, 196
indicator of multipurpose capabilities of a country, 109
within EEC, 191
Grotius, 204–5
Group of Ten, 40
Guptas, 92

Hague, the
Communique, 38
Congress, 1948, 59
Convention, 310
European 'relance' at in 1969, 344, 345
Summit Conference, 1969, 76, 77, 79
Hallstein, Walter, 14, 35, 74, 235, 306
Hallstein Commission, 231, 232, 233, 234
Hamburg, 80
Hapsburg Empire, 48, 111, 116

'High politics' *see* Regional
 integration
Historical unity of Europe, 92
Hitler, A., 47, 48, 349
Höchst Farbwerke, 437, 439, 448
Holy Roman Empire, 92, 365
Hugo, Victor, 43
Human rights, 100
 Human Rights Commission, 305

IBM, 424
Iceland, 102, 159
Immigration, comparative
 national policies on, 386–99
 cross national *see* Labour,
  mobility; Social aspects of
  integration; and under
  individual countries
India, 45, 111, 369
Industry, 24, 300
 coal and steel, 38, 56, 61, *see also*
  ECSC
 development, 101–2
 German, 23, 61, 298
 industrialism and integration,
  102–3, 106
 infant-industry theory, 132, 161
 productivity, 99
 research expenditure in
  European, 423, 430–31
 Union des Industries de la
  Communauté Européen, 298
Institutional change, as a factor
 in Integration, 215–16, 217
Instituto per la riconstruzione
 industriale (IRI), 450
intellectuals, 118
Interest groups, 20–21, 24–5, 96
 and amalgamation, 120
 and common transport policy in
  EEC, 271–2
 as force for integration, 117–19
 place in EEC method, 211,
  298–9
 political, 190
 supranational, 98

and transnational business
 ventures, 433
see also Pressure groups
International Civil Air Transport
 Organization, 311
International institutions, and
 community feeling, 206–8
 capacity of, 209–10
International Labour
 Organization, 23, 312, 380,
 382, 384, 389
International Monetary Fund, 40
International organizations, 21–3,
 23, 93–6, 104, 107, 108, 122
 legislative powers, 311–12
International relations, 17, 29, 66,
 93, 190
 study of, 184
Ireland, 102, 108, 115, 132
 emigration, 369
 English–Irish Union of 1801,
  116
 and functional amalgamation,
  116–17
 and migrant labour, 369, 375,
  383
ISCI, 407–8, 415
Islam, 92
Israel, 341, 364
Italy, 10, 40*n*, 44, 45, 50, 51, 60,
 64, 66, 70, 76–7, 102, 170
 and business in EEC, 426, 429,
  434, 435–7, 450
 consensus in favour of European
  integration, 334
 Corte Constituzionale, 316
 emigrants and labour mobility,
  366, 367, 368, 369, 377, 382,
  384, 389–91
 and EEC agricultural policy,
  282
 exports, 81
 integration of, 108, 114–15, 116,
  363
 labour unions, 444
 law courts, 315, 316

Mass media, 110
Mass observation, 18, 109, 327–8
  see also Public opinion
Mayer, Rene, 307
Mazzini, G., 43
Messina, 67, 197
Michelin, 435, 436
Michelin, François, 436
Middle East, 78
Ming Empire, 92
Minorities, 114, 119
Mitterand, François, 343
Monetary union, 28, 38, 40–41,
  70, 74, 76, 79, 300, 345
  and capital markets, 145–6
  and OEEC, 106
Monnet, Jean, 14, 35, 42, 46–7,
  56, 61, 62, 67, 215, 239
Monopolies, 165, 249
Montecatini–Edison, 450
Montreux, 55
Moon landing, 37
Multinational corporations, 40,
  82, 424–5
Munich, 77
Mussolini, B., 48

Nation states, 11, 13, 15, 18, 21–2,
  27, 29, 40, 55, 59, 82, 108
  decline of concept of, 48–9, 91
  in nineteenth century, 43
  as political communities, 92
  renunciation of sovereignty, 83
National government, as a model
  for the institutions of the
  EEC, 203, 204, 215, 216
  challenge to decision-making
  powers by EEC Commission,
  212
  impact of European Community
  on, 285; *see also* National
  policy making
National policy making,
  elite composition of national
    representatives to Community,
    290–91

European communities as an
  issue area in, 286–93
evolution of institutions
  designed to resolve national
  conflicts, 291–3
foreign policy role in dealings
  with community, 286–9, 295,
  296, 300
implications for, of growing area
  of community activity,
  299–301
national actors and European
  issue area, 293–9
'political' and 'technical' issues
  and EEC, 289–90, 295
role of finance ministers in
  dealings with EEC, 295–6
role of national domestic
  ministries in community
  structure, 289–90, 296
Nationalism, 21–2, 24, 46–50, 66,
  67–8, 73, 83–4, 366
  and age group differentials
    related to opinions on
    European integration, 329,
    349–54, 356–8
  decline of traditional forces of,
    in Europe, 51–2
  origins of, in individuals, 329,
    349
Neo-functionalism, 12, 20–28, 90,
  184, 189–90, 191, 194–5, 204
  and community method, 212,
    213, 215
  pluralistic model of society,
    207–9
  and relation between community
    and sovereignty, 208, 211
  and strategies for furthering
    integration, 218, 219, 220
Nestlé, 424
Netherlands, 40n, 46, 102, 170–71
  451
  agricultural policy, 271, 273, 282
  and business, in EEC, 426, 429,
    434, 440

Planning – *contd.*
  for long-range economic growth,
    94
  national, 50
  nuclear, 95
Pluralism, 20, 21, 123, 207
  and amalgamation, 120
  and federalism, 208–9
  pluralistic security communities,
    15, 16, 110, 114, 121, 123
  in Western Europe, 101
Poher, Alain, 344, 345, 452
Political aspects of integration,
    11–13, 151
  effect of transnational business
    collaboration on, 432–3
  leaders and issues, 117–19, 121–2
  political aspirations of major
    groups in society, 18
  role of political institutions of
    EEC, 230–40
  transfer of authority from
    nations to institutions of
    EEC, 201, 204; *and see*
    Individual institutions
Political community, concept of,
    92, 93, 99, 103
Political parties, 23, 24, 49–51, 58,
    96, 102, 115
  social identification with, 328,
    356
  and transnational business
    ventures, 433, 441
  and see Individual parties
Political Studies Association
    Conference, 203*n*
Political union, concept of, 76,
    77–8, 80, 85–6
  see also Political aspects of
    integration
Politicization, role in economic
    integration, 185–6, 189
Pollution, 37
Pompidou, Georges, 75, 77, 85,
    344–5, 360
Portugal, 49, 101, 102, 103

  migrant workers from, 368, 369,
    378
Potsdam, 57
Pressure groups, and the EEC
  activity of groups, 415–20
  birth of professional structures,
    404–7
  direct and indirect action by,
    409–10
  informal channels of influence,
    410–12
  official channels, 412–15
  phases of formation of groups,
    401–3
  relationship between groups and
    political parties, 419
  specialized action by technical
    organizations, 419–19
  structure of groups, 407–9
Price system in EEC, for cereals,
    249–50, 251, 252, 255
Protection, 132, 139, 151, 152–3,
    158, 159, 177, 179, 181
Public opinion,
  concept of 'cognitive
    mobilization', 346
  and consensus in favour of
    European integration,
    334–45, 362
  cross-sectional samples of, on
    European integration, 348,
    350–55
  shifts in, 355–9
  effects on national decision
    making, 325, 330–34
  and depth of feeling on issues,
    328–9, 332–3, 349
  and distribution of skills in a
    society, 327–8, 346
  on foreign policy, 325–6
  and pluralistic or monolithic
    decision-making structures,
    326–7
  leadership of, 326, 327

Referendums, 68, 344

United States of America – *contd.*
 decline in income disparity in,
  198
 Federal Constitution, 45
 Foreign policy, 39, 325, 353
 and immigration, 363, 364, 366,
  367, 398–9
 import surcharge, 40
 integration of, 108, 115, 116,
  119, 194*n*, 222, 363
 the New Deal, 329
 and NAFTA, 133
 and NATO, 104
 policy in Europe, 53–4, 57, 58,
  190, 193, 362
 size of market in, 177–8
 study of import tariff concessions
  in, 172–3
 and Tennessee Valley Authority,
  222
 'United States of Europe', 42, 67,
  336, 364
 Uniting of Europe, the, 184, 221
Universities, 73, 100
Urbanization, 102, 103, 106

Values, and attitudes to European
  unity, 20–21, 22, 42, 103,
  109–10, 232, 339, 448–9
Veto, in EEC, 26, 72, 106
Vietnam, US bombing, 325

Wales, 42, 108, 116
War, 9, 13–14, 21
 civil, 111–12
 First World War, 43, 46, 48, 51,
  54, 55, 56, 73, 92, 329, 349, 365
 and integration, 115, 121
 nuclear, 91, 111, 190–1
 Second World War, 11, 44, 46–7
  48, 50, 52, 54, 55, 56, 73, 92,
  192, 329, 349, 364, 365, 366,
  367, 369
Washington, 193

Weather control, 37
Welfare, 21, 22, 25, 79, 106, 125,
  126
 effects of customs unions on,
  127–8
 policy, 99, 100
 politics, and integration theory,
  188, 189–90, 192
 resources, 100
 state, 98
Werner Plan, 300, 302
West Indies, Federation of, 108
 and migrant labour from, 369
Western Europe, 37, 39, 58, 63
 and Eastern Europe, 52
 historical unity, 92–3
 influence of public opinion in,
  328
 and monetary policy, 40–41
 nationalism in, 329, 349
 national policies on
  immigration, 386–99
 pluralism of, 101
 prosperity, 38
 Western European Union, 95,
  99–100, 106, 305
Whigs, 116
Wilson, Harold, 325
Winnacker, Karl, 448
World Council of Churches, 381
World government, 13, 108, 122
World Health Organization
  (WHO), 311

Yalta, 53, 57
Yaounde Convention, 140
Youth, 18, 29, 37–8, 73, 221
 child–parent relations and
  opinion data on European
  integration, 353–4, 355
 see also Students
Yugoslavia, 368, 369

Zurich, 11, 58